ISBN: 9781313009188


Published by:
HardPress Publishing
8345 NW 66TH ST #2561
MIAMI FL 33166-2626

Email: info@hardpress.net
Web: http://www.hardpress.net

THE

# Book of Common Prayer,
# 1549.

COMMONLY CALLED

# The First Book of Edward vi.

TO WHICH IS ADDED

## THE ORDINAL OF 1549.

AND

## THE ORDER OF HOLY COMMUNION, 1548.

WITH AN INTRODUCTION BY

## MORGAN DIX, S. T. D.,

*Rector of Trinity Church, N. Y.,*

NEW YORK:
CHURCH KALENDAR PRESS,
No. 27 Rose Street.
1881.

This reprint has been read by the Secretary
of the Joint Committee in charge of the Stereo-
type Plates of the Standard Prayer Book.

Whitsuntide, 1881.

# INTRODUCTION

THIS is a reprint of the First Prayer Book of the Reformed Church of Christ in England; it has been commended by a high authority as "the noblest monument of piety, of prudence, and of learning which the sixteenth century constructed." Let every one who examines it bear the following points in mind as he reads:—

I. It was the result of study and long preparation, and essentially the work of English divines, such as would now be styled "Old Catholics:" it is therefore a correct exponent of the principles of the English Reformation.

II. It came into use on Whitsun-day, June 9th, A. D. 1549, by authority of the Church in Convocation and the State in Parliament; and no other Prayer Book had that joint sanction till 112 years afterwards.

III. They who put it forth declared, officially, their belief that it agreed in all particulars with the most sincere and pure Christian religion taught in Holy Scripture, and with the usages of the Primitive Church, and that its compilers had been aided by the Holy Ghost.

IV. In less than two years, another volume was substituted for it, by the authority of King and Parliament, with the assent of *some* of the Bishops and Clergy.

V. This Second Book of Edward VI., which was the First Book revised, defaced, and generally maltreated, was put forth in the vain hope of conciliating certain radicals and ultra-reformers in England, whom nothing would have satisfied but the extirpation of the whole Catholic system, and certain foreigners, who, having rejected the Episcopate and the Catholic traditions, were founding new "churches" on an independent basis, and inaugurating presbyteral and congregational disciplines, with inordinate boasts of their value and purity.

VI. They who, yielding to the violence of the radicals at home and the insolence of the reformers abroad, weakly consented to give up this Book, declared, at the moment of surrender, that there was no sound objection to it, and that those who wanted a change were a set of curious and mistaken men.

VII. The new book never came into use, but fell, stillborn, into its tomb.

VIII. It was, however, made the basis of a Prayer Book compiled on the accession of Queen Elizabeth, A.D. 1559; but some of its worst features were effaced, and many things that were in the First Book were restored.

IX. In each subsequent revision, the tendency has been to return to the old standard; and, little by little, things have been recovered which, in 1552, were recklessly thrown away.

Let the reader bear these points in mind, and if he make each the subject of intelligent study, he will have acquired a knowledge of Liturgiology worth having, and of great value to him as a preservative from the fallacies and prejudices of these days.

If it should be considered desirable to revise our American Book of Common Prayer, or deemed possible to improve it, revision ought to proceed on the lines drawn in this volume; any other revision would be clearly revolutionary. For us, real progress consists in drawing nearer to the ancient Catholic landmarks, not in departing still farther from them: this, only, is the progress which Churchmen should desire to see. To be spiritually minded with the Ancient Fathers and Doctors of the Church, is life: to be carnally minded, with the restless rationalists and self-sufficient critics of the present century, is death.

MORGAN DIX.

TRINITY RECTORY, NEW YORK,
     Whitsun-eve, A.D. 1881.

# THE

## booke of the common prayer and administracion of the Sacramentes, and other rites and Ceremonies of the Churche: after the use of the Churche of England.

LONDINI IN OFFICINA
*Edouardi Whitchurche.*
*Cum Priuilegio ad imprimendum solum*
ANNO DO. 1549, *Mense.*
*Junii.*

# THE CONTENTS OF THIS BOOK.

# THE PREFACE.

---

There was never any thing by the wit of man so well devised, or so surely established, which (in continuance of time) hath not been corrupted: as (among other things) it may plainly appear by the common Prayers in the Church, commonly called Divine Service: the first original and ground whereof, if a man would search out by the ancient fathers, he shall find that the same was not ordained, but of a good purpose, and for a great advancement of godliness: For they so ordered the matter, that all the whole Bible (or the greatest part thereof) should be read over once in the year, intending thereby, that the clergy, and specially such as were Ministers of the congregation, should (by often reading and meditation of God's word) be stirred up to godliness themselves, and be more able also to exhort other by wholesome doctrine, and to confute them that were adversaries to the truth. And further, that the people (by daily hearing of holy Scripture read in the Church) should continually profit more and more in the knowledge of God, and be the more inflamed with the love of his true religion. But these many years past, this godly and decent order of the ancient fathers hath been so altered, broken, and neglected, by planting in uncertain stories, legends, responds, verses, vain repetitions, commemorations, and synodals, that commonly when any book of the Bible was begun, before three or four chapters were read out, all the rest were unread. And in this sort, the book of Esaie was begun in Advent, and the book of Genesis in Septuagesima: but they were only begun, and never read through. After a like sort were other books of Holy Scripture used. And moreover, whereas S. Paul would have such language spoken to the people in the Church, as they might understand and have profit by hearing the same: the Service in this Church of England (these many years) hath been read in Latin to the people, which they understood not, so that they have heard with their ears only: and their hearts, spirit, and mind, have not been edified thereby. And furthermore, notwithstanding that the ancient fathers had divided the Psalms into seven portions; whereof every one was called a nocturn; now of late time a few of them have been daily said (and oft repeated) and the rest utterly omitted. Moreover, the number and hardness of the rules called the Pie, and the manifold changings of the Service, was the cause, that to turn the book only was so hard and intricate a matter, that many times there was more business to find out what should be read, than to read it when it was found out.

These inconveniences therefore considered, here is set forth such an order, whereby the same shall be redressed. And for a readiness in this matter, here is drawn out a Kalendar for that purpose, which is plain and easy to be understanded, wherein (so much as may be) the reading of Holy Scripture is so set forth, that all things shall be done in order, without breaking one piece thereof from another. For this cause be cut off Anthems, Responds, Invitatories, and such like things, as did break the continual course of the reading of the Scripture. Yet because there is no remedy, but that of necessity there must be some rules; therefore certain rules are here set forth, which as they be few in number, so they be plain and easy to be understanded. So that here you have an Order for Prayer (as touching the reading of Holy Scripture) much agreeable to the mind and purpose of the old fathers, and a great deal more profitable and commodious than that which of late was used. It is more profitable, because here are left out many things, whereof some be untrue, some uncertain, some vain and superstitious; and is ordained nothing to be read but the very pure word of God, the Holy Scriptures, or that which is evidently grounded upon the same: and that in such a language and order, as is most easy and plain for the understanding, both of the readers and hearers. It is also more commodious, both for the shortness thereof, and for the plainness of the Order, and for that the rules be few and easy. Furthermore, by this order, the curates shall need none other books for their public service, but this book and the Bible: by the means whereof the people shall not be at so great charge for books as in time past they have been.

And where heretofore there hath been great diversity in saying and singing in churches within this Realm: some following Salisbury use, some Hereford use, some the use of Bangor, some of York, and some of Lincoln: now from henceforth, all the whole realm shall have but one use. And if any would judge this way more painful because that all things must be read upon the book, whereas before, by the reason of so often repetition, they could say many things by heart: if those men will weigh their labour with the profit in knowledge which daily they shall obtain by reading upon the book, they will not refuse the pain, in consideration of the great profit that shall ensue thereof.

And forsomuch as nothing can almost be so plainly set forth, but doubts may rise in the use and practising of the same: to appease all such diversity, (if any arise,) and for the resolution of all doubts, concerning the manner how to understand, do, and execute the things contained in this Book, the parties that so doubt, or diversly take anything, shall alway resort to the Bishop of the Diocese, who by his discretion shall take order for the quieting and appeasing of the same: so that the same order be not contrary to any thing contained in this Book.

Though it be appointed in the afore written Preface, that all things shall be read and sung in the Church, in the English tongue, to the end that the congregation may be thereby edified: yet it is not meant, but when men say Matins and Evensong privately, they may say the same in any language that they themselves do understand. Neither that any man shall be bound to the saying of them. but such as from time to time, in Cathedral and Collegiate churches, Parish churches, and Chapels to the same annexed, shall serve the congregation.

# THE ORDER

## How the rest of the Holy Scripture (beside the Psalter) is appointed to be read.

THE Old Testament is appointed for the first Lessons, at Matins and Evensong, and shall be read through every year once, except certain books and chapters which be least edifying, and might best be spared, and therefore are left unread.

The New Testament is appointed for the second Lessons at Matins and Evensong, and shall be read over orderly every year thrice, beside the Epistles and Gospels; except the Apocalypse, out of the which there be only certain Lessons appointed upon divers proper Feasts.

And to know what Lessons shall be read every day, find the day of the month in the Kalendar following; and there ye shall perceive the books and chapters that shall be read for the Lessons, both at Matins and Evensong.

And here is to be noted, that whensoever there be any proper Psalms or Lessons appointed for any Feast, movable or unmovable, then the Psalms and Lessons appointed in the Kalendar shall be omitted for that time.

Ye must note also, that the Collect, Epistle and Gospel, appointed for the Sunday, shall serve all the week after, except there fall some Feast that hath his proper.

This is also to be noted, concerning the leap years, that the twenty-fifth day of February, which in leap years is counted for two days, shall in those two days alter neither Psalm nor Lesson; but the same Psalms and Lessons which be said the first day, shall serve also for the second day.

Also, wheresoever the beginning of any Lesson, Epistle, or Gospel is not expressed, there ye must begin at the beginning of the chapter.

| JANUARY KALENDAR. | | | MATINS. | | EVENSONG. | |
|---|---|---|---|---|---|---|
| | | PSALMS. | 1 LESSON. | 2 LESSON. | 1 LESSON. | 2 LESSON. |
| A | 1 | *Circumcision.* i. | Gen. —17 | Rom. — 2 | Deut. —10 | Col. — 2 |
| b | 2 | ———— ii. | Gen. — 1 | Matt. — 1 | Gen. — 2 | Rom. — 1 |
| c | 3 | ———— iii. | —— 3 | —— 2 | —— 4 | —— 2 |
| d | 4 | ———— iv. | —— 5 | —— 3 | —— 6 | —— 3 |
| e | 5 | ———— v. | —— 7 | —— 4 | —— 8 | —— 4 |
| f | 6 | *Epiphany—* vi. | Isa. —60 | Luke — 3 | Isa.——49 | John — 2 |
| g | 7 | ———— vii. | Gen. — 9 | Matt. — 5 | Gen. —11 | Rom. — 5 |
| A | 8 | ———— viii. | ——12 | —— 6 | ——13 | —— 6 |
| b | 9 | ———— ix. | ——14 | —— 7 | ——15 | —— 7 |
| c | 10 | ———— x. | ——16 | —— 8 | ——17 | —— 8 |
| d | 11 | ———— xi. | ——18 | —— 9 | ——19 | —— 9 |
| e | 12 | ———— xii. | ——20 | ——10 | ——21 | ——10 |
| f | 13 | ———— xiii. | ——22 | ——11 | ——23 | ——11 |
| g | 14 | ———— xiv. | ——24 | ——12 | ——25 | ——12 |
| A | 15 | ———— xv. | ——26 | ——13 | ——27 | ——13 |
| b | 16 | ———— xvi. | ——28 | ——14 | ——29 | ——14 |
| c | 17 | ———— xvii. | ——30 | ——15 | ——31 | ——15 |
| d | 18 | ———— xviii. | ——32 | ——16 | ——33 | ——16 |
| e | 19 | ———— xix. | ——34 | ——17 | ——35 | 1 Cor.— 1 |
| f | 20 | ———— xx. | ——36 | ——18 | ——37 | —— 2 |
| g | 21 | ———— xxi. | ——38 | ——19 | ——39 | —— 3 |
| A | 22 | ———— xxii. | ——40 | ——20 | ——41 | —— 4 |
| b | 23 | ———— xxiii. | ——42 | ——21 | ——43 | —— 5 |
| c | 24 | ———— xxiv. | ——44 | ——22 | ——45 | —— 6 |
| d | 25 | *Conversion of S. Paul.* xxv. | ——46 | Acts— 22 | ——47 | Acts —26 |
| e | 26 | ———— xxvi. | ——48 | Matt. —23 | ——49 | 1 Cor.— 7 |
| f | 27 | ———— xxvii. | ——50 | ——24 | Exod. — 1 | —— 8 |
| g | 28 | ———— xxviii. | Exod. — 2 | ——25 | —— 3 | —— 9 |
| A | 29 | ———— xxix. | —— 4 | ——26 | —— 5 | ——10 |
| b | 30 | ———— xxx. | —— 6 | ——27 | —— 7 | ——11 |
| c | 31 | ———— i. | —— 8 | ——28 | —— 9 | ——12 |

| FEBRUARY KALENDAR. | | | MATINS. | | EVENSONG. | |
|---|---|---|---|---|---|---|
| | | PSALMS. | 1 Lesson. | 2 Lesson. | 1 Lesson. | 2 Lesson. |
| d | 1 | | ii. | Exod. -10 | Mark — 1 | Exod. -11 | 1 Cor.—13 |
| e | 2 | *Purification of S. Mary.* | iii. | —12 | — 2 | —13 | —14 |
| f | 3 | | iv. | —14 | — 3 | —15 | —15 |
| g | 4 | | v. | —16 | — 4 | —17 | —16 |
| A | 5 | | vi. | —18 | — 5 | —19 | 2 Cor.— 1 |
| b | 6 | | vii. | —20 | — 6 | —21 | — 2 |
| c | 7 | | viii. | —22 | — 7 | —23 | — 3 |
| d | 8 | | ix. | —24 | — 8 | —32 | — 4 |
| e | 9 | | x. | —33 | — 9 | —34 | — 5 |
| f | 10 | | xi. | —35 | —10 | —40 | — 6 |
| g | 11 | | xii. | Lev. —18 | —11 | Lev. —19 | — 7 |
| A | 12 | | xiii. | —20 | —12 | Num. —10 | — 8 |
| b | 13 | | xiv. | Num. —11 | —13 | —12 | — 9 |
| c | 14 | | xv. | —13 | —14 | —14 | —10 |
| d | 15 | | xvi. | —15 | —15 | —16 | —11 |
| e | 16 | | xvii. | —17 | —16 | —18 | —12 |
| f | 17 | | xviii. | —19 | Luke *di* 1 | —20 | —13 |
| g | 18 | | xix. | —21 | —*di* 1 | —22 | Gal. — 1 |
| A | 19 | | xx. | —23 | — 2 | —24 | — 2 |
| b | 20 | | xxi. | —25 | — 3 | —26 | — 3 |
| c | 21 | | xxii. | —27 | — 4 | —28 | — 4 |
| d | 22 | | xxiii. | —29 | — 5 | —30 | — 5 |
| e | 23 | | xxiv. | —31 | — 6 | —32 | — 6 |
| f | 24 | *S. Matthias* | xxv. | —33 | — 7 | —34 | Eph. — 1 |
| g | 25 | | xxvi. | —35 | — 8 | —36 | — 2 |
| A | 26 | | xxvii. | Deut. — 1 | — 9 | Deut. — 2 | — 3 |
| b | 27 | | xxviii. | — 3 | —10 | — 4 | — 4 |
| c | 28 | | xxix. | — 5 | —11 | — 6 | — 5 |

| MARCH KALENDAR. | | | MATINS. | | EVENSONG. | |
|---|---|---|---|---|---|---|
| | | PSALMS. | 1 Lesson. | 2 Lesson. | 1 Lesson. | 2 Lesson. |
| d | 1 | xxx. | Deut. — 7 | Luke —12 | Deut. — 8 | Eph. — 6 |
| e | 2 | i. | ——— 9 | ———13 | ———10 | Phil.— 1 |
| f | 3 | ii. | ———11 | ———14 | ———12 | ——— 2 |
| g | 4 | iii. | ———13 | ———15 | ———14 | ——— 3 |
| A | 5 | iv. | ———15 | ———16 | ———16 | ——— 4 |
| b | 6 | v. | ———17 | ———17 | ———18 | Col. — 1 |
| c | 7 | vi. | ———19 | ———18 | ———20 | ——— 2 |
| d | 8 | vii. | ———21 | ———19 | ———22 | ——— 3 |
| e | 9 | viii. | ———23 | ———20 | ———24 | ——— 4 |
| f | 10 | ix. | ———25 | ———21 | ———26 | 1 Thess. 1 |
| g | 11 | x. | ———27 | ———22 | ———28 | ——— 2 |
| A | 12 | xi. | ———29 | ———23 | ———30 | ——— 3 |
| b | 13 | xii. | ———31 | ———24 | ———32 | ——— 4 |
| c | 14 | xiii. | ———33 | John — 1 | ———34 | ——— 5 |
| d | 15 | xiv. | Josh. — 1 | ——— 2 | Josh. — 2 | 2 Thess. 1 |
| e | 16 | xv. | ——— 3 | ——— 3 | ——— 4 | ——— 2 |
| f | 17 | xvi. | ——— 5 | ——— 4 | ——— 6 | ——— 3 |
| g | 18 | xvii. | ——— 7 | ——— 5 | ——— 8 | 1 Tim. - 1 |
| A | 19 | xviii. | ——— 9 | ——— 6 | ———10 | — 2 & 3 |
| b | 20 | xix. | ———11 | ——— 7 | ———12 | ——— 4 |
| c | 21 | xx. | ———13 | ——— 8 | ———14 | ——— 5 |
| d | 22 | xxi. | ———15 | ——— 9 | ———16 | ——— 6 |
| e | 23 | xxii. | ———17 | ———10 | ———18 | 2 Tim. - 1 |
| f | 24 | xxiii. | ———19 | ———11 | ———20 | ——— 2 |
| g | 25 | *Annunciation of B. V. M.* xxiv. | ———21 | ———12 | ———22 | ——— 3 |
| A | 26 | xxv. | ———23 | ———13 | ———24 | ——— 4 |
| b | 27 | xxvi. | Judges- 1 | ———14 | Judges- 2 | Titus — 1 |
| c | 28 | xxvii. | ——— 3 | ———15 | ——— 4 | — 2 & 3 |
| d | 29 | xxviii. | ——— 5 | ———16 | ——— 6 | Philem. 1 |
| e | 30 | xxix. | ——— 7 | ———17 | ——— 8 | Heb.— 1 |
| f | 31 | xxx. | ——— 9 | ———18 | ———10 | ——— 2 |

## APRIL.

| APRIL KALENDAR. | | MATINS. | | EVENSONG. | |
|---|---|---|---|---|---|
| | PSALMS. | 1 LESSON. | 2 LESSON. | 1 LESSON. | 2 LESSON. |
| 1 | i. | Judges-11 | John —19 | Judges-12 | Heb.—3 |
| 2 | ii. | —13 | —20 | —14 | —4 |
| 3 | iii. | —15 | —21 | —16 | —5 |
| 4 | iv. | —17 | Acts—1 | —18 | —6 |
| 5 | v. | —19 | —2 | —20 | —7 |
| 6 | vi. | —21 | —3 | Ruth—1 | —8 |
| 7 | vii. | Ruth—2 | —4 | —3 | —9 |
| 8 | viii. | —4 | —5 | 1 Sam.-1 | —10 |
| 9 | ix. | 1 Sam.-2 | —6 | —3 | —11 |
| 10 | x. | —4 | —7 | —5 | —12 |
| 11 | xi. | —6 | —8 | —7 | —13 |
| 12 | xii. | —8 | —9 | —9 | James-1 |
| 13 | xiii. | —10 | —10 | —11 | —2 |
| 14 | xiv. | —12 | —11 | —13 | —3 |
| 15 | xv. | —14 | —12 | —15 | —4 |
| 16 | xvi. | —16 | —13 | —17 | —5 |
| 17 | xvii. | —18 | —14 | —19 | 1 Peter-1 |
| 18 | xviii. | —20 | —15 | —21 | —2 |
| 19 | xix. | —22 | —16 | —23 | —3 |
| 20 | xx. | —24 | —17 | —25 | —4 |
| 21 | xxi. | —26 | —18 | —27 | —5 |
| 22 | xxii. | —28 | —19 | —29 | 2 Peter-1 |
| 23 | xxiii. | —30 | —20 | —31 | —2 |
| 24 | xxiv. | 2 Sam.-1 | —21 | 2 Sam.-2 | —3 |
| 25 *S. Mark the Evangelist.* | xxv. | —3 | —22 | —4 | 1 John-1 |
| 26 | xxvi. | —5 | —23 | —6 | —2 |
| 27 | xxvii. | —7 | —24 | —8 | —3 |
| 28 | xxviii. | —9 | —25 | —10 | —4 |
| 29 | xxix. | —11 | —26 | —12 | —5 |
| 30 | xxx. | —13 | —27 | —14 | 2 & 3 John |

| MAY KALENDAR. | | | MATINS. | | EVENSONG. | |
|---|---|---|---|---|---|---|
| | | PSALMS. | 1 Lesson. | 2 Lesson. | 1 Lesson. | 2 Lesson. |
| b | 1 | *S. Philip and S. James.* i. | 2 Sam. -15 | Acts — 8 | 2 Sam. -16 | Jude— 1 |
| c | 2 | ii. | ——17 | ——28 | ——18 | Rom. — 1 |
| d | 3 | iii. | ——19 | Matt. — 1 | ——20 | —— 2 |
| e | 4 | iv. | ——21 | —— 2 | ——22 | —— 3 |
| f | 5 | v. | ——23 | —— 3 | ——24 | —— 4 |
| g | 6 | vi. | 1 Kings 1 | —— 4 | 1 Kings 2 | —— 5 |
| A | 7 | vii. | —— 3 | —— 5 | —— 4 | —— 6 |
| b | 8 | viii. | —— 5 | —— 6 | —— 6 | —— 7 |
| c | 9 | ix. | —— 7 | —— 7 | —— 8 | —— 8 |
| d | 10 | x. | —— 9 | —— 8 | ——10 | —— 9 |
| e | 11 | xi. | ——11 | —— 9 | ——12 | ——10 |
| f | 12 | xii. | ——13 | ——10 | ——14 | ——11 |
| g | 13 | xiii. | ——15 | ——11 | ——16 | ——12 |
| A | 14 | xiv. | ——17 | ——12 | ——18 | ——13 |
| b | 15 | xv. | ——19 | ——13 | ——20 | ——14 |
| c | 16 | xvi. | ——21 | ——14 | ——22 | ——15 |
| d | 17 | xvii. | 2 Kings 1 | ——15 | 2 Kings 2 | ——16 |
| e | 18 | xviii. | —— 3 | ——16 | —— 4 | 1 Cor.— 1 |
| f | 19 | xix. | —— 5 | ——17 | —— 6 | —— 2 |
| g | 20 | xx. | —— 7 | ——18 | —— 8 | —— 3 |
| A | 21 | xxi. | —— 9 | ——19 | ——10 | —— 4 |
| b | 22 | xxii. | ——11 | ——20 | ——12 | —— 5 |
| c | 23 | xxiii. | ——13 | ——21 | ——14 | —— 6 |
| d | 24 | xxiv. | ——15 | ——22 | ——16 | —— 7 |
| e | 25 | xxv. | ——17 | ——23 | ——18 | —— 8 |
| f | 26 | xxvi. | ——19 | ——24 | ——20 | —— 9 |
| g | 27 | xxvii. | ——21 | ——25 | ——22 | ——10 |
| A | 28 | xxviii. | ——23 | ——26 | ——24 | ——11 |
| b | 29 | xxix. | ——25 | ——27 | 1Chron. 1 | ——12 |
| c | 30 | xxx. | 1Chron. 2 | ——28 | —— 3 | ——13 |
| d | 31 | xxx. | —— 4 | Mark — 1 | —— 5 | ——14 |

| JUNE KALENDAR. | | | MATINS. | | EVENSONG. | |
|---|---|---|---|---|---|---|
| | | PSALMS. | 1 LESSON. | 2 LESSON. | 1 LESSON. | 2 LESSON. |
| e | 1 | | i. | 1Chron. 6 | Mark — 2 | 1Chron. 7 | 1 Cor.—15 |
| f | 2 | | ii. | ——— 8 | ——— 3 | ——— 9 | ———16 |
| g | 3 | | iii. | ———10 | ——— 4 | 2Chron. 1 | 2 Cor.— 1 |
| A | 4 | | iv. | 2Chron. 2 | ——— 5 | ——— 3 | ——— 2 |
| b | 5 | | v. | ——— 4 | ——— 6 | ——— 5 | ——— 3 |
| c | 6 | | vi. | ——— 6 | ——— 7 | ——— 7 | ——— 4 |
| d | 7 | | vii. | ——— 8 | ——— 8 | ——— 9 | ——— 5 |
| e | 8 | | viii. | ———10 | ——— 9 | ———11 | ——— 6 |
| f | 9 | | ix. | ———12 | ———10 | ———13 | ——— 7 |
| g | 10 | | x. | Esther– 1 | ———11 | Esther– 2 | ——— 8 |
| A | 11 | *S. Barnabas the Apostle.* | xi. | ——— 3 | Acts —14 | ——— 4 | Acts —15 |
| b | 12 | | xii. | ——— 5 | Mark —12 | ——— 6 | 2 Cor.— 9 |
| c | 13 | | xiii. | ——— 7 | ———13 | ——— 8 | ———10 |
| d | 14 | | xiv. | ——— 9 | ———14 | Job— 1 | ———11 |
| e | 15 | | xv. | Job. — 2 | ———15 | ——— 3 | ———12 |
| f | 16 | | xvi. | ——— 4 | ———16 | ——— 5 | ———13 |
| g | 17 | | xvii. | ——— 6 | Luke — 1 | ——— 7 | Gal. — 1 |
| A | 18 | | xviii. | ——— 8 | ——— 2 | ——— 9 | ——— 2 |
| b | 19 | | xix. | ———10 | ——— 3 | ———11 | ——— 3 |
| c | 20 | | xx. | ———12 | ——— 4 | ———13 | — — 4 |
| d | 21 | | xxi. | ———14 | ——— 5 | ———15 | ——— 5 |
| e | 22 | | xxii. | ———16 | ——— 6 | —17 & 18 | ——— 6 |
| f | 23 | | xxiii. | ———19 | ——— 7 | ———20 | Eph.— 1 |
| g | 24 | *S. John the Baptist.* | xxiv. | Malachi 3 | Matt. — 3 | Malachi 4 | Matt. —14 |
| A | 25 | | xxv. | Job—21 | Luke — 8 | Job—22 | Eph.— 2 |
| b | 26 | | xxvi. | ———23 | ——— 9 | —24 & 25 | ——— 3 |
| c | 27 | | xxvii. | —26 & 27 | ———10 | ———28 | ——— 4 |
| d | 28 | | xxviii. | ———29 | ———11 | ———30 | ——— 5 |
| e | 29 | *S. Peter the Apostle.* | xxix. | ———31 | Acts— 3 | ———32 | Acts— 4 |
| f | 30 | | xxx. | ———33 | Luke —12 | ———34 | Eph.— 1 |

| JULY KALENDAR. | | | MATINS. | | EVENSONG. | |
|---|---|---|---|---|---|---|
| | | PSALMS. | 1 LESSON. | 2 LESSON. | 1 LESSON. | 2 LESSON. |
| g | 1 | ——————— i. | Job. —35 | Luke —13 | Job ——36 | Phil.— 1 |
| A | 2 | ——————— ii. | ——37 | ——14 | ——38 | —— 2 |
| b | 3 | ——————— iii. | ——39 | ——15 | ——40 | —— 3 |
| c | 4 | ——————— iv. | ——41 | ——16 | ——42 | —— 4 |
| d | 5 | ——————— v. | Prov.— 1 | ——17 | Prov.— 2 | Colos. - 1 |
| e | 6 | ——————— vi. | —— 3 | ——18 | —— 4 | —— 2 |
| f | 7 | ——————— vii. | —— 5 | ——19 | —— 6 | —— 3 |
| g | 8 | ——————— viii. | —— 7 | ——20 | —— 8 | —— 4 |
| A | 9 | ——————— ix. | —— 9 | ——21 | ——10 | 1 Thes. 1 |
| b | 10 | ——————— x. | ——11 | ——22 | ——12 | —— 2 |
| c | 11 | ——————— xi. | ——13 | ——23 | ——14 | —— 3 |
| d | 12 | ——————— xii. | ——15 | ——24 | ——16 | —— 4 |
| e | 13 | ——————— xiii. | ——17 | John — 1 | ——18 | —— 5 |
| f | 14 | ——————— xiv. | ——19 | —— 2 | ——20 | 2 Thes. 1 |
| g | 15 | ——————— xv. | ——21 | —— 3 | ——22 | —— 2 |
| A | 16 | ——————— xvi. | ——23 | —— 4 | ——24 | —— 3 |
| b | 17 | ——————— xvii. | ——25 | —— 5 | ——26 | 1 Tim.- 1 |
| c | 18 | ——————— xviii. | ——27 | —— 6 | ——28 | —2 & 3 |
| d | 19 | ——————— xix. | ——29 | —— 7 | ——30 | —— 4 |
| e | 20 | ——————— xx. | ——31 | —— 8 | Eccles. 1 | —— 5 |
| f | 21 | ——————— xxi. | Eccles. 2 | —— 9 | —— 3 | —— 6 |
| g | 22 | S. Mary Magdalen. xxii. | —— 4 | ——10 | —— 5 | 2 Tim - 1 |
| A | 23 | ——————— xxiii. | —— 6 | ——11 | —— 7 | —— 2 |
| b | 24 | ——————— xxiv. | —— 8 | ——12 | —— 9 | —— 3 |
| c | 25 | S. James the Apostle. xxv. | ——10 | ——13 | ——11 | —— 4 |
| d | 26 | ——————— xxvi. | ——12 | ——14 | Jer.— 1 | Titus— 1 |
| e | 27 | ——————— xxvii. | Jer.— 2 | ——15 | —— 3 | —2 & 3 |
| f | 28 | ——————— xxviii. | —— 4 | ——16 | —— 5 | Philem. 1 |
| g | 29 | ——————— xxix. | —— 6 | ——17 | —— 7 | Heb. — 1 |
| A | 30 | ——————— xxx. | —— 8 | ——18 | —— 9 | —— 2 |
| b | 31 | ——————— xxx. | ——10 | ——19 | ——11 | —— 3 |

# AUGUST.

| AUGUST KALENDAR. | | MATINS. | | EVENSONG. | |
|---|---|---|---|---|---|
| | PSALMS. | 1 Lesson. | 2 Lesson. | 1 Lesson. | 2 Lesson. |
| 1 | i. | Jer. ——12 | John —20 | Jer. ——13 | Heb. — 4 |
| 2 | ii. | ——14 | ———21 | ——15 | ——— 5 |
| 3 | iii. | ——16 | Acts — 1 | ——17 | ——— 6 |
| 4 | iv. | ——18 | —— 2 | ——19 | ——— 7 |
| 5 | v. | ——20 | —— 3 | ——21 | ——— 8 |
| 6 | vi. | ——22 | —— 4 | ——23 | ——— 9 |
| 7 | vii. | ——24 | —— 5 | ——25 | ——10 |
| 8 | viii. | ——26 | —— 6 | ——27 | ——11 |
| 9 | ix. | ——28 | —— 7 | ——29 | ——12 |
| 10 | x. | ——30 | —— 8 | ——31 | ——13 |
| 11 | xi. | ——32 | —— 9 | ——33 | James – 1 |
| 12 | xii. | ——34 | ——10 | ——35 | —— 2 |
| 13 | xiii. | ——36 | ——11 | ——37 | —— 3 |
| 14 | xiv. | ——38 | ——12 | ——39 | —— 4 |
| 15 | xv. | ——40 | ——13 | ——41 | —— 5 |
| 16 | xvi. | ——42 | ——14 | ——43 | 1 Pet. – 1 |
| 17 | xvii. | ——44 | ——15 | —45 & 46 | —— 2 |
| 18 | xviii. | ——47 | ——16 | ——48 | —— 3 |
| 19 | xix. | ——49 | ——17 | ——50 | —— 4 |
| 20 | xx. | ——51 | ——18 | ——52 | —— 5 |
| 21 | xxi. | Lam. — 1 | ——19 | Lam. — 2 | 2 Pet. – 1 |
| 22 | xxii. | —— 3 | ——20 | —— 4 | —— 2 |
| 23 | xxiii. | —— 5 | ——21 | Ezek.— 2 | —— 3 |
| 24 | S. Bartholo-mew, Apostle. xxiv. | Ezek.— 3 | ——22 | —— 6 | 1 John– 1 |
| 25 | xxv | —— 7 | ——23 | ——13 | —— 2 |
| 26 | xxvi. | ——14 | ——24 | ——18 | —— 3 |
| 27 | xxvii. | ——33 | ——25 | ——34 | —— 4 |
| 28 | xxviii. | —— 1 | ——26 | Dan.— 2 | —— 5 |
| 29 | xxix. | —— 3 | ——27 | —— 4 | 2 & 3 John |
| 30 | xxx. | —— 5 | ——28 | —— 6 | Jude— 1 |
| 31 | xxx. | —— 7 | Matt. — 1 | —— 8 | Rom. — 1 |

| SEPTEMBER KALENDAR. | | | MATINS. | | EVENSONG. | |
|---|---|---|---|---|---|---|
| | | PSALMS. | 1 LESSON. | 2 LESSON. | 1 LESSON. | 2 LES |
| f | 1 | ———— i. | Dan.—— 9 | Matt. — 2 | Dan.——10 | Rom. |
| g | 2 | ———— ii. | ————11 | ———— 3 | ————12 | —·— |
| A | 3 | ———— iii. | ————13 | ———— 4 | ————14 | ———— |
| b | 4 | ———— iv. | Hosea - 1 | ———— 5 | Hosea 2 3 | ———— |
| c | 5 | ———— v. | ———— 4 | ———— 6 | -—— 5 6 | ———— |
| d | 6 | ———— vi. | ———— 7 | ———— 7 | ———— 8 | ———— |
| e | 7 | ———— vii. | ———— 9 | ———— 8 | ————10 | ———— |
| f | 8 | ———— viii. | ————11 | ———— 9 | ————12 | ———— |
| g | 9 | ———— ix. | ————13 | ————10 | ————14 | ———— |
| A | 10 | ———— x. | Joel — 1 | ————11 | Joel — 2 | ———— |
| b | 11 | ———— xi. | ———— 3 | ————12 | Amos— 1 | ———— |
| c | 12 | ———— xii. | Amos. - 2 | ————13 | ———— 3 | ———— |
| d | 13 | ———— xiii. | ———— 4 | ————14 | ———— 5 | ———— |
| e | 14 | ———— xiv. | ———— 6 | ————15 | ———— 7 | ———— |
| f | 15 | ———— xv. | ———— 8 | ————16 | ———— 9 | ———— |
| g | 16 | ———— xvi. | Obadia. 1 | ————17 | Jonas— 1 | 1 Cor |
| A | 17 | ———— xvii. | Jonas 2 3 | ————18 | ———— 4 | ———— |
| b | 18 | ———— xviii. | Micha – 1 | ————19 | Micha - 2 | ———— |
| c | 19 | ———— xix. | ———— 3 | ————20 | ———— 4 | ———— |
| d | 20 | ———— xx. | ———— 5 | ————21 | ———— 6 | ———— |
| e | 21 | *S. Matthew.* xxi. | ———— 7 | ————22 | Nahum. 1 | ———— |
| f | 22 | ———— xxii. | Nahum. 2 | ————23 | ———— 3 | ———— |
| g | 23 | ———— xxiii. | Hab.— 2 | ————24 | Hab.— 2 | ———— |
| A | 24 | ———— xxiv. | ———— 3 | ————25 | Zeph.— 1 | ———— |
| b | 25 | ———— xxv. | Zeph. - 2 | ————26 | ———— 3 | ———— |
| c | 26 | ———— xxvi. | Hag — 1 | ————27 | Hag.— 2 | ———— |
| d | 27 | ———— xxvii. | Zach.— 1 | ————28 | Zech.-2 3 | ———— |
| e | 28 | ———— xxviii. | —— 4 & 5 | Mark — 1 | ———— 6 | ———— |
| f | 29 | ———— xxix. | ———— 7 | ———— 2 | ———— 8 | ———— |
| g | 30 | *S. Michael & All Angels.* xxx. | ———— 9 | ———— 3 | ————10 | ———— |

| OCTOBER KALENDAR. | | | MATINS. | | EVENSONG. | |
|---|---|---|---|---|---|---|
| | | PSALMS. | 1 LESSON. | 2 LESSON. | 1 LESSON. | 2 LESSON. |
| A | 1 | i. | Zech. —11 | Mark — 4 | Zech. —12 | 1 Cor. -16 |
| b | 2 | ii. | ——13 | —— 5 | ——14 | 2 Cor. - 1 |
| c | 3 | iii. | Mal. — 1 | —— 6 | Mal. — 2 | —— 2 |
| d | 4 | iv. | —— 3 | —— 7 | —— 4 | —.— 3 |
| e | 5 | v. | Tobit. - 1 | —— 8 | Tobit — 2 | —— 4 |
| f | 6 | vi. | —— 3 | —— 9 | —— 4 | —— 5 |
| g | 7 | vii. | —— 5 | ——10 | —— 6 | —— 6 |
| A | 8 | viii. | —— 7 | ——11 | —— 8 | —— 7 |
| b | 9 | ix. | —— 9 | ——12 | ——10 | —— 8 |
| c | 10 | x. | ——11 | ——13 | ——12 | —— 9 |
| d | 11 | xi. | ——13 | ——14 | ——14 | ——10 |
| e | 12 | xii. | Judith - 1 | ——15 | Judith - 2 | ——11 |
| f | 13 | xiii. | —— 3 | ——16 | —— 4 | ——12 |
| g | 14 | xiv. | —— 5 | Luke *di* 1 | —— 6 | ——13 |
| A | 15 | xv. | —— 7 | —*di* 1 | —— 8 | Gal. — 1 |
| b | 16 | xvi. | —— 9 | —— 2 | ——10 | —— 2 |
| c | 17 | xvii. | ——11 | —— 3 | ——12 | —— 3 |
| d | 18 | *S. Luke* *Evangelist.* xviii. | ——13 | —— 4 | ——14 | —— 4 |
| e | 19 | xix. | ——15 | —— 5 | ——16 | —— 5 |
| f | 20 | xx. | Wisd'm 1 | —— 6 | Wisd'm 2 | —— 6 |
| g | 21 | xxi. | —— 3 | —— 7 | —— 4 | Eph.— 1 |
| A | 22 | xxii. | —— 5 | —— 8 | —— 6 | —— 2 |
| b | 23 | xxiii. | —— 7 | —— 9 | —— 8 | —— 3 |
| c | 24 | xxiv. | —— 9 | ——10 | ——10 | —— 4 |
| d | 25 | xxv. | ——11 | ——11 | ——12 | —— 5 |
| e | 26 | xxvi. | ——13 | ——12 | ——14 | —— 6 |
| f | 27 | xxvii. | ——15 | ——13 | ——16 | Phil.— 1 |
| g | 28 | *S. Simon and* *S. Jude.* xxviii. | ——17 | ——14 | ——18 | —— 2 |
| A | 29 | xxix. | ——19 | ——15 | Ecclus. 1 | —— 3 |
| b | 30 | xxx. | Ecclus. 2 | ——16 | —— 3 | —— 4 |
| c | 31 | xxx. | —— 4 | ——17 | —— 5 | Colos. - 1 |

| NOVEMBER KALENDAR. | | PSALMS. | MATINS. 1 LESSON. | 2 LESSON. | EVENSONG. 1 LESSON. | 2 LES |
|---|---|---|---|---|---|---|
| d | 1 | *All Saints' Day.* i. | Wisd'm 3 | Heb. 11 12 | Wisd'm 5 | Rev. |
| e | 2 | ——— ii. | Ecclus. 6 | Luke —18 | Ecclus. 7 | Colos. |
| f | 3 | ——— iii. | ——— 8 | ———19 | ——— 9 | ——— |
| g | 4 | ——— iv. | ———10 | ———20 | ———11 | - —— |
| A | 5 | ——— v. | ———12 | ———21 | ———13 | 1 The |
| b | 6 | ——— vi. | ———14 | ———22 | ———15 | ——— |
| c | 7 | ——— vii. | ———16 | ———23 | ———17 | ——— |
| d | 8 | ——— viii. | ———18 | ———24 | ———19 | ——— |
| e | 9 | ——— ix. | ———20 | John — 1 | ———21 | ——— |
| f | 10 | ——— x. | ———22 | ——— 2 | ———23 | 2 The |
| g | 11 | ——— xi. | ———24 | ——— 3 | ———25 | ——— |
| A | 12 | ——— xii. | ———26 | ——— 4 | ———27 | ——— |
| b | 13 | ——— xiii. | ———28 | ——— 5 | ———29 | 1 Tim |
| c | 14 | ——— xiv. | ———30 | ——— 6 | ———31 | ———2 |
| d | 15 | ——— xv. | ———32 | ——— 7 | ———33 | ——— |
| e | 16 | ——— xvi. | ———34 | ——— 8 | ———35 | ——— |
| f | 17 | ——— xvii. | ———36 | ——— 9 | ———37 | ——— |
| g | 18 | ——— xviii. | ———38 | ———10 | ———39 | 2 Tim |
| A | 19 | ——— xix. | ———40 | ———11 | ———41 | ——— |
| b | 20 | ——— xx. | ———42 | ———12 | ———43 | ——— |
| c | 21 | ——— xxi. | ———44 | ———13 | ———45 | ——— |
| d | 22 | ——— xxii. | ———46 | ———14 | ———47 | Titus |
| e | 23 | ——— xxiii. | ———48 | ———15 | ———49 | ———2 |
| f | 24 | ——— xxiv. | ———50 | ———16 | ———51 | Philem |
| g | 25 | ——— xxv. | Bar. — 1 | ———17 | Bar. — 2 | Heb.- |
| A | 26 | ——— xxvi. | ——— 3 | ———18 | ——— 4 | ——— |
| b | 27 | ——— xxvii. | ——— 5 | ———19 | ——— 6 | ——— |
| c | 28 | ——— xxviii. | Isa.—— 1 | ———20 | Isa.—— 2 | ——— |
| d | 29 | ——— xxix. | ——— 3 | ———21 | ——— 4 | ——— |
| e | 30 | *S. Andrew, Apostle.* xxx. | ——— 5 | Acts— 1 | ——— 6 | ——— |

| DECEMBER KALENDAR. | | | | MATINS. | | EVENSONG. | |
|---|---|---|---|---|---|---|---|
| | | | PSALMS. | 1 LESSON. | 2 LESSON. | 1 LESSON. | 2 LESSON. |
| f | 1 | | i. | Isa. —— 7 | Acts —— 2 | Isa. —— 8 | Heb.—— 7 |
| g | 2 | | ii. | —— 9 | —— 3 | —— 10 | —— 8 |
| A | 3 | | iii. | —— 11 | —— 4 | —— 12 | —— 9 |
| b | 4 | | iv. | —— 13 | —— 5 | —— 14 | —— 10 |
| c | 5 | | v. | —— 15 | —— 6 | —— 16 | —— 11 |
| d | 6 | | vi. | —— 17 | —— *di* 7 | —— 18 | —— 12 |
| e | 7 | | vii. | —— 19 | —— *di* 7 | —20 & 21 | —— 13 |
| f | 8 | | viii. | —— 22 | —— 8 | —— 23 | James – 1 |
| g | 9 | | ix. | —— 24 | —— 9 | —— 25 | —— 2 |
| A | 10 | | x. | —— 26 | —— 10 | —— 27 | —— 3 |
| b | 11 | | xi. | —— 28 | —— 11 | —— 29 | —— 4 |
| c | 12 | | xii. | —— 30 | —— 12 | —— 31 | —— 5 |
| d | 13 | | xiii. | —— 32 | —— 13 | —— 33 | 1 Peter 1 |
| e | 14 | | xiv. | —— 34 | —— 14 | —— 35 | —— 2 |
| f | 15 | | xv. | —— 36 | —— 15 | —— 37 | —— 3 |
| g | 16 | | xvi. | —— 38 | —— 16 | —— 39 | —— 4 |
| A | 17 | | xvii. | —— 40 | —— 17 | —— 41 | —— 5 |
| b | 18 | | xviii. | —— 42 | —— 18 | —— 43 | 2 Pet. r 1 |
| c | 19 | | xix. | —— 44 | —— 19 | —— 45 | —— 2 |
| d | 20 | | xx. | —— 46 | —— 20 | —— 47 | —— 3 |
| e | 21 | *S. Thomas, Apostle.* | xxi. | —— 48 | —— 21 | —— 49 | 1 John 1 |
| f | 22 | | xxii. | —— 50 | —— 22 | —— 51 | —— 2 |
| g | 23 | | xxiii. | —— 52 | —— 23 | —— 53 | —— 3 |
| A | 24 | | xxiv. | —— 54 | —— 24 | —— 55 | —— 4 |
| b | 25 | *Christmas.* | xxv. | Isa. —— 9 | Matt. — 1 | Isa. —— 7 | Titus — 3 |
| c | 26 | *S. Stephen.* | xxvi. | —— 56 | Acts 6 & 7 | —— 57 | Acts —— 7 |
| d | 27 | *S. John.* | xxvii. | —— 58 | Rev. — 1 | —— 59 | Rev. —22 |
| e | 28 | *Innocents.* | xxviii. | Jer. —31 | Acts —25 | Isa. —60 | 1 John 5 |
| f | 29 | | xxix. | Isa. —61 | —— 26 | —— 62 | 2 John 1 |
| g | 30 | | xxx. | —— 63 | —— 27 | —— 64 | 3 John 1 |
| A | 31 | | xxx. | —— 65 | —— 28 | —— 66 | Jude— 1 |

# AN ORDER

## FOR

## Matins daily through the Year.

The Priest being in the Quire, shall begin with a loud voice the Lord's Prayer, called the *Pater noster*.

OUR FATHER, which art in heaven, Hallowed be thy Name. Thy kingdom come. Thy will be done in earth, as it is in heaven, Give us this day our daily bread. And forgive us our trespasses, as we forgive them that trespass against us. And lead us not into temptation; But deliver us from evil. Amen.

Then likewise he shall say,

O Lord, open thou my lips.

*Answer.*

And my mouth shall shew forth thy praise.

*Priest.*

O God, make speed to save me.

*Answer.*

O Lord, make haste to help me.

*Priest.*

Glory be to the Father, and to the Son, and to the Holy Ghost.

As it was in the beginning, is now, and ever shall be: world without end. Amen.

Praise ye the Lord.

And from Easter to Trinity Sunday.

Alleluia.

Then shall be said or sung, without any Invitatory, this Psalm, *Venite, exultemus,* &c. in English, as followeth: Psalm xcv.

O COME, let us sing unto the Lord: let us heartily rejoice in the strength of our salvation.

Let us come before his presence with thanksgiving: and shew our self glad in him with Psalms.

For the Lord is a great God: and a great King above all gods.

In his hand are all the corners of the earth: and the strength of the hills is his also.

The sea is his, and he made it: and his hands prepared the dry land.

O come, let us worship, and fall down: and kneel before the Lord our Maker.

For he is the Lord our God: and we are the people of his pasture, and the sheep of his hands.

To day if ye will hear his voice, harden not your hearts: as in the provocation, and as in the day of temptation in the wilderness.

When your fathers tempted me: proved me, and saw my works.

Forty years long was I grieved with this generation. and said: It is a people that do err in their hearts, for they have not known my ways.

Unto whom I sware in my wrath: that they should not enter into my rest.

Glory be to the Father, and to the Son: and to the Holy Ghost.

As it was in the beginning, is now, and ever shall be: world without end. Amen.

¶ Then shall follow certain Psalms in order as they be appointed in a Table made for that purpose, except there be proper Psalms appointed for that day. And at the end of every Psalm throughout the year, and likewise in the end of *Benedictus*, *Benedicite*, *Magnificat*, and *Nunc dimittis*, shall be repeated,

Glory be to the Father, and to the Son, and to the Holy Ghost.

As it was in the beginning, is now, and ever shall be: world without end. Amen.

¶ Then shall be read two Lessons distinctly with a loud voice, that the people may hear. The first of the Old Testament, the second of the New; like as they be appointed by the Kalendar, except there be proper Lessons assigned for that day: the Minister that readeth the Lesson standing and turning him so as he may best be heard of all such as be present. And before every Lesson, the Minister shall say thus: *The first, second, third* or *fourth chapter of Genesis* or *Exodus, Matthew, Mark,* or other like, as is appointed in the Kalendar. And in the end of every chapter he shall say,

Here endeth such a chapter of such a book.

And (to the end the people may the better hear) in such places where they do sing, there shall the Lessons be sung in a plain tune, after the manner of distinct reading: and likewise the Epistle and Gospel.

¶ After the first Lesson shall follow *Te Deum laudamus* in English, daily throughout the year, except in Lent, all the which time, in the place of *Te Deum,* shall be used *Benedicite omnia Opera Domini Domino,* in English as followeth.

## Te Deum laudamus.

WE praise thee, O God, we knowledge thee to be the Lord.

All the earth doth worship thee, the Father everlasting.

To thee all angels cry aloud, the Heavens and all the Powers therein.

To thee Cherubin, and

Seraphin continually do cry, Holy, Holy, Holy, Lord God of Sabaoth.

Heaven and earth are replenished with the Majesty, of thy Glory.

The glorious company of the Apostles, praise thee.

The goodly fellowship of the Prophets, praise thee.

The noble army of Martyrs, praise thee.

The holy Church throughout all the world doth knowledge thee.

The Father of an infinite Majesty.

Thy honourable, true, and only Son.

The Holy Ghost also being the Comforter.

Thou art the King of Glory, O Christ.

Thou art the everlasting Son of the Father.

When thou tookest upon thee to deliver man, thou didst not abhor the Virgin's womb.

When thou hadst overcome the sharpness of death, thou didst open the Kingdom of Heaven to all believers.

Thou sittest on the right hand of God, in the glory of the Father.

We believe that thou shalt come to be our Judge.

We therefore pray thee, help thy servants, whom thou hast redeemed with thy precious blood.

Make them to be numbered with thy saints, in glory everlasting.

O Lord, save thy people: and bless thine heritage.

Govern them, and lift them up for ever.

Day by day we magnify thee.

And we worship thy Name ever world without end.

Vouchsafe, O Lord, to keep us this day without sin.

O Lord, have mercy upon us: have mercy upon us.

O Lord, let thy mercy lighten upon us: as our trust is in thee.

O Lord, in thee have I trusted: let me never be confounded.

### *Benedicite, omnia Opera Domini Domino.*

O ALL ye Works of the Lord, speak good of the Lord: praise him, and set him up for ever.

O ye Angels of the Lord, speak good of the Lord: praise him, and set him up for ever.

O ye Heavens, speak good of the Lord: praise him, and set him up for ever.

O ye Waters, that be above the Firmament, speak good

of the Lord: praise him, and set him up for ever.

O all ye Powers of the Lord, speak good of the Lord: praise him, and set him up for ever.

O ye Sun, and Moon: speak good of the Lord: praise him, and set him up for ever.

O ye Stars of Heaven, speak good of the Lord: praise him, and set him up for ever.

O ye Showers and Dew, speak good of the Lord: praise him, and set him up for ever.

O ye Winds of God, speak good of the Lord: praise him, and set him up for ever.

O ye Fire and Heat, praise ye the Lord: praise him, and set him up for ever.

O ye Winter and Summer, speak good of the Lord: praise him, and set him up for ever.

O ye Dews and Frosts, speak good of the Lord: praise him, and set him up for ever.

O ye Frost and Cold, speak good of the Lord: praise him, and set him up for ever.

O ye Ice and Snow, speak good of the Lord: praise him, and set him up for ever.

O ye Nights and Days, speak good of the Lord:

praise him, and set him up for ever.

O ye Light and Darkness, speak good of the Lord: praise him, and set him up for ever.

O ye Lightnings and Clouds, speak good of the Lord: praise him, and set him up for ever.

O let the Earth speak good of the Lord: yea, let it praise him, and set him up for ever.

O ye Mountains and Hills, speak good of the Lord: praise him, and set him up for ever.

O all ye Green Things upon the Earth, speak good of the Lord: praise him, and set him up for ever.

O ye Wells, speak good of the Lord: praise him, and set him up for ever.

O ye Seas and Floods, speak good of the Lord: praise him, and set him up for ever.

O ye Whales, and all that move in the Waters, speak good of the Lord: praise him, and set him up for ever.

O all ye Fowls of the Air, speak good of the Lord: praise him, and set him up for ever.

O all ye Beasts and Cattle, speak ye good of the Lord: praise him, and set him up for ever.

O ye Children of Men, speak good of the Lord: praise him, and set him up for ever.

O let Israel speak good of the Lord: praise him, and set him up for ever.

O ye Priests of the Lord, speak good of the Lord: praise him, and set him up for ever.

O ye Servants of the Lord, speak good of the Lord: praise him, and set him up for ever.

O ye Spirits and Souls of the righteous, speak good of the Lord: praise him, and set him up for ever.

O ye holy and humble Men of heart, speak ye good of the Lord: praise ye him, and set him up for ever.

O Ananias, Azarias, and Misael, speak ye good of the Lord: praise ye him, and set him up for ever.

Glory be to the Father, and to the Son, and to the Holy Ghost;

As it was in the beginning, is now, and ever shall be: world without end. Amen.

¶ And after the second Lesson, throughout the whole year, shall be used *Benedictus Dominus Deus Israël*, &c., in English, as followeth.

*Benedictus.* Luke, i: 68-80.

Blessed be the Lord God of Israel: for he hath visited and redeemed his people;

And hath lifted up an horn of salvation to us: in the house of his servant David;

As he spake by the mouth of his holy Prophets: which have been since the world began;

That we should be saved from our enemies: and from the hands of all that hate us;

To perform the mercy promised to our fathers: and to remember his holy covenant.

To perform the oath which he sware to our father Abraham: that he would give us;

That we being delivered out of the hands of our enemies: might serve him without fear:

In holiness and righteousness before him: all the days of our life.

And thou, Child, shalt be called the Prophet of the Highest: for thou shalt go before the face of the Lord to prepare his ways;

To give knowledge of salvation unto his people: for the remission of their sins,

Through the tender mercy of our God: whereby the dayspring from on high hath visited us;

To give light to them that sit in darkness, and in the

shadow of death: and to guide our feet into the way of peace.

Glory be to the Father, &c.

As it was in the beginning, &c.

Then shall be said daily through the year, the Prayers follow-ing, as well at Evensong as at Matins, all devoutly kneeling.

Lord, have mercy upon us.

*Christ, have mercy upon us.*

Lord, have mercy upon us.

Then the Minister shall say the *Creed* and the *Lord's Prayer* in English, with a loud voice, &c.

*Answer.*

But deliver us from evil. Amen.

*Priest.*

O Lord, shew thy mercy upon us.

*Answer.*

And grant us thy salvation.

*Priest.*

O Lord, save the king.

*Answer.*

And mercifully hear us when we call upon thee.

*Priest.*

Indue thy Ministers with righteousness.

*Answer.*

And make thy chosen peo-ple joyful.

*Priest.*

O Lord, save thy people.

*Answer.*

And bless thine inheri-tance.

*Priest.*

Give peace in our time, O Lord.

*Answer.*

Because there is none other that fighteth for us, but only thou, O God.

*Priest.*

O God, make clean our hearts within us.

*Answer.*

And take not thine Holy Spirit from us.

*Priest.*

The Lord be with you.

*Answer.*

And with thy spirit.

¶ Then shall daily follow three Collects; the first of the day, which shall be the same that is appointed at the Communion; the second for peace; the third for grace to live well. And the last two Collects shall never al-ter, but daily be said at Matins throughout all the year, as fol-loweth. The Priest standing up, and saying,

Let us pray.

¶ Then the Collect of the day.

*The second Collect, for peace.*

O GOD, which art author of peace, and lover of concord, in knowledge of whom standeth our eternal life, whose service is perfect freedom: Defend us thy humble servants in all assaults of our enemies; that we, surely trusting in thy defence, may not fear the power of any adversaries, through the might of Jesu Christ our Lord.

Amen.

*The third Collect, for grace.*

O LORD, our heavenly Father, Almighty and ever living God, which hast safely brought us to the beginning of this day: Defend us in the same with thy mighty power; and grant that this day we fall into no sin, neither run into any kind of danger; but that all our doings may be ordered by thy governance, to do always that is righteous in thy sight; through Jesus Christ our Lord. Amen.

# AN ORDER

## FOR

## Evensong throughout the Year.

The Priest shall say,

OUR FATHER, which art in heaven, Hallowed be thy Name. Thy kingdom come. Thy will be done in earth as it is in heaven, Give us this day our daily bread. And forgive us our trespasses, as we forgive them that trespass against us. And lead us not into temptation; But deliver us from evil. Amen.

Then likewise he shall say,

O God, make speed to save me.

*Answer.*

O Lord, make haste to help me.

*Priest.*

Glory be to the Father, and to the Son: and to the Holy Ghost.

As it was in the beginning, is now, and ever shall be: world without end. Amen.

Praise ye the Lord.

And from Easter to Trinity Sunday.

Alleluia.

As before is appointed at Matins.

Then Psalms in order as they be appointed in the Table for Psalms, except there be proper Psalms appointed for that day. Then a Lesson of the Old Testament, as it is appointed likewise in the Kalendar, except there be proper Lessons appointed for that day. After that (*Magnificat anima mea Dominum*) in English, as followeth.

*Magnificat*, Luke, i: 46–56.

MY soul doth magnify the Lord.

And my spirit hath rejoiced in God my Saviour.

For he hath regarded the lowliness of his handmaiden.

For behold, from henceforth all generations shall call me blessed.

For he that is mighty hath magnified me: and holy is his Name.

And his mercy is on them that fear him: throughout all generations.

He hath shewed strength with his arm: he hath scattered the proud in the imagination of their hearts.

He hath put down the mighty from their seat: and

hath exalted the humble and meek.

He hath filled the hungry with good things: and the rich he hath sent empty away.

He remembering his mercy hath holpen his servant Israel: as he promised to our fathers, Abraham and his seed, for ever.

Glory be to the Father, and to the Son: and to the Holy Ghost;

As it was in the beginning, is now, and ever shall be: world without end. Amen.

Then a lesson of the New Testament. And after that, (*Nunc dimittis servum tuum,*) in English, as followeth.

*Nunc dimittis.* Luke ii 29-33.

LORD, now lettest thou thy servant depart in peace: according to thy word.

For mine eyes have seen thy salvation,

Which thou hast prepared: before the face of all people.

To be a light to lighten the Gentiles: and to be the glory of thy people Israel.

Glory be to the Father, and to the Son: and to the Holy Ghost;

As it was in the beginning, is now, and ever shall be: world without end. Amen.

Then the suffrages before assigned at Matins, the Clerks kneeling likewise; with three

Collects. First of the day, second of peace, third for aid against all perils, as here followeth: which last two Collects shall be daily said at Evensong without alteration.

*The Second Collect at Evensong.*

O GOD, from whom all holy desires, all good counsels, and all just works do proceed: Give unto thy servants that peace which the world cannot give; that both our hearts may be set to obey thy commandments, and also that by thee we being defended from the fear of our enemies may pass our time in rest and quietness; through the merits of Jesu Christ, our Saviour. Amen.

*The Third Collect, for aid against all perils.*

LIGHTEN our darkness, we beseech thee, O Lord; and by thy great mercy defend us from all perils and dangers of this night: for the love of thy only Son, our Saviour, Jesu Christ. Amen.

¶ In the Feasts of *Christmas*, the *Epiphany, Easter*, the *Ascension, Pentecost*, and upon *Trinity Sunday*, shall be sung or said immediately after *Benedictus*, this Confession of our Christian Faith.

*Quicunque vult, &c.*

WHOSOVER will be saved: before all things it is necessary that he hold the ~~Cath-olic~~ Faith.

Which Faith except every one do keep holy and undefiled: without doubt he shall perish everlastingly.

And the ~~Catholic~~ Faith is this: That we worship one God in Trinity, and Trinity in Unity;

Neither confounding the Persons: nor dividing the Substance.

For there is one Person of the Father, another of the Son: and another of the Holy Ghost.

But the Godhead of the Father, of the Son, and of the Holy Ghost, is all one: the Glory equal, the Majesty co-eternal.

Such as the Father is, such is the Son: and such is the Holy Ghost.

The Father uncreate, the Son uncreate: and the Holy Ghost uncreate.

The Father incomprehensible, the Son incomprehensible: and the Holy Ghost incomprehensible.

The Father eternal, the Son eternal: and the Holy Ghost eternal.

And yet they are not three eternals: but one eternal.

As also there be not three incomprehensibles, nor three uncreated: but one uncrea-

ted, and one incomprehensible.

So likewise the Father is Almighty, the Son Almighty: and the Holy Ghost Almighty.

And yet they are not three Almighties: but one Almighty.

So the Father is God, the Son God: and the Holy Ghost God.

And yet are they not three Gods: but one God.

So likewise the Father is Lord, the Son Lord: and the Holy Ghost Lord.

And yet not three Lords: but one Lord.

For like as we be compelled by the Christian verity: to acknowledge every Person by himself to be God and Lord;

So are we forbidden by the ~~Catholic~~ Religion: to say, There be three Gods, or three Lords.

The Father is made of none: neither created, nor begotten.

The Son is of the Father alone: not made, nor created, but begotten.

The Holy Ghost is of the Father ~~and of the Son~~: neither made, nor created, nor begotten, but ~~proceeding.~~

So there is one Father, not three Fathers; one Son, not

three Sons: one Holy Ghost, not three Holy Ghosts.

And in this Trinity none is afore, nor after other: none is greater, nor less than other;

But the whole three Persons: be co-eternal together and co-equal;

So that in all things, as it is aforesaid: the Unity in Trinity, and the Trinity in Unity is to be worshipped.

He therefore that will be saved: must thus think of the Trinity.

Furthermore, it is necessary to everlasting salvation: that he also believe rightly in the Incarnation of our Lord Jesu Christ.

For the right faith is, that we believe and confess: that our Lord Jesus Christ, the Son of God, is God and Man;

God, of the Substance of the Father, begotten before the worlds: and Man, of the Substance of his Mother, born in the world.

Perfect God, and perfect Man: of a reasonable soul and human flesh subsisting;

Equal to the Father, as touching his Godhead: and inferior to the Father, touching his Manhood.

Who although he be God and Man: yet he is not two, but one Christ;

One; not by conversion of the Godhead into flesh: but by taking of the Manhood into God;

One altogether; not by confusion of Substance: but by unity of Person.

For as the reasonable soul and flesh is one man: so God and Man is one Christ;

Who suffered for our salvation: descended into hell; rose again the third day from the dead.

He ascended into heaven, he sitteth on the right hand of the Father, God Almighty: from whence he shall come to judge the quick and dead.

At whose coming all men shall rise again with their bodies: and shall give account of their own works.

And they that have done good shall go into life everlasting: and they that have done evil into everlasting fire.

This is the Catholic Faith: which except a man believe faithfully, he cannot be saved.

Glory be to the Father, and to the Son: and to the Holy Ghost;

As it was in the beginning, is now, and ever shall be: world without end. Amen.

*Thus endeth the Order of Matins and Evensong.*

# The Introits, Collects, Epistles and Gospels.

*To be used at the Celebration of the Lord's Supper and Holy Communion, through the Year: with proper Psalms and Lessons for divers Feasts and Days.*

## The First Sunday in Advent.

*Beatus vir*, Psalm i.

BLESSED is that man, that hath not walked in the counsel of the ungodly, nor stand in the way of sinners: and hath not sit in the seat of the scornful;

But his delight is in the law of the Lord: and in his law will he exercise himself day and night.

And he shall be like a tree planted by the water-side: that will bring forth his fruit in due season.

His leaf also shall not wither: and look, whatsoever he doth, it shall prosper.

As for the ungodly, it is not so with them: but they are like the chaff, which the wind scattereth away (from the face of the earth).

Therefore the ungodly shall not be able to stand in the judgment: neither the sinners in the congregation of the righteous.

But the Lord knoweth the way of the righteous: and the way of the ungodly shall perish.

Glory be to the Father, and to the Son: and to the Holy Ghost;

As it was in the beginning, is now, and ever shall be: world without end.   Amen.

And so must every Introit be ended.

Let us pray.

### The Collect.

ALMIGHTY God, give us grace that we may cast away the works of darkness, and put upon us the armour of light, now in the time of this mortal life, (in the which thy Son Jesus Christ came to visit us in great humility;) that in the last day, when he shall come again in his glorious majesty, to judge both the quick and the dead, we may rise to the life immortal, through him who liveth and reigneth with thee and the

Holy Ghost, now and ever. *Amen.*

*The Epistle,* Rom. xiii.

Owe nothing to any man but this, that ye love one another: for he that loveth another fulfilleth the law. For these commandments, Thou shalt not commit adultery, Thou shalt not kill, Thou shalt not steal, Thou shalt bear no false witness, Thou shalt not lust, and so forth; (if there be any other commandment) it is all comprehended in this saying, namely, Love thy neighbour as thyself. Love hurteth not his neighbour; therefore is love the fulfilling of the law. This also, we know the season, how that it is time that we should now awake out of sleep: for now is our salvation nearer than when we believed. The night is passed, the day is come nigh; let us therefore cast away the deeds of darkness, and let us put on the armour of light. Let us walk honestly as it were in the day light; not in eating and drinking, neither in chambering and wantonness, neither in strife and envying. But put ye on the Lord Jesus Christ. And make not provision for the flesh, to fulfil the lusts of it.

*The Gospel,* Matt. xxi.

And when they drew nigh to Jerusalem, and were come to Bethphage unto mount Olivet, then sent Jesus two disciples, saying unto them, Go into the town that lieth over against you, and anon ye shall find an ass bound, and a colt with her: loose them, and bring them unto me. And if any man say ought unto you, say ye, The Lord hath need of them; and straightway he will let them go. All this was done, that it might be fulfilled which was spoken by the Prophet, saying, Tell ye the daughter of Sion, Behold, thy King cometh unto thee, meek, sitting upon an ass, and a colt, the foal of the ass used to the yoke. The disciples went, and did as Jesus commanded them; and brought the ass, and the colt, and put on them their clothes, and set him thereon. And many of the people spread their garments in the way; other cut down branches from the trees, and strewed them in the way. Moreover the people that went before, and they that came after, cried, saying, Hosanna to the Son of David: Blessed is he that cometh in the name of the Lord; Hosanna in the highest. And when he was come to Jerusalem all the city was moved, saying, Who is this? And the people said, This is Jesus the Prophet of Nazareth a city of Galilee. And Jesus went into the temple of God, and cast out all them that sold and bought in the temple; and overthrew the tables of the money-changers, and the seats of them that sold doves; and said unto them, It is written, My house shall be called the house of prayer, but ye have made it a den of thieves.

## The Second Sunday in Advent.

*Ad Dominum cum tribularer,* Psalm cxx.

WHEN I was in trouble I called upon the Lord: and he heard me.

Deliver my soul, O Lord, from lying lips: and from a deceitful tongue.

What reward shall be given unto thee, thou false tongue: even mighty and sharp arrows, with hot burning coals.

Woe is me, that I am constrained to dwell with Mesech: and to have mine habitation among the tents of Cedar.

My soul hath long dwelt among them: that be enemies unto peace.

I labour for peace, but when I speak unto them thereof: they make them to battle.

Glory be to the Father, and to the Son, and to the Holy Ghost.

As it was in the beginning, is now, and ever shall be: world without end. Amen.

*The Collect.*

BLESSED Lord, which hast caused all holy Scriptures to be written for our learning; Grant us that we may in such wise hear them, read, mark, learn, and inwardly digest them, that by patience and comfort of thy holy Word, we may embrace and ever hold fast the blessed hope of everlasting life, which thou hast given us in our Saviour Jesus Christ.

*The Epistle,* Rom. xv.

WHATSOEVER things are written aforetime, they are

written for our learning, that we through patience, and comfort of the Scriptures, might have hope. The God of patience and consolation grant you to be likeminded one towards another, after the ensample of Christ Jesu: that ye all agreeing together, may with one mouth praise God, the Father of our Lord Jesus Christ. Wherefore receive ye one another, as Christ received us, to the praise of God. And this I say, that Jesus Christ was a minister of the circumcision for the truth of God, to confirm the promises made unto the fathers: And that the Gentiles might praise God for his mercy; as it is written, For this cause I will praise thee among the Gentiles, and sing unto thy Name. And again he saith, Rejoice, ye Gentiles, with his people. And again, Praise the Lord, all ye Gentiles, and laud him, all ye nations together. And again, Esai saith, There shall be the root of Jesse, and he that shall rise to reign over the Gentiles, in him shall the Gentiles trust. The God of hope fill you with all joy and peace in believing, that ye may be rich in hope, through the power of the Holy Ghost.

*The Gospel*, Luke xxi.

THERE shall be signs in the sun, and in the moon, and in the stars; and in the earth the people shall be at their wits' end through despair: the sea and the water shall roar, and men's hearts shall fail them for fear, and for looking after those things which shall come on the earth: for the powers of heaven shall move. And then shall they see the Son of Man come in a cloud with power and great glory. When these things begin to come to pass, then look up, and lift up your heads; for your redemption draweth nigh. And he shewed them a similitude, Behold the fig-tree, and all other trees; when they shoot forth their buds, ye see and know of your own selves that summer is then nigh at hand. So likewise ye also (when ye see these things come to pass) be sure that the Kingdom of God is nigh. Verily I say unto you, This generation shall not pass, till all be fulfilled: heaven and earth shall pass, but my words shall not pass.

## The Third Sunday in Advent.

*Cum invocarem*, Psalm iv.

HEAR me when I call, O God of my righteousness: thou hast set me at liberty when I was in trouble : have mercy upon me, and hearken unto my prayer.

O ye sons of men, how long will ye blaspheme mine honour : and have such pleasure in vanity, and seek after leasing?

Know this also, that the Lord hath chosen to himself the man that is godly : when I call upon the Lord, he will hear me.

Stand in awe, and sin not : commune with your own heart, and in your chamber, and be still.

Offer the sacrifice of righteousness : and put your trust in the Lord.

There be many that will say : Who will shew us any good?

Lord, lift thou up : the light of thy countenance upon us.

Thou hast put gladness in mine heart: since the time that their corn, and wine, (and oil) increased.

I will lay me down in peace, and take my rest : for it is thou, Lord, only, that makest me to dwell in safety.

Glory be to the Father, and to the Son, and to the Holy Ghost.

As it was in the beginning, is now, and ever shall be : world without end.    Amen.

### The Collect.

LORD, we beseech thee, give ear to our prayers, and by thy gracious visitation lighten the darkness of our heart, by our Lord Jesus Christ.

### The Epistle, 1 Cor. iv.

LET a man this wise esteem us, even as the ministers of Christ, and stewards of the secrets of God.    Furthermore, it is required of the stewards, that a man be found faithful.    With me it is but a very small thing that I should be judged of you, either of man's judgment : no, I judge not mine own self.    For I know nought by myself, yet am I not thereby justified ; it is the Lord that judgeth me.    Therefore judge nothing before the time, until the Lord come, which will lighten things that are hid in darkness, and open the counsels of the hearts ; and then shall every man have praise of God.

*The Gospel*, Matt. xi.

WHEN John being in prison heard the works of Christ, he sent two of his disciples, and said unto him, Art thou he that shall come, or do we look for another? Jesus answered and said unto them, go and shew John again what ye have heard and seen: The blind receive their sight, the lame walk, the lepers are cleansed, and the deaf hear, the dead are raised up, and the poor receive the glad tidings of the Gospel: And happy is he that is not offended by me. And as they depart-ed, Jesus began to say unto the people concerning John, What went ye out into the wilderness to see? A reed that is shaken with the wind? Or what went ye out for to see? A man clothed in soft raiment? behold, they that wear soft clothing are in kings' houses. But what went ye out for to see? A prophet? verily I say unto you, and more than a prophet. For this is he of whom it is written, Behold, I send my messenger before thy face, which shall prepare thy way before thee.

## The Fourth Sunday in Advent.

*Verba mea auribus.* Psalm v.

PONDER my words, O Lord: consider my meditation.

O hearken thou unto the voice of my calling, my King, and my God: for unto thee will I make my prayer.

My voice shalt thou hear betimes, O Lord: early in the morning will I direct my prayer unto thee, and will look up.

For thou art the God that hath no pleasure in wickedness: neither shall any evil dwell with thee.

Such as be foolish shall not stand in thy sight: for thou hatest all them that work vanity.

Thou shalt destroy them that speak leasing: the Lord will abhor both the blood-thirsty and deceitful man.

But as for me, I will come into thy house, even upon the multitude of thy mercy: and in thy fear will I worship toward thy holy temple.

Lead me, O Lord, in thy righteousness, because of mine enemies: make thy way plain before my face.

For there is no faithfulness in his mouth: their inward parts are very wickedness.

Their throat is an open sepulchre: they flatter with their tongue.

Destroy thou them, O God; let them perish through their own imaginations: cast them out in the multitude of their ungodliness; for they have rebelled against thee.

And let all them that put their trust in thee rejoice: they shall ever be giving of thanks, because thou defendest them; they that love thy Name shall be joyful in thee.

For thou, Lord, wilt give thy blessing unto the righteous: and with thy favourable kindness wilt thou defend him as with a shield.

Glory be to the Father, and to the Son: and to the Holy Ghost.

As it was in the beginning, is now, and ever shall be: world without end. Amen.

### The Collect.

LORD, raise up (we pray thee) thy power, and come among us, and with great might succour us; that whereas, through our sins and wickedness, we be sore let and hindered, thy bounti-

ful grace and mercy, through the satisfaction of thy Son our Lord, may speedily deliver us; to whom with thee and the Holy Ghost be honour and glory, world without end.

### The Epistle, Phil. iv.

REJOICE in the Lord alway, and again I say, Rejoice. Let your softness be known unto all men. The Lord is even at hand. Be careful for nothing: but in all prayer and supplication, let your petitions be manifest unto God, with giving of thanks. And the peace of God (which passeth all understanding) keep your hearts and minds through Christ Jesu.

### The Gospel, John i.

THIS is the record of John, when the Jews sent Priests and Levites from Jerusalem to ask him, What art thou? And he confessed, and denied not; and said plainly, I am not Christ. And they asked him, What then? Art thou Helias? And he saith, I am not. Art thou that Prophet? And he answered, No. Then said they unto him, What art thou? that we may give an answer unto them that sent us. What sayest thou of thyself? He said, I am the voice of a crier in the wilderness, Make straight the way of the Lord, as said the prophet Esai. And they which were sent were of the Pharisees. And they asked him, and said unto him, Why baptizest thou then, if thou be not Christ, nor Helias, neither that Prophet? John answered them, saying, I baptize with water: but there standeth one among you, whom ye know not: He it is which though he came after me was before me, whose shoe latchet I am not worthy to unloose. These things were done at Bethabara beyond Jordan, where John did baptize.

## PROPER PSALMS AND LESSONS ON

## Christmas Day.

### At Matins.

Psalm xix. ⎫ THE FIRST LESSON, Isa. ix.
Psalm xlv. ⎬
Psalm lxxxv. ⎭ THE SECOND LESSON, Matt. i.

## At the First Communion.

*Cantate Domino*, Psalm xcviii.

O SING unto the Lord a new song: for he hath done marvellous things.

With his own right hand, and with his holy arm: hath he gotten himself the victory.

The Lord declared his salvation: his righteousness hath he openly shewed in the sight of the heathen.

He hath remembered his mercy and truth toward the house of Israel: and all the ends of the world have seen the salvation of our God.

Shew yourselves joyful unto the Lord, all ye lands: sing, rejoice, and give thanks.

Praise the Lord upon the harp: sing to the harp with a psalm of thanksgiving.

With trumpets also and shawms: O shew yourselves joyful before the Lord the King.

Let the sea make a noise, and all that therein is: the round world, and they that dwell therein.

Let the floods clap their hands, and let the hills be joyful together before the Lord:

for he is come to judge the earth.

With righteousness shall he judge the world: and the people with equity.

Glory be to the Father, and to the Son: and to the Holy Ghost.

As it was in the beginning, is now, and ever shall be: world without end. Amen.

### The Collect.

God, which makest us glad with the yearly remembrance of the birth of thy only Son Jesus Christ; grant that as we joyfully receive him for our Redeemer, so we may with sure confidence behold him, when he shall come to be our judge, who liveth and reigneth, etc.

### The Epistle, Titus ii.

T н e grace of G o d that bringeth salvation unto all men hath appeared, and teacheth us that we should deny ungodliness and worldly lusts, and that we should live soberly, and righteously, and godly, in this present world; looking for that blessed hope, and appearing of the glory of the great God and of our Saviour Jesu Christ; which gave himself for us, to redeem us from all unrighteousness, and to purge us a peculiar people unto himself, fervently given unto good works. T h e s e things speak, and exhort, and rebuke with all ferventness of commanding. See that no man despise thee.

### The Gospel, Luke ii.

And it chanced in those days, that there went out a commandment from Augustus the Emperor, that all the world should be taxed. And this taxing was the first, and executed when Sirenius was lieutenant in S i r i a. And every man went unto his own city to be taxed. And Joseph also ascended from Galilee, out of a city called Nazareth, into Jewry, unto the city of David, which is called Bethleem; because he was of the house and lineage of David; to be taxed with Mary, his spoused wife, which was with child. And it fortuned, that, while they were there, her time was come that she should be d e l i v e r e d. And s h e brought forth her first-begotten son, and wrapped him in swaddling clothes, and laid him in a manger; because there was no room for them in the inn. And there were in the same region shepherds watching and keeping their flock by n i g h t. And, lo, the angel of the Lord stood hard by them, and the brightness of the Lord shone round about them: and they were sore afraid. And the angel said unto them, Be not afraid: for, behold, I bring you tidings of great joy, that shall come to all people. For unto you is born this day in the city of David a Saviour, which is Christ the Lord. And take this for a sign; Ye shall find the child wrapped in swaddling clothes, and laid in a manger. And straightway there was with the angel a multitude of heavenly soldiers, praising God, and saying, Glory to God on high, and peace on the earth, and unto men a good will.

## Christmas Day.
### At the Second Communion.

*Domine Dominus noster.*
Psalm viii.

O LORD our Governor, how excellent is thy Name in all the world: thou that hast set thy glory above the heavens.

Out of the mouth of very babes and sucklings hast thou ordained strength, because of thine enemies: that t h o u mightest still the enemy and the avenger.

For I will consider t h y heavens, even the works of thy fingers: the moon and the stars, which thou hast ordained.

What is man, that thou art so mindful of him: and the son of man, that thou visitest him?

Thou madest him lower than the angels: to crown him with glory and worship.

Thou makest him to have dominion of the works of thy hands: and thou hast put all things in subjection under his feet;

All sheep and oxen: yea, and the beasts of the field;

The fowls of the air, and the fishes of the sea: and whatsoever walketh through the paths of the seas.

O Lord our Governor: how excellent is thy Name in all the world.

Glory be to the Father, and to the Son: and to the Holy Ghost;

As it was in the beginning, is now, and ever shall be: world without end. Amen.

### The Collect.

ALMIGHTY God, which hast given us thy only-begotten

Son to take our nature upon him, and this day to be born of a pure Virgin; Grant that we being regenerate, a n d made thy children by adoption and grace, may daily be renewed by thy Holy Spirit; through the same our Lord Jesus Christ, who liveth and reigneth, etc.

### The Epistle, Heb. i.

God, in times past diversely and many ways spake unto the fathers by prophets, but in these last days he hath spoken to us by his own Son, whom he hath made heir of all things, by whom also he made the world; which (Son) being the brightness of his glory, and the very image of his substance, ruling all things with the word of his power, hath by his own person purged our sins, and sitteth on the right hand of the Majesty on high; being so much more excellent than the angels, as he hath by inheritance obtained a` more excellent Name than they. For unto which of the angels said he at any time, Thou art my Son, this day have I begotten thee? And again, I will be his Father, and he shall be my Son? And again, when he bringeth in the first-begotten Son into the world,

he saith, And let all the angels of God worship him. And unto the angels he saith, He maketh his angels spirits, and his ministers a flame of fire. But unto the Son he saith, Thy seat (O God) shall be for ever and ever; the sceptre of thy kingdom is a right sceptre: Thou hast loved righteousness and hated iniquity; wherefore God, even thy God, hath anointed thee with the oil of gladness above thy fellows. And thou, Lord, in the beginning hast laid the foundation of the earth; and the heavens are the works of thy hands: they shall perish, but thou endurest; but they all shall wax old as doth a garment; and as a vesture shalt thou change them, and they shall be changed: but thou art even the same, and thy years shall not fail.

### The Gospel, John i.

In the beginning was the Word, and the Word was with God, and God was the Word. The same was in the beginning with God. All things were made by it; and without it was made nothing that was made. In it was life, and the life was the light of men. And the light shineth in darkness, and the darkness comprehended it not. There was sent from God a man, whose name was John. The same came as a witness, to bear witness of the light, that all men through him might believe. He was not that light, but was sent to bear witness of that light. That light was the true light, which lighteth every man that cometh into the world. He was in the world, and the world was made by him, and the world knew him not. He came among his own, and his own received him not. But as many as received him, to them gave he power to be the sons of God, even them that believed on his Name: which were born, n o t o f blood, nor of the will of the flesh, nor yet of the will of man, but of God. And the same Word became flesh, and dwelt among us; and we saw the glory of it, as the glory of the only-begotten Son of the Father, full of grace and truth.

### Proper Psalms and Lessons at Evensong.

Psalm lxxxix.　⎫　THE FIRST LESSON, Isaiah vii.
Psalm cx.　　 ⎬
Psalm cxxxii.　⎭　THE SECOND LESSON, Titus iii.

# Saint Stephen's Day.

## At Matins.

THE SECOND LESSON, Acts vi, *v.* 8 to vii, *v.* 30.

## At the Communion.

*Quid gloriaris in malicia?*
Psalm lii.

WHY boastest thou thyself, thou tyrant: that thou canst do mischief;

Whereas the goodness of God: endureth yet daily;

Thy tongue i m a g i n e t h wickedness: and with lies thou cuttest like a sharp razor.

Thou hast loved ungraciousness more than goodness: and to talk of lies more than righteousness.

Thou hast loved to speak all words that may do hurt: O thou false tongue.

Therefore shall God destroy thee for ever: he shall take thee, and pluck thee out of thy dwelling, and root thee out of the land of the living.

The righteous also shall see this, and fear: and shall laugh him to scorn;

Lo, this is the man that took not God for his strength: but trusted unto the multitude of his riches, and strengthen himself in his wickedness.

As for me, I am like a green olive tree in the house of God: my trust is in the tender mercy of God for ever and ever.

I will alway give thanks unto thee for that thou hast done: and I will hope in thy Name, for thy saints like it well.

Glory be to the Father, and to the Son: and to the Holy Ghost.

As it was in the beginning, is now, and ever shall be: world without end. Amen.

### The Collect.

GRANT us, O Lord, to learn to love our enemies, by the example of thy martyr Saint Stephen, who prayed to thee for his persecutors; which livest and reignest, etc.

¶Then shall follow a Collect of the Nativity.

### The Epistle, Acts vii.

AND Stephen, being full of the Holy Ghost, looked up stedfastly with his eyes into heaven, and saw the glory of God, and Jesus standing on the right hand of God, and said, Behold, I see the heavens open, and the Son of Man standing on the right hand of God. Then they gave a shout with a loud voice, and stopped their ears, and ran upon him all at once, and cast him out of the city, and stoned him: and the witnesses laid down their clothes at a young man's feet, whose name was Saul. And they stoned Stephen, calling on and saying, Lord Jesu, receive my spirit, And he kneeled down, and cried with a loud voice, Lord, lay not this sin to their charge. And when he had thus spoken, he fell asleep.

### The Gospel, Matt. xxiii.

BEHOLD, I send unto you prophets, and wise men, and scribes; and some of them ye shall kill and crucify; and some of them shall ye scourge in your synagogues, and persecute them from city to city; that upon you may come all the righteous blood which hath been shed upon the earth, from the blood of righteous Abel unto the blood of Zacharias, the son of Barachias, whom ye slew between the temple and the altar. Verily I say unto you, All these things shall come upon this generation. O Jerusalem, Jerusalem, thou that killest the prophets, and stonest them which are sent unto thee: how often would I have gathered thy children together, even as the hen gathereth her chickens under her wings, and ye would not! Behold, your house is left unto you desolate. For I say unto you, Ye shall not see me henceforth, till that ye say, Blessed is he that cometh in the Name of the Lord.

### At Evensong.
THE SECOND LESSON, Acts vii

---

# Saint John Evangelist's Day.

### At Matins.
THE SECOND LESSON, Rev. i.

## At the Communion.

*In Domino confido.* Psal. xi.

In the Lord put I my trust. how say ye then to my soul, that she should fly as a bird to the hill?

For lo, the ungodly bend their bow, and make ready their arrows within the quiver: that they may privily shoot at them which are true of heart.

For the foundations will be cast down: and what hath the righteous done?

The Lord is in his holy temple: the Lord's seat is in heaven.

His eyes consider the poor: and his eyelids trieth the children of men.

The Lord alloweth the righteous: but the ungodly, and him that delighteth in wickedness, doth his soul abhor.

Upon the ungodly he shall rain snares, fire and brimstone, storm and tempest: this shall be their portion to drink.

For the righteous Lord loveth righteousness: his countenance will behold the thing that is just.

Glory be to the Father, and

to the Son: and to the Holy Ghost.

As it was in the beginning, is now, and ever shall be: world without end. Amen.

### The Collect.

MERCIFUL Lord, we beseech thee to cast thy bright beams of light upon thy Church, that it being lightened by the doctrine of thy blessed Apostle and Evangelist John may attain to thy everlasting gifts; through Jesus Christ our Lord.

### The Epistle. 1 John i.

THAT which was from the beginning, which we have heard, which we have seen with our eyes, which we have looked upon, and our hands have handled of the Word of life; and the Life appeared, and we have seen and bear witness, and shew unto you that eternal Life, which was with the Father, and appeared unto us; that which we have seen and heard declare we unto you, that ye also may have fellowship with us, and that our fellowship may be with the Father, and his Son Jesus Christ. And this write we unto you, that ye may rejoice, and that your joy may be full. And this is the tidings which we have heard of him, and declare unto you, That God is Light, and in him is no darkness at all. If we say that we have fellowship with him, and walk in darkness, we lie, and do not the truth: but and if we walk in light, even as he is in light, then have we fellowship with him, and the blood of Jesus Christ his Son cleanseth us from all sin. If we say we have no sin, we deceive ourselves, and the truth is not in us. If we knowledge our sins, he is faithful and just to forgive us our sins, and cleanse us from all unrighteousness. If we say we have not sinned, we make him a liar, and his word is not in us.

### The Gospel. John xxi.

JESUS said unto Peter, Follow thou me. Peter turned about, and saw the disciple whom Jesus loved following; (which also leaned on his breast at supper, and said, Lord, which is he that betrayeth thee?); when Peter therefore saw him, he said to Jesus, Lord, what shall he here do? Jesus said unto him, If I will have him to tarry till I come, what is that to thee? follow thou me. Then went this saying abroad among the brethren, That that disciple should not die; yet Jesus said not to him, He shall not die: but, If I will that he tarry till I come, what is that to thee? The same disciple is he which testifieth of these things, and wrote these things, and we know that his testimony is true. There are also many other things which Jesus did, the which if they should be written every one, I suppose the world could not contain the books that s h o u l d be written.

### At Evensong.

THE SECOND LESSON, Rev. xxii.

---

# The Innocents' Day.

### At Matins.

THE FIRST LESSON, Jer. xxxi: 1-18.

*Deus, venerunt gentes.*
Psalm lxxix.

O GOD, the heathen are come into thine inheritance: thy holy temple have they defiled, and made Jerusalem an heap of stones.

The dead bodies of t h y servants have they given to be meat unto the fowls of the air: and the flesh of thy saints unto the beasts of the land.

Their blood have they shed like water on every side of Jerusalem: and there was no man to bury them.

We are become an open shame to our enemies: a very scorn and derision unto them that are round about us.

Lord, how long wilt thou be angry: shall thy jealousy burn like fire for ever?

Pour out thine indignation upon the heathen that have not known thee: and upon the kingdoms that have not called upon thy Name.

For they have devoured Jacob: and laid waste his dwelling-place.

O remember not our old sins, but have mercy upon us, and that soon: for we are come to great misery.

Help us, O God of our salvation, for the glory of thy Name: O deliver us, and be merciful unto our sins, for thy Name's sake.

Wherefore do the heathen

say: Where is now their God?

O let the vengeance of thy servant's blood that is shed: be openly shewed upon the heathen in our sight.

O let the sorrowful sighing of the prisoners come before thee: according unto the greatness of thy power, preserve thou those that are appointed to die.

And as for the blasphemy (wherewith our neighbours have blasphemed thee:) reward thou them, O Lord, sevenfold into their bosom.

So we, that be thy people, and sheep of thy pasture, shall give thee thanks for ever: and will alway be shewing forth thy praise from generation to generation.

Glory be to the Father, and to the Son: and to the Holy Ghost.

As is was in the beginning, is now, and ever shall be: world without end. Amen.

### The Collect.

ALMIGHTY God, whose praise this day the young innocents thy witnesses hath confessed and shewed forth, not in speaking but in dying: Mortify and kill all vices in us, that in our conversation our life may express thy faith, which with our tongues we do confess; through Jesus Christ our Lord.

### The Epistle. Rev. xiv.

I LOOKED, and lo, a Lamb stood on the mount Sion, and with him an hundred and xliv. thousand, having his name and his Father's name written in their foreheads. And I heard a voice from heaven, as the sound of many waters, and as the voice of a great thunder: and I heard the voice of harpers harping with their harps: and they sung as it were a new song before the seat, and before the iv. beasts, and the elders; and no man could learn the song, but the C. xliv. thousand, which were redeemed from the earth. These are they which were not defiled with women, for they are virgins: these follow the Lamb whithersoever he goeth: these were redeemed from men, being the first-fruits unto God, and to the Lamb. And in their mouths was found no guile; for they are without spot before the throne of God.

### The Gospel. Matt. ii.

THE angel of the Lord appeared to Joseph in a sleep, saying, Arise, and take the child, and his mother, and fly into Egypt, and be thou there till I bring thee word; for it will come to pass that Herode shall seek the child to destroy him. So when he awoke, he took the child and his mother by night, and departed into Egypt, and was there unto the death of Herode; that it might be fulfilled which was spoken of the Lord by the prophet, saying, Out of Egypt have I called my Son. Then Herode, when he saw that he was mocked of the wise men, he was exceeding wroth; and sent forth men of war, and slew all the children that were in Bethleem, and in all the coasts, (as many as were ii. year old or under,) according to the time which he had diligently known out of the wise men. Then was fulfilled that which was spoken by the prophet Jeremy, where as he said, In Rama was there a voice heard, lamentation, weeping, and great mourning, Rachel weeping for her children, and would not be comforted, because they were not.

## The Sunday after Christmas Day.

*Levavi oculos.* Psalm cxxi.

I WILL lift up mine eyes unto the hills: from whence cometh my help.

My help cometh even from the Lord: which hath made heaven and earth.

He will not suffer thy foot to be moved: and he that keepeth thee will not sleep.

Behold, he that keepeth Israel: shall neither slumber nor sleep.

The Lord himself is thy keeper; the Lord is thy defence upon thy right hand.

So that the sun shall not burn thee by day: neither the moon by night.

The Lord shall preserve thee from all evil: yea, it is even he that shall keep thy soul.

The Lord shall preserve thy going out, and thy coming in: from this time forth for evermore.

Glory be to the Father, and to the Son: and to the Holy Ghost.

As it was in the beginning, is now, and ever shall be: world without end. Amen.

*The Collect.*

ALMIGHTY God, which hast given us, etc., *As upon Christmas Day.*

*The Epistle.* Gal. iv.

AND I say, that the heir (as long as he is a child) differeth not from a servant, though he be Lord of all; but is under tutors and governors, until the time that the father hath appointed. Even so we, also, when we were children, were in bondage under the ordinances of the world: but when the time was full come, God sent his Son, made of a woman and made bond unto the law, to redeem them which were bond unto the law, that we through election might receive the inheritance that belongeth unto the natural sons. Because ye are sons, God hath sent the Spirit of his Son into our hearts, which crieth, Abba, Father. Wherefore now thou art not a servant, but a son; if thou be a son, thou art also an heir of God through Christ.

*The Gospel.* Matt. 1.

THIS is the book of the generation of Jesu Christ, the son of David, the son of Abraham. Abraham begat Isaac; Isaac begat Jacob; Jacob begat Judas and his brethren: Judas begat Phares and Zaram of Thamar; Phares begat Esrom; Esrom begat Aram; Aram begat Aminadab; Aminadab begat Naasson; Naasson begat Salmon; Salmon begat Boos of Rahab; Boos begat Obed of Ruth; Obed begat Jesse; Jesse begat David the king; David the king begat Salomon of her that was the wife of Urie; Salomon begat Roboam; Roboam begat Abia; Abia begat Asa; Asa begat Josaphat; Josaphat begat Joram; Joram begat Osias; Osias begat Joatham; Joatham begat Achas; Achas begat Ezechias; Ezechias begat Manasses; Manasses begat Amon; Amon begat Josias; Josias begat Jeconias and his brethren, about the time that they were carried away to Babilon: and after they were brought to Babilon, Jeconias begat Salathiel; Salathiel begat Zorobabel; Zorobabel begat Abiud; Abiud begat Eliachim; Eliachim begat Azor; Azor begat Sadoc; Sadoc begat Achin; Achin begat Eliud; Eliud begat Eleasar; Eleasar begat Matthan; Matthan begat Jacob; Jacob begat Joseph the husband of Mary, of whom was born Jesus, even he that is called Christ. And so all the generations from Abraham to David are xiv. generations; and from David unto the captivity of Babilon are xiv. generations; and from the captivity of Babilon unto Christ are xiv. generations.

The birth of Jesus Christ was on this wise: When his mother Mary was married to Joseph, (before they came to dwell together,) she was found with child by the Holy Ghost. Then Joseph her husband (because he was a righteous man, and would not put her to shame) was minded privily to depart from her. But while he thus thought, behold, the angel of the Lord appeared unto him in sleep, saying, Joseph, thou son of David, fear not to take unto thee Mary thy wife: for that which is conceived in her cometh of the Holy Ghost. She shall bring forth a son, and thou shalt call his name JESUS; for he shall save his people from their sins.

All this was done, that it might be fulfilled which was spoken of the Lord by the prophet, saying, Behold, a maid shall be with child, and shall bring forth a son, and they shall call his name Emanuel, which if a man interpret is as much to say as, God with us. And Joseph as soon as he awoke out of sleep did as the angel of the Lord had bidden him, and he took his wife unto him: and knew her not till she had brought forth her first-begotten son: and called his name JESUS.

## The Circumcision of Christ.

### At Matins.

THE FIRST LESSON, Gen. xvii.    THE SECOND LESSON, Rom. ii.

### At the Communion.

*Lœtatus sum.* Psalm cxxii.

I WAS glad when they said unto me: We will go into the house of the Lord.

Our feet shall stand in thy gates: O Jerusalem.

Jerusalem is builded as a city: that is at unity in itself.

For thither the tribes go up, even the tribes of the Lord: to testify unto Israel, to give thanks unto the Name of the Lord.

For there is the seat of judgment: even the seat of the house of David.

O pray for the peace of Jerusalem: they shall prosper that love thee.

Peace be within thy walls: and plenteousness within thy palaces.

For my brethren and companions' sakes: I will wish thee prosperity.

Yea, because of the house of the Lord our God: I will seek to do thee good.

Glory be to the Father, and to the Son: and to the Holy Ghost.

As it was in the beginning, is now, and ever shall be: world without end. Amen.

### The Collect.

ALMIGHTY God, which madest thy blessed Son to be circumcised, and obedient to the law for man; Grant us the true circumcision of thy Spirit; that our hearts, and all our members, being mortified from all worldly and carnal lusts, may in all things obey thy blessed will; through the same thy Son Jesus Christ our Lord.

### The Epistle. Rom. iv.

BLESSED is that man to whom the Lord will not impute sin. Came this blessedness then upon the uncircumcision, or upon the circumcision also? For we say, that faith was reckoned to Abraham for righteousness. How was it then reckoned? when he was in the circumcision, or when he was in the uncircumcision? Not in the time of circumcision, but when he was yet uncircumcised. And he received the sign of circumcision, as a seal of the righteousness of faith, which he had yet being uncircumcised; that he should be the father of all them that believe, though they be not circumcised; that righteousness might be imputed to them also: and that he might be the father of circumcision, not unto them only which came of the circumcised, but unto them also that walk in the steps of the faith that was in our father Abraham before the time of circumcision. For the promise (that he should be the heir of the world) happened not to Abraham, or to his seed, through the law, but through the righteousness of faith. For if they which are of the law be heirs, then is faith but vain, and the promise of none effect.

### The Gospel. Luke ii.

AND it fortuned, as soon as the angels were gone away from the shepherds into heaven, they said one to another,

Let us go now even unto Bethleem, and see this thing that we hear say is happened, which the Lord hath shewed unto us. And they came with haste, and found Mary and Joseph, and the babe laid in a manger. And when they had seen it, they published abroad the saying which was told them of that child. And all they that heard it wondered at those things which were told them of the shepherds. But Mary kept all those sayings, and pondered them in her heart. And the shepherds returned, praising and lauding God for all the things that they had heard and seen, even as it was told unto them. And when the eight day was come that the child should be circumcised, his Name was called JESUS, which was named of the angel before he was conceived in the womb.

### At Evensong.

THE FIRST LESSON, Deut. x:12.  THE SECOND LESSON, Col. ii.

# The Epiphany.

### At Matins.

THE FIRST LESSON, Isaiah lx.  THE SECOND LESSON, Luke iii:15-23.

### At the Communion.

*Cantate Domino.*

### Psal. xcvi.

O SING unto the Lord a new song: sing unto the Lord all the whole earth.

Sing unto the Lord, and praise his Name: be telling of his salvation from day to day.

Declare his honour unto the heathen: and his wonders unto all people.

For the Lord is great, and cannot worthily be praised: he is more to be feared than all gods.

As for all the gods of the heathen, they be but idols: but it is the Lord that made the heavens.

Glory and worship are before him: power and honour are in his sanctuary.

Ascribe unto the Lord, O ye kindreds of the people: ascribe unto the Lord worship and power.

Ascribe unto the Lord the honour due unto his Name:

bring presents, and come into his courts.

O worship the Lord in the beauty of holiness: let the whole earth stand in awe of him.

Tell it out among the heathen that the Lord is King, and that it is he which hath made the round world so fast that it cannot be moved: and how that he shall judge the people righteously.

Let the heavens rejoice, and let the earth be glad: let the sea make a noise, and all that therein is.

Let the field be joyful, and all that is in it: then shall all the trees of the wood rejoice before the Lord.

For he cometh, for he cometh to judge the earth: and with righteousness to judge the world, and the people with his truth.

Glory be to the Father, and to the Son: and to the Holy Ghost.

As it was in the beginning, is now, and ever shall be: world without end. Amen.

### The Collect.

O GOD, which by the leading of a star didst manifest thy only-begotten Son to the Gentiles; . Mercifully grant, that we, which know thee now by faith, may after this life have the fruition of thy glorious God-head; through Christ our Lord.

### The Epistle. Eph. iii.

FOR this cause, I Paul am a prisoner of Jesus Christ for you heathen; if ye have heard of the ministration of the grace of God, which is given me to you-ward: for by revelation shewed he the mystery unto me, as I wrote afore in few words, whereby, when ye read, ye may understand my knowledge in the mystery of Christ; which mystery in times past was not opened unto the sons of men, as it is now declared unto his holy Apostles and Prophets by the Sprit; That the Gentiles should be inheritors also, and of the same body, and partakers of his promise in Christ, by the means of the gospel: whereof I am made a minister, according to the gift of the grace of God which is given unto me after the working of his power. Unto me, the least of all saints, is this grace given, that I should preach among the Gentiles the unsearchable riches of Christ; and to make all men see what the fellowship of the mystery is, which from the beginning of the world hath been hid in God, which made all things through Jesus Christ: to the intent that now unto the rulers and powers in heavenly things, might be known by the congregation the manifold wisdom of God, according to the eternal purpose which he wrought in Christ Jesu our Lord: by whom we have boldness and entrance with the confidence which is by the faith of him.

*The Gospel.* Matt. iii.

WHEN Jesus was born in Bethleem, a city of Jewry, in the time of Herode the king, behold, there came wise men from the east to Jerusalem, saying, Where is he that is born King of Jews? for we have seen his star in the east, and are come to worship him. When Herode the king had heard these things, he was troubled, and all the city of Jerusalem with him. And when he had gathered all the chief priests and scribes of the people together, he demanded of them, where Christ should be born. And they said unto him, At Bethleem in Jewry, for thus it is written by the prophet, And thou, Bethleem, in the land of Jewry, art not the least among the princes of Juda: for out of thee there shall come unto me the Captain that shall govern my people Israel. Then Herode (when he had privily called the wise men) he inquired of them diligently what time the star appeared. And he bade them to go to Bethleem, and said, go your way thither, and search diligently for the child, and when ye have found him, bring me word again, that I may come and worship him also. When they had heard the king, they departed; and lo, the star which they saw in the east went before them, till it came and stood over the place wherein the child was. When they saw the star, they were exceeding glad; and went into the house, and found the child with Mary his mother, and fell down flat, and worshipped him; and opened their treasures, and offered unto him gifts; gold, frankincense, and myrrh. And after they were warned of God in sleep, (that they should not go again to Herode,) they returned into their own country another way.

## At Evensong.

THE FIRST LESSON, Isaiah xlix.   THE SECOND LESSON, John ii:12.

## The First Sunday after the Epiphany.

*Usquequo, Domine?* Psl. xiii.

How long wilt thou forget me, O Lord, for ever: how long wilt thou hide thy face from me?

How long shall I seek counsel in my soul, and be so vexed in my heart: how long shall mine enemy triumph over me?

Consider, and hear me, O Lord my God: lighten mine eyes, that I sleep not in death.

Lest mine enemy say, I have prevailed against him: for if I be cast down, they that trouble me will rejoice at it.

But my trust is in thy mercy: and my heart is joyful in thy salvation.

I will sing of the Lord, because he hath dealt so lovingly with me: (yea, I will praise the Name of the Lord most Highest.)

Glory be to the Father, and to the Son: and to the Holy Ghost.

As it was in the beginning, is now, and ever shall be: world without end.    Amen.

### The Collect.

LORD, we beseech thee mercifully to receive the prayers of thy people which call upon thee; and grant that they may both perceive and know what things they ought to do, and also have grace and power faithfully to fulfil the same.

### The Epistle. Rom. xii.

I BESEECH you therefore, brethren, by the mercifulness of God, that ye make your bodies a quick sacrifice, holy, and acceptable unto God, which is your reasonable serving of God. And fashion not yourselves like unto this world; but be ye changed in your shape by the renewing of your mind, that ye may prove what thing that good, and acceptable, and perfect will of God is. For I say (through the grace that unto me given is) to every man among you, that no man stand high in his own conceit, more than it becometh him to esteem of himself; but so judge of himself, that he be gentle and sober, according as God hath dealt to every man the measure of faith. For as we have many members in one body, and all members have not one office; so we, being many, are one body in Christ, and every man among ourselves one another's members.

### The Gospel. Luke ii.

THE father and mother of

Jesus went to Jerusalem, after the custom of the feast day. And when they had fulfilled the days, as they returned home, the child Jesus abode still in Jerusalem, and his father and his mother knew not of it. But they, supposing him to have been in the company, came a day's journey, and sought him among their kinsfolk and acquaintance. And when they found him not, they went back again to Jerusalem, and sought him. And it fortuned, that after three days they found him in the temple, sitting in the midst of the doctors, hearing them, and posing them. And all that heard him were astonied at his understanding and answers. And when they saw him, they marvelled: and his mother said unto him, Son, why hast thou thus dealt with us? behold, thy father and I have sought thee sorrowing. And he said unto them, How happened it that ye sought me? wist ye not that I must go about my Father's business? And they understood not that saying which he spake unto them. And he went down with them, and came to Nazareth, and was obedient unto them: but his mother kept all these sayings together in her heart. And Jesus prospered in wisdom, and age, and in favour with God and men.

## The Second Sunday after the Epiphany.

*Dixit insipiens.* Psalm xiv.

THE fool hath said in his heart: There is no God.

They are corrupt, and become abominable in their doings: there is not one that doeth good, (no not one.)

The Lord looked down from heaven upon the children of men: to see if there were any that would understand and seek after God.

But they are all gone out of the way, they are altogether become abominable: there is none that doeth good, (no not one.)

Their throat is an open sepulchre, with their tongues they have deceived: the poison of asps is under their lips.

Their mouth is full of cursing and bitterness: their feet are swift to shed blood.

Destruction and unhappiness is in their ways, and the way of peace have they not known: there is no fear of God before their eyes.

Have they no knowledge, that they are all such workers of mischief: eating up my people as it were bread, and call not upon the Lord?

There were they brought in great fear (even where no fear was): for God is in the generation of the righteous.

As for you, ye have made a mock at the counsel of the poor: because he putteth his trust in the Lord.

Who shall give salvation unto Israel out of Sion? when the Lord turneth the captivity of his people: then shall Jacob rejoice, and Israel be glad.

Glory be to the Father, and to the Son: and to the Holy Ghost.

As it was in the beginning, is now, and ever shall be: world without end. Amen.

### The Collect.

ALMIGHTY and everlasting God, which dost govern all things in heaven and earth; Mercifully hear the supplications of thy people, and grant us thy peace all the days of our life.

*The Epistle.* Rom. xii.

SEEING that we have divers gifts, according to the grace that is given unto us, if any man have the gift of prophecy, let him have it, that it be agreeing to the faith. Let him that hath an office, wait on his office; let him that teacheth, take heed to his doctrine; let him that exhorteth, give attendance to his exhortation. If any man give, let him do it with singleness. Let him that ruleth, do it with diligence. If any man shew mercy, let him do it with cheerfulness. Let love be without dissimulation. Hate that which is evil, and cleave unto that which is good. Be kind one to another with brotherly love. In giving honour, go one before another. Be not slothful in the business which ye have in hand; be frevent in the spirit; apply yourselves to the time; rejoice in hope; be patient in tribulation; continue in prayer; distribute unto the necessity of the saints; be ready to harbour. Bless them which persecute you; bless, I say, and curse not. Be merry with them that are merry; weep also with them that weep. Be of like affection one towards another. Be not high minded, but make yourself equal to them of the lower sort.

*The Gospel.* John ii.

AND the third day was there a marriage in Cana, a city of Galilee, and the mother of Jesus was there. And Jesus was called (and his disciples) unto the marriage. And when the wine failed, the mother of Jesus said unto him, They have no wine. Jesus said unto her, Woman, what have I to do with thee? mine hour is not yet come. His mother said unto the ministers, Whatsoever he saith unto you, do it. And there were standing there vi. waterpots of stone, after the manner of the purifying of the Jews, containing ii. or iii. firkins apiece. Jesus said unto them, Fill the waterpots with water. And they filled them up to the brim. And he said unto them, Draw out now, and bear unto the governor of the feast. And they bare it. When the ruler of the feast had tasted the water that was turned into wine, and knew not whence it was, (but the ministers which drew the water knew), he called the bridegroom, and said unto him, Every man at the beginning doth set forth good wine, and when men be drunk then that which is worse : but thou hast kept the good wine until now. This beginning of miracles did Jesus in Cana of Galilee, and shewed his glory, and his disciples believed on him.

## The Third Sunday after the Epiphany.

*Domine, quis habitabit?*

Psalm xv.

LORD, who shall dwell in thy tabernacle : who shall rest upon thy holy hill?

Even he that leadeth an uncorrupt life : and doeth the thing which is right, and speaketh the truth from his heart.

He that hath used no deceit in his tongue, nor done evil to his neighbour : and hath not slandered his neighbours.

He that setteth not by himself, but is lowly in his own eyes : and maketh much of them that fear the Lord.

He that sweareth unto his neighbour, and disappointeth him not : though it were to his own hinderance.

He that hath not given his money unto usury : nor taken reward against the innocent.

Whoso doeth these things : shall never fall.

Glory be to the Father, and to the Son : and to the Holy Ghost.

As it was in the beginning, is now, and ever shall be : world without end. Amen.

### The Collect.

ALMIGHTY and everlasting God, mercifully look upon our infirmities, and in all our dangers and necessities stretch forth thy right hand to help and defend us; through Christ our Lord.

### The Epistle. Rom. xii.

BE not wise in your own opinions. Recompense to no man evil for evil. Provide aforehand things honest, not only before God, but also in the sight of all men. If it be possible (as much as is in you) live peaceably with all men. Dearly beloved, avenge not yourselves, but rather give place unto wrath; for it is written, Vengeance is mine; I will reward, saith the Lord. Therefore, if thine enemy hunger, feed him; if he thirst, give him drink; for in so doing thou shalt heap coals of fire on his head. Be not overcome of evil, but overcome evil with goodness.

### The Gospel. Matt. viii.

WHEN he was come down from the mountain, much people followed him. And behold, there came a leper and worshipped him, saying, Master, ·if thou wilt, thou canst make me clean. And Jesus put forth his hand, and touched him, saying, I will, be thou clean. And immediately his leprosy was cleansed. And Jesus said unto him, See thou tell no man, but go, and shew thyself to the priest, and offer the gift (that Moses commanded to be offered) for a witness unto him. And when Jesus was entered into Capernaum, there came unto him a centurion, and besought him, saying, Master, my servant lieth at home sick of the palsy, and is grievously pained. And Jesus said, When I come unto him, I will heal him. The centurion answered and said, Sir, I am not worthy that thou shouldest come under my roof; but speak the word only, and my servant shall be healed. For I also myself am a man subject to the authority of another, and have soldiers under me: and I say to this man, Go, and he goeth; and to another man, Come, and he cometh; and to my servant: Do this, and he doeth it. When Jesus heard these words, he marvelled, and said to them that followed him, Verily I say unto you, I have not found so great faith in Israel. I say unto you, That many shall come from the east and west, and shall rest with

Abraham, and Isaac, and Jacob, in the kingdom of heaven. But the children of the kingdom shall be cast out into utter darkness: there shall be weeping and gnashing of teeth. And Jesus said unto the centurion, Go thy way, and as thou believest, so be it unto thee. And his servant was healed in the selfsame hour.

---

## The Fourth Sunday after the Epiphany.

*Quare fremuerunt gentes?*

Psalm ii.

WHY do the heathen so furiously rage together: and why do the people imagine a vain thing?

The kings of the earth stand up, and the rulers take counsel together: against the Lord and against his Anointed.

Let us break their bonds asunder: and cast away their cords from us.

He that dwelleth in heaven shall laugh them to scorn: the Lord shall have them in derision.

Then shall he speak unto them in his wrath: and vex them in his sore displeasure.

Yet have I set my king: upon my holy hill of Sion.

I will preach the law, whereof the Lord hath said unto me: Thou art my Son, this day have I begotten thee.

Desire of me, and I shall give thee the heathen for thine inheritance: and the uttermost parts of the earth for thy possession.

Thou shalt bruise them with a rod of iron: and break them in pieces like a potter's vessel.

Be wise now therefore, O ye kings: be learned, ye that are judges of the earth.

Serve the Lord in fear: and rejoice (unto him) with reverence.

Kiss the Son, lest he be angry, and so ye perish from the right way: if his wrath be kindled, (yea, but a little,) blessed are all they that put their trust in him.

Glory be to the Father, and to the Son: and to the Holy Ghost.

As it was in the beginning, is now, and ever shall be: world without end. Amen.

### The Collect.

GOD, which knowest us to be set in the midst of so many and great dangers, that for man's frailness we cannot always stand uprightly; Grant to us the health of body and soul, that all those things which we suffer for sin, by thy help we may well pass and overcome; through Christ our Lord.

*The Epistle.* Rom. xiii.

LET every soul submit himself unto the authority of the higher powers; for there is no power but of God: the powers that be are ordained of God. Whosoever therefore resisteth power resisteth the ordinance of God: but they that resist shall receive to themselves damnation. For rulers are not fearful to them that do good, but to them that do evil. Wilt thou be without fear of the power? do well then, and so shalt thou be praised of the same: for he is the minister of God for thy wealth. But and if thou do that which is evil, then fear; for he beareth not the sword for nought: for he is the minister of God, to take vengeance on him that doeth evil. Wherefore ye must needs obey, not only for fear of vengeance, but also because of conscience. And even for this cause pay ye tribute; for they are God's ministers, serving for the

same purpose. Give to every man therefore his duty; tribute to whom tribute belongeth, custom to whom custom is due, fear to whom fear belongeth, honour to whom honour pertaineth.

*The Gospel.* Matt. viii.

AND when he entered into a ship, his disciples followed him. And behold, there arose a great tempest in the sea, insomuch that the ship was covered with waves: but he was asleep. And his disciples came to him, and awoke him, saying, Master, save us, we perish. And he saith unto them, Why are ye fearful, O ye of little faith? Then he arose, and rebuked the winds and the sea, and there followed a great calm. But the men marvelled, saying, What manner of man is this, that both winds and sea obey him. And when he was come to the other side into the country of the Gergesites, there met him ii. possessed of devils, which came out of the graves, and were out of measure fierce, so that no man might go by that way. And behold, they cried out, saying, O Jesu, thou Son of God, what have we to do with thee? art thou come hither to torment us before the time? And there was a good way off from them a herd of many swine, feeding. So the devils besought him, saying, If thou cast us out, suffer us to go into the herd of swine. And he said unto them, Go your ways. Then went they out, and departed into the herd of swine: and behold, the whole herd of swine was carried headlong into the sea, and perished in the waters. Then they that kept them fled, and went their ways into the city, and told every thing, and what had happened unto the possessed of the devils. And behold, the whole city came out to meet Jesus: and when they saw him, they besought him that he would depart out of their coasts.

## The Fifth Sunday after the Epiphany.

*Exaudiat te Dominus.*

Psalm xx.

THE Lord hear thee in the day of trouble: the Name of the God of Jacob defend thee;

Send thee help from the sanctuary: and strength thee out of Sion;

Remember all thy offerings: and accept thy brent sacrifice;

Grant thee thy heart's desire: and fulfil all thy mind.

We will rejoice in thy salvation, and triumph in the Name of the Lord our God: the Lord perform all thy petitions.

Now know I that the Lord helpeth his anointed, and will hear him from his holy heaven: even with the wholesome strength of his right hand.

Some put their trust in chariots, and some in horses: but we will remember the name of the Lord our God.

They are brought down and fallen: but we are risen and stand upright.

Save, Lord, and hear us, O King of heaven: when we call upon thee.

Glory be to the Father, and to the Son: and to the Holy Ghost.

As it was in the beginning, is now, and ever shall be: world without end. Amen.

*The Collect.*

LORD, we beseech thee to keep thy Church and household continually in thy true religion; that they which do lean only upon hope of thy heavenly grace may evermore be defended by thy mighty power; through Christ our Lord.

### The Epistle. Col. iii.

PUT upon you, as the elect of God, tender mercy, kindness, humbleness of mind, meekness, long-suffering; forbearing one another, and forgiving one another, if any man have a quarrel against another; as Christ forgave you, even so do ye. Above all these things put on love, which is the bond of perfectness. And the peace of God rule in your hearts, to the which peace ye are called in one body; and see that ye be thankful. Let the word of Christ dwell in you plenteously with all wisdom. Teach and exhort your own selves in psalms, and hymns, and spiritual songs, singing with grace in your hearts to the Lord. And whatsoever ye do, in word or deed, do all in the Name of the Lord Jesu, giving thanks to God the Father by him.

### The Gospel. Matt. xiii.

THE kingdom of heaven is like unto a man which sowed good seed in his field. But while men slept, his enemy came and sowed tares among the wheat, and went his way. But when the blade was sprung up, and had brought forth fruit then appeared the tares also. So the servants of the householder came, and said unto him, Sir, didst not thou sow good seed in thy field? from whence then hath it tares? He said unto them, The envious man hath done this. The servants said unto him, Wilt thou then that we go and weed them up? But he said, Nay; lest while ye gather up the tares, ye pluck up also the wheat with them. Let both grow together until the harvest; and in time of harvest I will say to the reapers, Gather ye first the tares, and bind them together in sheaves to be brent: but gather the wheat into my barn.

The Sixth Sunday (if there be so many) shall have the same Psalm, Collect, Epistle, and Gospel, that was upon the Fifth.

## The Sunday called Septuagesima.

*Dominus regit.* Psalm xxiii.

THE Lord is my shepherd : therefore can I lack nothing.

He shall feed me in a green pasture: and lead me forth beside the waters of comfort.

He shall convert my soul: and bring me forth in the paths of righteousness, for his Name's sake.

Yea, though I walk through the valley of the shadow of death, I will fear no evil: for thou art with me; thy rod and thy staff comfort me.

Thou shalt prepare a table before me against them that trouble me: thou hast anointed my head with oil, and my cup shall be full.

But thy loving-kindness and mercy shall follow me all the days of my life: and I will dwell in the house of the Lord for ever.

Glory be to the Father, and to the Son: and to the Holy Ghost.

As it was in the beginning, is now, and ever shall be: world without end. Amen.

### The Collect.

O Lord, we beseech thee favourably to hear the prayers of thy people; that we, which are justly punished for our offences, may be mercifully delivered by thy goodness, for the glory of thy Name; through Jesu Christ our Saviour, who liveth and reigneth, etc.

### The Epistle. 1. Cor. ix.

Perceive ye not, how that they which run in a course run all, but one receiveth the reward? So run that ye may obtain. Every man that proveth masteries abstaineth from all things: and they do it to obtain a crown that shall perish, but we to obtain an everlasting crown. I therefore so run, not as at an uncertain thing; so fight I, not as one that beateth the air; but I tame my body, and bring it into subjection, lest by any means it come to pass, that when I have preached to other, I myself should be a cast-away.

### The Gospel. Matt. xx.

The kingdom of heaven is like unto a man that is an householder, which went out early in the morning to hire labourers into his vineyard. And when the agreement was made with the labourers for a penny a day, he sent them into his vineyard. And he went out about the third hour, and saw other standing idle in the market place, and said unto them, Go ye also into the vineyard, and whatsoever is right I will give you. And they went their way. Again he went out about the vi. and ix. hour, and did likewise. And about the xi. hour he went out, and found other standing idle, and said unto them, Why stand ye here all the day idle? They said unto him, Because no man hath hired us. He saith unto them, Go ye also into the vineyard, and whatsoever is right, that shall ye receive. So when even was come, the lord of the vineyard said unto his steward, Call the labourers and give them their hire, beginning at the last until the first. And when they did come that came about the xi. hour, they received every man a penny. But when the first came also, they supposed that they should have received more; and they likewise received every man a penny. And when they had received it, they murmured against the goodman of the house, saying, These last have wrought but one hour, and thou hast made them equal with us, which have borne the burthen and heat of the day But he answered unto one of them, and said, Friend, I do thee no wrong; didst thou not agree with me for a penny? Take that thine is, and go thy way; I will give unto this last even as unto thee. Is it not lawful for me to do as me lusteth with mine own goods? Is thine eye evil, because I am good? So the last shall be first, and the first shall be last: for many be called, but few be chosen.

## The Sunday called Sexagesima.

*Domini est terra*　Psl. xxiv.

THE earth is the Lord's, and all that therein is: the compass of the world, and they that dwell therein.

For he hath founded it upon the seas: and prepared it upon the floods.

Who shall ascend into the hill of the Lord: or who shall rise up in his holy place?

Even he that hath clean hands, and a pure heart: and that hath not lift up his mind unto vanity, nor sworn to deceive his neighbour.

He shall receive the blessing from the Lord: and righteousness from the God of his salvation.

This is the generation of them that seek him: even of them that seek thy face, O Jacob.

Lift up your heads (O ye gates), and be ye lift up ye

everlasting doors: and the King of glory shall come in.

Who is this King of glory: it is the Lord, strong and mighty, even the Lord mighty in battle.

Lift up your heads (O ye gates), and be ye lift up ye everlasting doors: and the King of glory shall come in.

Who is this King of glory: even the Lord of hosts, he is the King of glory.

Glory be to the Father, and to the Son: and to the Holy Ghost.

As it was in the beginning, is now, and ever shall be: world without end. Amen.

### The Collect.

LORD GOD, which seest that we put not our trust in any thing that we do; Mercifully grant that by thy power we may be defended against all adversity; through Jesus Christ our Lord.

### The Epistle. ii. Cor. xi.

YE suffer fools gladly, seeing ye yourselves are wise. For ye suffer if a man bring you into bondage, if a man devour, if a man take, if a man exalt himself, if a man smite you on the face. I speak as concerning rebuke, as though we had been weak in this behalf: howbeit, whereinsoever any man dare be bold, (I speak foolishly,) I dare be bold also. They are Hebrues, even so am I. They are Israelites; even so am I. They are the seed of Abraham; even so am I. They are the ministers of Christ; (I speak as a fool;) I am more: in labours more abundant; in stripes above measure; in prison more plenteously; in death oft. Of the Jews five times received I xl. stripes save one; thrice was I beaten with rods; I was once stoned; I suffered thrice shipwrack; night and day have I been in the deep sea; in journeying often; in perils of waters; in perils of robbers; in jeopardies of mine own nation; in jeopardies among the heathen; in perils in the city; in perils in wilderness; in perils in the sea; in perils among false brethren; in labour and travail; in watchings often; in hunger and thirst; in fastings often; in cold and nakedness; beside the things which outwardly happen unto me, I am cumbered daily, and do care for all congregations. Who is weak, and I am not weak? who is offended, and I burn not? If I must needs boast, I will boast of the things that concern mine infirmities. The God and Father of our Lord Jesus Christ, which is blessed for evermore, knoweth that I lie not.

### *The Gospel.* Luke viii.

WHEN much people were gathered together, and were come to him out of all cities, he spake by a similitude: The sower went out to sow his seed; and as he sowed, some fell by the way-side, and it was trodden down, and the fowls of the air devoured it up. And some fell on stones, and as soon as it was sprung up, it withered away, because it lacked moistness. And some fell among thorns, and the thorns sprang up with it and choked it. And some fell on good ground, and sprang up, and bare fruit an hundred-fold. And as he said these things, he cried. He that hath ears to hear, let him hear. And his disciples asked him, saying, What manner of similitude is this? And he said, Unto you it is given to know the secrets of the kingdom of God: but to other by parables; that when they see they should not see, and when they hear they should not understand. The parable is this: The seed is the word of God. Those that are beside the way are they that hear; then cometh the devil and taketh away the word out of their hearts, lest they should believe, and be saved. They on the stones are they, which, when they hear, receive the word with joy; and these have no roots, which for a while believe, and in time of temptation go away. And that which fell among thorns, are they, which, when they have heard, go forth, and are choked with cares, and riches, and voluptuous living, and bring forth no fruit. That which fell in the good ground, are they, which with a pure and good heart, hear the word, and keep it, and bring forth fruit through patience.

## The Sunday called Quinquagesima.

### *Judica me Domine.*
### Psalm xxvi.

BE thou my judge, O Lord, for I have walked innocently: my trust hath been also in the Lord, therefore shall I not fall.

Examine me, O Lord, and prove me: try out my reins and my heart.

For thy loving-kindness is

before mine eyes: and I will walk in thy truth.

I have not dwelt with vain persons: neither will I have fellowship with the deceitful.

I have hated the congregation of the wicked: and will not sit among the ungodly.

I will wash my hands in innocency, O Lord: and so will I go to thine altar;

That I may shew the voice of thanksgiving: and tell of all thy wondrous works.

Lord, I have loved the habitation of thy house: and the place where thine honour dwelleth.

O shut not up my soul with the sinners: nor my life with the bloodthirsty;

In whose hands is wickedness: and their right hand is full of gifts.

But as for me: I will walk innocently: O Lord deliver me, and be merciful unto me.

My foot standeth right: I will praise the Lord in the congregations.

Glory be to the Father, and to the Son: and to the Holy Ghost.

As it was in the beginning, is now, and ever shall be: world without end. Amen.

### The Collect.

O LORD, which dost teach us that all our doings without charity are nothing worth; Send thy Holy Ghost, and pour into our hearts that most excellent gift of charity, the very bond of peace and all virtues, without the which whosoever liveth is counted dead before thee; Grant this for thy only Son Jesus Christ's sake.

### The Epistle. 1 Cor. xiii.

THOUGH I speak with the tongues of men and of angels, and have no love, I am even as sounding brass, or as a tinkling cymbal. And though I could prophesy, and understood all secrets, and all knowledge; yea, if I have all faith, so that I can move mountains out of their places, and yet have no love, I am nothing. And though I bestow all my goods to feed the poor, and though I gave my body even that I burned, and yet have no love, it profiteth me nothing. Love suffereth long, and is courteous; love envieth not; love doth not frowardly, swelleth not, dealeth not dishonestly, seeketh not her own, is not provoked to anger, thinketh none evil, rejoiceth not in iniquity, but rejoiceth in the truth; suffereth all things, believeth all things, hopeth all things, endureth all things: though that prophesying fail, either tongues cease, or knowledge vanish away, yet love falleth never away. For our knowledge is unperfect, and our prophesying is unperfect. But when that which is perfect is come, then that which is unperfect shall be done away. When I was a child, I spake as a child, I understood as a child, I imagined as a child; but as soon as I was a man, I put away childishness. Now we see in a glass, even in a dark speaking; but then shall we see face to face: now I know unperfectly; but then shall I know even as I am known. Now abideth faith, hope, and love, even these three; but the chief of these is love.

*The Gospel.* Luke xviii.

JESUS took unto him the xii., and said unto them, Behold, we go up to Hierusalem, and all shall be fulfilled that are written by the prophets of the Son of Man. For he shall be delivered unto the Gentiles, and shall be mocked, and despitefully intreated, and spitted on. And when they have scourged him, they will put him to death; and the third day he shall rise again. And they understood none of these things; and this saying was hid from them, so that they perceived not the things which were spoken. And it came to pass, that as he was come nigh unto Jericho, a certain blind man sat by the highway-side begging: and when he heard the people pass by, he asked what it meant. And they said unto him, that Jesus of Nazareth passed by. And he cried, saying, Jesu, thou Son of David, have mercy on me. And they which went before rebuked him, that he should hold his peace: but he cried so much the more, Thou Son of David, have mercy on me. And Jesus stood still and commanded him to be brought unto him: and when he was come near, he asked him, saying, What wilt thou that I do unto thee? And he said, Lord, that I may receive my sight. And Jesus said unto him, Receive thy sight; thy faith hath saved thee. And immediately he received his sight, and followed him, praising God: and all the people, when they saw it, gave praise unto God.

# The First day of Lent commonly called Ashwednesday.

*Domine ne.* Psalm vi.

O LORD, rebuke me not in thine indignation: neither chasten me in thy displeasure.

Have mercy upon me, O Lord, for I am weak: O Lord, heal me, for my bones are vexed.

My soul also is sore troubled: but, Lord, how long wilt thou punish me?

Turn thee, O Lord, and deliver my soul: O save me for thy mercy's sake.

For in death no man remembereth thee: and who will give thee thanks in the pit?

I am weary of my groaning; every night wash I my bed: and water my couch with my tears.

My beauty is gone for very trouble: and worn away because of all mine enemies.

Away from me, all ye that work vanity: for the Lord hath heard the voice of my weeping.

The Lord hath heard my petition: the Lord will receive my prayer.

All mine enemies shall be confounded, and sore vexed: they shall be turned back, and put to shame suddenly.

Glory be to the Father, and to the Son: and to the Holy Ghost.

As it was in the beginning, is now, and ever shall be: world without end. Amen.

### The Collect.

ALMIGHTY and everlasting God, which hatest nothing that thou hast made, and dost forgive the sins of all them that be penitent; Create and make in us new and contrite hearts, that we worthily lamenting our sins, and knowledging our wretchedness, may obtain of thee, the God of all mercy, perfect remission and forgiveness; through Jesus Christ.

### The Epistle. Joel ii.

TURN you unto me with all your hearts, with fasting, weeping, and mourning. Rent your hearts, and not your clothes. Turn you unto the Lord your God: for he is gracious and merciful, long-suffering, and of great compassion, and ready to pardon wickedness. Then (no doubt) he also shall turn and forgive: and after his chastening, he shall let your increase remain for meat and drink offerings unto the Lord your God. Blow out with the trumpet in Sion, proclaim a fasting, call the congregation, and gather the people together; warn the congregation; gather the elders, bring the children and sucklings together; let the bridegroom go forth of his chamber, and the bride out of her closet; let the priests serve the Lord between the porch and the altar, weeping and saying, Be favourable, O Lord, be favourable unto thy people; let not thine heritage be brought to such confusion, lest the heathen be lords thereof: wherefore should they say among the heathen, Where is now their God?

*The Gospel.* Matt. vi.

WHEN ye fast, be not sad, as the hypocrites are: for they disfigure their faces, that it may appear unto men how that they fast. Verily I say unto you, They have their reward. But thou, when thou fastest, anoint thine head, and wash thy face, that it appear not unto men how that thou fastest, but unto thy Father which is in secret; and thy Father, which seeth in secret, shall reward thee openly. Lay not up for ourselves treasure upon earth, where the rust and moth doth corrupt, and where thieves break through and steal: but lay up for you treasures in heaven, where neither rust nor moth doth corrupt, and where thieves do not break through nor steal. For where your treasure is, there will your hearts be also.

---

# The First Sunday in Lent.

*Beati, quorum.* Psalm xxxii.

BLESSED is he whose unrighteousness is forgiven: and whose sin is covered.

Blessed is the man unto whom the Lord imputeth no sin: and in whose spirit there is no guile.

For while I held my tongue: my bones consumed away through my daily complaining.

For thy hand is heavy upon me both day and night: and my moisture is like the drought in summer.

I will knowledge my sin unto thee: and mine unrighteonsness have I not hid.

I said, I will confess my sins unto the Lord: and so

thou forgavest the wickedness of my sin.

For this shall every one that is godly make his prayer unto thee, in a time when thou mayest be found: but in the great water-floods they shall not come nigh him.

Thou art a place to hide me in, thou shalt preserve me from trouble: thou shalt compass me about with songs of deliverance.

I will inform thee, and teach thee in the way wherein thou shalt go: and I will guide thee with mine eye.

Be not ye like horse and mule, which have no understanding: whose m o u t h s must be holden with bit and bridle, lest they fall upon thee.

Great plagues remain for the ungodly: but whoso putteth his trust in the Lord, mercy embraceth him on every side.

Be glad, O ye righteous, and rejoice in the Lord: and be joyful all, ye that are true of heart.

Glory be to the Father, and to the Son: and to the Holy Ghost.

As it was in the beginning, is now, and ever shall be: world without end.　Amen.

*The Collect.*

O LORD, which for our sake didst fast forty days and forty nights; Give us grace to use such abstinence, that, our flesh being subdued to the Spirit, we may ever obey thy godly motions in righteousness, and true holiness, to thy honour and glory, which livest and reignest, etc.

*The Epistle.* ii. Cor. vi.

WE, as helpers, exhort you, that ye receive not the grace of God in vain; for he saith, I have heard thee in a time accepted, and in the day of salvation have I succoured thee: behold, now is that accepted time; behold, now is that day of salvation. Let us give no occasion of evil, that in o u r office be found no faute; but in all things let us behave ourselves as the ministers of God, in much patience, in afflictions, in necessities, in anguishes, in stripes, in prisonments, in strifes, in labours, in watchings, in fastings, in pureness, in knowledge, in long-suffering, in kindness, in the Holy Ghost, in love unfeigned, in the word of truth, in the power of God, by the armour of righteousness on the right hand and on the left, by honour and dishonour, by evil report and good report; as deceivers, and yet true; as unknown, and yet known; as dying, and behold, we live; as chastened, and not killed; as sorrowing, and yet alway merry; as poor, and yet make many rich; as having nothing, and yet possessing all things.

*The Gospel.* Matt. iv.

THEN was Jesus led away of the Spirit into wilderness, to be tempted of the Devil. And when he had f a s t e d forty days and forty nights, he was at the last an hungered. And when the tempter came to him, he said, If thou be the Son of God, command that these stones be made bread. But he answered and said, It is written, Man shall not live by bread only, but by every word that proceedeth out of the mouth of God. Then the Devil taketh him up into the holy city, and setteth him on a pinnacle of the temple, and saith unto him, If thou be the Son of God, cast thyself down headlong; for it is written, He shall give his angels charge over thee, and with their hands they shall hold thee up, lest at any time thou dash thy foot against a stone. And Jesus said unto him, It is written again, Thou shalt not tempt the Lord thy God. Again, the Devil taketh him up into an exceeding high mountain, and sheweth him all the kingdoms of the world, and the glory of them; and saith unto h i m, All these will I give thee, if thou wilt fall down and worship me. Then saith Jesus unto him, Avoid, S a t h a n; for it is written, Thou shalt worship the Lord thy God, and him only shalt thou serve. Then the Devil leaveth him, and behold, the angels came and ministered unto him.

---

## The Second Sunday in Lent.

*De profundis.* Psalm cxxx.

OUT of the deep have I called unto thee, O Lord: Lord, hear my voice.

O let thine ears consider well: the voice of my complaint.

If thou, Lord, wilt be extreme to mark what is done amiss: O Lord, who may abide it?

For there is mercy with thee: therefore shalt thou be feared.

I look for the Lord; my soul doth wait for him: in his word is my trust.

My soul flieth unto the Lord, before the morning watch: I say, before the morning watch.

O Israel, trust in the Lord, for with the Lord there is mercy: and with him is plenteous redemption.

And he shall redeem Israel: from all his sins.

Glory be to the Father, and to the Son: and to the Holy Ghost.

As it was in the beginning, is now, and ever shall be: world without end. Amen.

### The Collect.

ALMIGHTY God, which dost see that we have no power of ourselves to help ourselves; Keep thou us both outwardly in our bodies, and inwardly in our souls; that we may be defended from all adversities which may happen to the body, and from all evil thoughts which may assault and hurt the soul; through Jesus Christ, etc.

### The Epistle. i. Thess. iv.

WE beseech you, brethren, and exhort you by the Lord Jesus, that ye increase more and more, even as ye have received of us, how ye ought to walk and to please God. For ye know what commandments we gave you by our Lord Jesu Christ. For this is the will of God, even your holiness, that ye should abstain from fornication; and that every one of you should know how to keep his vessel in holiness and honour; and not in the lust of concupiscence, as do the heathen which know not God: that no man oppress and defraud his brother in bargaining: because that the Lord is the avenger of all such things. as we told you before, and testified. For God hath not called us unto uncleanness, but unto holiness. He therefore that despiseth despiseth not man, but God, which hath sent his Holy Spirit among you.

### The Gospel. Matt. xv.

JESUS went thence and departed into the coasts of Tyre and Sidon. And behold, a woman of Canaan (which came out of the same coasts) cried unto him, saying, Have mercy on me, O Lord, thou Son of David; my daughter is piteously vexed with a devil. But he answered her nothing at all. And his disciples came and besought him, saying, Send her away; for she crieth after us. But he answered and said, I am not sent, but to the lost sheep of the house of Israel. Then came she and worshipped him, saying, Lord, help me. He answered and said, It is not meet to take the children's bread, and cast it to dogs. She answered and said, Truth, Lord; for the dogs eat of the crumbs which fall from their master's table. Then Jesus answered and said unto her, O woman, great is thy faith: be it unto thee even as thou wilt. And her daughter was made whole even at the same time.

## The Third Sunday in Lent.

*Judica me, Deus.* Psalm xliii.

GIVE sentence with me, (O God,) and defend my cause against the ungodly people: O deliver me from the deceitful and wicked man.

For thou art the God of my strength, why hast thou put me from thee: and why go I so heavily, while the enemy oppresseth me?

O send out thy light and thy truth, that they may lead me: and bring me unto thy holy hill, and to thy dwelling.

And that I may go unto the altar of God, even unto the God of my joy and gladness: and upon the harp will I give thanks unto thee (O God) my God.

Why art thou so heavy (O my soul): and why art thou so disquieted within me?

O put thy trust in God: for I will yet give him thanks, which is the help of my countenance, and my God.

Glory be to the Father, and to the Son : and to the Holy Ghost.

As it was in the beginning, is now, and ever shall be: world without end. Amen.

### The Collect.

WE beseech thee, Almighty God, look upon the hearty desires of thy humble servants, and stretch forth the right hand of thy Majesty, to be our defence against all our enemies; through Jesus Christ our Lord.

### The Epistle, Eph. v.

BE you the followers of God, as dear children; and walk in love, even as Christ loved us, and gave himself for us, an offering and a sacrifice of a sweet savour to God. As for fornication, and all uncleanness, or covetousness, let it not be once named among you, as it becometh saints; or filthiness, or foolish-talking, or jesting, which are not comely; but rather giving of thanks: for this ye know, that no whoremonger, either unclean person, or covetous person, (which is a worshipper of images,) hath any inheritance in the kingdom of Christ and of God. Let no man deceive you with vain words: for because of such things cometh the wrath of God upon the children of disobedience. Be not ye therefore companions of them. Ye were sometime darkness, but now are ye light in the Lord: walk as children of light; for the fruit of the Spirit consisteth in all goodness, and righteousness, and truth. Accept that which is pleasing unto the Lord; and have no fellowship with the unfruitful works of darkness, but rather rebuke them: for it is a shame even to name those things which are done of them in secret. But all things when they are brought forth by the light are manifest: for whatsoever is manifest the same is light. Wherefore he saith, Awake, thou that sleepest, and stand up from death; and Christ shall give thee light.

*The Gospel.* Luke xi.

JESUS was casting out a devil that was dumb. And when he cast out the devil, the dumb spake; and the people wondered. But some of them said, He casteth out devils through Beelzebub, the chief of the devils. And other tempted him, and required of him a sign from heaven. But he, knowing their thoughts, said unto them, Every kingdom divided against itself is desolate; and one house doth fall upon another. If Sathan also be divided against himself, how shall his kingdom endure? because ye say that I cast out devils through Beelzebub. If I by the help of Beelzebub cast out devils, by whose help do your children cast them out: therefore shall they be your judges. But if I with the finger of God cast out devils, no doubt the kingdom of God is come upon you. When a strong man armed watcheth his house, the things that he possesseth are in peace; but when a stronger than he cometh upon him, and overcometh him, he taketh from him all his harness (wherein he trusted) and divideth his goods. He that is not with me is against me: and he that gathereth not with me scattereth abroad. When the unclean spirit is gone out of a man, he walketh through dry places, seeking rest; and when he findeth none, he saith, I will return again into my house whence I came out. And when he cometh, he findeth it swept and garnished. Then goeth he and taketh to him vii. other spirits worse than himself, and they enter in, and dwell there; and the end of that man is worse than the beginning. And it fortuned that as he spake these things, a certain woman of the company lift up her voice, and said unto him, Happy is the womb that bare thee, and the paps which gave thee suck. But he said, Yea, happy are they that hear the word of God, and keep it.

## The Fourth Sunday in Lent.

*Deus noster refugiam.*
Psalm xlvi.

GOD is our hope and strength : a very present help in trouble.

Therefore will not we fear, though the earth be moved : and though the hills be carried into the midst of the sea.

Though the waters thereof rage and swell : and though the mountains shake at the tempest of the same.

The rivers of the flood thereof shall make glad the city of God : the holy place of the tabernacle of the most Highest.

God is in the midst of her, therefore shall she not be removed : God shall help her, and that right early.

The heathen make much ado, and the kingdoms are moved : but God hath shewed his voice, and the earth shall melt away.

The Lord of hosts is with us : the God of Jacob is our refuge.

O come hither, and behold the works of the Lord : what destruction he hath brought upon the earth.

He maketh wars to cease in all the world : he breaketh the bow, and knappeth the spear in sunder, and burneth the chariots in the fire.

Be still then and know that I am God : I will be exalted among the heathen, and I will be exalted in the earth.

The Lord of hosts is with us : the God of Jacob is our defence.

Glory be to the Father, and

to the Son : and to the Holy Ghost.

As it was in the beginning, is now, and ever shall be : world without end. Amen.

### The Collect.

GRANT, we beseech thee, Almighty God, t h a t we, which for our evil deeds are worthily punished by the comfort of thy grace may mercifully be relieved ; through our Lord Jesus Christ.

### The Epistle. Gal. iv.

TELL me, (ye that desire to be under the law,) do ye not hear of the law ? For it is written, that Abraham had ii. sons, the one by a bondmaid, the other by a freewoman. Yea, and he which was born of the bond-woman was born after the flesh ; but he which was born of the freewoman was born by promise. Which things are spoken by an allegory ; for these are two testaments ; the one f r o m the mount Sina, which gendereth unto bondage, which is Agar. For mount Sina is Agar in Arabia, and bordereth upon the city which is now called Jerusalem, and is in bondage with her children. But Jerusalem which is above is free ; which is the mother of us all. For it is written, Rejoice, thou barren ᵗh a t

bearest no children ; break forth and cry, thou that travailest not : for the desolate hath many more children than she which hath an husband. Brethren, we are after Isaac the children of promise. But as then he that was born after the flesh persecuted him that was born after the Spirit ; even so is it now. Nevertheless, what saith the Scripture ? Put away the bond-woman and her son ; for the son of the bond-woman shall not be heir with the son of the freewoman. So then, brethren, we are not children of the bond-woman, but of the freewoman.

### The Gospel. John vi.

JESUS departed over the sea of Galilee, which is the sea of Tiberias. And a great multitude followed him, because they saw his miracles which he did on them that were diseased. And Jesus went up into a mountain, and there h e s a t with his disciples. And Easter, a feast of the Jews, was nigh. When Jesus then lift up his eyes, and saw a great company come unto him, he saith unto Philip, Whence shall we b u y bread, that these may eat ? This he said to prove him ; for he himself knew what he would do. Philip answered him, Two hundred penny-worth of bread are not suffi-cient for them, that every man may take a little. One of his disciples (Andrew, Simon Peter's brother) saith unto him, There is a lad here, which hath five barley-loaves and two fishes: but what are they among so many? And Jesus said, Make the people sit down. There was much grass in the place. So the men sat down, in number about five thousand. And Jesus took the bread, and when he had given thanks he gave to the disciples, and the disciples to them that were set down; and likewise of the fishes as much as they would. When they had eat-en enough, he said unto his disciples, Gather up the bro-ken meat which remaineth, that nothing be lost. And they gathered it together, and filled xii. baskets with the broken meat of the five barley-loaves, which broken meat remained unto them that had eaten. Then those men (when they had seen the miracle that Jesus did) said, This is of a truth the same Prophet that should come in-to the world.

## The Fifth Sunday in Lent.

*Deus, in nomine tuo.*
Psalm liv.

SAVE me (O God) for thy Name's sake : and avenge me in thy strength.

Hear my prayer (O God:) and hearken unto the words of my mouth.

For strangers are risen up against me : and tyrants (which have not God before their eyes) seek after my soul.

Behold, God is my helper : the Lord is with them that uphold my soul.

He shall reward evil unto mine enemies : destroy thou them in thy truth.

An offering of a free heart will I give thee, and praise thy Name (O Lord :) because it is so comfortable.

For he hath delivered me out of all my trouble: and mine eye hath seen his desire upon mine enemies.

Glory be to the Father, and to the Son: and to the Holy Ghost.

As it was in the beginning, is now, and ever shall be: world without end. Amen.

*The Collect.*

WE beseech thee, Almighty God, mercifully to look upon thy people; that by thy great goodness they may be governed and preserved evermore, both in body and soul; through Jesus Christ our Lord.

*The Epistle.* Heb. ix.

CHRIST being an High Priest of good things to come, came by a greater and a more perfect tabernacle, not made with hands; that is to say, not of this building; neither by the blood of goats and calves; but by his own Blood he entered in once into the holy place, and found eternal redemption. For if the blood of oxen and of goats, and the ashes of a young cow, when it was sprinkled, purifieth the unclean as touching the purifying of the flesh; how much more shall the Blood of Christ (which through the eternal Spirit offered himself without spot to God) purge your conscience from dead works for to serve the living God? And for this cause is he the Mediator of the new testament, that through death, which chanced for the redemption of those trangressions that were under the first testament, they which are

called might receive the promise of eternal inheritance

*The Gospel.* John viii.

WHICH of you can rebuke me of sin? If I say the truth, why do ye not believe me? He that is of God heareth God's words: ye therefore hear them not, because ye are not of God. Then answered the Jews, and said unto him, Say we not well, that thou art a Samaritan, and hast the devil? Jesus answered, I have not the devil; but I honour my Father, and ye have dishonoured me. I seek not mine own praise; there is one that seeketh and judgeth. Verily, verily, I say unto you, If a man keep my saying, he shall never see death. Then said the Jews unto him, Now know we that thou hast the devil: Abraham is dead, and the prophets; and thou sayest, If a man keep my saying, he shall never taste of death. Art thou greater than our father Abraham, which is dead? and the prophets are dead: whom makest thou thyself? Jesus answered, If I honour myself, mine honour is nothing; it is my Father that honoureth me, which ye say is your God:

and yet ye have not known him; but I know him: and if I say, I know him not, I shall be a liar like unto you; but I know him, and keep his saying. Your father Abraham was glad to see my day, and he saw it, and rejoiced. Then said the Jews unto him, Thou art not yet l. year old, and hast thou seen Abraham? Jesus said unto them, Verily, verily, I say unto you, Ere Abraham was born, I am. Then took they up stones to cast at him: and Jesus hid himself, and went out of the temple.

## The Sunday next before Easter.

*Exaudi, Deus deprecationem.*
Psalm lxi.

HEAR my crying, O God: give ear unto my prayer.

From the ends of the earth will I call unto thee: when my heart is in heaviness.

O set me up upon the rock that is higher than I: for thou hast been my hope, and a strong tower for me against the enemy.

I will dwell in thy tabernacle for ever: and my trust shall be under the covering of thy wings.

For thou, O Lord, hast heard my desires: and hast given an heritage unto those that fear thy Name.

Thou shalt grant the King a long life: that his years may endure throughout all generations.

He shall dwell before God for ever: O prepare thy loving mercy and faithfulness, that they may preserve him.

So will I alway sing praise unto thy Name: that I may daily perform my vows.

Glory be to the Father, and to the Son: and to the Holy Ghost.

As it was in the beginning, is now, and ever shall be: world without end. Amen.

### The Collect.

ALMIGHTY and everlasting God, which, of thy tender love toward man, has sent our Saviour Jesus Christ, to take upon him our flesh, and to suffer death upon the Cross, that all mankind should follow the example of his great humility: Mercifully grant that we both follow the example of his patience, and be made partakers of his resurrection; through the same Jesus Christ our Lord.

*The Epistle.* Phil. ii.

LET the same mind be in you, that was also in Christ Jesu: which, when he was in the shape of God, thought it no robbery to be equal with God; nevertheless he made himself of no reputation, taking on him the shape of a servant, and became like unto men, and was found in his apparel as a man: he humbled himself, and became obedient unto the death, even the death of the cross. Wherefore God hath also exalted him on high, and given him a Name which is above all names; that in the Name of Jesus every knee should bow, both of things in heaven, and things in earth, and things under the earth; and that all tongues should confess that Jesus Christ is the Lord. unto the praise of God the Father.

*The Gospel.*
Matt. xxvi., xxvii.

AND it came to pass, when Jesus had finished all these sayings, he said unto his disciples, Ye know that after two days shall be Easter, and the Son of Man shall be delivered over to be crucified. Then assembled together the chief priests, and the scribes, and the elders of the people; unto the palace of the high priest, (which was called Caiphas,) and held a council that they might take Jesus by subtilty, and kill him. But they said, Not on the holy day, lest there be an uproar among the people. When Jesus was in Bethany, in the house of Simon the leper, there came unto him a woman having an alabaster box of precious ointment, and poured it on his head, as he sat at the board. But when his disciples saw it, they had indignation, saying, Whereto serveth this waste? This ointment might have been well sold, and given to the poor. When Jesus understood that, he said unto them, Why trouble ye the woman? for she hath wrought a good work upon me. For ye have the poor always with you; but me shall ye not have always. And in that she hath cast this ointment on my body, she did it to bury me. Verily I say unto you, Wheresoever this gospel shall be preached in all the world, there shall also this, that she hath done, be told for a memorial of her. Then one of the xii. (which was called Judas Iscarioth) went unto the chief priests, and said unto them, What will ye give me, and I will deliver him unto you? And they appointed unto him xxx. pieces of silver. And from that time forth he sought opportunity to betray him. The first day of sweet bread the disciples came to Jesus, saying unto him, Where wilt thou that we prepare for thee to eat the passover? And he said, Go into the city to such a man, and say unto him, The Master saith, My time is at hand; I will keep my Easter by thee with my disciples. And the disciples did as Jesus had appointed them; and they made ready the passover. When the even was come, he sat down with the xii. And as they did eat, he said, Verily I say unto you, that one of you shall betray me. And they were exceeding sorrowful, and began every one of them to say unto him, Lord, is it I? He answered and said, He that dippeth his hand with me in the dish, the same shall betray me. The Son of Man truly goeth as it is written of him: but woe unto that man by whom the Son of Man is betrayed! it had been good for that man if he had not been born. Then Judas, which betrayed him, answered and said, Master, is it I? He said unto him, Thou hast said. When they were eating, Jesus took bread, and when he had given thanks, he brake it, and gave it to the disciples, and said, Take, eat, this is my body. And he took the cup, and thanked, and gave it them, saying, Drink ye all of this; for this is my blood (which is of the new testament) that is shed for many for the remission of sins. But I say unto you, I will not drink henceforth of this fruit of the vine tree, until that day when I shall drink it new with you in my Father's kingdom. And when they had said grace, they went out unto mount Olivet. Then said Jesus unto them, All ye shall be offended because of me this night: for it is written, I will smite the shepherd, and the sheep of the flock shall be scattered abroad. But after I am risen again, I will go before you into Galilee. Peter answered and said unto him, Though all men be offended because of thee, yet will not I be offended. Jesus said unto him, Verily I say unto thee, That in this same night, before the cock crow, thou shalt deny me thrice. Peter said unto him, Yea, though I should die with thee, yet will I not deny thee. Likewise also said all the disciples. Then came Jesus with them unto a farm place, (which is called

Gethsemane,) and said unto the disciples, Sit ye here, while I go and pray yonder. And he took with him Peter and the two sons of Zebede, and began to wax sorrowful and heavy. Then said Jesus unto them, my soul is heavy even unto the death: tarry ye here, and watch with me. And he went a little further, and fell flat on his face, and prayed, saying, O my Father, if it be possible, let this cup pass from me: nevertheless not as I will, but as thou wilt. And he came unto the disciples, and found them asleep, and said unto Peter, What, could ye not watch with me one hour? Watch and pray, that ye enter not into temptation: the spirit is willing, but the flesh is weak. He went away once again, and prayed, saying, O my Father, if this cup may not pass away from me, except I drink of it, thy will be fulfilled. And he came and found them asleep again: for their eyes were heavy. And he left them, and went again, and prayed the third time, saying the same words. Then cometh he to his disciples, and saith unto them, Sleep on now, and take your rest: behold the hour is at hand, and the Son of Man is betrayed into the hands of sinners. Rise, let us be going: behold, he is at hand that doth betray me. While he yet spake, lo, Judas, one of the number of the xii., came, and with him a great multitude with swords and staves, sent from the chief priests and elders of the people. But he that betrayed him gave them a token saying, Whomsoever, I kiss, the same is he: hold him fast. And forthwith he came to Jesus, and said, Hail, master; and kissed him. And Jesus said unto him, Friend, wherefore art thou come? Then came they, and laid hands on Jesus, and took him. And behold, one of them which were with Jesus stretched out his hand, and drew his sword, and struck a servant of the high priest, and smote off his ear. Then said Jesus unto him, Put up thy sword into the sheath: for all they that take the sword shall perish with the sword. Thinkest thou that I cannot now pray to my Father, and he shall give me even now more than xii. legions of angels? But how then shall the Scriptures be fulfilled? for thus must it be. In that same hour said Jesus to the multitude, Ye be come out as it were to a thief with swords and staves for to take me. I sat daily with you teaching in the temple, and ye took me not. But all this is done, that the scriptures of the prophets might be fulfilled. Then all the disciples forsook him, and fled. And they took Jesus, and led him to Caiphas the high priest, where the scribes and the elders were assembled. But Peter followed him afar off unto the high priest's palace, and went in, and sat with the servants to see the end. The chief priests, and the elders, and all the council, sought false witness against Jesus, (for to put him to death,) but found none: yea, when many false witnesses came, yet found they none. At the last came ii. false witnesses, and said, This fellow said, I am able to destroy the temple of God, and to build it again in iii. days. And the chief priest arose, and said unto him, Answerest thou nothing? why do these bear witness against thee? But Jesus held his peace. And the chief priest answered and said unto him, I charge thee by the living God, that thou tell us whether thou be Christ, the Son of God. Jesus said unto him, Thou hast said; nevertheless I say unto you, Hereafter shall ye see the Son of Man sitting on the right hand

of power, and coming in the clouds of the sky. Then the high priest rent his clothes, saying, He hath spoken blasphemy; what need we of any more witnesses? behold, now ye have heard his blasphemy. What think ye? They answered and said, He is worthy to die. Then did they spit in his face, and buffeted him with fists; and other smote him on the face with the palm of their hands, saying, Tell us, thou Christ, Who is he that smote thee? Peter sat without in the palace: and a damosel came to him, saying, Thou also wast with Jesus of Galilee. But he denied before them all, saying, I wot not what thou sayest. When he was gone out into the porch, another wench saw him, and said unto them that were there, This fellow was also with Jesus of Nazareth. And again he denied with an oath, saying, I do not know the man. And after a while came unto him they that stood by, and said unto Peter, Surely thou art even one of them; for thy speech bewrayeth thee. Then began he to curse and to swear, that he knew not the man. And immediately the cock crew. And Peter remembered the word of Jesu, which said unto him, Before the cock crow, thou shalt deny me thrice. And he went out, and wept bitterly. When the morning was come, all the chief priests and the elders of the people held a council against Jesus, to put him to death; and brought him bound, and delivered him unto Poncius Pilate the deputy. Then Judas (which had betrayed him) seeing that he was condemned, repented himself, and brought again the xxx. plates of silver to the chief priests and elders, saying, I have sinned, betraying the innocent blood. And they said, What is that to us? see thou to that. And he cast down the silver plates in the temple, and departed, and went and hanged himself. And the chief priests took the silver plates, and said, It is not lawful for to put them into the treasure, because it is the price of blood. And they took counsel, and bought with them a potter's field, to bury strangers in. Wherefore the field is called Haceldama, that is, the field of blood, until this day. Then was fulfilled that which was spoken by Jeremy the prophet, saying, And they took xxx. silver plates, the price of him that was valued, whom they bought of the children of Is-

rael, and gave them for the potter's field, as the Lord appointed me. Jesus stood before the deputy; and the deputy asked him, saying, Art thou the King of the Jews? Jesus said unto him, Thou sayest. And when he was accused of the chief priests and elders, he answered nothing. Then said Pilate unto him, Hearest thou not how many witnesses they lay against thee? And he answered him to never a word, insomuch that the deputy marvelled greatly. At that feast the deputy was wont to deliver unto the people a prisoner, whom they would desire. He had then a notable prisoner, called Barabbas. Therefore when they were gathered together, Pilate said, Whether will ye that I give loose unto you, Barabbas, or Jesus which is called Christ? For he knew that for envy they had delivered him. When he was set down to give judgment, his wife sent unto him, saying, Have thou nothing to do with that just man: for I have suffered many things this day in my sleep because of him. But the chief priests and elders persuaded the people that they should ask Barabbas, and destroy Jesus. The deputy answered and said unto them, Whether of the twain will ye that I let loose unto you? They said Barabbas. Pilate said unto them, What shall I do then with Jesus, which is called Christ? They all said unto him, Let him be crucified! The deputy said, What evil hath he done? But they cried the more, saying, Let him be crucified! When Pilate saw that he could prevail nothing, but that more business was made, he took water, and washed his hands before the people, saying, I am innocent of the blood of this just person: ye shall see. Then answered all the people, and said, His blood be on us, and on our children. Then let he Barabbas loose unto them, and scourged Jesus, and delivered him to be crucified. Then the soldiers of the deputy took Jesus into the common hall, and gathered unto him all the company. And they stripped him, and put on him a purple robe, and platted a crown of thorns, and put it upon his head, and a reed in his right hand: and bowed the knee before him, and mocked him, saying, Hail, King of the Jews! And when they had spit upon him, they took the reed, and smote him on the head. And after that they had mocked him, they took

the robe off him again, and put his own raiment on him, and led him away to crucify him. And as they came out, they found a man of Cirene (named Simon); him they compelled to bear his cross. And they came unto the place which is called Golgotha, (that is to say, the place of dead men's skulls,) and gave him vinegar to drink mingled with gall: and when he had tasted thereof, he would not drink. When they had crucified him, they parted his garments, and did cast lots: that it might be fulfilled which was spoken by the prophet, They parted my garments among them, and upon my vesture did they cast lots. And they sat and watched him there, and set up over his head the cause of his death, written, THIS IS JESUS THE KING OF THE JEWS. Then were there ii. thieves crucified with him: one on the right hand, and another on the left. They that passed by reviled him, wagging their heads and saying, Thou that destroyedst the temple of God, and didst built it in three days, save thyself: if thou be the Son of God, come down from the cross. Likewise also the high priests mocking him, with the scribes and elders, said, He saved other, himself he cannot save: If he be the King of Israel, let him now come down from the cross, and we will believe him. He trusted in God; let him deliver him now, if he will have him: for he said, I am the Son of God. The thieves also, which were crucified with him cast the same in his teeth. From the sixth hour was there darkness all over the land until the ninth hour. And about the ninth hour, Jesus cried with a loud voice, saying, *Eli, Eli, lamasabathany?* that is to say, My God, My God, why hast thou forsaken me? Some of them that stood there, when they heard that, said, This man calleth for Helias. And straightway one of them ran, and took a sponge, and when he had filled it full of vinegar, he put it on a reed, and gave him to drink. Other said, Let be, let us see whether Helias will come and deliver him.

Jesus, when he had cried again with a loud voice, yielded up the ghost. And behold, the vail of the temple did rent into two parts from the top to the bottom, and the earth did quake, and the stones rent and graves did open, and many bodies of saints which slept arose and went out of the graves after his resurrection, and came into the holy city, and appeared unto many. When the centurion, and they that were with him watching Jesus, saw the earthquake, and those things which happened, they feared greatly, saying, Truly this was the Son of God. And many women were there, (beholding him afar off,) which followed Jesus from Galilee, ministering unto him: among which was Mary Magdalene, and Mary the mother of James and Joses, and the mother of Zebede's children.

## * Monday before Easter.

*The Epistle.* Isaiah lxiii.

WHAT is he this that cometh from Edom, with red-coloured clothes of Bosra, (which is so costly cloth,) and cometh in so mightily with all his strength? I am he that teacheth righteousness, and am of power to help. Wherefore then is thy clothing red, and thy raiment like his that treadeth in the wine press? I have trodden the press myself alone, and of all people there is not one with me. Thus will I tread down mine enemies in my wrath, and set my feet upon them in mine indignation; and their blood shall bespring my clothes, and so will I stain all my raiment. For the day of vengeance is assigned in my heart, and the year when my people shall be delivered is come. I looked about me, and there was no man to shew me any help; I marvelled that no man held me up: then I held me by mine own arm, and my ferventness sustained me. And thus will I tread down the people in my wrath, and bathe them in my displeasure, and upon the earth will I lay their strength. I will declare the goodness of the Lord, yea and the praise of the Lord, for all that he hath given us, for the great good that he hath done for Israel, which he hath given them of his own favour, and according to the multitude of his loving-kindnesses. For he said, These no doubt are my people, and no shrinking children; and so he was their Saviour. In their troubles he was also troubled with them, and the angel that went forth from his presence delivered them: of very love

and kindness that he had unto them he redeemed them: he hath borne them, and carried them up, ever since the world began. But after they provoked him to wrath, and vexed his holy mind, he was their enemy, and fought against them himself. Yet remembered Israel the old time of Moses and his people, saying, Where is he that brought them from the water of the sea, with them that fed his sheep? where is he that hath given his Holy Spirit among them? he led them by the right hand of Moses, with his glorious arm, dividing the water before them, (whereby he gat himself an everlasting Name;) he led them in the deep as an horse is led in the plain, that they should not stumble; as a tame beast goeth in the field: and the breath given of God giveth him rest. Thus (O God) hast thou led thy people, to make thyself a glorious Name withal. Look down then from heaven, and behold the dwelling place of thy sanctuary and thy glory. How is it that thy jealousy, thy strength, the multitude of thy mercies, and thy loving-kindness, will not be entreated of us? Yet art thou our Father: for Abraham knoweth us not, neither is Israel acquainted with us: but thou, Lord, art our Father and Redeemer, and thy Name is everlasting. O Lord, wherefore hast thou led us out of thy way? wherefore hast thou hardened o u r hearts, that we fear thee not? Be at one with us again, for thy servant's sake, and for the generation of thine heritage. Thy people have had but a little of thy sanctuary in possession: for our enemies have trodden down the holy place. And we were thine from the beginning, when thou was not their Lord, for they have not called upon thy Name.

*The Gospel.* Mark xiv.

AFTER two days was Easter, and the days of sweet bread: and the high priests and the scribes sought h o w t h e y might take him by craft, and put him to death. But they said, Not in the feast day, lest any business arise among the people. And when he was at Bethany, in the house of Simon the leper, even as he sat at meat, there came a woman having an alabaster box of ointment called nard, that was pure and costly; and she brake the box, and poured it on his head. And there were some that were not content within t h e m - selves, and said, What needed this waste of ointment? for it might have been sold for more than ccc. pence, and have been given unto the poor: and they grudged against her. And Jesus said, Let her alone; why trouble ye her? she hath done a good work on me: for ye have poor with you always, and whensoever ye will ye may do them good; but me have ye not always. She hath done that she could; s h e came aforehand to anoint my body to the burying. Verily I say unto you, Wheresoever this gospel shall be preached throughout the whole world, this also that she hath done shall be rehearsed in remembrance of her. And Judas Iscarioth, one of the twelve, went away unto the high priests t o betray him unto them. When they h e a r d t h a t they were glad, and promised t h a t they would give him money. And he sought how he might conveniently betray him. And the first day of sweet b r e a d, (when they offered passover,) his disciples said unto him, Where wilt thou that we go and prepare, that thou mayest eat the passover? And he sent forth two of his disciples, and said unto them, Go ye unto the city, and there shall meet you a man bearing a pitcher of water; follow him. And whithersoever he goeth in say ye unto the goodman of the house, Th e Master saith, Where is the guest-chamber, where I shall eat passover with my disciples? And he will shew you a great parlour paved and prepared: there make ready for us. And his disciples went forth, and came into the city, and found as he had said unto them: and they made ready the passover. And when it was now eventide he came with the xii. And as they sat at board, and did eat, Jesus said, Verily I say unto you, One of you (that eateth with me) shall betray me. And they began to be sorry, and to say to him one by one, Is it I? and another said, Is it I? He answered and said unto them, It is one of the xii., even he that dippeth with me in the platter. The Son of Man truly goeth, as it is written of him: but woe to that man by whom the Son of Man is betrayed: good were it for that man if he had never been born. And as they did eat, Jesus took bread, and when he had given thanks he brake it, and gave to them,

and said, Take, eat: this is my body. And he took the cup, and when he had given thanks he took it to them: and they all drank of it. And he said unto them, This is my blood of the new testament, which is shed for many. Verily I say unto you, I will drink no more of the fruit of the vine, until that day that I drink it new in the king-dom of God. And when they had said grace, they went out to mount Olivet. And Jesus saith unto them, All ye shall be offended be-cause of me this night: for it is written, I will smite the shepherd, and the sheep shall be scattered. But after that I am risen again, I will go in-to Galilee before you. Peter said unto him, And though all men be offended, yet will not I. And Jesus saith unto him, Verily I say unto thee, That this day, even in this night, before the cock crow twice, thou shalt deny me three times. But he spake more vehemently, No, if I should die with thee, I will not deny thee. Likewise al-so said they all. And they came into a place which was named Gethsemany: and he said to his disciples, Sit ye here, while I go aside and pray. And he taketh with him Peter, and James, and John, and began to wax abashed, and to be in an agony, and said unto them, My soul is heavy even unto the death; tarry ye here, and watch. And he went forth a little, and fell 'down flat on the ground, and prayed, that, if it were possible, the hour might pass from him. And he said, Abba, Father, all things are possible unto thee; take away this cup from me; nevertheless, not that I will, but that thou wilt be done. And he came and found them sleeping, and saith to Peter, Simon, sleepest thou? couldst not thou watch one hour? Watch ye and pray, lest ye enter into temptation: the spirit truly is ready, but the flesh is weak. And again he went aside and prayed, and spake the same words. And he returned and found them asleep again, for their eyes were heavy, neither wist they what to answer him. And he came the third time, and said unto them, Sleep henceforth, and take your ease: it is enough, the hour is come; behold, the Son of Man is betrayed into the hands of sinners. Rise up, let us go; lo, he that betrayeth me is at hand. And immediately, while he yet spake, cometh Judas, (which was one of the xii.,) and with him a great number of people with swords and staves, from the high priests, and scribes, and elders. And he that betrayed him had given them a general token, saying, Whosoever I do kiss, the same is he; take him, and lead him away warily. And as soon as he was come he goeth straightway to him, and saith unto him, Master, master; and kissed him. And they laid their hands on him, and took him. And one of them that stood by drew out a sword, and smote a servant of the high priest, and cut off his ear. And Jesus answered, and said unto them, Ye be come out as unto a thief, with swords and staves, for to take me. I was daily with you in the temple teaching, and ye took me not: but these things come to pass that the Scriptures should be fulfilled. And they all forsook him, and ran away. And there followed him a certain young man, clothed in linen upon the bare; and the young men caught him: and he left his linen garment, and fled from them naked. And they led Jesus away to the highest priest of all: and and with him came all the high priests, and the elders, and the scribes. And Peter followed him a great way off, (even till he was come into the palace of the high priest,) and he sat with the servants, and warmed himself at the fire. And the high priests and all the council sought for witness against Jesu to put him to death; and found none. For many bare false witness against him, but their witnesses agreed not together. And there arose certain, and brought false witness against him, saying, We heard him say, I will destroy this temple that is made with hands, and within iii. days I will build another made without hands. But yet their witnesses agreed not together. And the high priest stood up among them, and asked Jesus, saying, Answerest thou nothing? how is it that these bear witness against thee? But he held his peace, and answered nothing. Again the high priest asked him, and said unto him, Art thou Christ, the Son of the Blessed? And Jesus said, I am; and ye shall see the Son of Man sitting on the right hand of power, and coming in the clouds of heaven. Then the high priest rent his clothes, and said, What need we any further of witnesses? ye have heard blasphemy: what think ye? And they all condemned him to be worthy of death. And some began to spit at him, and to cover his face, and to beat him with fists, and to say unto him, Areade: and the servants buffeted him on the face. And as Peter was beneath in the palace, there came one of the wenches of the highest priest; and when she saw Peter warming himself she looked on him, and said, Wast not thou also with Jesus of Nazareth? And he denied, saying, I know him not, neither wot I what thou sayest. And he went out into the porch; and the cock crew. And a damosel (when she saw him) began again to say to them that stood by, This is one of them. And he denied it again. And anon after, they that stood by said again unto Peter, Surely thou art one of them; for thou art of Galilee, and thy speech agreeth thereto. But he began to curse and to swear, saying, I know not this man of whom ye speak. And again the cock crew. And Peter remembered the word that Jesus had said unto him, Before the cock crow twice, thou shalt deny me three times. And he began to weep.

## Tuesday before Easter,

### *The Epistle.* Isaiah l.

THE Lord God hath opened mine ear, therefore can I not say nay, neither withdraw myself. But I offer my back unto the smiters, and my cheeks to the nippers: I turn not my face from shame and spitting; and the Lord God shall help me, therefore shall I not be confounded. I have hardened my face like a flint stone, for I am sure that I shall not come to confusion. He is at hand that justifieth me; who will then go to law with me? Let us stand one against another; if there be any that will reason with me, let him come here forth unto me. Behold, the Lord God standeth by me; what is he then that can condemn me? Lo, they shall be all like as an old cloth: the moth shall eat them up. Therefore, whoso feareth the Lord among you, let him hear the voice of his servant: whoso walketh in darkness, and no light shineth upon him, let him put his trust in the Name of the Lord, and hold him by his God. But take heed, ye all kindle a fire of the wrath of God, and stir up the coals: walk on in the glistering of your own fire, and in the coals that ye have kindled. This cometh unto you from my hand, namely, that ye shall sleep in sorrow.

### *The Gospel.* Mark xv.

AND anon in the dawning, the high priests held a council with the elders, and the scribes, and the whole congregation, and bound Jesus, and led him away, and delivered him to Pilate. And Pilate asked him, Art thou the King of the Jews? And he answered and said unto him, Thou sayest it. And the high priests accused him of many things. So Pilate asked him again, saying, Answerest thou nothing? behold how many things they lay unto thy charge. Jesus yet answered nothing: so that Pilate marvelled. At that feast Pilate did deliver unto them a prisoner, whomsoever they would desire. And there was one that was named Barabbas, which lay bound with them that made insurrection: he had committed murther. And the people called unto him, and began to desire him that he would do according as he had ever done unto them. Pilate answered them, saying, Will ye that I let loose unto you the King of the Jews? For he knew that the high priests had delivered him of envy. But the high priests moved the people, that he should rather deliver Barabbas unto them. Pilate answered again, and said unto them, What will ye that I then do unto him whom ye call the King of the Jews? And they cried again, Crucify him. Pilate said unto them, What evil hath he done? And they cried the more fervently, Crucify him. And so Pilate, willing to content the people, let loose Barabbas unto them, and delivered up Jesus (when he had scourged him) for to be crucified. And the soldiers led him away into the common hall; and called together the whole multitude. And they clothed him with purple, and they platted a crown of thorns, and crowned him withal; and began to salute him, Hail, King of the Jews! And they smote him on the head with a reed, and did spit upon him, and bowed their knees and worshipped him. And when they had mocked him they took the purple off him, and put his own clothes on him, and led him out to crucify him. And they compelled one that passed by, called Simon of Cirene (the father of Alexander and Rufus), which came out of the field, to bear his cross. And they brought him to a place named Golgotha, (which, if a man interpret it, is the place of dead men's skulls:) and they gave him to drink wine mingled with myrrh; but he received it not. And when they had crucified him, they parted his garments, casting lots upon them, what every man should take. And it was about the third hour, and they crucified him. And the title of his cause was written, THE KING OF THE JEWS. And they crucified with him two thieves, the one on his right hand, and the other on his left. And the scripture was fulfilled, which saith, He was counted among the wicked. And they that went by railed on him, wagging their heads, and saying, A wretch! thou that destroyest the temple and buildest it again in three days, save thyself, and come down from the cross. Likewise also mocked him the high priests among themselves, with the scribes, and said, He saved other men; himself he cannot save. Let Christ the King of Israel descend now from the cross, that we may see and believe.

And they that were crucified with him checked him also. And when the sixth hour was come, darkness arose over all the earth until the ninth hour. And at the ninth hour Jesus cried with a loud voice, saying, *Eloy, Eloy, lamasabathany?* which is, (if one interpret it,) My God, My God, why hast thou forsaken me? And some of them that stood by, when they heard that, said, Behold, he calleth for Helias. And one ran and filled a spunge full of vinegar, and put it on a reed, and gave him to drink, saying, Let him alone; let us see whether Helias will come and take him down. But Jesus cried with a loud voice, and gave up the ghost. And the vail of the temple rent in two pieces from the top to the bottom. And when the centurion (which stood before him) saw that he so cried and gave up the ghost, he said, Truly this man was the Son of God. There were also women a good way off beholding him : among whom was Mary Magdalene and Mary the mother of James the little and of Joses, and Mary Salome ; (which also, when he was in Galilee, had followed him, and ministered unto him;) and many other women which came up with him to Jerusalem. And now when the even was come, (because it was the day of preparing that goeth before the sabbath,) Joseph of the city of Aramathia, a noble counsellor, which also looked for the kingdom of God, came, and went in boldly unto Pilate and begged of him the body of Jesu. And Pilate marvelled that he was already dead ; and called unto him the centurion, and asked of him whether he had been any while dead. And when he knew the truth of the centurion, he gave the body to Joseph. And he bought a linen cloth, and took him down and wrapped him in the linen cloth, and laid him in a sepulchre that was hewn out of a rock, and rolled a stone before the door of the sepulchre. And Mary Magdalene and Mary Joses beheld where he was laid.

## Wednesday before Easter.

*The Epistle.* Heb. ix.

WHEREAS is a testament, there must also (of necessity) be the death of him that maketh the testament: for the testament taketh authority when men are dead; for it is yet of no value as long as he that maketh the testament is alive. For which cause also, neither the first testament was ordained without blood: for when Moses had declared all the commandment to all the people, according to the law, he took the blood of calves and of goats, with water, and purple wool, and hyssop, and sprinkled both the book, and all the people, saying, This is the blood of the testament, which God hath appointed unto you. Moreover, he sprinkled the tabernacle with blood also, and all the ministering vessels. And almost all things are by the law purged with blood; and without shedding of blood is no remission. It is need then that the similitudes of heavenly things be purified with such things; but that the heavenly things themselves be purified with better sacrifices than are those. For Christ is not entered into the holy places that are made with hands, (which are similitudes of true things,) but is entered into very heaven, for to appear now in the sight of God for us; not to offer himself often, as the high priest entereth into the holy place every year with strange blood: for then must he have often suf-fered since the world began; but now in the end of the world hath he appeared once to put sin to flight by the offering up of himself. And as it is appointed unto all men that they shall once die, and then cometh the judgment: even so Christ was once offered to take away the sins of many; and unto them that look for him shall he appear again without sin unto salvation.

*The Gospel.* Luke xxii.

THE feast of sweet bread drew nigh, which is called Easter. And the high priests and scribes sought how they might kill him; for they feared the people. Then entered Sathan into Judas, whose surname was Iscarioth, (which was of the number of the xii.) And he went his way, and commoned with the high priests and officers, how he might betray him unto them. And they were glad, and promised to give him money. And he consented, and sought opportunity to betray him unto them when the people were away. Then came the day of sweet bread, when of necessity passover must be offered. And he sent Peter and John, saying, Go and prepare us the passover, that we may eat.

They said unto him, Where wilt thou that we prepare? And he said unto them, Behold, when ye enter into the city, there shall a man meet you bearing a pitcher of water; him follow into the same house that he entereth in. And ye shall say unto the goodman of the house, The Master saith unto thee, Where is the guest-chamber, where I shall eat the passover with my disciples? And he shall shew you a great parlour paved; there make ready. And they went, and found as he had said unto them: and they made ready the passover. And when the hour was come, he sat down, and the xii. apostles with him. And he said unto them, I have inwardly desired to eat this passover with you before that I suffer: for I say unto you, Henceforth I will not eat of it any more, until it be fulfilled in the kingdom of God. And he took the cup, and gave thanks, and said, Take this, and divide it among you. For I say unto you, I will not drink of the fruit of the vine, until the kingdom of God come. And he took bread, and when he had given thanks, he brake it, and gave unto them, saying, this is my body, which is given for you: this do in the remembrance of me. Likewise also when he had supped, he took the cup, saying, This cup is the new testament in my blood, which is shed for you. Yet behold, the hand of him that betrayeth me is with me on the table. And truly the Son of Man goeth as it is appointed; but woe unto that man by whom he is betrayed. And they began to inquire among themselves which of them it was that should do it. And there was a strife among them, which of them should seem to be greatest. And he said unto them, The kings of nations reign over them, and they that have authority upon them are called gracious lords. But ye shall not be so: but he that is greatest among you, shall be as the younger; and he that is chief, shall be as he that doth minister. For whether is greater, he that sitteth at meat, or he that serveth? is not he that sitteth at meat? But I am among you as he that ministereth. Ye are they which have bidden with me in my temptations. And I appoint unto you a kingdom, as my Father hath appointed to me; that ye may eat and drink at my table in my kingdom, and sit on seats, judging the xii. tribes of Israel. And the Lord said, Simon, Simon, behold, Sathan hath desired to sift you, as it were wheat; but I have prayed for thee, that thy faith fail not; and when thou art converted, strength thy brethren. And he said unto him, Lord, I am ready to go with thee into prison and to death. And he said, I tell thee Peter, the cock shall not crow this day, till thou have thrice denied that thou knowest me. And he said unto them, When I sent you without wallet, and scrip, and shoes, lacked ye any thing? And they said, No. Then said he unto them, But now, he that hath a wallet, let him take it up, and likewise his scrip: and he that hath no sword, let him sell his coat, and buy one. For I say unto you, That yet the same which is written must be performed in me, Even among the wicked was he reputed: for those things which are written of me have an end. And they said, Lord, behold, here are two swords. And he said unto them, It is enough. And he came out, and went (as he was wont) to mount Olivet, and the disciples followed him. And when he came to the place, he said unto them, Pray, lest ye fall into temptation. And he gat himself from them

about a stone's cast, and kneeled down and prayed, saying, Father, if thou wilt, remove this cup from me: nevertheless, not my will, but thine be fulfilled. And there appeared an angel unto him from heaven, comforting him. And he was in an agony, and prayed the longer; and his sweat was like drops of blood trickling down to the ground. And when he arose from prayer, and was come to his disciples, he found them sleeping for heaviness, and he said unto them, Why sleep ye? rise and pray, lest ye fall into temptation. While he yet spake, behold, there came a company, and he that was called Judas, one of the xii., went before them, and pressed nigh unto Jesus to kiss him. But Jesus said unto him, Judas, betrayest thou the Son of Man with a kiss? When they which were about him saw what would follow, they said unto him, Lord, shall we smite with the sword? And one of them smote a servant of the high priest, and struck off his right ear. Jesus answered and said, Suffer ye thus far forth. And when he touched his ear he healed him. Then Jesus said unto the high priests, and rulers of the temple, and the elders which were come to him, Ye be come out as unto a thief, with swords and staves. When I was daily with you in the temple, ye stretched forth no hands against me: but this is even your very hour, and the power of darkness. Then took they him, and led him, and brought him to the high priest's house: but Peter followed afar off. And when they had kindled a fire in the midst of the palace, and were set down together, Peter also sat down among them. But when one of the wenches beheld him, as he sat by the fire, (and looked upon him,) she said, This same fellow was also with him. And he denied him, saying, Woman, I know him not. And after a little while another saw him, and said, Thou art also of them. And Peter said, Man, I am not. And about the space of an hour after, another affirmed, saying, Verily this fellow was with him also; for he is of Galilee. And Peter said, Man, I wot not what thou sayest. And immediately, while he yet spake, the cock crew. And the Lord turned back, and looked upon Peter; and Peter remembered the word of the Lord, how he had said unto him, Before the cock crow, thou shalt deny me thrice. And Peter went out, and wept bitterly. And the men that took Jesus mocked him, and smote him. And when they had blindfolded him, they struck him on the face, and asked him, saying, Areade, who is it that smote thee? And many other things despitefully said they against him. And as soon as it was day, the elders of the people, and the high priests, and scribes, came together, and led him into their council, saying, art thou very Christ? tell us. And he said unto them, If I tell you, ye will not believe me; and if I ask you, you will not answer me, nor let me go. Hereafter shall the Son of Man sit on the right hand of the power of God. Then said they all, Art thou then the Son of God? He said, Ye say that I am. And they said, What need we of any further witness? for we ourselves have heard of his own mouth.

## At Evensong.

### THE FIRST LESSON, LAM. i.

## Thursday before Easter.

### At Matins.
#### THE FIRST LESSON, LAM. ii.

*The Epistle.* i. Cor. xi.

THIS I warn you of, and commend not, that ye come not together after a better manner, but after a worse. For first of all, when ye come together in the congregation, I hear that there is dissension among you, and I partly believe it. For there must be sects among you, that they which are perfect among you may be known. When ye come together therefore into one place, the Lord's supper cannot be eaten: for every man beginneth afore to eat his own supper; and one is hungry and another is drunken. Have ye not houses to eat and drink in? despise ye the congregation of God, and shame them that have not? What shall I say unto you? shall I praise you? In this I praise you not. That which I delivered unto you I received of the Lord. For the Lord Jesus, the same night in which he was betrayed, took bread; and when he had given thanks, he brake it, and said, Take ye, and eat; this is my body, which is broken for you: this do ye in the remembrance of me. After the same manner also he took the cup when supper was done, saying, This cup is the new testament in my blood: this do, as oft as ye drink it, in remembrance of me. For as often as ye shall eat this bread, and drink this cup, ye shall shew the Lord's death till he come. Wherefore, whosoever shall eat of this bread, or drink of the cup of the Lord unworthily, shall be guilty of the body and blood of the Lord But let a man examine himself, and so let him eat of the bread, and drink of the cup. For he that eateth and drinketh unworthily eateth and drinketh his own damnation, because he maketh no difference of the Lord's body. For this cause many are weak and sick among you, and many sleep. For if we had judged ourselves, we should not have been judged. But when we are judged of the Lord, we are chastened, that we should not be damned with the world.

Wherefore, my b r e t h r e n, when ye come together to eat, tarry one for another. If any man hunger, let him eat at home; that ye come not together unto condemnation. Other things will I set in order when I come.

*The Gospel.* Luke xxiii.

THE whole multitude of them arose, and led him unto Pilate. And they began to accuse him, saying, We found this fellow perverting the people, and forbidding to pay tribute to Cesar, saying, That he is Christ a King. And Pilate apposed him, saying, Art thou the King of the Jews? He answered him, and said, Thou sayest it. Then said Pilate to the high priests and to the people, I find no faute in this man. And they were the more fierce, saying, He moveth the people, teaching throughout all Jewry, and began at Galilee, even to this place. When Pilate heard mention of Galilee, he asked whether t h e man were of Galilee. And as soon as he knew that he belonged unto Herode's jurisdiction, he sent him to Herode, which was also at Jerusalem at that time. And when Herode saw Jesus he was exceeding glad; for he was desirous to see him of a long season, because he had heard many things of him, and he trusted to have seen some miracle done by him. Then he questioned with him many words; but he answered him nothing. The high priests and scribes stood forth and accused him straightly. And Herode with his men of war despised him: and when he had mocked him he arrayed him in white clothing, and sent him a g a i n to Pilate. And the same day Pilate and Herode were made friends together; for before t h e y were at variance. And Pilate called together the high priests, and the rulers, and t h e people, and said unto them, Ye have brought this man unto me, as one that perverteth the people: and, behold, I examine him before you, and find no faute in this man of those things whereof ye accuse him, no, nor yet Herode: for I sent you unto him; and lo, nothing worthy of death is done unto him. I will therefore chasten him and let him loose. For of necessity he must have let one loose unto them at that feast. · And all the people cried at once, saying, Away with him, and deliver us Barabbas: (which for a certain insurrection made in the city, and for a murther, was cast in prison.) Pilate s p a k e again unto them, willing to let Jesus loose. But they cried, saying, Crucify him, crucify him. He said unto them the third time, What evil hath he done ? I find no cause of death in him : I will therefore chasten him and let him go. And they cried with loud voices, requiring that he might be crucified : and the voices of them and of the high priests prevailed. And Pilate gave sentence that it should be as they required. And he let loose unto them him that (f o,r insurrection and murther) was cast into prison, whom they had desired; and he delivered to them Jesus, to do with him what they would. And as they led him away, they caught one Simon of Cirene coming out of the field, and on him laid they the cross, that he might bear it after Jesus. And there followed him a great company of people, and of women, which bewailed and lamented him. But Jesus turned back unto them, and said, Ye daughters of Jerusalem, weep not for me, but weep for yourselves, and for your children. For behold, the days will come, in which they shall say, Happy are the barren, and the wombs that never bare, and the paps which never gave suck. Then shall they begin to say to the mountains, Fall on us; and to the hills, Cover us. For if they do this in a green tree, what shall be done in the dry ? And there were two evildoers led with him to be slain. And after that they were come to the place (which is called Calvarie), there they crucified him, and the evildoers, one on the right hand, and the other on the left. Then said Jesus, Father, forgive them, for they wot not what they do. And they parted h i s raiment, and cast lots. And the people stood and beheld; and the rulers mocked him with them, saying, He saved other men; let him save himself, if he be very Christ, the chosen of God. The soldiers also mocked him, and came and offered him vinegar, and said, If thou be the King of the Jews, save thyself. And a superscription was written over him with l e t t e r s of Greke, and Latin, and Hebrue, THIS IS THE KING OF THE JEWS. And one of the evildoers, which were hanged, railed on him, saying, If thou be Christ, save thyself, and us. But the other answered and rebuked him, saying,

Fearest thou not God, seeing thou art in the same damnation? We are righteously punished; for we receive according to our deeds: but this man hath done nothing amiss. And he said unto Jesus, Lord, remember me when thou comest into thy kingdom. And Jesus said unto him, Verily I say unto thee, To-day shalt thou be with me in Paradise. And it was about the vi. hour: and there was darkness over all the earth until the ix. hour. And the sun was darkened, and the vail of the temple did rent even through the midst. And when Jesus had cried with a loud voice, he said, Father, into thy hands I commend my spirit: and when he thus had said, he gave up the ghost. When the centurion saw what had happened, he glorified God, saying, Verily this was a righteous man. And all the people that came together to that sight, and saw the things which had happened, smote their breasts, and returned.

And all his acquaintance, and the women that followed him from Galilee, stood afar off, beholding these things. And, behold, there was a man named Joseph, a counsellor: and he was a good man, and a just: the same had not consented to the counsel and deed of them; which was of Aramathia, a city of the Jews: which same also waited for the kingdom of God. He went unto Pilate, and begged the body of Jesus; and took it down, and wrapped it in a linen cloth, and laid it in a sepulchre that was hewn in stone, wherein never man before had been laid. And that day was the preparing of the sabbath, and the sabbath drew on. The women that followed after, which had come with him from Galilee, beheld the sepulchre, and how his body was laid. And they returned, and prepared sweet odours and ointments; but rested on the sabbath day according to the commandment.

## At Evensong.

### THE FIRST LESSON, LAM. iii.

# On Good Friday.

## At Matins.

### THE FIRST LESSON, GEN. xxii.

*The Collect.*

ALMIGHTY God, we beseech thee graciously to behold this thy family, for the which our Lord Jesus Christ was con- tented to be betrayed, and given up into the hands of wicked men, and to suffer death upon the cross; who liveth and reigneth, etc.

## At the Communion.

*Deus, Deus meus.* Psalm xxii.

MY God, my God, (look upon me,) why hast thou forsaken me: and art so far from my health, and from the words of my complaint?

O my God, I cry in the daytime, but thou hearest not: and in the night season also I take no rest.

And thou continuest holy: O thou worship of Israel.

Our fathers hoped in thee: they trusted in thee, and thou didst deliver them.

They called upon thee, and were helped: they put their trust in thee, and were not confounded.

But as for me, I am a worm and no man: a very scorn of men, and the outcast of the people.

All they that see me laugh me to scorn: they shoot out their lips, and shake the head, saying,

He trusted in God that he would deliver him: let him deliver him, if he will have him.

But thou art he that took me out of my mother's womb: thou wast my hope when I hanged yet upon my mother's breasts.

I have been left unto thee ever since I was born: thou art my God even from my mother's womb.

O go not from me, for trouble is here at hand: and there is none to help me.

Many oxen are come about me: fat bulls of Basan close me in on every side.

They gape upon me with their mouths: as it were a ramping and roaring lion.

I am poured out like water,

and all my bones are out of joint: my heart also in the midst of my body is even like melting wax.

My strength is dried up like a potsherd, and my tongue cleaveth to my gums: and thou shalt bring me into the dust of death.

For (many) dogs are come about me: and the council of the wicked lay siege against me.

They pierced my hands and my feet; I may tell all my bones: they stand staring and looking upon me.

They part my garments among them: and cast lots upon my vesture.

But be not thou far from me, O Lord: thou art my succour, haste thee to help me.

Deliver my soul from the sword: my darling from the power of the dog.

Save me from the lion's mouth: thou hast heard me also from among the horns of the unicorns.

I will declare thy Name unto my brethren: in the midst of the congregation will I praise thee.

O praise the Lord, ye that fear him: magnify him, all ye of the seed of Jacob, and fear ye him, all ye seed of Israel.

For he hath not despised nor abhorred the low estate of the poor: he hath not hid his face from him, but when he called unto him he heard him.

My praise is of thee in the great congregation : my vows will I perform in the sight of them that fear him.

The poor shall eat, and be satisfied: they that seek after the Lord shall praise him; your heart shall live for ever.

All the ends of the world shall remember themselves, and be turned unto the Lord: and all the kynreds of the nations shall worship before him.

For the kingdom is the Lord's: and he is the Governor among the people.

All such as be fat upon earth: have eaten, and worshipped.

All they that go down into the dust shall kneel before him : and no man hath quickened his own soul.

My seed shall serve him: they shall be counted unto the Lord for a generation.

They shall come, and the heavens shall declare his righteousness: unto a people that shall be born, whom the Lord hath made.

Glory be to the Father,

and to the Son: and to the Holy Ghost.

As it was in the beginning, is now, and ever shall be: world without end. Amen.

After the two Collects at the Communion shall be said these two Collects following.

### The Collect.

ALMIGHTY and everlasting God, by whose Spirit the whole body of the Church is governed and sanctified; Receive our supplications and prayers, which we offer before thee for all estates of men in thy holy congregation, that every member of the same, in his vocation and ministry, may truly and godly serve thee; through our Lord Jesus Christ.

MERCIFUL God, who hast made all men, and hatest nothing that thou hast made, nor wouldest the death of a sinner, but rather that he should be converted and live; Have mercy upon all Jews, Turks, Infidels, and Heretics, and take from them all ignorance, hardness of heart, and contempt of thy word: and so fetch them home, blessed Lord, to thy flock, that they may be saved among the remnant of the true Israelites, and be made one fold under one shepherd,

Jesus Christ our Lord; who liveth and reigneth, etc.

### The Epistle. Heb. x.

THE law (which hath but a shadow of good things to come, and not the very fashion of things themselves) can never with those sacrifices, which they offer year by year continually, make the comers thereunto perfect: for would not then those sacrifices have ceased to have been offered? because that the offerers once purged should have had no more conscience of sins. Nevertheless in those sacrifices is there mention made of sins every year. For the blood of oxen and of goats cannot take away sins. Wherefore, when he cometh into the world, he saith, Sacrifice and offering thou wouldest not have, but a body hast thou ordained me: burnt-offerings also for sin hast thou not allowed. Then said I, Lo, I am here: in the beginning of the book it is written of me, that I should do thy will, O God. Above, when he saith, Sacrifice and offering, and burnt sacrifices, and sin-offerings thou wouldest not have, neither hast thou allowed them, (which yet are offered by the law,) then said he, Lo, I am here to do thy will, O God.

He taketh away the first to establish the latter. By the which will we are made holy, even by the offering of the body of Jesu Christ once for all. And every priest is ready, daily ministering and offering oftentimes one manner of oblation, which can never take away sins. But this man, after he hath offered one sacrifice for sins, is set down for ever on the right hand of God; and from henceforth tarrieth till his foes be made his footstool. For with one offering hath he made perfect forever them that are sanctified: the Holy Ghost himself also beareth us record, even when he told before: This is the testament that I will make unto them: After those days (saith the Lord) I will put my laws in their hearts, and in their minds will I write them; and their sins and iniquities will I remember no more. And where remission of these things is, there is no more offering for sin. Seeing therefore, brethren, that by the means of the blood of Jesu, we have liberty to enter into the holy place, by the new and living way, which he hath prepared for us, through the vail, (that is to say, by his flesh;) and seeing also that we have an High Priest which is ruler over the house of God; let us draw nigh with a true heart in a sure faith, sprinkled in our hearts from an evil conscience, and washed in our bodies with pure water. Let us keep the profession of our hope without wavering; (for he is faithful that promised;) and let us consider one another, to the intent that we may provoke unto love and to good works; not forsaking the fellowship that we have among ourselves, as the manner of some is; but let us exhort one another: and that so much the more, because ye see that the day draweth nigh.

*The Gospel.* John xviii. xix.

WHEN Jesus had spoken these words, he went forth with his disciples over the brook Cedron, where was a garden, into the which he entered, with his disciples. Judas also, which betrayed him, knew the place: for Jesus ofttimes resorted thither with his disciples. Judas then, after he had received a band of men, (and ministers of the high priests and Pharisees,) came thither with lanterns and firebrands and weapons. And Jesus, knowing all things that should come on him, went forth, and said unto them, Whom seek ye?

They answered him, Jesus of Nazareth. Jesus saith unto them, I am he. Judas also, which betrayed him, stood with them. As soon then as he had said unto them, I am he, they went backward, and fell to the ground. Then asked he them again, Whom seek ye? They said, Jesus of Nazareth. Jesus answered, I have told you that I am he: if ye seek me therefore, let these go their way: that the saying might be fulfilled, which he spake, Of them which thou gavest me have I not lost one. Then Simon Peter having a sword drew it, and smote the high priest's servant, and cut off his right ear. The servant's name was Malchus. Therefore saith Jesus unto Peter, Put up thy sword into the sheath: shall I not drink of the cup which my Father hath given me? Then the company and the captain and the ministers of the Jews took Jesus, and bound him, and led him away to Annas first; for he was father in law to Caiphas, which was the high priest the same year. Caiphas was he that gave counsel to the Jews, that it was expedient that one man should die for the people. And Simon Peter followed Jesus, and so did another disciple: that dis-ciple was known to the high priest, and went in with Jesus into the palace of the high priest. But Peter stood at the door without. Then went out that other disciple, (which was known to the high priest,) and spake to the damosel that kept the door, and brought in Peter. Then said the damosel that kept the door unto Peter, Art not thou also one of this man's disciples? He said, I am not. The servants and ministers stood there, which had made a fire of coals; for it was cold: and they warmed themselves: Peter also stood among them, and warmed himself. The high priest then asked Jesus of his disciples, and of his doctrine. Jesus answered him, I spake openly in the world; I ever taught in the synagogue, and in the temple, whither all the Jews have resorted; and in secret have I said nothing. Why askest thou me? ask them which heard me, what I said unto them: behold they can tell what I said. When he had thus spoken, one of the ministers which stood by smote Jesus on the face, saying, Answerest thou the high priest so? Jesus answered him, If I have evil spoken, bear witness of the evil: but if I have well spoken, why smitest thou me? And Annas sent him bound unto Caiphas the high priest. Simon Peter stood and warmed himself. Then said they unto him, Art not thou also one of his disciples? He denied it, and said, I am not. One of the servants of the high priest (his cousin whose ear Peter smote off) said unto him, Did not I see thee in the garden with him? Peter therefore denied again: and immediately t h e cock crew. Then led they Jesus from Caiphas into the hall of judgment: it was in the morning; a n d t h e y themselves went not into the judgment hall, lest they should be defiled; but that they might eat the passover. Pilate then went out to them, and said, What accusation bring you against this man? They answered and said unto him, If he were not an evildoer, we would not have delivered him unto thee. Then said Pilate unto them, Take ye him, and judge him after your own law. The Jews therefore said unto him, It is not lawful for us to put any man to death: that the words of Jesus might be fulfilled, which he spake, signifying what d e a t h h e should die. Then Pilate entered into the judgment hall again, and called Jesus, and said unto him, Art thou the King of the Jews? Jesus answered, Sayest thou that of thyself, or did other tell it thee of me? Pilate answered, Am I a Jew? Thine own nation and high priests have delivered thee unto me: what hast thou done? Jesus answered, My kingdom is not of this world: if my kingdom were of this world, then would my ministers surely fight, that I should not be delivered to the Jews: but now is my kingdom not from hence. Pilate therefore said unto him, Art thou a king then? Jesus answered, Thou sayest that I am a king. For this cause was I born, and for this cause came I into the world, that I should bear witness unto the truth. And all that are of the truth hear my voice. Pilate said unto him, What thing is truth? And when he had said this, he went out again unto the Jews, and saith unto them, I find in him no cause at all. Ye have a custom, that I should deliver you one loose at Easter: will ye that I loose unto you the King of the Jews? Then cried they all again, saying, Not him but Barabbas. The same Barabbas was a murtherer. Then Pilate took Jesus therefore and scourged him. And the soldiers wound a crown of thorns, and put it on his head, and they put on him a purple garment, and came unto him, and said, Hail, King of the Jews! and they smote him on the face. Pilate went forth again, and said unto them, Behold, I bring him forth to you, that ye may know that I find no fault in him. Then came Jesus forth, wearing a crown of thorn, and a robe of purple. And he saith unto them, Behold the man! When the high priests therefore and ministers saw him, they cried, saying, Crucify him, crucify him. Pilate saith unto them, Take ye him, and crucify him: for I find no cause in him. The Jews answered him, We have a law, and by our law he ought to die, because he made himself the Son of God. When Pilate heard that saying, he was the more afraid: and went again into the judgment hall, and saith unto Jesus, Whence art thou? But Jesus gave him none answer. Then said Pilate unto him, Speakest thou not unto me? knowest thou not that I have power to crucify thee, and have power to loose thee? Jesus answered, Thou couldest have no power at all against me, except it were given thee from above:

therefore he that delivered me unto thee hath the more sin. And from thenceforth sought Pilate means to loose him: but the Jews cried, saying, If thou let him go, thou art not Cesar's friend: for whosoever maketh himself a king is against Cesar. When Pilate heard that saying, he brought Jesus forth, and sat down to give sentence in a place that is called the Pavement, but in the Hebrue tongue Gabbatha. It was the preparing day of Easter, about the vi. hour: and he saith unto the Jews, Behold your King! They cried, saying, Away with him, away with him, crucify him. Pilate saith unto them, Shall I crucify your King? The high priests answered, We have no king but Cesar. Then delivered he him unto them to be crucified: and they took Jesus and led him away. And he bare his cross, and went forth into a place which is called the place of dead men's skulls, but in Hebrue, Golgotha: where they crucified him, and two other with him, on either side one, and Jesus in the midst. And Pilate wrote a title, and put it on the cross. The writing was, JESUS OF NAZARETH KING OF THE JEWS. This title read many of the Jews: for the place where Jesus was crucified was nigh to the city: and it was written in Hebrue, Greke, and Latin. Then said the high priests of the Jews to Pilate, Write not, King of the Jews; but that he said, I am King of the Jews. Pilate answered, What I have written, that have I written. Then the soldiers when they had crucified Jesus, took his garments, and made iv. parts, to every soldier a part; and also his coat: the coat was without seam, wrought upon throughout. They said therefore among themselves, Let us not divide it, but cast lots for it, who shall have it: that the scripture might be fulfilled, saying, They have parted my raiment among them, and for my coat did they cast lots. And the soldiers did such things in deed. There stood by the cross of Jesus, his mother, and his mother's sister, Mary the wife of Cleophas, and Mary Magdalene. When Jesus therefore saw his mother, and the disciple standing, whom he loved, he saith unto his mother, Woman, behold thy son! Then said he to the disciple, Behold thy mother! And from that hour the disciple took her for his own.

After these things, Jesus knowing that all things were now performed, that the scripture might be fulfilled, he saith, I thirst. So there stood a vessel by full of vinegar: therefore they filled a spunge with vinegar, and wound it about with hyssop, and put it to his mouth. As soon as Jesus then received of the vinegar, he said, It is finished; and bowed his head and gave up the ghost. The Jews therefore, because it was the preparing of the sabbath, that the bodies should not remain upon the cross on the sabbath day, (for that sabbath day was an high day,) besought Pilate that their legs might be broken, and that they might be taken down. Then came the soldiers, and brake the legs of the first, and of the other which was crucified with him. But when they came to Jesus, and saw that he was dead already, they brake not his legs. But one of the soldiers with a spear thrust him into the side, and forthwith came there out blood and water. And he that saw it bare record, and his record is true: and he knoweth that he saith true, that ye might believe also. For these things were done that the scripture should be fulfilled, Ye shall not break a bone of him.

And again another scripture saith, They shall look upon him whom they have pierced. After this Joseph of Aramathia (which was a disciple of Jesus, but secretly for fear of the Jews) besought Pilate that h e might take down the body of Jesus: and Pilate gave him license. He came therefore, and took the body of Jesus. And there came also Nicodemus, (which at the beginning came to Je-sus by night,) and brought of myrrh and aloes mingled together, a b o u t an hundred pound weight. Then took they the body of Jesus, and wound it in linen clothes with the odours, as the manner of the Jews is to bury. And in the place where he was crucified there was a garden; and in the garden a new sepulchre, wherein was never man laid. There laid they Jesus therefore because of the preparing of the sabbath of the Jews; for the sepulchre was nigh at hand.

### At Evensong.
THE FIRST LESSON, Isaiah liii.

---

# Easter Even.

### At Matins.
THE FIRST LESSON, Lam. iv and v.

## At the Communion.

*Domine Deus salutis.*
Psalm lxxxviii.

O LORD GOD of my salvation, I have cried day and night before thee: O let my prayer enter into thy presence, incline thine ear unto my calling.

For my soul is f u l l of trouble: and my life draweth nigh unto hell.

I am counted as one of them that go down unto the pit: and I have been even as a man that hath no strength.

Free among the dead, like unto them that be wounded, and lie in the grave: which be out of remembrance, and are c u t away f r o m thy hand.

Thou hast laid me in the

lowest pit: in a place of darkness, and in the deep.

Thine indignation lieth hard upon me: and thou hast vexed me with all thy storms.

Thou hast put away mine acquaintance far from me: and made me to be abhorred of them.

I am so fast in prison: that I cannot get forth.

My sight faileth for very trouble: Lord, I have called daily upon thee, I have stretched out my hands unto thee.

Dost thou shew wonders among the dead: or shall the dead rise up again, and praise thee?

Shall thy loving kindness be shewed in the grave: or thy faithfulness in destruction?

Shall thy wondrous works be known in the dark: and thy righteousness in the land where all things are forgotten?

Unto thee have I cried, O Lord: and early shall my prayer come before thee.

Lord, why abhorrest thou my soul: and hidest thou thy face from me?

I am in misery, and like unto him that is at the point to die: (even from my youth up) thy terrors have I suffered with a troubled mind.

Thy wrathful displeasure goeth over me: and the fear of thee hath undone me.

They came round about me daily like water: and compassed me together on every side.

My lovers and friends hast thou put away from me: and hid mine acquaintance out of my sight.

Glory be to the Father, and to the Son: and to the Holy Ghost.

As it was in the beginning, is now, and ever shall be: world without end. Amen.

### *The Epistle.* 1. Pet. iii.

IT is better (if the will of God be so) that ye suffer for well doing than for evil doing. Forasmuch as Christ hath once suffered for sins, the just for the unjust, to bring us to God; and was killed as pertaining to the flesh; but was quickened in the Spirit. In which Spirit he also went and preached to the spirits that were in prison; which sometime had been disobedient, when the long-suffering of God was once looked for in the days of Noe, while the ark was a preparing; wherein a few, that is to say, eight souls, were saved by the water; like as Baptism also now saveth us; not the putting away of the filth of the flesh, but in that a good conscience consenteth to God, by the resurrection of Jesus Christ: which is on the right hand of God, and is gone into heaven, angels, powers, and might, subdued unto him.

*The Gospel.* Matt. xxvii.

WHEN the even was come, there came a rich man of Aramathia, named Joseph, which also was Jesu's disciple. He went unto Pilate and begged the body of Jesus. Then Pilate commanded the body to be delivered. And when Joseph had taken the body, he wrapped it in a clean linen cloth, and laid it in his new tomb, which he had hewn out even in the rock; and rolled a great stone to the door of the sepulchre, and departed. And there was Mary Magdalene, and the other Mary, sitting over against the sepulchre. The next day that followed the day of preparing, the high priests and Pharisees came together unto Pilate, saying, Sir, we remember that this deceiver said while he was yet alive, After iii. days I will rise again. Command, therefore, that the sepulchre be made sure until the third day, lest his disciples come and steal him away, and say unto the people, He is risen from the dead: and the last error shall be worse than the first. Pilate said unto them, Ye have the watch; go your way, make it as sure as ye can. So they went and made the sepulchre sure with the watchmen, and sealed the stone.

# Easter Day.

In the Morning afore Matins, the people being assembled in the Church, these Anthems shall be first solemnly sung or said.

CHRIST rising again from the dead, now dieth not: Death from henceforth hath no power upon him. For in that he died, he died but once to put away sin: but in that he liveth, he liveth unto God. And so likewise count yourselves dead unto sin: but living unto God in Christ Jesus our Lord. Alleluia. Alleluia.

CHRIST is risen again: the first fruits of them that sleep. For seeing that by man came death: by man also cometh the resurrection of the dead. For as by Adam all men do die, so by Christ all men shall be restored to life. Alleluia.

*The Priest.*

Shew forth to all nations the glory of God.

*The Answer.*

And among all people his wonderful works.

Let us pray.

O GOD, who for our redemption didst give thine only begotten Son to the death of the Cross; and by his glorious resurrection hast delivered us from the power of our enemy: Grant us so to die daily from sin, that we may evermore live with him in the joy of his resurrection; through the same Christ our Lord. Amen.

## Proper Psalms and Lessons.

### At Matins.

Psalm ii.  
Psalm lvii.  } THE FIRST LESSON, Exod. xii.  
Psalm cxi.  } THE SECOND LESSON, Rom. vi.

## At the First Communion.

*Conserva me, Domine.*  
Psalm xvi.

PRESERVE me, O God; for in thee have I put my trust.

O my soul, thou hast said unto the Lord: Thou art my God, my goods are nothing unto thee.

All my delight is upon the saints that are in the earth: and upon such as excel in virtue.

But they that run after another god: shall have great trouble.

Their drink-offerings of blood will not I offer: neither make mention of their names within my lips.

The Lord himself is the portion of mine inheritance, and of my cup: thou shalt maintain my lot.

The lot is fallen unto me in a fair ground: yea, I have a goodly heritage.

I will thank the Lord for giving me warning: my reins also chasten me in the night-season.

I have set God always before me: for he is on my right hand, therefore I shall not fall.

Wherefore my heart was glad, and my glory rejoiced: my flesh also shall rest in hope.

For why? thou shalt not leave my soul in hell: neither shalt thou suffer thy Holy One to see corruption.

Thou shalt shew me the path of life; in thy presence is the fulness of joy: and at thy right hand there is pleasure for evermore.

Glory be to the Father, and to the Son: and to the Holy Ghost.

As it was in the beginning, is now, and ever shall be: world without end.    Amen.

### The Collect.

ALMIGHTY God, which through thy only begotten Son Jesus Christ hast overcome death, and opened unto us the gate of everlasting life; We humbly beseech thee, that, as by thy special grace preventing us thou dost put in our minds good desires, so by thy continual help we may bring the same to good effect; through Jesus Christ our Lord, who liveth and reigneth, etc.

### The Epistle. Col. iii.

IF ye be risen again with Christ, seek those t h i n g s w h i c h are above, where Christ sitteth on the right hand of God. Set your affection on heavenly things, and not on earthly things: for ye are dead, and your life is hid with Christ in God. Whensoever Christ (which is our life) shall shew himself, then shall ye a l s o appear with him in glory.    Mortify therefore your earthly members, fornication, uncleanness, unnatural lust, evil concupiscence, a n d covetousness, which is worshipping of idols: for which things' sake the wrath of God useth to come on the disobedient children; among whom ye walked sometime when ye lived in them.

### The Gospel. John xx.

THE first day of the sabbaths came Mary Magdelene early (when it was yet dark) unto the sepulchre, and saw the stone taken away from the grave.    Then she r a n and came to Simon Peter, and to the other disciple whom Jesus loved, and saith unto them, They have taken away the Lord out of the grave, and we cannot t e l l where they have laid him. Peter therefore went forth, and that other disciple, and came u n t o the sepulchre. They ran both together; and the other disciple did outrun Peter, and came first to the sepulchre: and when he had stooped down, he saw the linen clothes lying; yet went he not in. Then came Simon Peter following him, and went into the sepulchre, and saw the linen clothes lie; and the napkin that was about his head, not lying with the linen clothes, but wrapped together in a place by itself. Then went in also that other disciple which came first to the sepulchre, and he saw, and believed. For as yet they knew not the scripture, that he should rise again from death. Then the disciples went away again unto their own home.

## Easter Day
## At the Second Communion,

*Domine, quid multiplicati.*
Psalm iii.

LORD, how are they increased that trouble me many are they that rise against me.

Many one there be that say of my soul: There is no help for him in his God.

But thou, O Lord, art my defender: thou art my worship, and the lifter up of my head.

I did call upon the Lord with my voice: and he heard me out of his holy hill.

I laid me down and slept, and rose up again: for the Lord sustained me.

I will not be afraid for ten thousands of the people that have set themselves against me round about.

Up, Lord, and help me, O my God: for thou smitest all mine enemies upon the cheek bone; thou hast broken the teeth of the ungodly.

Salvation belongeth unto thy Lord: and thy blessing is upon thy people.

Glory be to the Father, and to the Son: and to the Holy Ghost.

As it was in the beginning, is now, and ever shall be: world without end. Amen.

### The Collect.

ALMIGHTY Father, which hast given thy only Son to die for our sins, and to rise again for our justification; Grant us so to put away the leaven of malice and wickedness, that we may alway serve thee in pureness of living and truth; through Jesus Christ our Lord.

### The Epistle. 1. Cor. v.

KNOW ye not that a little leaven soureth the whole

lump of dough? Purge therefore the old leaven, that ye may be new dough, as ye are sweet bread. For Christ our passover is offered up for us: therefore let us keep holy day, not with old leaven, neither with the leaven of maliciousness and wickedness; but with the sweet bread of pureness and truth.

*The Gospel.* Mark xvi.

WHEN the sabbath was past, Mary Magdalene, and Mary Jacoby, and Salome, bought sweet odours, that they might come and anoint him. And early in the morning, the first day of the sabbath, they came unto the sepulchre when the sun was risen. And they said among themselves, Who shall roll us away the stone from the door of the sepulchre? And when they looked, they saw how that the stone was rolled away: for it was a very great one. And they went into the sepulchre, and saw a young man sitting on the right side, clothed in a long white garment; and they were afraid. And he said unto them, Be not afraid: ye seek Jesus of Nazareth, which was crucified: he is risen; he is not here: behold the place where they had put him. But go your way, and tell his disciples and Peter that he goeth before you into Galilee: there shall ye see him, as he said unto you. And they went out quickly, and fled from the sepulchre; for they trembled and were amazed: neither said they anything to any man; for they were afraid.

Proper Psalms and Lessons at Evensong.

Psalms cxiii; cxiv and cxviii.     THE SECOND LESSON, Acts II.

## Monday in Easter Week.

### At Matins.
THE SECOND LESSON, Matt. xxviii.

## At the Communion.

*Nonne Deo subjecta.* Ps. lxii.

MY soul truly waiteth still upon God: for of him cometh my salvation.

He verily is my strength and my salvation: he is my defence, so that I shall not greatly fall.

How long will ye imagine mischief against every man: ye shall be slain all the sort of you; yea, as a tottering wall shall ye be, and like a broken hedge.

Their device is only how to put him out whom God will exalt: their delight is in lies; they give good words with their mouth, but curse with their heart.

Nevertheless, my soul, wait thou still upon God: for my hope is in him.

He truly is my strength and my salvation: he is my defence, so that I shall not fall.

In God is my health and my glory: the rock of my might, and in God is my trust.

O put your trust in him alway, ye people: pour out your hearts before him, for God is our hope.

As for the children of men, they are but vain, the children of men are deceitful: upon the weights, they are altogether lighter than vanity itself.

O trust not in wrong and robbery, give not yourselves unto vanity: if riches increase set not your heart upon them.

God spake once and twice: I have also heard the same, that power belongeth unto God.

And that thou, Lord, art merciful: for thou rewardest every man according to his work.

Glory be to the Father, and to the Son: and to the Holy Ghost.

As it was in the beginning, is now, and ever shall be: world without end. Amen.

### The Collect.

ALMIGHTY God, which through thy only-begotten Son Jesus Christ hast overcome death, and opened unto us the gate of everlasting life; We humbly beseech thee, that as by thy special grace preventing us thou dost put in our minds good desires, so by thy continual help we may bring the same to good effect; through Jesus Christ our Lord, who liveth and reigneth, etc.

### The Epistle. Acts x.

PETER opened his mouth, and said, Of a truth I perceive that there is no respect of persons with God; but in all people he that feareth him, and worketh righteousness, is accepted with him. Ye know the preaching that God sent unto the children of Israel, preaching peace by Jesu Christ, which is Lord over all things; which preaching was published throughout all Jewry, (and began in Galilee, after the baptism which John preached;) how God anointed Jesus of Nazareth with the Holy Ghost, and with power; which went about doing good, and healing all that were oppressed of the devil: for God was with him. And we are witnesses of all things which he did in the land of the Jews, and at Jerusalem; whom they slew, and hanged on tree: him God raised up the third day, and shewed him openly; not to all the people, but unto us witnesses (chosen before of God for the same intent,) which did eat and drink with him after he rose from death. And he commanded us to preach unto the people, and to testify that it is he which was ordained of God to be the judge of the quick and dead. To him gave all the prophets witness, that through his name whosoever believeth in him shall receive remission of sins.

*The Gospel.* Luke xxiv.

BEHOLD, two of the disciples went that same day to a town called Emaus, which was from Jerusalem about lx. furlongs. And they talked together of all the things that had happened. And it chanced, that while they commoned together and reasoned, Jesus himself drew near, and went with them. But their eyes were holden, that they should not know him. And he said unto them, What manner of communications are these that ye have one to another, as ye walk and are sad? And the one of them (whose name was Cleophas) answered, and said unto him, Art thou only a stranger in Jerusalem, and hast not known the things which have chanced there in these days? He said unto them, What things? And they said unto him, of Jesus of Nazareth, which was a prophet mighty in deed and word before God and all the people: and how the high priests and our rulers delivered him to be condemned to death and have crucified him. But we trusted that it had been he which should have redeemed Israel: and as touching all these things, to-day is even the third day that they were done. Yea, and certain women also of our company made us astonied, which came early unto the sepulchre, and found not his body, and came, saying, that they had seen a vision of angels, which said that he was alive. And certain of them which were with us went to the sepulchre, and found it even so as the women had said; but him they saw not. And he said unto them, O fools, and slow of heart to believe all that the prophets have spoken: ought not Christ to have suffered these things, and to enter into his glory? And he began at Moses and all the prophets, and interpreted unto them in all Scriptures which were written of him. And they drew nigh unto the town which they went unto; and he made as though he would have gone further: and they constrained him, saying, Abide with us, for it draweth towards night, and the day is far passed. And he went in to tarry with them. And it came to pass, as he sat at meat with them, he took bread, and blessed it, and brake, and gave unto them. And their eyes were opened, and they knew him, and he vanished out of their sight. And they said between themselves, Did not our hearts burn within us, while he talked with us by the way, and opened to us the Scriptures? And they rose up the same hour, and returned to Jerusalem, and found the eleven gathered together, and them that were with them, saying, The Lord is risen in deed, and hath appeared to Simon. And they told what things were done in the way, and how they knew him in breaking of the bread.

At Evensong.

THE SECOND LESSON, Acts iii.

---

## Tuesday in Easter Week.

### At Matins.

THE SECOND LESSON, Luke xxiv:1-13.

### At the Communion.

*Laudate, pueri.*
Psalm cxiii.

PRAISE the Lord (ye servants:) O praise the Name of the Lord.

Blessed is the Name of the Lord: from this time forth for evermore.

The Lord's Name is praised: from the rising up of the sun unto the going down of the same.

The Lord is high above all heathen : and his glory above the heavens.

Who is like unto the Lord our God, that hath his dwelling so high: and yet humbleth himself to behold the things that are in heaven and earth ?

He taketh up the simple out of the dust: and lifteth the poor out of the mire;

That he may set him with the princes: even with the princes of his people.

He maketh the barren woman to keep house: and to be a joyful mother of children.

Glory be to the Father, and to the Son : and to the Holy Ghost.

As it was in the beginning, is now, and ever shall be; world without end.    Amen.

### The Collect.

ALMIGHTY Father, which hast given thy only Son to die for our sins, and to rise again for our justification; Grant us so to put away the leaven of malice and wickedness, that we may alway serve thee in pureness of living and truth; through Jesus Christ our Lord.

### The Epistle. Acts xiii.

YE men and brethren, children of the generation of Abraham, and whosoever among you feareth God, to you is this word of salvation sent.    For the inhabiters of Jerusalem, and their rulers, because they knew him not, nor yet the voices of the prophets which are read every sabbath day, they have fulfilled them in condemning him.    And when they found no cause of death in him, yet desired they Pilate to kill him.    And when they had fulfilled all that were written of him, they took him down from the tree, and put him in a sepulchre.    But God raised him again from death the third day: and he was seen many days of them which went with him from Galilee to Jerusalem, which are his witnesses unto the people.    And we declare unto you, how that the promise, (which was made unto the fathers,) God hath fulfilled unto their children, (even unto us,) in that he raised up Jesus again; even as it is written in the second Psalm, Thou art my Son, this day have I begotten thee.    As concerning that he raised him up from death, now no more to return to corruption, he said on this wise, The holy promises made to David will I give faithfully to you.

Wherefore he saith also in another place, Thou shalt not suffer thine Holy to see corruption. For David (after that he had in his time fulfilled the will of God) fell on sleep, and was laid unto his fathers, and saw corruption: but he whom God raised again saw no corruption. Be it known unto you therefore, (ye men and brethren,) that through this man is preached unto you the forgiveness of sins: and that by him all that believe are justified from all things, from which ye could not be justified by the law of Moses. Beware therefore, lest that fall on you which is spoken of in the prophets; Behold, ye despisers, and wonder and perish ye: for I do a work in your days, which ye shall not believe, though a man declare it you.

*The Gospel.* Luke xxiv.

JESUS stood in the midst of his disciples, and said unto them, Peace be unto you. It is I; fear not. But they were abashed and afraid, and supposed that they had seen a spirit. And he said unto them, Why are ye troubled, and why do thoughts arise in your hearts? Behold my hands and my feet, that it is even I myself; handle me, and see; for a spirit hath not flesh and bones, as ye see me have. And when he had thus spoken, he shewed them his hands and his feet. And while they yet believed not for joy, and wondered, he said unto them, Have ye here any meat? And they offered him a piece of a broiled fish, and of an honey-comb. And he took it, and did eat before them. And he said unto them, These are the words which I spake unto you, while I was yet with you, that all must needs be fulfilled which were written of me in the law of Moses, and in the Prophets, and in the Psalms. Then opened he their wits, that they might understand the Scriptures, and said unto them, Thus it is written, and thus it behoved Christ to suffer, and to rise again from death the third day; and that repentance and remission of sins should be preached in his Name among all nations, and must begin at Jerusalem. And ye are witnesses of these things.

### At Evensong.

THE SECOND LESSON, 1 Cor. xv.

## The First Sunday after Easter.

*Beatus vir.* Psalm cxii.

BLESSED is the man that feareth the Lord: he hath great delight in his commandments.

His seed shall be mighty upon earth: the generation of the faithful shall be blessed.

Riches and plenteousness shall be in his house: and his righteousness endureth for ever.

Unto the godly there ariseth up light in the darkness; he is merciful, loving, and righteous.

A good man is merciful, and lendeth: and will guide his words with discretion.

For he shall never be moved: and the righteous shall be had in everlasting remembrance.

He will not be afraid for any evil tidings: for his heart standeth fast, and believeth in the Lord.

His heart is established, and will not shrink: until he see his desire upon his enemies.

He hath sparsed abroad, and given to the poor: and his righteousness remaineth for ever; his horn shall be exalted with honour.

The ungodly shall see it, and it shall grieve him: he shall gnash with his teeth, and consume away; the desire of the ungodly shall perish.

Glory be to the Father, and to the Son: and to the Holy Ghost.

As it was in the beginning, is now, and ever shall be: world without end. Amen.

*The Collect.*

ALMIGHTY Father, etc., *as at the second Communion on Easter Day.*

*The Epistle.* 1 John v.

ALL that is born of God overcometh the world; and this is the victory that overcometh the world, even our faith. Who is it that overcometh the world, but he which believeth that Jesus is the Son of God? This Jesus Christ is he that came by water and blood; not by water only, but by water and blood: and it is the Spirit that beareth witness, because the Spirit is truth. For there are three which bare record in heaven, the Father, the Word, and the Holy Ghost; and these three are one. And there are three which bare record in earth, the Spirit, and Water, and Blood: and these three are one. If we receive the witness of men, the witness of God is greater: for this is the witness of God that is greater, which he testified of his Son. He that believeth on the Son of God hath the witness in himself: he that believeth not God hath made him a liar, because he believeth not the record that God gave of his Son. And this is the record, how that God hath given unto us eternal life: and this life is in his Son. He that hath the Son hath life; and he that hath not the Son of God hath not life.

*The Gospel.* John xx.

THE same day at night, which was the first day of the sabbaths, when the doors were shut, (where the disciples were assembled together for fear of the Jews,) came Jesus and stood in the midst, and said unto them, Peace be unto you. And when he had so said, he shewed unto them his hands and his side. Then were the disciples glad when they saw the Lord. Then said Jesus to them again, Peace be unto you: as my Father sent me, even so send I you also. And when he had said those words, he breathed on them, and said unto them, Receive ye the Holy Ghost. Whosoever's sins ye remit, they are remitted unto them; and whosoever's sins ye retain, they are retained.

## The Second Sunday after Easter.

*Deus in adjutorium.*
Psalm lxx.

Haste thee, O God, to deliver me: make haste to help me, O Lord.

Let them be ashamed and confounded that seek after my soul: let them be turned backward and put to confusion that wish me evil.

Let them (for their reward) be soon brought to shame: that cry over me, There, there.

But let all those that seek thee be joyful and glad in thee: and let all such as delight in thy salvation say alway, The Lord be praised.

As for me, I am poor and in misery: haste thee unto me, O God.

Thou art my help, and my redeemer: O Lord, make no long tarrying.

Glory be to the Father, and to the Son: and to the Holy Ghost.

As it was in the beginning, is now, and ever shall be: world without end. Amen.

### The Collect.

ALMIGHTY God, which hast given thy holy Son to be unto us both a sacrifice for sin, and also an example of godly life; Give us the grace that we may always most thankfully receive that his inestimable benefit, and also daily endeavour ourselves to follow the blessed steps of his most holy life.

### The Epistle. 1 Peter ii.

THIS is thankworthy, if a man for conscience toward God endure grief, and suffer wrong undeserved. For what praise is it, if, when ye be buffeted for your fautes, ye take it patiently? But and if, when ye do well, ye suffer wrong, and take it patiently, then is there thank with God. For hereunto verily were ye called: for Christ also suffered for us, leaving us an ensample that ye should follow his steps: which did no sin, neither was there guile found in his mouth: which when he was reviled, reviled not again: when he suffered, he threatened not; but committed the vengeance to him that judgeth righteously: which his own self bare our sins in his body on the tree, that we being delivered from sin should live unto righteousness; by whose stripes ye were healed. For ye were as sheep going astray; but are now turned unto the Shepherd and Bishop of your souls.

### The Gospel. John x.

CHRIST said to his disciples, I am the good Shepherd: a good shepherd giveth his life for the sheep. An hired servant, and he which is not the shepherd, (neither the sheep are his own,) seeth the wolf coming, and leaveth the sheep, and flieth; and the wolf catcheth and scattereth the sheep. The hired servant flieth, because he is an hired servant, and careth not for the sheep. I am the good Shepherd, and know my sheep, and am known of mine. As my Father knoweth me, even so know I also my Father: and I give my life for the sheep. And other sheep I have, which are not of this fold; them also must I bring, and they shall hear my voice; and there shall be one fold, and one shepherd.

## The Third Sunday after Easter.

*Confitebimur.* Psalm lxxv.

UNTO thee (O God) do we give thanks: yea, unto thee do we give thanks.

Thy Name also is so nigh: and that do thy wondrous works declare.

When I receive the congregation: I shall judge according unto right.

The earth is weak, and all the inhabiters thereof: I bear up the pillars of it.

I said unto the fools, Deal not so madly: and to the ungodly, Set not up your horn.

Set not up your horn on high: and speak not with a stiff neck.

For promotion cometh neither from the east, nor from the west: nor yet from the south.

And why? God is the Judge: he putteth down one, and setteth up another.

For in the hand of the Lord there is a cup, and the wine is red: it is full mixed, and he poureth out of the same.

As for the dregs thereof: all the ungodly of the earth shall drink them, and suck them out.

But I will talk of the God of Jacob; and praise him for ever.

All the horns of the ungodly also will I break: and the horns of the righteous shall be exalted.

Glory be to the Father, and to the Son: and to the Holy Ghost.

As it was in the beginning, is now, and ever shall be: world without end. Amen.

### The Collect.

ALMIGHTY God, which shewest to all men that be in error the light of thy truth, to the intent that they may return into the way of righteousness; Grant unto all them that be admitted into the fellowship of Christ's religion, that they may eschew those things that be contrary to their profession, and follow all such things as be agreeable to the same; through our Lord Jesus Christ.

### The Epistle. 1. Pet. ii.

DEARLY beloved, I beseech you as strangers and pilgrims, abstain from fleshly lusts, which fight against the soul; and see that ye have honest conversation among the Gentiles; that, whereas they backbite you as evildoers, they may see your good works, and praise God in the day of visitation. Submit yourselves therefore unto all manner ordinance of man for the Lord's sake, whether it be unto the king, as unto the chief head; either unto rulers, as unto them that are sent of him, for the punishment of evildoers, but for the laud of them that do well. For so is the will of God, that with well-doing ye may stop the mouths of foolish and ignorant men: free, and not as having the liberty for a cloak of maliciousness; but even as the servants of God. Honour all men. Love brotherly fellowship. Fear God. Honour the king.

*The Gospel.* John xvi.

JESUS said to his disciples, After a while ye shall not see me; and again, after a while ye shall see me; for I go to the Father. Then said some of his disciples between themselves, What is this that he saith unto us, After a while ye shall not see me; and again, after a while ye shall see me: and that I go to the Father? They said therefore, What is this that he saith, After a while? we cannot tell what he saith. Jesus perceived that they would ask him, and said unto them, Ye inquire of this between yourselves, because I said, After a while ye shall not see me; and again, after a while ye shall see me. Verily, verily I say unto you, Ye shall weep and lament, but contrariwise the world shall rejoice: ye shall sorrow, but your sorrow shall be turned to joy. A woman, when she travaileth, hath sorrow, because her hour is come: but as soon as she is delivered of the child, she remembereth no more the anguish, for joy that a man is born into the world. And ye now therefore have sorrow: but I will see you again, and your hearts shall rejoice, and your joy shall no man take from you.

## The Fourth Sunday after Easter.

*Deus stetit in synagoga.*
Psalm lxxxii.

GOD standeth in the congregation of princes: he is Judge among gods.

How long will ye give wrong judgment: and accept the persons of the ungodly?

Defend the poor and fatherless: see that such as be in need and necessity have right.

Deliver the outcast and poor: save them from the hand of the ungodly.

They will not be learned nor understand, but walk on still in darkness: all the foundations of the earth be out of course.

I have said, Ye are gods: and ye all are children of the most Highest.

But ye shall die like men: and fall like one of the princes.

Arise, O God, and judge thou the earth: for thou shalt take all the heathen to thine inheritance.

Glory be to the Father, and to the Son: and to the Holy Ghost.

As it was in the beginning, is now, and ever shall be: world without end. Amen.

### The Collect.

ALMIGHTY God, which dost make the minds of all faithful men to be of one will; Grant unto thy people, that they may love the thing which thou commandest, and desire that which thou dost promise; that among the sundry and manifold changes of the world, our hearts may surely there be fixed, where as true joys are to be found; through Christ our Lord.

### The Epistle. James i.

EVERY good gift, and every perfect gift is from above, and cometh down from the Father of lights, with whom is no variableness, neither is he changed unto darkness. Of his own will begat he us with the Word of truth, that we should be the first-fruits of his creatures. Wherefore (dear brethren) let every man be swift to hear, slow to speak, slow to wrath; for the wrath of man worketh not that which is righteous before God. Wherefore lay apart all filthiness and superfluity of maliciousness, and receive with meekness the Word that is graffed in you, which is able to save your souls.

### The Gospel. John xvi.

JESUS said unto his disciples, Now I go my way to him that sent me, and none of you asketh me whither I go. But, because I have said such things unto you, your hearts are full of sorrow. Nevertheless I tell you the truth; it is expedient for you that I go away: for if I go not away, that Comforter will not come unto you; but if I depart, I will send him unto you. And when he is come, he will rebuke the world of sin, and of righteousness, and of judgment: of sin, because they believe not on me; of righteousness, because I go to my Father, and ye shall see me no more; of judgment, because the prince of this world is judged already. I have yet many things to say unto you, but ye cannot bear them away now. Howbeit, when he is come, (which is the Spirit of truth,) he will lead you into all truth. He shall not speak of himself; but whatsoever he shall hear, that shall he speak: and he will shew you things to come. He shall glorify me: for he shall receive of mine, and shall shew unto you. All things that the Father hath are mine: therefore said I unto you, that he shall take of mine, and shew unto you.

## The Fifth Sunday after Easter,

*Quam dilecta tabernacula!*
Psalm lxxxiv.

O how amiable are thy dwellings: thou Lord of hosts!

My soul hath a desire and longing to enter into the courts of the Lord: my heart and my flesh rejoice in the living God.

Yea, the sparrow hath found her an house, and the swallow a nest where she may lay her young: even altars, O Lord of hosts, my King and my God.

Blessed are they that dwell in thy house: they will be alway praising thee.

Blessed is that man whose strength is in thee: in whose heart are thy ways.

Which going through the vale of misery use it for a well: and the pools are filled with water.

They will go from strength to strength: and unto the God of gods appeareth every one of them in Sion.

O Lord God of hosts, hear my prayer: hearken, O God of Jacob.

Behold, O God our defender: and look upon the face of thine Anointed.

For one day in thy courts: is better than a thousand.

I had rather be a doorkeeper in the house of my God: than to dwell in the tents of ungodliness.

For the Lord God is a light and defence: the Lord will give grace and worship, and no good thing shall he withhold from them that live a godly life.

O Lord God of hosts: blessed is the man that putteth his trust in thee.

Glory be to the Father, and to the Son: and to the Holy Ghost.

As it was in the beginning, is now, and ever shall be: world without end. Amen.

### The Collect.

LORD, from whom all good things do come; Grant us, thy humble servants, that by thy holy inspiration we may think those things that be good, and by thy merciful guiding may perform the same; through our Lord Jesus Christ.

### The Epistle. James i.

SEE that ye be doers of the Word, and not hearers only, deceiving your own selves. For if any man hear the Word, and declareth not the same by his works, he is like unto a man beholding his bodily face in a glass. For as soon as he hath looked on himself, he goeth his way, and forgetteth immediately what his fashion was. But whoso looketh in the perfect law of liberty, and continueth therein, (if he be not a forgetful hearer, but a doer of the work,) the same shall be happy in his deed. If any

man among you seem to be devout, and refraineth not his tongue, but deceiveth his own heart, this man's devotion is in vain. Pure devotion, and undefiled before God the Father, is this, To visit the fatherless and widows in their adversity, and to keep himself unspotted of the world.

### The Gospel. John xvi.

VERILY, verily I say unto you, Whatsoever, ye shall ask the Father in my Name, he will give it you. Hitherto have ye asked nothing in my Name: ask, and ye shall receive, that your joy may be full. These things have I spoken unto you by proverbs: the time will come when I shall no more speak unto you by proverbs, but I shall shew you plainly from my Father. At that day shall ye ask in my Name: and I say not unto you that I will speak unto my Father for you; for the Father himself loveth you, because ye have loved me, and have believed that I came out from God. I went out from the Father, and came into the world: again, I leave the world, and go to the Father.

His disciples said unto him, Lo, now talkest thou plainly, and speakest no proverb.

Now are we sure that thou knowest all things, and needest not that any man should ask thee any question : therefore believe we that thou camest from God. Jesus answered them, Now ye do believe. Behold, the hour draweth nigh, and is already come, that ye shall be scattered every man to his own, and shall leave me alone : and yet am I not alone, for the Father is with me. These words have I spoken unto you, that in me ye might have peace, for in the world shall ye have tribulation ; but be of good cheer, I have overcome the world.

# The Ascension Day.

### Proper Psalms and Lesson at Matins.

Psalms viii; xv and xxi.   THE SECOND LESSON, John xiv.

## At the Communion.

#### · *Omnes gentes, plaudite.*
#### Psalm xlvii.

O CLAP your hands together (all ye people :) O sing unto God with the voice of melody.

For the Lord is high, and to be feared : he is the great King upon all the earth.

He shall subdue the people under us : and the nations under our feet.

He shall choose out an heritage for us : even the worship of Jacob whom he loved.

God is gone up with a merry noise : and the Lord with the sound of the trump.

O sing praises, sing praises unto our God : O sing praises, sing praises unto our King.

For God is the King of all the earth : sing ye praises with understanding.

God reigneth over the heaven : God sitteth upon his holy seat.

The princes of the people are joined to the people of the God of Abraham : for God (which is very high exalted) doth defend the earth, as it were with a shield.

Glory be to the Father, and to the Son : and to the Holy Ghost.

As it was in the beginning, is now, and ever shall be : world without end.   Amen.

## The Collect.

GRANT, we beseech thee, Almighty God, that like as we do believe thy only-begotten Son our Lord to have ascended into the heavens; so we may also in heart and mind thither ascend, and with him continually dwell.

## The Epistle. Acts i.

IN the former treatise (dear Theophilus) we have spoken of all that Jesus began to do and teach, until the day in which he was taken up, after that he through the Holy Ghost had given commandments unto the apostles whom he had chosen: to whom also he shewed himself alive after his passion, (and that by many tokens,) appearing unto them xl. days, and speaking of the kingdom of God; and gathered them together, and commanded them that they should not depart from Jerusalem, but to wait for the promise of the Father, whereof (saith he) ye have heard of me. For John truly baptized with water, but ye shall be baptized with the Holy Ghost after these few days. When they therefore were come together, they asked him, saying, Lord, wilt thou at this time restore again the kingdom to Israel? And he said unto them, It is not for you to know the times or the seasons, which the Father hath put in his own power. But ye shall receive power after that the Holy Ghost is come upon you; and ye shall be witnesses unto me, not only in Jerusalem, but also in all Jewry, and in Samaria, and even unto the world's end. And when he had spoken these things, while they beheld, he was taken up on high, and a cloud received him up out of their sight. And while they looked stedfastly up toward heaven as he went, behold, two men stood by them in white apparel, which also said, Ye men of Galilee, why stand ye gazing up into heaven? This same Jesus, which is taken up from you into heaven, shall so come, even as ye have seen him go into heaven.

## The Gospel. Mark xvi.

JESUS appeared unto the eleven as they sat at meat, and cast in their teeth their unbelief and hardness of heart, because they believed not them which had seen that he was risen again from the dead. And he said unto them, Go ye into all the world, and preach the gospel to all creatures. He that believeth, and is baptized shall be saved; but he that believeth not shall be damned. And these tokens shall follow them that believe: in my Name they shall cast out devils; they shall speak with new tongues; they shall drive away serpents; and if they drink any deadly thing, it shall not hurt them; they shall lay their hands on the sick, and they shall recover. So then when the Lord had spoken unto them, he was received into heaven, and is on the right hand of God. And they went forth and preached every where, the Lord working with them, and confirming the word with miracles following.

### Proper Psalms and Lesson at Evensong.

Psalms, xxiv; lxviii and cxlviii. THE SECOND LESSON, Eph. iv.

## The Sunday after the Ascension.

*Dominus regnavit.*
Psalm xciii.

THE Lord is King, and hath put on glorious apparel: the Lord hath put on his apparel, and girded himself with strength.

He hath made the round world so sure: that it cannot be moved.

Ever since the world began hath thy seat been prepared: thou art from everlasting.

The floods are risen, O Lord, the floods have lift up their noise: the floods lift up their waves.

The waves of the sea are mighty, and rage horribly: but yet the Lord that dwelleth on high is mightier.

Thy testimonies, O Lord, are very sure: holiness becometh thine house for ever.

Glory be to the Father, and to the Son: and to the Holy Ghost.

As it was in the beginning, is now, and ever shall be: world without end. Amen.

### The Collect.

O GOD, the King of Glory, which hast exalted thine only Son Jesus Christ with great triumph unto thy kingdom in heaven; we beseech thee, leave us not comfortless: but send to us thine Holy Ghost to comfort us, and exalt us unto the same place whither our Saviour Christ is gone before; who liveth and reigneth, etc.

*The Epistle.* 1 Peter iv.

THE end of all things is at hand; be ye therefore sober, and watch unto prayer. But above all things have fervent love among yourselves: for love shall cover the multitude of sins. Be ye herberous one to another without grudging. As every man hath received the gift, even so minister the same one to another, as good ministers of the manifold grace of God. If any man speak, let him talk as the words of God: if any man minister, let him do it as of the ability which God ministereth unto him; that God in all things may be glorified through Jesus Christ; to whom be praise and dominion for ever and ever. Amen.

*The Gospel.* John xv. xvi.

WHEN the Comforter is come, whom I will send unto you from the Father, (even the Spirit of truth, which proceedeth of the Father,) he shall testify of me. And ye shall bear witness also, because ye have been with me from the beginning. These things have I said unto you, because ye should not be offended. They shall excommunicate you: yea, the time shall come, that whosoever killeth you will think that he doeth God service. And such things will they do unto you, because they have not known the Father, neither yet me. But these things have I told you, that, when the time is come, ye may remember then that I told you. These things said I not unto you at the beginning, because I was present with you.

## Whitsunday.

### Proper Psalms and Lesson at Matins.

Psalms xlviii; lxvii and cxlv.    THE SECOND LESSON, Acts x.34.

### At the Communion.

*Exultate justi in Domino.*
Psalm xxxiii.
REJOICE in the Lord, O ye righteous: for it becom-

eth well the just to be thankful.

Praise the Lord with harp: sing psalms unto him with the

lute, and instrument of ten strings.

Sing unto the Lord a new song: sing praises lustily (unto him) with a good courage.

For the word of the Lord is true: and all his works are faithful.

He loveth righteousness and judgment: the earth is full of the goodness of the Lord.

By the word of the Lord were the heavens made: and all the hosts of them by the breath of his mouth.

He gathereth the waters of the sea together as it were upon a heap: and layeth up the deep as it were in a treasure-house.

Let all the earth fear the Lord: stand in awe of him, all ye that dwell in the world.

For he spake, and it was done: he commanded, and it stood fast.

The Lord bringeth the counsel of the heathen to nought: and maketh the devices of the people to be of none effect, (and casteth out the counsels of princes.)

The counsel of the Lord shall endure for ever: and the thoughts of his heart from generation to generation.

Blessed are the people, whose God is the Lord Jehovah: and blessed are the folk that have chosen him to be their inheritance.

The Lord looked down from heaven, and beheld all the children of men: from the habitation of his dwelling he considereth all them that dwell in the earth.

He fashioneth all the hearts of them: and understandeth all their works.

There is no king that can be saved by the multitude of an host: neither is any mighty man delivered by much strength.

A horse is counted but a vain thing to save a man: neither shall he deliver any man by his great strength.

Behold, the eye of the Lord is upon them that fear him: and upon them that put their trust in his mercy.

To deliver their souls from death: and to feed them in the time of dearth.

Our soul hath patiently tarried for the Lord: for he is our help and our shield.

For our heart shall rejoice in him: because we have hoped in his holy Name.

Let thy merciful kindness, O Lord, be upon us: like as we have put our trust in thee.

Glory be to the Father, and to the Son: and to the Holy Ghost.

As it was in the beginning,

is now, and ever shall be: world without end.   Amen.

### The Collect.

GOD, which as upon this day hast taught the hearts of thy faithful people, by the sending to them the light of thy Holy Spirit; Grant us by the same Spirit to have a right judgment in all things, and evermore to rejoice in his holy comfort; through the merits of Christ Jesus our Saviour, who liveth and reigneth with thee, in the unity of the same Spirit, one God, world without end.

### The Epistle. Acts ii.

WHEN the fifty days were come to an end, they were all with one accord together in one place.   And suddenly there came a sound from heaven, as it had been the coming of a mighty wind, and it filled all the house where they sat.   And there appeared unto them cloven tongues, like as they had been of fire, and it sat upon each one of them; and they were all filled with the Holy Ghost, and began to speak with other tongues, even as the same Spirit gave them utterance. There were dwelling at Jerusalem Jews, devout men, out of every nation of them that are under heaven.   When this was noised about, the multitude came together, and were astonied, because that every man heard them speak with his own language.   They wondered all, and marvelled, saying among themselves, Behold, are not all these which speak of Galilee?   And how hear we every man his own tongue wherein we were born?   Parthians, and Medes, and Elamites, and the inhabiters of Mesopotamia, and of Jewry, and of Capadocia, of Pontus and Asia, Phrygia and Pamphilia, of Egypt, and of the parties of Libia which is beside Siren, and strangers of Rome, Jews and Proselites, Grekes and Arabians, we have heard them speak in our own tongues the great works of God.

### The Gospel. John xiv.

JESUS said unto his disciples, If ye love me, keep my commandments.   And I will pray the Father, and he shall give you another Comforter, that he may abide with you for ever; even the Spirit of truth, whom the world cannot receive, because the world seeth him not, neither knoweth him: but ye know him; for he dwelleth with you, and shall be in you.   I will not leave you comfortless; but will come to you. Yet a little while, and the world seeth me no more; but ye see me, for I live, and ye shall live. That day shall ye know that I am in the Father, and you in me, and I in you. He that hath my commandments, and keepeth them, the same is he that loveth me; and he that loveth me shall be loved of my Father, and I will love him, and will shew mine own self unto him.

### Proper Psalms and Lesson at Evensong.

Psalms, civ and cxlv.　　THE SECOND LESSON, Acts xix:1-21.

## Monday in Whitsun Week.

*Jubilate Deo.* Psalm c.

O BE joyful in the Lord (all ye lands:) serve the Lord with gladness, and come before his presence with a song.

Be ye sure that the Lord he is God: it is he that hath made us, and not we ourselves; we are his people, and the sheep of his pasture.

O go your way into his gates with thanksgiving, and into his courts with praise: be thankful unto him, and speak good of his Name.

For the Lord is gracious, his mercy is everlasting: and his truth endureth from generation to generation.

Glory be to the Father, and to the Son: and to the Holy Ghost.

As it was in the beginning, is now, and ever shall be: world without end. Amen.

*The Collect.*

GOD, which, etc., *as upon Whitsunday.*

*The Epistle.* Acts x.

THEN Peter opened his mouth, and said, Of a truth I perceive that there is no respect of persons with God; but in all people, he that feareth him, and worketh righteousness, is accepted with him. Ye know the preaching that God sent unto the children of Israel, preaching peace by Jesu Christ, which is Lord over all things; which preaching was published throughout all Jewry (and began in Galilee, after the baptism which John preached:) how God anointed Jesus of Nazareth with the Holy Ghost, and with power; which Jesus went about doing good, and healing all that were oppressed of the devil: for God was with him. And we are witnesses of all things which he did in the land of the Jews and at Jerusalem; whom they slew, and hanged on tree: him God raised up the third day, and shewed him openly; not to all the people, but unto us witnesses (chosen before of God for the same intent;) which did eat and drink with him after he arose from death. And he commanded us to preach unto the people, and to testify that it is he which was ordained of God to be the Judge of quick and dead. To him give all the prophets witness, that through his Name whosoever believeth in him shall receive remission of sins. While Peter yet spake these words, the Holy Ghost fell on all them which heard the preaching. And they of the circumcision, which believed, were astonied, as many as came with Peter, because that on the Gentiles also was shed out the gift of the Holy Ghost. For they heard them speak with tongues, and magnify God. Then answered Peter, Can any man forbid water, that these should not be baptized, which have received the Holy Ghost as well as we? And he commanded them to be baptized in the Name of the Lord. Then prayed they him to tarry a few days.

*The Gospel.* John iii.

So God loved the world, that he gave his only-begotten Son, that whosoever believeth in him should not perish, but have everlasting life. For God sent not his Son into the world to condemn the world, but that the world through him might be saved. He that believeth on him is not condemned: but he that believeth not is condemned already; because he hath not believed in the Name of the only-begotten Son of God. And this is the condemnation, that light is come into the world, and men loved darkness more than light, because their deeds were evil. For every one that evil doeth hateth the light, neither cometh to the light, lest his deeds should be reproved. But he that doeth truth cometh to the light, that his deeds may be known, how that they are wrought in God.

## Tuesday in Whitsun Week.

## At the Communion.

*Misericordiam.* Psalm ci.

My song shall be of mercy and judgment: unto thee (O Lord) will I sing.

O let me have understanding: in the way of godliness.

When wilt thou come unto me: I will walk in my house with a perfect heart.

I will take no wicked thing in hand; I hate the sins of unfaithfulness: there shall no such cleave unto me.

A froward heart shall depart from me: I will not know a wicked person.

Whoso privily slandereth his neighbour: him will I destroy.

Whoso hath also a proud look and an high stomach: I will not suffer him.

Mine eyes look unto such as be faithful in the land: that they may dwell with me.

Whoso leadeth a godly life: he shall be my servant.

There shall no deceitful person dwell in my house: he that telleth lies shall not tarry in my sight.

I shall soon destroy all the ungodly that are in the land: that I may root out all wicked doers from the city of the Lord.

Glory be to the Father, and to the Son: and to the Holy Ghost.

As it was in the beginning, is now, and ever shall be: world without end. Amen.

*The Collect.*

GOD, which, etc., *as upon Whitsunday.*

*The Epistle.* Acts. viii.

WHEN the apostles, which were at Jerusalem, heard say that Samaria had received the word of God, they sent unto them Peter and John; which, when they were come down, prayed for them, that they might receive the Holy Ghost: for as yet he was come on none of them; but they were baptized only in the Name of Christ Jesu. Then laid they their hands on them, and they received the Holy Ghost.

*The Gospel.* John x.

VERILY, verily I say unto you, He that entereth not in by the door into the sheepfold, but climbeth up some other way, the same is a thief and a murtherer. But he that entereth in by the door is the shepherd of the sheep: to him the porter openeth, and the sheep hear his voice, and he calleth his own sheep by name, and leadeth them out. And when he hath sent forth his own sheep, he goeth before them, and the sheep follow him; for they know his voice. A stranger will they not follow; but will fly from him; for they know not the voice of strangers. This proverb spake Jesus unto them: but they understood not what things they were which he spake unto them. Then said Jesus unto them again; Verily, verily, I say unto you, I am the door of the sheep. All (even as many as came before me) are thieves and murtherers but the sheep did not hear them. I am the door; by me, if any enter in, he shall be safe, and shall go in and out, and find pasture. A thief cometh not but for to steal, kill, and destroy: I am come that they might have life, and that they might have it more abundantly.

# Trinity Sunday.

## At Matins.

THE FIRST LESSON, Gen. xviii.     THE SECOND LESSON, Matt. iii.

## At the Communion.

*Deus misereatur.* Psal. lxvii.

GOD be merciful unto us, and bless us: and shew us the light of his countenance, and be merciful unto us:

That thy way may be known upon earth: thy saving health among all nations.

Let the people praise thee, O God: yea, let all the people praise thee.

O let the nations rejoice and be glad: for thou shalt judge the folk righteously, and govern the nations upon earth.

Let the people praise thee, O God: let all the people praise thee.

Then shall the earth bring forth her increase: and God, even our own God, shall give us his blessing.

God shall bless us: and all

the ends of the world shall fear him.

Glory be to the Father, and to the Son : and to the Holy Ghost.

As it was in the beginning, is now, and ever shall be; world without end. Amen.

### The Collect.

ALMIGHTY and everlasting God, which hast given unto us thy servants grace by the confession of a true faith to acknowledge the glory of the eternal Trinity, and in the power of the Divine Majesty to worship the Unity: We beseech thee, that through the stedfastness of this faith, we may evermore be defended from all adversity, which livest and reignest one God, world without end.

### The Epistle. Rev. iv.

AFTER this I looked, and behold a door was open in heaven : and the first voice which I heard was as it were of a trumpet talking with me ; which said, Come up hither, and I will shew thee things which must be fulfilled hereafter. And immediately I was in the Spirit; and behold, a seat was set in heaven, and one sat on the seat: and he that sat was to look upon like unto a jasper stone and a sardine stone : and there was a rainbow about the seat, in sight like unto an emerald. And about the seat were xxiv. seats; and upon the seats xxiv. elders sitting, clothed in white raiment, and had on their heads crowns of gold : and out of the seat proceeded lightnings, and thunderings, and voices. And there were vii. lamps of fire burning before the seat, which are the vii. Spirits of God. And before the seat there was a sea of glass like unto crystal : and in the midst of the seat, and round about the seat, were iv. beasts full of eyes before and behind. And the first beast was like a lion, and the second beast like a calf, and the third beast had a face as a man, and the fourth beast was like a flying eagle. And the iv. beasts had each one of them six wings about him; and they were full of eyes within : and they had no rest day neither night. saying, Holy, Holy, Holy, Lord God Almighty, which was, and is, and is to come. And when those beasts gave glory, and honour, and thanks to him that sat on the seat, (which liveth for ever and ever,) the xxiv. elders fell down before him that sat on the throne, and worshipped him that liveth for ever, and cast their crowns before the throne, saying; Thou art worthy, O Lord, (our God,) to receive glory, and honour, and power; for thou hast created all things, and for thy will's sake they are and were created.

*The Gospel.* John iii.

THERE was a man of the Pharisees, named Nicodemus, a ruler of the Jews: the same came to Jesus by night, and said unto him, Rabbi, we know that thou art a teacher come from God: for no man could do such miracles, as thou doest, except God were with him. Jesus answered and said unto him, Verily, verily, I say unto thee, Except a man be born from above, he cannot see the kingdom of God. Nicodemus said unto him, How can a man be born when he is old? can he enter into his mother's womb, and be born again? Jesus answered, Verily, verily, I say unto thee, Except a man be born of water, and of the Spirit, he cannot enter into the kingdom of God. That which is born of the flesh is flesh; and that which is born of the Spirit is spirit. Marvel not thou that I said to thee, Ye must be born from above. The wind bloweth where it lusteth, and thou hearest the sound thereof, but canst not tell whence it cometh, and whither it goeth; so is every one that is born of the Spirit. Nicodemus answered and said unto him, How can these things be? Jesus answered and said unto him, Art thou a master in Israel, and knowest not these things? Verily, verily, I say unto thee, We speak that we do know, and testify that we have seen: and ye receive not our witness. If I have told you earthly things, and ye believe not; how shall ye believe if I tell you of heavenly things? And no man ascendeth up to heaven, but he that came down from heaven, even the Son of Man, which is in heaven. And as Moses lift up the serpent in the wilderness, even so must the Son of Man be lift up; that whosoever believeth in him perish not, but have everlasting life.

## The First Sunday after Trinity Sunday,

*Beati immaculati.*
Psalm cxix : 1-8.

BLESSED are those that be undefiled in the way : and walk in the law of the Lord.

Blessed are they that keep his testimonies : and seek him with their whole heart.

For they which do no wickedness : walk in his ways.

Thou hast charged, that we shall diligently keep thy commandments.

O that my ways were made so direct, that I might keep thy statutes !

So shall I not be confounded : while I have respect unto all thy commandments.

I will thank thee with an unfeigned heart : when I shall have learned the judgments of thy righteousness.

I will keep thy ceremonies : O forsake me not utterly.

Glory be to the Father, and to the Son : and to the Holy Ghost.

As it was in the beginning, is now, and ever shall be : world without end.　Amen.

### The Collect.

GOD, the strength of all them that trust in thee, mercifully accept our prayers; and because the weakness of our mortal nature can do no good thing without thee, grant us the help of thy grace, that in keeping of thy commandments we may please thee, both in will and deed; through Jesus Christ our Lord.

### The Epistle. 1. John iv.

DEARLY beloved, let us love one another : for love cometh of God; and every one that loveth is born of God, and knoweth God. He that loveth not, knoweth not God; for God is love. In this appeared the love of God to usward, because that God sent his only-begotten Son into the world, that we might live through him. Herein is love, not that we loved God, but that he loved us, and sent his Son to be the agreement for our sins. Dearly beloved, if God so loved us, we ought also to love one another. No man hath seen God at any time. If we love one another, God dwelleth in us, and his love is perfect in us. Hereby know we that we dwell in him, and he in us, because he hath given us of his Spirit. And we have seen, and do testify, that the Father sent the Son to be the Saviour of the world. Whosoever confesseth that Jesus is the Son of God, in him dwelleth God, and he in God. And we have known and believed the love that God hath to us. God is love; and he that dwelleth in love dwelleth in God, and God in him. Herein is the love perfect in us, that we should have trust in the day of judgment; for as he is, even so are we in this world. There is no fear in love; but perfect love casteth out fear; for fear hath painfulness: he that feareth is not perfect in love. We love him, for he loved us first. If a man say, I love God, and yet hate his brother, he is a liar: for how can he that loveth not his brother, whom he hath seen, love God whom he hath not seen? And this commandment have we of him, That he which loveth God should love his brother also.

### *The Gospel.* Luke xvi.

THERE was a certain rich man, which was clothed in purple and fine white, and fared deliciously every day. And there was a certain beggar, named Lazarus, which lay at his gate full of sores, desiring to be refreshed with the crumbs which fell from the rich man's board: and no man gave unto him. The dogs came also and licked his sores. And it fortuned, that the beggar died, and was carried by the angels into Abraham's bosom. The rich man also died, and was buried: and being in hell in torments, he lift up his eyes and saw Abraham afar off, and Lazarus in his bosom. And he cried and said, Father Abraham, have mercy on me, and send Lazarus, that he may dip the tip of his finger in water, and cool my tongue; for I am tormented in this flame. But Abraham said, Son, remember that thou in thy lifetime receivedst thy pleasure, and contrariwise Lazarus received pain; but now is he comforted, and thou art punished. Beyond all this, between us and you there is a great space set: so that they which would go from hence to you cannot; neither may come from thence to us. Then he said, I pray thee therefore, father, send him to my father's house, (for I have five brethren,) for to warn them, lest they also come into this place of torment. Abraham said unto him, They have Moses and the prophets; let them hear them. And he said, Nay, father Abraham; but if one come unto them from the dead, they will repent. He said unto him, If they hear not Moses and the prophets, neither will they be lie ve, though one rose from death again.

---

## The Second Sunday after Trinity Sunday.

*In quo corriget?*

Psalm cxix : 9-16.

WHEREWITHAL shall a young man cleanse his way: even by ruling himself after thy word.

With my whole heart have I sought thee: O let me not go wrong out of thy commandments.

Thy words have I hid within my heart: that I should not sin against thee.

Blessed art thou, O Lord: O teach me thy statutes.

With my lips have I been telling: of all the judgments of thy mouth.

I have had as great delight in the way of thy testimonies: as in all manner of riches.

I will talk of thy commandments: and have respect unto thy ways.

My delight shall be in thy statutes: and I will not forget thy word.

Glory be to the Father, and to the Son: and to the Holy Ghost.

As it was in the beginning, is now, and ever shall be: world without end. Amen.

### The Collect.

LORD, make us to have a perpetual fear and love of thy holy Name: for thou never failest to help and govern them whom thou dost bring up in thy stedfast love: Grant this, etc.

### The Epistle. 1. John iii.

MARVEL not, my brethren, though the world hate you. We know that we are translated from death unto life, because we love the brethren. He that loveth not his brother abideth in death. Whosoever hateth his brother is a manslayer: and ye know that no manslayer hath eternal life abiding in him. Hereby perceive we love, because he gave his life for us: and we ought to give our lives for the brethren. But whoso hath this world's good, and seeth his brother have need, and shutteth up his compassion from him; how dwelleth the love of God in him? My babes, let us not love in word, neither in tongue; but in deed, and in verity. Hereby we know that we are of the verity, and can quiet our hearts before him. For if our heart condemn us, God is greater than out heart, and knoweth all things. Dearly beloved, if our heart condemn us not, then have we trust to Godward. And whatsoever we ask, we receive of him, because we keep his commandments, and do those things which are pleasant in his sight. And this is his commandment, That we believe on the Name of his Son Jesus Christ, and love one another, as he gave commandment. And he that keepeth his commandments dwelleth in him, and he in him: and hereby we know that he abideth in us, even by the Spirit which he hath given us.

*The Gospel.* Luke xiv.

A CERTAIN man ordained a great supper, and bade many; and sent his servant at suppertime to say to them that were bidden, Come, for all things are now ready. And they all at once began to make excuse. The first said unto him, I have bought a farm, and I must needs go and see it; I pray thee have me excused. And another said, I have bought v. yoke of oxen, and I go to prove them; I pray thee have me excused. And another said, I have married a wife, and therefore I cannot come. And the servant returned, and brought his master word again thereof. Then was the goodman of the house displeased, and said to his servant, Go out quickly into the streets and quarters of the city, and bring in hither the poor, and the feeble, and the halt, and the blind. And the servant said, Lord, it is done as thou hast commanded, and yet there is room. And the lord said to the servant, Go out unto the highways and hedges, and compel them to come in, that my house may be filled. For I say unto you, That none of those men which were bidden shall taste of my supper.

## The Third Sunday after Trinity Sunday.

*Retribue servo tuo.* Psalm cxix: 17-24.

O DO well unto thy servant: that I may live, and keep thy word.

Open thou mine eyes: that

I may see the wondrous things of thy law.

I am a stranger upon earth: O hide not thy commandments from me.

My soul breaketh out for the very fervent desire: that it hath alway unto thy judgments.

Thou hast rebuked the proud: and cursed are they that do err from thy commandments.

O turn from me shame and rebuke: for I have kept thy testimonies.

Princes also did sit and speak against me: but thy servant is occupied in thy statutes.

For thy testimonies are my delight: and my counsellors.

Glory be to the Father, and to the Son: and to the Holy Ghost.

As it was in the beginning, is now, and ever shall be: world without end. Amen.

### The Collect.

LORD, we beseech thee mercifully to hear us, and unto whom thou hast given an hearty desire to pray; Grant that by thy mighty aid we may be defended; through Jesus Christ our Lord.

*The Epistle.* 1 Peter v.

SUBMIT yourselves every man one to another; knit yourselves together in lowliness of mind : for God resisteth the proud, and giveth grace to the humble. Submit yourselves therefore under the mighty hand of God, that he may exalt you when the time is come. Cast all your care upon him, for he careth for you. Be sober, and watch; for your adversary the Devil, as a roaring lion, walketh about seeking whom he may devour : whom resist stedfast in the faith, knowing that the same afflictions are appointed unto your brethren that are in the world. But the God of all grace, which hath called us into his eternal glory by Christ Jesu, shall his own self (after that ye have suffered a little affliction) make you perfect, settle,strength, and stablish you. To him be glory and dominion for ever and ever.

### The Gospel. Luke xv.

THEN resorted unto him all the publicans and sinners for to hear him. And the Pharisees and Scribes murmured, saying, He receiveth sinners, and eateth with them. But he put forth this parable unto them, saying, What man among you having an hundred sheep, (if he lose one of them,) doth not leave ninety and nine in the wilderness, and goeth after that which is lost, until he find it? And when he hath found it, he layeth it on his shoulders with joy. And as soon as he cometh home, he calleth together his lovers and neighbours, saying unto them, Rejoice with me, for I have found my sheep which was lost. I say unto you, That likewise joy shall be in heaven over one sinner that repenteth, more than over ninety and nine just persons, which need no repentance. Either what woman having ten groats, (if she lose one,) doth not light a candle, and sweep the house, and seek diligently till she find it? And when she hath found it, she calleth her lovers and her neighbours together, saying, Rejoice with me, for I have found the groat which I had lost. Likewise, I say unto you, shall there be joy in the presence of the angels of God over one sinner that repenteth.

## The Fourth Sunday after Trinity Sunday.

## At the Communion.

*Adhæsit pavimento anima.*
Psalm cxix: 25-32.

MY soul cleaveth to the dust: O quicken thou me, according to thy word.

I have knowledged my ways, and thou heardest me: O teach me thy statutes.

Make me to understand the way of thy commandments: and so shall I talk of thy wondrous works.

My soul melteth away for very heaviness: comfort thou me according unto thy word.

Take from me the way of lying: and cause thou me to make much of thy law.

I have chosen the way of truth: and thy judgments have I laid before me.

I have sticken unto thy testimonies: O Lord, confound me not.

I will run the way of thy commandments: when thou hast set my heart at liberty.

Glory be to the Father, and to the Son: and to the Holy Ghost.

As it was in the beginning, is now, and ever shall be: world without end. Amen.

*The Collect.*

GOD, the protector of all that trust in thee, without

whom nothing is strong, nothing is holy, Increase and multiply upon us thy mercy; that, thou being our ruler and guide, we may so pass through things temporal, that we finally lose not the things eternal : Grant this, heavenly Father, for Jesu Christ's sake our Lord.

*The Epistle.* Rom. viii.

I SUPPOSE that the afflictions of this life are not worthy of the glory which shall be shewed upon us. For the fervent desire of the creature abideth, looking when the sons of God shall appear. Because the creature is subdued to vanity against the will thereof, but for his will which has subdued the same in hope : for the same creature shall be delivered from the bondage of corruption, into the glorious liberty of the sons of God. For we know that every creature groaneth with us also, and travaileth in pain, even unto this time. Not only it, but we also which have the first-fruits of the Spirit, mourn in ourselves also, and wait for the adoption, (of the children of God,) even the deliverance of our bodies.

*The Gospel.* Luke vi.

BE ye merciful, as your Father also is merciful. Judge not, and ye shall not be judged: condemn not, and ye shall not be condemned : forgive, and ye shall be forgiven : give, and it shall be given unto you; good measure, and pressed down, and shaken together, and running over, shall men give into your bosoms. For with the same measure that ye mete withal, shall other men mete to you again. And he put forth a similitude unto them, Can the blind lead the blind? do they not both fall into the ditch? the disciple is not above his master; every man shall be perfect, even as his master is. Why seest thou a mote in thy brother's eye, but considerest not the beam that is in thine own eye? Either how canst thou say to thy brother, Brother, let me pull out the mote that is in thine eye, when thou seest not the beam that is in thine own eye? Thou hypocrite, cast out the beam out of thine own eye first, and then shalt thou see perfectly to pull out the mote that is in thy brother's eye.

# The Fifth Sunday after Trinity Sunday.

*Legem pone.* Psalm cxix : 33-40.

TEACH me, O Lord, the way of thy statutes: and I shall keep it unto the end.

Give me understanding, and I shall keep thy law: yea, I shall keep it with my whole heart.

Make me to go in the path of thy commandments: for therein is my desire.

Incline my heart unto thy testimonies: and not to covetousness.

O turn away mine eyes, lest they behold vanity : and quicken thou me in thy way.

O stablish thy word in thy servant: that I may fear thee.

Take away the rebuke that I am afraid of: for thy judgments are good.

Behold, my delight is in thy commandments: O quicken me in thy righteousness.

Glory be to the Father, and to the Son : and to the Holy Ghost.

As it was in the beginning, is now, and ever shall be : world without end.    Amen.

### The Collect.

GRANT, Lord, we beseech thee, that the course of this world may be so peaceably ordered by thy governance, that thy congregation may joyfully serve thee in all godly quietness; through Jesus Christ our Lord.

### The Epistle. 1 Peter iii.

BE you all of one mind and of one heart; love as brethren, be pitiful, be courteous, (meek,) not rendering evil for evil, or rebuke for rebuke; but contrariwise bless; knowing that ye are thereunto called, even that ye should be heirs of the blessing.  For he that doth long after life, and loveth to see good days, let him refrain his tongue from evil, and his lips that they speak no guile.  Let him eschew evil, and do good; let him seek peace, and ensue it.  For the eyes of the Lord are over the righteous, and his ears are open unto their prayers: again, the face of the Lord is over them that do evil. Moreover, who is it that will harm you, if ye follow that which is good?  Yea, happy are ye if any trouble happen unto you for righteousness' sake:  be not ye afraid for any terror of them, neither be ye troubled; but sanctify the Lord God in your hearts.

*The Gospel.* Luke v.

IT came to pass that (when the people pressed upon him to hear the word of God) he stood by the lake of Genezareth, and saw two ships stand by the lake's side; but the fishermen were gone out of them, and were washing their nets. And he entered into one of the ships, (which pertained to Simon,) and prayed him that he would thrust out a little from the land: and he sat down, and taught the people out of the ship. When he had left speaking, he said unto Simon, Launch out into the deep, and let slip your nets to make a draught. And Simon answered and said unto him, Master, we have laboured all night, and have taken nothing; nevertheless, at thy commandment I will loose forth the net. And when they had this done, they inclosed a great multitude of fishes; but their net brake. And they beckoned to their fellows (which where in the other ship) that they should come and help them. And they came, and filled both the ships, that they sunk again. When Simon Peter saw this, he fell down at Jesu's knees, saying, Lord, go from me, for I am a sinful man. For he was astonied, and all that were with him, at the draught of fishes which they had taken; and so was also James and John the sons of Zebede, which were partners with Simon. And Jesus said unto Simon, Fear not, from henceforth thou shalt catch men. And they brought the ships to land, and forsook all, and followed him.

---

## The Sixth Sunday after Trinity Sunday,

*Et veniat super me.* Psalm cxix : 41-48.

LET thy loving mercy come also unto me, O Lord: even thy salvation, according unto thy word.

So shall I make answer unto my blasphemers: for my trust is in thy word.

O take not the word of truth utterly out of my mouth: for my hope is in thy judgments.

So shall I alway keep thy law: yea, for ever and ever.

And I will walk at liberty: for I seek thy commandments.

I will speak of thy testimonies also, even before kings: and will not be ashamed.

And my delight shall be in thy commandments: which I have loved.

My hands also will I lift up unto thy commandments, which I have loved: and my study shall be in thy statutes.

Glory be to the Father, and to the Son: and to the Holy Ghost.

As it was in the beginning, is now, and ever shall be: world without end. Amen.

### The Collect.

GOD, which hast prepared to them that love thee such good things as pass all man's understanding; pour into our hearts such love toward thee, that we, loving thee in all things, may obtain thy promises, which exceed all that we can desire; through Jesus Christ our Lord.

### The Epistle. Rom. vi.

KNOW ye not, that all we which are baptized in Jesu Christ are baptized to die with him? We are buried then with him by Baptism for to die; that likewise as Christ was raised from death by the glory of the Father, even so we also should walk in a new life. For if we be graffed in death like unto him, even so shall we be partakers of the resurrection: knowing this, that our old man is crucified with him also, that the body of sin might utterly be destroyed, that henceforth we should not be servants unto sin. For he that is dead is justified from sin. Wherefore if we be dead with Christ, we believe that we shall also live with him; knowing that Christ being raised from death, dieth no more; death hath no more power over him. For as touching that he died, he died concerning sin once; and as touching that he liveth, he liveth unto God. Likewise consider ye also that ye are dead as touching sin, but are alive unto God through Jesus Christ our Lord.

### The Gospel. Matt. v.

JESUS said unto his disciples, Except your righteousness exceed the righteousness of the Scribes and Pharisees, ye cannot enter into the kingdom of heaven. Ye have heard that it was said unto them of the old time, Thou shalt not kill: whosoever killeth shall be in danger of judgment. But I say unto you, that whosoever is angry with his brother (unadvisedly) shall be in danger of judgment: and whosoever say unto his brother, Racha, shall be in danger of a council: but whosoever saith, Thou fool, shall be in danger of hell-fire. Therefore if thou offerest thy gift at the altar, and there rememberest that thy brother hath ought against thee; leave there thine offering before the altar, and go thy way first, and be reconciled to thy brother, and then come and offer thy gift. Agree with thine adversary quickly whiles thou art in the way with him; lest at any time the adversary deliver thee to the judge, and the judge deliver thee to the minister, and then thou be cast into prison. Verily I say unto thee, Thou shalt not come out thence, till thou have paid the uttermost farthing.

## The Seventh Sunday after Trinity Sunday.

*Memor esto.*

Psalm cxix: 49-56.

O THINK upon thy servant, as concerning thy word: wherein thou hast caused me to put my trust.

The same is my comfort in my trouble: for thy word hath quickened me.

The proud have had me exceedingly in derision: yet have I not shrinked from thy law.

For I remembered thine everlasting judgments, O Lord: and received comfort.

I am horribly afraid: for the ungodly that forsake thy law.

Thy statutes have been my songs: in the house of my pilgrimage.

I have thought upon thy Name, O Lord, in the night-season: and have kept thy law.

This I had: because I kept thy commandments.

Glory be to the Father, and to the Son: and to the Holy Ghost.

As it was in the beginning, is now, and ever shall be: world without end. Amen.

### The Collect.

LORD of all power and might, which art the author and giver of all good things; Graff in our hearts the love of thy Name, increase in us true religion, nourish us with all goodness, and of thy great mercy keep us in the same; through Jesus Christ our Lord.

*The Epistle.* Rom. vi.

I SPEAK grossly, because of the infirmity of your flesh: as ye have given your members servants to uncleanness, and to iniquity (from one iniquity to another); even so now give over your members servants unto righteousness, that ye may be sanctified. For when ye were the servants of sin, ye were void of righteousness. What fruit had you then in those things whereof ye are now ashamed? for the end of those things is death. But now are ye delivered from sin, and made the servants of God, and have your fruit to be sanctified, and the end everlasting life. For the reward of sin is death: but eternal life is the gift of God, through Jesus Christ our Lord.

*The Gospel.* Mark viii.

IN those days, when there was a very great company, and had nothing to eat, Jesus called his disciples unto him, and said unto them, I have compassion on the people, because they have now been with me three days, and have nothing to eat: and if I send them away fasting to their own houses, they shall faint by the way; for divers of them came from far. And his disciples answered him, Where should a man have bread here in the wilderness to satisfy these? And he asked them, How many loaves have ye? They said, Seven. And he commanded the people to sit down on the ground. And he took the seven loaves; and when he had given thanks, he brake, and gave to his disciples to set before them; and they did set them before the people. And they had a few small fishes; and when he had blessed, he commanded them also to be set before them. And they did eat, and were sufficed: and they took up of the broken meat that was left seven baskets full. And they that did eat were about four thousand. And he sent them away

---

## The Eighth Sunday after Trinity Sunday.

*Portio meo, Domine.* Psalm cxix : 57-64.

THOU art my portion, O Lord: I have promised to keep thy law.

I made mine humble petition in thy presence with my whole heart: O be merciful unto me, according unto thy word.

I call mine own ways to remembrance: and turn my feet into thy testimonies.

I made haste, and prolonged not the time: to keep thy commandments.

The congregations of the ungodly have robbed me: but I have not forgotten thy law.

At midnight will I rise to give thanks unto thee: because of thy righteous judgments.

I am a companion of all them that fear thee: and keep thy commandments.

The earth, O Lord, is full of thy mercy: O teach me thy statutes.

Glory be to the Father, and to the Son: and to the Holy Ghost.

As it was in the beginning, is now, and ever shall be: world without end. Amen.

### The Collect.

GOD, whose providence is never deceived; We humbly beseech thee that thou wilt put away from us all hurtful things, and give those things which be profitable for us; through Jesus Christ our Lord.

### The Epistle. Rom. viii.

BRETHREN, we are debtors, not to the flesh, to live after the flesh. For if ye live after the flesh, ye shall die; but if ye through the Spirit do mortify the deeds of the body, ye shall live. For as many as are led by the Spirit of God, they are the sons of God. For ye have not received the spirit of bondage to fear any more, but ye have received the spirit of adoption, whereby we cry, Abba, Father. The same Spirit certifieth our spirit, that we are the sons of God. If we be sons, then are we also heirs; the heirs I mean of God, and heirs annexed with Christ: if so be that we suffer with him, that we may be also glorified with him.

### The Gospel. Matt. vii.

BEWARE of false prophets, which come to you in sheep's clothing, but inwardly they are ravening wolves. Ye shall know them by their fruits: do men gather grapes of thorns, or figs of thistles? Even so every good tree bringeth forth good fruits; but a corrupt tree bringeth forth evil fruits. A good tree cannot bring forth bad fruits; neither can a bad tree bring forth good fruits. Every tree that bringeth not forth good fruit is hewn down, and cast into the fire. Wherefore by their fruits ye shall know them. Not every one that saith unto me, Lord, Lord, shall enter into the kingdom of heaven; but he that doeth the will of my Father which is in heaven, he shall enter the kingdom of heaven.

## The Ninth Sunday after Trinity Sunday.

*Bonitatem.*
Psalm cxix: 65 72

O LORD, thou hast dealt graciously with thy servant: according unto thy word.

O learn me true understanding and knowledge: for I have believed thy commandments.

Before I was troubled I went wrong: but now I have kept thy word.

Thou art good and gracious: O teach me thy statutes.

The proud have imagined a lie against me: but I will keep thy commandments with my whole heart.

Their heart is as fat as brawn: but my delight hath been in thy law.

It is good for me that I have been in trouble: that I may learn thy statutes.

The law of thy mouth is dearer unto me: than thousands of gold and silver.

Glory be to the Father, and to the Son: and to the Holy Ghost.

As it was in the beginning, is now, and ever shall be: world without end. Amen.

### The Collect.

GRANT to us, Lord, we beseech thee, the spirit to think and do always such things as be rightful; that we, which cannot be without thee, may by thee be able to live according to thy will: through Jesus Christ our Lord.

### The Epistle. 1. Cor. x.

BRETHREN, I would not that ye should be ignorant, how that our fathers were all under the cloud, and all passed through the sea; and were all baptized under Moses in the cloud, and in the sea; and did all eat of one spiritual meat, and did all drink of one spiritual drink: and they drank of the spiritual Rock that followed them, which Rock was Christ. But in many of them had God no delight; for they were overthrown in the wilderness. These are ensamples to us, that we should not lust after evil things, as they lusted: and that ye should not be worshippers of images, as were some of them: according as it is written, The people sat down to eat and drink, and rose up to play. Neither let us be defiled with fornication, as some of them were defiled with fornication, and fell in one day three and twenty thousand. Neither let us tempt Christ, as some of them tempted, and were destroyed of serpents. Neither murmur ye, as some of them murmured, and were destroyed of the destroyer. All these things happened unto them for ensamples: but are written to put us in remembrance, whom the ends of the world are come upon. Wherefore let him that thinketh he standeth take heed lest he fall. There hath none other temptation taken you, but such as followeth the nature of man: but God is faithful, which shall not suffer you to be tempted above your strength: but shall in the midst of the temptation make a way, that ye may be able to bear it.

*The Gospel.* Luke xvi.

Jesus said unto his disciples, There was a certain rich man which had a steward; and the same was accused unto him that he had wasted his goods. And he called him, and said unto him, How is it that I hear this of thee? Give accounts of thy stewardship, for thou mayest be no longer steward. The steward said within himself, What shall I do? for my master taketh away from me the stewardship: I cannot dig, and to beg I am ashamed. I wot what to do, that when I am put out of the stewardship they may receive me into their houses. So when he had called all his master's debtors together, he said unto the first, How much owest thou unto my master? And he said, An hundred tons of oil. And he said unto him, Take thy bill, and sit down quickly, and write fifty. Then said he to another, How much owest thou? And he said, an hundred quarters of wheat. He said unto him, Take thy bill, and write fourscore. And the lord commended the unjust steward, because he had done wisely: for the children of this world are in their nation wiser than the children of light. And I say unto you, Make you friends of the unrighteous mammon, that when ye shall have need, they may receive you into everlasting habitations.

---

## The Tenth Sunday after Trinity Sunday.

*Manus tuæ.*
Psalm cxix: 73-80.

THY hands have made me and fashioned me: O give me understanding, that I may learn thy commandments.

They that fear thee will be glad when they see me: because that I have put my trust in thy word.

I know, O Lord, that thy judgments are right: and thou of very faithfulness hast caused me to be troubled.

O let thy merciful kindness be my comfort: according to thy word unto thy servant.

O let thy loving mercies come unto me, that I may live: for thy law is my delight.

Let the proud be confounded, for they go wickedly about to destroy me: but I will be occupied in thy commandments.

Let such as fear thee and have known thy testimonies: be turned unto me.

O let my heart be sound in thy statutes: that I be not ashamed.

Glory be to the Father, and to the Son: and to the Holy Ghost.

As it was in the beginning, is now, and ever shall be: world without end. Amen.

### The Collect.

LET thy merciful ears, O Lord, be open to the prayers of thy humble servants; and that they may obtain their petitions, make them to ask such things as shall please thee; through Jesus Christ our Lord.

### The Epistle. 1. Cor. xii.

CONCERNING spiritual things (brethren) I would not have you ignorant. Ye know that ye were Gentiles, and went your ways unto dumb images, even as ye were led. Wherefore I declare unto you, that no man, speaking by the Spirit of God, defieth Jesus; also no man can say that Jesus is the Lord, but by the Holy Ghost.

There are diversities of gifts, yet but one Spirit. And there are differences of administrations, and yet but one Lord. And there are divers manners of operations, and yet but one God, which worketh all in all. The gift of the Spirit is given to every man to edify withal. For to one is given through the Spirit the utterance of wisdom; to another is given the utterance of knowledge by the same Spirit; to another is given faith by the same Spirit; to another the gift of healing by the same Spirit; to another power to do miracles; to another prophecy; to another judgment to discern spirits; to another divers tongues; to another the interpretation of tongues. But these all worketh even the selfsame Spirit, dividing to every man a several gift even as he will.

*The Gospel.* Luke xix.

AND when he was come near to Hierusalem, he be- held the city, and wept on it, saying, If thou hadst known those things which belong unto thy peace, even in this thy day, thou wouldest take heed! but now are they hid from thine eyes. For the days shall come upon thee, that thy enemies also shall cast a bank about thee, and compass thee round, and keep thee in on every side, and make thee even with the ground, and thy children which are in thee; and they shall not leave in thee one stone upon another; because thou knowest not the time of thy visitation. And he went into the temple, and began to cast out them that sold therein, and them that bought, saying unto them, It is written, My house is the house of prayer; but ye have made it a den of thieves. And he taught daily in the temple.

---

## The Eleventh Sunday after Trinity Sunday,

*Defecit.*

Psalm cxix : 81-88.

My soul hath longed for thy salvation : and I have a good hope, because of thy word.

Mine eyes long sore for thy word : saying, O when wilt thou comfort me?

For I am become like a bottle in the smoke : yet do I not forget thy statutes.

How many are the days of thy servant : when wilt thou be avenged of them that persecute me?

The proud have digged pits

for me : which are not after thy law.

All thy commandments are true : they persecute me falsely ; O be thou my help.

They had almost made an end of me upon earth : but I forsook not thy commandments.

O quicken me after thy loving-kindness : and so shall I keep the testimonies of thy mouth.

Glory be to the Father, and to the Son : and to the Holy Ghost.

As it was in the beginning, is now, and ever shall be : world without end. Amen.

### The Collect.

God, which declarest thy almighty power most chiefly in shewing mercy and pity ; Give unto us abundantly thy grace, that we, running to thy promises, may be made partakers of thy heavenly treasure ; through Jesus Christ our Lord.

### The Epistle. 1. Cor. xv.

Brethren, as pertaining to the gospel which I preached unto you, which ye have also accepted, and in the which ye continue, by the which also ye are saved ; I do you to wit after what manner I preached unto you, if ye keep it, except ye have believed in vain. For first of all I delivered unto you that which I received, how that Christ died for our sins, agreeing to the scriptures ; and that he was buried ; and that he arose again the third day, according to the scriptures ; and that he was seen of Cephas, then of the xii. : after that he was seen of more than five hundred brethren at once ; of which many remain unto this day, and many are fallen asleep : after that appeared he to James ; then to all the apostles : and last of all, he was seen of me, as of one that was born out of due time. For I am the least of the apostles, which am not worthy to be called an apostle, because I have persecuted the congregation of God. But by the grace of God I am that I am : and his grace which is in me was not in vain ; but I laboured m or e abundantly than they all ; yet not I, but the grace of God which is with me. Therefore, whether it were I or t h e y, so we preached, and so ye have believed.

### The Gospel. Luke xviii.

Christ told t h i s parable unto certain which trusted in themselves t h a t they were perfect, and despised other :

Two men went up into the temple to pray; the one a Pharisee, and the o t h e r a Publican. The Pharisee stood and prayed thus with himself, God, I thank thee, that I am not as other men are, extortioners, unjust, adulterers, or as this Publican: I fast twice in the week, I give tithe of all that I possess. And the Pub-

lican, standing afar off, would not lift up his eyes to heaven, but smote upon his breast, saying, God, be merciful to me a sinner. I tell you, this man departed home to his house justified more than the other: for every man that exalteth himself shall be brought low; and he that humbleth himself shall be exalted.

## The Twelfth Sunday after Trinity Sunday.

*In æternum, Domine.*
Psalm cxix : 89-96.

O LORD, thy word: endureth for ever in heaven.

Thy truth also remaineth from one generation to another: thou hast laid the foundation of the earth, and it abideth.

They continue this day according to thine ordinance: for all things serve thee.

If my delight had not been in thy law: I should have perished in my trouble.

I will never forget thy commandments: for with them thou hast quickened me.

I am thine, O save me: for I have sought thy commandments.

The ungodly laid wait for me to destroy me: but I will consider thy testimonies.

I see that all things come to an end: but thy commandments are exceeding broad.

Glory be to the Father, and to the Son: and to the Holy Ghost.

As it was in the beginning, is now, and ever shall be: world without end. Amen.

### *The Collect.*

ALMIGHTY and everlasting God, which art always more ready to hear than we to pray, and art wont to give more than either we desire or deserve; Pour down upon us the abundance of thy mercy; forgiving us those t h i n g s whereof o u r conscience is afraid, and giving unto us that that our prayer dare not presume to ask; t h r o u g h Jesus Christ our Lord.

*The Epistle.* 2. Cor. iii.

SUCH trust have we through Christ to God-ward; not that we are sufficient of ourselves to think any thing as of ourselves; but if we be able unto any thing, the same cometh of God; which hath made us able to minister the new testament; not of the letter, but of the spirit: for the letter killeth, but the Spirit giveth life. If the ministration of death, through the letters figured in stones, was glorious, so that the children of Israel could not behold the face of Moses for the glory of his countenance; (which glory is done away;) why shall not the ministration of the Spirit be much more glorious? For if the ministration of condemnation be glorious, much more doth the ministration of righteousness exceed in glory.

*The Gospel.* Mark vii.

JESUS departed from the coasts of Tyre and Sidon, and came unto the sea of Galilee, through the midst of the coasts of the x. cities. And they brought unto him one that was deaf, and had an impediment in his speech; and they prayed him to put his hand upon him. And when he had taken him aside from the people, he put his fingers into his ears, and did spit, and touched his tongue, and looked up to heaven, and sighed, and said unto him, Ephata, that is to say, Be opened. And straightway his ears were opened, and the string of his tongue was loosed, and he spake plain. And he commanded them that they should tell no man: but the more he forbade them, so much the more a great deal they published, saying, He hath done all things well; he hath made both the deaf to hear, and the dumb to speak.

# The Thirteenth Sunday after Trinity Sunday.

*Quomodo dilexi!*

Psalm cxix: 97-104.

LORD, what love have I unto thy law: all the day long is my study in it.

Thou through thy commandments hast made me wiser than mine enemies: for they are ever with me.

I have more understanding than my teachers: for thy testimonies are my study.

I am wiser than the aged:

because I kept thy commandments.

I have refrained my feet from every evil way: that I may keep thy word.

I have not shrinked from thy judgments: for thou teachest me.

O how sweet are thy words unto my throat: yea, sweeter than honey unto my mouth.

Through thy commandments I get understanding: therefore I hate all wicked ways.

Glory be to the Father, and to the Son: and to the Holy Ghost.

As it was in the beginning, is now, and ever shall be: world without end. Amen.

### *The Collect.*

ALMIGHTY and merciful God, of whose only gift it cometh that thy faithful people do unto thee true and laudable service; Grant, we beseech thee, that we may so run to thy heavenly promises, that we fail not finally to attain the same; through Jesus Christ our Lord.

### *The Epistle.* Gal. iii.

To Abraham and his seed were the promises made. He saith not, In the seeds, as many; but, In thy seed, as of one, which is Christ. This I say, That the law which began afterward, beyond iv. C. and xxx. years, doth not disannul the testament that was confirmed afore of God unto Christ-ward, to make the promise of none effect. For if the inheritance come of the law, it cometh not now of promise; but God gave it to Abraham by promise. Wherefore then serveth the law? The law was added because of transgression, (till the seed came, to whom the promise was made,) and it was ordained by angels in the hand of a mediator. A mediator is not a mediator of one; but God is one. Is the law then against the promise of God? God forbid: for if there had been a law given which could have given life, then no doubt righteousness should have come by the law. But the scripture concludeth all things under sin, that the promise by the faith of Jesus Christ should be given unto them that believe.

### *The Gospel.* Luke x.

HAPPY are the eyes which see the things that ye see. For I tell you, That many prophets and kings have desired to see those things which ye see, and have not seen them; and to hear those things which ye hear, and have not heard them. And behold, a certain lawyer stood up, and tempted him, saying, Master, what shall I do to inherit eternal life? He said unto him, What is written in the law? how readest thou? And he answered and said, Love the Lord thy God with all thy heart, and with all thy soul, and with all thy strength, and with all thy mind; and thy neighbour as thyself. And he said unto him, Thou hast answered right; this do, and thou shalt live. But he, willing to justify himself, said unto Jesus, And who is my neighbour? Jesus answered and said, A certain man descended from Jerusalem to Hierico, and fell among thieves, which robbed him of his raiment, and wounded him, and departed, leaving him half dead. And it chanced that there came down a certain priest that same way, and when he saw him, he passed by. And likewise a Levite, when he went nigh to the place, came and looked on him, and passed by. But a certain Samaritan, as he journeyed, came unto him; and when he saw him, he had compassion on him, and went to, and bound up his wounds, and poured in oil and wine, and set him on his own beast, and brought him to a common inn, and made provision for him. And on the morrow, when he departed, he took out two pence, and gave them to the host, and said unto him, Take cure of him; and whatsoever thou spendest more, when I come again I will recompense thee. Which now of these three, thinkest thou, was neighbour unto him that fell among the thieves? And he said, He that shewed mercy upon him. Then said Jesus unto him, Go, and do thou likewise.

## The Fourteenth Sunday after Trinity Sunday.

*Lucerna pedibus meis.* Psalm cxix: 105-112.

Thy word is a lantern unto my feet: and a light unto my paths.

I have sworn, and am stedfastly purposed: to keep thy righteous judgments.

I am troubled above measure: quicken me, O Lord, according unto thy word.

Let the freewill offerings

of my mouth please thee, O Lord: and teach me thy judgments.

My soul is alway in my hand: yet do not I forget thy law.

The ungodly have laid a snare for me: but yet swerved not I from thy commandments.

Thy testimonies have I claimed as mine heritage for ever: and why? they are the very joy of my heart.

I have applied my heart to fulfill thy statutes alway: even unto the end.

Glory be to the Father, and to the Son: and to the Holy Ghost.

As it was in the beginning, is now, and ever shall be: world without end. Amen.

### The Collect.

ALMIGHTY and everlasting God, give unto us the increase of faith, hope, and charity; and, that we may obtain that which thou dost promise, make us to love that which thou dost command; through Jesus Christ our Lord.

### The Epistle. Gal. v.

I SAY, walk in the Spirit, and fulfil not the lust of the flesh. For the flesh lusteth contrary to the Spirit, and the Spirit contrary to the flesh; these are contrary one to the other; so that ye cannot do whatsoever ye would. But and if ye be led of the Spirit, then are ye not under the law. The deeds of the flesh are manifest, which are these; adultery, fornication, uncleanness, watonness, worshipping of images, witchcraft, hatred, variance, zeal, wrath, strife, seditions, sects, envying, murder, drunkenness, gluttony, and such like: of the which I tell you before, as I have told you in times past, that they which commit such things shall not be inheritors of the kingdom of God. Contrarily, the fruit of the Spirit is love, joy, peace, long-suffering, gentleness, goodness, faithfulness, meekness, temperance. Against such there is no law. They truly that are Christ's have crucified the flesh, with the affections and lusts.

### The Gospel. Luke xvii.

AND it chanced, as Jesus went to Jerusalem, that he passed through Samaria and Galilee. And as he entered into a certain town, there met him x. men that were lepers, which stood afar off, and put forth their voices, and said, Jesu, Master, have mercy upon us. When he saw them, he said unto them, Go, shew yourselves unto the priests. And it came to pass, that, as they went, they were cleansed. And one of them, when he saw that he was cleansed, turned back again, and with a loud voice praised God, and fell down on his face at his feet, and gave him thanks; and the same was a Samaritan. And Jesus answered and said, Are there not x. cleansed? but where are those ix.? There are not found that returned again to give God praise, save only this stranger. And he said unto him, Arise, go thy way, thy faith hath made thee whole.

## The Fifteenth Sunday after Trinity Sunday,

*Iniquos odio habui.* Psalm cxix : 113-120.

I HATE them that imagine evil things: but thy law do I love.

Thou art my defence and shield: and my trust is in thy word.

Away from me, ye wicked: I will keep the commandments of my God.

O stablish me according unto thy word, that I may live: and let me not be disappointed of my hope.

Hold thou me up, and I shall be safe: yea, my delight shall ever be in thy statutes.

Thou hast trodden down all them that depart from thy statutes: for they imagine but deceit.

Thou puttest away all the ungodly of the earth like dross: therefore I love thy testimonies.

My flesh trembleth for fear of thee: and I am afraid of thy judgments.

Glory be to the Father, and to the Son: and to the Holy Ghost.

As it was in the beginning, is now, and ever shall be: world without end. Amen.

### The Collect.

KEEP, we beseech thee, O Lord, thy Church with thy perpetual mercy: and, because the frailty of man without thee cannot but fall, keep us ever by thy help, and lead us to all things profitable to our salvation; through Jesus Christ our Lord.

### The Epistle. Gal. vi.

YE see how large a letter I have written unto you with mine own hand. As many as desire with outward appearance to please carnally, the same constrain you to be circumcised; only lest they should suffer persecution for the cross of Christ. For they themselves which are circumcised keep not the law; but desire to have you circumcised, that they might rejoice in your flesh. God forbid that I should rejoice, but in the cross of our Lord Jesu Christ, whereby the world is crucified unto me, and I unto the world. For in Christ Jesu neither circumcision availeth anything at all, nor uncircumcision, but a new creature. And as many as walk according unto this rule, peace be on them, and mercy, and upon Israel that pertaineth to God. From henceforth let no man put me to business; for I bear in my body the marks of the Lord Jesu. Brethren, the grace of our Lord Jesu Christ be with your spirit. Amen.

*The Gospel.* Matt. vi.

No man can serve two masters: for either he shall hate the one, and love the other; or else lean to the one, and despise the other. Ye cannot serve God and Mammon. Therefore I say unto you, Be not careful for your life, what ye shall eat or drink, nor yet for your body, what raiment ye shall put on: is not the life more worth than meat, and the body more of value than raiment? Behold the fowls of the air; for they sow not, neither do they reap, nor carry into the barns; and your heavenly Father feedeth them. Are ye not much better than they? Which of you, (by taking careful thought) can add one cubit unto his stature: And why care ye for raiment? Consider the lilies of the field how they grow: they labour not, neither do they spin: and yet I say unto you, That even Salomon in all his royalty was not clothed like one of these. Wherefore, if God so clothe the grass of the field (which though it stand to-day, is to-morrow cast into the furnace), shall he not much more do the same for you, O ye of little faith? Therefore take no thought, saying, What shall we eat? or what shall we drink? or wherewith shall we be clothed? After all these things do the Gentiles seek. For your heavenly Father knoweth that ye have need of all these things. But rather seek ye first the kingdom of God, and the righteousness thereof, and all things shall be ministered unto you. Care not then for the morrow; for the morrow day shall care for itself: | sufficient unto the day is the travail thereof.

---

## The Sixteenth Sunday after Trinity Sunday.

*Feci judicium.* Psalm cxix: 121-128.

I deal with the thing that is lawful and right: O give me not over unto mine oppressors.

Make thou thy servant to delight in that which is good: that the proud do me no wrong.

Mine eyes are wasted away with looking for thy health: and for the word of thy righteousness.

O deal with thy servant according unto thy loving mercy: and teach me thy statutes.

I am thy servant: O grant me understanding that I may know thy testimonies.

It is time for thee, Lord, to lay to thine hand: for they have destroyed thy law.

For I love thy commandments: above gold and precious stone.

Therefore hold I straight all thy commandments: and all false ways I utterly abhor.

Glory be to the Father, and to the Son: and to the Holy Ghost.

As it was in the beginning, is now, and ever shall be: world without end. Amen.

### The Collect.

LORD, we beseech thee, let thy continual pity cleanse and defend thy congregation; and, because it cannot continue in safety without thy succour, preserve it evermore by thy help and goodness; through Jesus Christ our Lord.

### The Epistle. Eph. iii.

I DESIRE that you faint not because of my tribulations that I suffer for your sakes, which is your praise. For this cause I bow my knees unto the Father of our Lord Jesus Christ, which is Father over all that is called father in heaven and in earth, that he would grant you, according to the riches of his glory, that ye may be strengthed with might by his Spirit in the inner man: that Christ may dwell in your hearts by faith; that ye, being rooted and grounded in love, might be able to comprehend with all saints, what is the breadth and length, depth and height, and to know the excellent love of the knowledge of Christ, that ye might be fulfilled with all fulness which cometh of God. Unto him that is able to do exceeding abundantly above all that we ask or think, according to the power that worketh in us, be praise in the congregation by Christ Jesus, throughout all generations, from time to time. Amen.

*The Gospel.* Luke vii.

AND it fortuned, that Jesus went into a city called Naim ; and many of his disciples went with him, and much people. When he came nigh to the gate of the city, behold, there was a dead man carried out, which was the only son of his mother, and she was a widow; and much people of the city was with her. And when the Lord saw her, he had compassion on her, and said unto her, Weep not. And he came nigh, and touched the coffin, and they that bare him stood still ; and he said, Young man, I say unto thee, arise. And he that was dead sat up, and began to speak : and he delivered him to his mother. And there came a fear on them all, and they gave the glory unto God, saying, A great prophet is risen up among us, and God hath visited his people. And this rumour of him went forth throughout all Jewry, and throughout all the regions which lie round about.

## The Seventeenth Sunday after Trinity Sunday.

*Mirabilia.*
Psalm cxix : 129-136.

THY testimonies are wonderful : therefore doth my soul keep them.

When thy word goeth forth : it giveth light and understanding even unto the simple.

I opened my mouth and drew in my breath : for my delight was in thy commandments.

O look thou upon me, and be merciful unto me : as thou usest to do unto those that love thy Name.

Order my steps in thy word : and so shall no wickedness have dominion over me.

O deliver me from the

wrongful dealings of men: and so shall I keep thy commandments.

Shew the light of thy countenance upon thy servant: and teach me thy statutes.

Mine eyes gush out with water: because men keep not thy law.

Glory be to the Father, and to the Son : and to the Holy Ghost.

As it was in the beginning, is now, and ever shall be: world without end. Amen.

### The Collect.

LORD, we pray thee that thy grace may always prevent and follow us, and make us continually to be given to all good works; through Jesus Christ our Lord.

### The Epistle. Eph. iv.

I (which am a prisoner of the Lord's) exhort you that ye walk worthy of the vocation wherewith ye are called, with all lowliness and meekness, with humbleness of mind, forbearing one another through love; and be diligent to keep the unity of the spirit through the bond of peace : being one body and one spirit, even as ye are called in one hope of your calling: let there be but one Lord, one faith, one baptism, one God and Father of all, which is above all, and through all, and in you all.

### The Gospel. Luke xiv.

IT chanced that Jesus went into the house of one of the chief Pharisees to eat bread on the sabbath day, and they watched him. And behold, there was a certain man before him which had the dropsy. And Jesus answered and spake unto the lawyers and Pharisees, saying, Is it lawful to heal on the sabbath day? And they held their peace. And he took him, and healed him, and let him go; and answered them, saying, Which of you shall have an ass or an ox fallen into a pit, and will not straightway pull him out on the sabbath day? And they could not answer him again to these things. He put forth also a similitude to the guests, when he marked how they pressed to be in the highest rooms, and said unto them, When thou art bidden of any man to a wedding, sit not down in the highest room; lest a more honourable man than thou be bidden of him; and he (that bade him and thee) come and say to thee, Give this man room; and thou then begin with shame to take the lowest room. But rather, when thou art bidden, go and sit in the lowest room, that when he that bade thee cometh, he may say unto thee, Friend, sit up higher: then shalt thou have worship in the presence of them that sit at meat with thee. For whosoever exalteth himself shall be brought low, and he that humbleth himself shall be exalted.

## The Eighteenth Sunday after Trinity Sunday.

*Justus es, Domine.*

Psalm cxix: 137-144.

RIGHTEOUS art thou, O Lord: and true is thy judgment.

The testimonies that thou hast commanded: are exceeding righteous and true.

My zeal hath even consumed me: because mine enemies have forgotten thy words.

Thy word is tried to the uttermost: and thy servant loveth it.

I am small, and of no reputation: yet do not I forget thy commandments.

Thy righteousness is an everlasting righteousness: and thy law is the truth.

Trouble and heaviness have taken hold upon me: yet is my delight in thy commandments.

The righteousness of thy testimonies is everlasting: O grant me understanding, and I shall live.

Glory be to the Father, and to the Son: and to the Holy Ghost.

As it was in the beginning, is now, and ever shall be: world without end. Amen.

### The Collect.

LORD, we beseech thee, grant thy people grace to avoid the infections of the devil, and with pure heart and mind to follow thee the only God; through Jesus Christ our Lord.

### The Epistle. 1 Cor. i.

I THANK my God, always on your behalf, for the grace of God which is given you by Jesus Christ; that in all things ye are made rich by him, in all utterance, and in all knowledge; by the which things the testimony of Jesus Christ was confirmed in you; so that ye are behind in no gift; waiting for the appearing of our Lord Jesus Christ, which shall also strength you unto the end, that ye may be blameless in the day of the coming of our Lord Jesus Christ.

*The Gospel.* Matt. xxii.

WHEN the Pharisees had heard that Jesus did put the Sadducees to silence, they came together: and one of them (which was a doctor of law) asked him a question, tempting him, and saying, Master, which is the greatest commandment in the law? Jesus said unto him, Thou shalt love the Lord thy God with all thy heart, and with all thy soul, and with all thy mind. This is the first and greatest commandment. And the second is like unto it, Thou shalt love thy neighbour as thyself. In these two commandments hang all the law and the prophets. While the Pharisees were gathered together, Jesus asked them, saying, What think ye of Christ? whose son is he? They said unto him, The son of David. He said unto them, How then doth David in spirit call him Lord, saying, The Lord said unto my Lord, Sit thou on my right hand, till I make thine enemies thy footstool? If David then call him Lord, how is he then his son? And no man was able to answer him any thing, neither durst any man (from that day forth) ask him any more questions.

# The Nineteenth Sunday after Trinity Sunday.

*Clamavi.*
Psalm cxix: 145-152.

I CALL with my whole heart: hear me, O Lord, I will keep thy statutes.

Yea, even upon thee do I call: help me, and I shall keep thy testimonies.

Early in the morning do I cry unto thee: for in thy word is my trust.

Mine eyes prevent the night-watches: that I might be occupied in thy words.

Hear my voice, (O Lord,) according unto thy loving-kindness: quicken me, according as thou art wont.

They draw nigh that of malice persecute me: and are far from thy law.

Be thou nigh at hand, O Lord: for all thy commandments are true.

As concerning thy testimonies, I have known long since: that thou hast grounded them for ever.

Glory be to the Father, and to the Son: and to the Holy Ghost.

As it was in the beginning, is now, and ever shall be: world without end. Amen.

### The Collect.

O GOD, forasmuch as without thee we are not able to please thee; Grant that the working of thy mercy may in all things direct and rule our hearts; through Jesus Christ our Lord.

### The Epistle. Eph. iv.

THIS I say, and testify through the Lord, that ye henceforth walk not as other Gentiles walk, in vanity of their mind, while they are blinded in their understanding, being far from a godly life, by the means of the ignorance that is in them, and because of the blindness of their hearts; which, being past repentance, have given themselves over unto wantonness, to work all manner of uncleanness even with greediness. But ye have not so learned Christ; if so be that ye have heard of him, and have been taught in him, as the truth is in Jesu: (as concerning the conversation in time past:) to lay from you that old man, which is corrupt according to the deceivable lusts: to be renewed also in the spirit of your mind; and to put on that new man, which after God is shapen in righteousness and true holiness. Wherefore put away lying, and speak every man truth unto his neighbour: forasmuch as we are members one of another. Be angry and sin not: let not the sun go down upon your wrath: neither give place to the backbiter. Let him that stole steal no more; but let him rather labour with his hands the thing which is good, that he may give unto him that needeth. Let no filthy communication proceed out of your mouth, but that which is good to edify withal, as oft as need is, that it may minister grace unto the hearers. And grieve not ye the Holy Spirit of God, by whom ye are sealed unto the day of redemption. Let all bitterness, and fierceness, and wrath, and roaring, and cursed speaking, be put away from you, with all maliciousness. Be ye courteous one to another, merciful, forgiving one another, even as God for Christ's sake hath forgiven you.

*The Gospel.* Matt. ix.

JESUS entered into a ship, and passed over, and came into his own city. And behold, they brought to him a man sick of the palsy, lying in a bed. And when Jesus saw the faith of them, he said unto the sick of the palsy, Son, be of good cheer, thy sins be forgiven thee. And behold, certain of the Scribes said within themselves, This man blasphemeth. And when Jesus saw their thoughts, he said, Wherefore think ye evil in your hearts? Whether is it easier to say, Thy sins be forgiven thee? or to say, Arise, and walk? But that ye may know that the Son of Man hath power to forgive sins in earth, then saith he unto the sick of the palsy, Arise, take up thy bed, and go unto thine house. And he arose, and departed to his house. But the people that saw it marvelled, and glorified God, which had given such power unto men.

## The Twentieth Sunday after Trinity Sunday.

*Vide humilitatem meam.*
Psalm cxix: 153-160.

O CONSIDER mine adversity, and deliver me: for I do not forget thy law.

Avenge thou my cause, and deliver me: quicken me, according unto thy word.

Health is far from the ungodly: for they regard not thy statutes.

Great is thy mercy, O Lord: quicken me, as thou art wont.

Many there are that trouble me, and persecute me: yet do not I swerve from thy testimonies.

It grieveth me when I see the transgressors: because they keep not thy law.

Consider, O Lord, how I love thy commandments: O quicken me, according to thy loving-kindness.

Thy word is true from everlasting: all the judgments of thy righteousness endure for evermore.

Glory be to the Father, and to the Son: and to the Holy Ghost.

As it was in the beginning, is now, and ever shall be: world without end. Amen.

*The Collect.*

ALMIGHTY and merciful God, of thy bountiful goodness keep us from all things that may hurt us; that we, being ready both in body and soul, may with free hearts accomplish those things that thou wouldest have done; through Jesus Christ our Lord.

### *The Epistle.* Eph. v.

Take heed, therefore, how ye walk circumspectly, not as unwise, but as wise men, winning occasion, because the days are evil. Wherefore be ye not unwise, but understand what the will of the Lord is. And be not drunken with wine, wherein is excess; but be filled with the Spirit: speaking unto yourselves in psalms, and hymns, and spiritual songs; singing and making melody to the Lord in your hearts; giving thanks always for all things unto God the Father, in the Name of our Lord Jesus Christ; submitting yourselves one to another in the fear of God.

### *The Gospel.* Matt. xxii.

JESUS said to his disciples, The kingdom of heaven is like unto a man that was a king, which made a marriage for his son; and sent forth his servants to call them that were bid to the wedding; and they would not come. Again, he sent forth other servants, saying, Tell them which are bidden, Behold, I have prepared my dinner; mine oxen and my fatlings are killed, and all things are ready; come unto the marriage. But they made light of it, and went their ways, one to his farm place, another to his merchandise: and the remnant took his servants, and entreated them shamefully, and slew them. But when the king heard thereof, he was wroth; and sent forth his men of war, and destroyed those murtherers, and brent up their city. Then said he to his servants, The marriage in deed is prepared, but they which were bidden were not worthy. Go ye therefore out into the highways, and as many as ye find bid them to the marriage. And the servants went forth into the highways, and gathered together all, as many as they could find, both good and bad, and the wedding was furnished with guests. Then the king came in to see the guests; and when he spied there a man which had not on a wedding garment, he said unto him, Friend how camest thou in hither, not having a wedding garment? And he was even speechless. Then said the king to the ministers, Take and bind him hand and foot, and cast him into utter darkness: there shall be weeping and gnashing of teeth. For many be called, but few are chosen.

---

# The Twenty-first Sunday after Trinity Sunday,

*Principes persecuti.*

Psalm cxix: 161-168.

PRINCES have persecuted me without cause: but my heart standeth in awe of thy words.

I am as glad of thy word: as one that findeth great spoils.

As for lies, I hate and abhor them: but thy law do I love.

Seven times a day do I praise thee: because of thy righteous judgments.

Great is the peace that they have which love thy law: and they are not offended at it.

Lord, I have looked for thy saving health: and done after thy commandments.

My soul hath kept thy testimonies: and loved them exceedingly.

I have kept thy commandments and testimonies: for all my ways are before thee.

Glory be to the Father, and to the Son: and to the Holy Ghost.

As it was in the beginning, is now, and ever shall be: world without end. Amen.

*The Collect.*

GRANT, we beseech thee, merciful Lord, to thy faithful people pardon, and peace, that they may be cleansed from all their sins, and serve thee with a quiet mind; through Jesus Christ our Lord.

*The Epistle.* Eph. vi.

My brethren, be strong through the Lord, and through the power of his might. Put on all the armour of God, that ye may stand against the assaults of the devil. For we wrestle not against blood and flesh, but against rule, against power, against worldly rulers, even governors of the darkness of this world, against spiritual craftiness in heavenly things. Wherefore take unto you the whole armour of God, that ye may be able to resist in the evil day, and stand perfect in all things. Stand, therefore, and your loins gird with the truth; having on the breastplate of righteousness, and having shoes on your feet, that ye may be prepared for the gospel of peace; above all, take to you the shield of faith, wherewith ye may quench all the fiery darts of the wicked; and take the helmet of salvation, and the sword of the spirit, which is the word of God: and pray always with all manner of prayer and supplication in the Spirit; and watch thereunto with all instance and supplication for all saints; and for me, that utterance may be given unto me, that I may open my mouth freely, to utter the secrets of my gospel (whereof I am a messenger in bonds), that therein I may speak freely, as I ought to speak.

*The Gospel.* John iv.

THERE was a certain ruler, whose son was sick at Capernaum. As soon as the same heard that Jesus was come out of Jewry into Galilee, he went unto him, and besought him that he would come down and heal his son, for he was even at the point of death. Then said Jesus unto him, Except ye see signs and wonders, ye will not believe. The ruler saith unto him, Sir, come down or ever that my son die. Jesus saith unto him, Go thy way, thy son liveth. The man believed the word that Jesus had spoken unto him, and he went his way. And, as he was going down, the servants met him, and told him, saying, Thy son liveth. Then inquired he of them the hour when he began to amend: and they said unto him, Yesterday at the seventh hour the fever left him. So the father knew that it was the same hour in the which Jesus said unto him, Thy son liveth; and he believed and all his household. This is again the second miracle that Jesus did, when he was come out of Jewry into Galilee.

# The Twenty-second Sunday after Trinity Sunday.

*Appropinquet deprecatio.*
Psalm cxix: 169-176.

LET my complaint come before thee, O Lord: give me understanding, according unto thy word.

O let my supplication come before thee: deliver me, according to thy word.

My lips shall speak of thy praise: when thou hast taught me thy statutes.

Yea, my tongue shall sing of thy word: for all thy commandments are righteous.

Let thine hand help me: for I have chosen thy commandments.

I have longed for thy saving health, O Lord: and in thy law is my delight.

O let my soul live, and it shall praise thee: and thy judgments shall help me.

I have gone astray like a sheep that is lost: O seek thy servant, for I do not forget thy commandments.

Glory be to the Father, and to the Son: and to the Holy Ghost.

As it was in the beginning, is now, and ever shall be: world without end. Amen.

### The Collect.

LORD, we beseech thee to keep thy household the Church in continual godliness; that through thy protection it may be free from all adversities, and devoutly given to serve thee in good works, to the glory of thy Name; through Jesus Christ our Lord.

### The Epistle. Phil. i.

I THANK my God with all remembrance of you always in all my prayers for you, and pray with gladness; because ye are come into the fellowship of the gospel, from the first day unto now; and am surely certified of this, that he which hath begun a good work in you shall perform it until the day of Jesus Christ; as it becometh me, so judge I of you all, because I have you in my heart, forasmuch as ye are all companions of grace with me, even in my bonds, and in the defending and stablishing of the gospel. For God is my record, how greatly I long after you all from the very heart root in Jesus Christ. And this I pray, that your love may increase yet more and more in knowledge, and in all understanding: that ye may accept the things that are most excellent, that ye may be pure, and such as offend no man, until the day of Christ: being filled with the fruit of righteousness, which cometh by Jesus Christ, unto the glory and praise of God.

### The Gospel. Matt. xviii.

PETER said unto Jesus, Lord, how oft shall I forgive my brother, if he sin against me? till seven times? Jesus saith unto him, I say not unto thee, Until seven times; but, Seventy times seven times. Therefore is the kingdom of heaven likened unto a certain man that was a king, which would take accounts of his servants. And when he had begun to reckon, one was brought unto him which ought him ten M. talents. But forasmuch as he was not able to pay, his lord commanded him to be sold, and his wife and children, and all that he had, and payment to be made. The servant fell down, and besought him, saying, Sir, have patience with me, and I will pay thee all. Then had the lord pity on that servant, and loosed him, and forgave him the debt. So the same servant went out, and found one of his fellows, which ought him an C. pence; and he laid hands on him, and took him by the throat, saying, Pay that thou owest. And his fellow fell down, and be-sought him, saying, Have patience with me, and I will pay thee all. And he would not; but went and cast him into prison till he should pay the debt. So when his fellows saw what was done, they were very sorry, and came and told unto their lord all that had happened. Then his lord called him, and said unto him, O thou ungracious servant, I forgave thee all that debt, when thou desiredst me: shouldest not thou also have had compassion on thy fellow, even as I had pity on thee? And his lord was wroth, and delivered him to the jailors, till he should pay all that was due unto him. So likewise shall my heavenly Father do also to you, if ye from your hearts forgive not (every one his brother) their trespasses.

# The Twenty-third Sunday after Trinity Sunday.

*Nisi quia Dominus.*
Psal. cxxiv.

IF the Lord himself had not been on our side (now may Israel say): if the Lord himself had not been on our side, when men rose up against us;
They had swallowed us up quick: when they were so wrathfully displeased at us.
Yea, the waters had drowned us: and the stream had gone even over our soul.
The deep waters of the proud: had gone even over our soul.
But praised be the Lord:

which hath not given us over for a prey unto their teeth.

Our soul is escaped even as a bird out of the snare of the fowler: the snare is broken, and we are delivered.

Our help standeth in the Name of the Lord: which hath made heaven and earth.

Glory be to the Father, and to the Son: and to the Holy Ghost.

As it was in the beginning, is now, and ever shall be: world without end. Amen.

### The Collect.

GOD, our refuge and strength. which art the author of all godliness, be ready to hear the devout prayers of thy Church; and grant that those things which we ask faithfully we may obtain effectually; through Jesu Christ our Lord.

### The Epistle. Phil. iii.

BRETHREN, be followers together of me, and look on them which walk even so as ye have us for an example. For many walk; (of whom I have told you often, and now tell you weeping), that they are the enemies of the cross of Christ; whose end is damnation, whose belly is their god, and glory to their shame, which are worldly minded.

But our conversation is in heaven; from whence we look for the Saviour, even the Lord Jesus Christ; which shall change our vile body, that he may make it like unto his glorious body, according to the working whereby he is able also to subdue all things unto himself.

### The Gospel. Matt. xxii.

THEN the Pharisees went out and took counsel how they might tangle him in his words. And they sent out unto him their disciples, with Herode's servants, saying, Master, we know that thou art true, and teachest the way of God truly, neither carest thou for any man: for thou regardest not the outward appearance of men. Tell us therefore, how thinkest thou? Is it lawful that tribute be given unto Cesar, or not? But Jesus, perceiving their wickedness, said, Why tempt ye me, ye hypocrites? shew me the tribute-money. And they took him a penny. And he said unto them, Whose is this image and superscription? They said unto him, Cesar's. Then said he unto them, Give therefore unto Cesar the things which are Cesar's; and unto God those things that are God's. When they heard these words, they marvelled, and left him, and went their way.

---

# The Twenty-fourth Sunday after Trinity Sunday.

*Qui confidunt.* Psalm cxxv.

THEY that put their trust in the Lord shall be even as the mount Sion : which may not be removed, but standeth fast for ever.

The hills stand about Jerusalem : even so standeth the Lord round about his people, from this time forth for evermore.

For the rod of the ungodly cometh not into the lot of the righteous : lest the righteous put their hand unto wickedness.

Do well (O Lord) : unto those that be good and true of heart.

As for such as turn back into their own wickedness : the Lord shall lead them forth with the evildoers; but peace shall be upon Israel.

Glory be to the Father, and to the Son : and to the Holy Ghost.

As it was in the beginning, is now, and ever shall be : world without end. Amen.

### The Collect.

LORD, we beseech thee, assoil thy people from their offences; that through thy bountiful goodness we may be delivered from the bands of all those sins, which by our frailty we have committed : Grant this, etc.

### The Epistle. Col. i.

WE give thanks to God, the Father of our Lord Jesus Christ, always for you in our prayers; for we have heard of your faith in Christ Jesu, and of the love which ye bear to all saints; for the hope's sake which is laid up in store for you in heaven; of which hope ye heard before by the true word of the gospel; which is come unto you even as it is, fruitful, and groweth as it is also among you, from the day in the which ye heard of it, and had experience in the grace of God through the truth. As ye learned of Epaphra, our dear fellow-servant, which is for you a faithful minister of Christ; which also declared unto us your love which ye have in the Spirit. For this cause we also, ever since the day we heard of it, have not ceased to pray for you, and to desire that ye might be fulfilled with the knowledge of his will in all wisdom and spiritual understanding : that ye might walk worthy of the Lord, that in all things ye may please, being fruitful in all good works, and increasing in the knowledge of God; strengthed with all might, through his glorious power, unto all patience and longsuffering with joyfulness; giving thanks unto the Father, which hath made us meet to be partakers of the inheritance of saints in light.

*The Gospel.* Matt. ix.

WHILE Jesus spake unto the people, behold, there came a certain ruler, and worshipped him, saying, My daughter is even now deceased; but come, and lay thy hand upon her, and she shall live. And Jesus arose and followed him, and so did his disciples. And behold, a woman which was diseased with an issue of blood twelve years, came behind him, and touched the hem of his vesture ; for she said within herself, If I may touch but even his vesture only, I shall be safe. But Jesus turned him about, and when he saw her, he said, Daughter, be of good comfort, thy faith hath made thee safe. And the woman was made whole even that same time. And when Jesus came into the ruler's house, and saw the minstrels and the people making a noise, he said unto them, Get you hence ; for the maid is not dead, but sleepeth. And they laughed him to scorn. But when the people were put forth, he went in, and took her by the hand, and said, Damosel, arise. And the damosel arose. And this noise went abroad into all that land.

# The Twenty-fifth Sunday after Trinity Sunday.

*Nisi Dominus.* Psalm cxxvii.

EXCEPT the Lord build the house : their labour is but lost that build it.

Except the Lord keep the city : the watchman waketh but in vain.

It is but lost labour that ye haste to rise up early, and so late take rest, and eat the bread of carefulness : for so he giveth his beloved sleep.

Lo, children and the fruit of the womb are an heritage

and gift: that cometh of the Lord.

Like as the arrows in the hand of the giant: even so are the young children.

Happy is the man that hath his quiver full of them: they shall not be ashamed when they speak with their enemies in the gate.

Glory be to the Father, and to the Son: and to the Holy Ghost.

As it was in the beginning, is now, and ever shall be: world without end. Amen.

### The Collect.

STIR up, we beseech thee, O Lord, the wills of thy faithful people; that they plenteously bringing forth the fruit of good works, may of thee be plenteously rewarded; through Jesus Christ our Lord.

### The Epistle. Jer. xxiii.

BEHOLD, the time cometh, saith the Lord, that I will raise up the righteous Branch of David, which King shall bear rule, and he shall prosper with wisdom, and shall set up equity and righteousness again in the earth. In his time shall Juda be saved, and Israel shall dwell without fear: and this is the Name that they shall call him, even

THE LORD OUR RIGHTEOUSNESS. And therefore behold, the time cometh, saith the Lord, that it shall no more be said, The Lord liveth, which brought the children of Israel out of the land of Egypt; but, The Lord liveth, which brought forth and led the seed of the house of Israel out of the north land, and from all countries where I had scattered them; and they shall dwell in their own land again.

### The Gospel. John vi.

WHEN Jesus lift up his eyes, and saw a great company come unto him, he saith unto Philip, Whence shall we buy bread that these may eat? This he said to prove him; for he himself knew what he would do. Philip answered him, Two hundred pennyworth of bread are not sufficient for them, that every man may take a little. One of his disciples (Andrew, Simon Peter's brother) said unto him, There is a lad here, which hath five barley loaves, and two fishes; but what are they among so many? And Jesus said, Make the people sit down. There was much grass in the place. So the men sat down, in number about five thousand. And

Jesus took the bread, and when he had given thanks, he gave to the disciples, and the disciples to them that were set down, and likewise of the fishes, as much as they would. When they had eaten enough, he saith unto his disciples, Gather up the broken meat which remaineth, that nothing be lost. And they gathered it together, and filled twelve baskets with the broken meat of the five barley loaves, which broken meat remained unto them that had eaten. Then those men (when they had seen the miracle that Jesus did) said, This is of a truth the same prophet that should come into the world.

## Saint Andrew's Day.

### At the Communion.

*Sæpe expugnaverunt.*

#### Psalm cxxix.

MANY times have they fought against me from my youth up: may Israel now say.

Yea, many a time have they vexed me from my youth up: but they have not prevailed against me.

The plowers plowed upon my back: and made long furrows.

But the righteous Lord: hath hewn the snares of the ungodly in pieces.

Let them be confounded and turned backward: as many as have evil will at Sion.

Let them be even as the grass growing upon the house-tops: which withereth afore it be plucked up;

Whereof the mower filleth not his hand: neither he that bindeth up the sheaves his bosom.

So that they which go by say not so much as, The Lord prosper you: we wish you good luck in the Name of the Lord.

Glory be to the Father, and to the Son: and to the Holy Ghost.

As it was in the beginning, is now, and ever shall be: world without end. Amen.

### The Collect.

ALMIGHTY God, which hast given such grace to thy

Apostle Saint Andrew, that he counted the sharp and painful death of the cross to be an high honour, and a great glory; Grant us to take and esteem all troubles and adversities which shall come unto us for thy sake, as things profitable for us toward the obtaining of everlasting life; through Jesus Christ our Lord.

### *The Epistle.* Rom. x.

If thou knowledge with thy mouth that Jesus is the Lord, and believe in thy heart that God raised him up from death, thou shalt be safe. For to believe with the heart justifieth; and to knowledge with the mouth maketh a man safe. For the scripture saith, Whosoever believeth on him shall not be confounded. There is no difference between the Jew and the Gentile: for one is Lord of all, which is rich unto all that call upon him. For whosoever doth call on the Name of the Lord shall be safe. How then shall they call on him, on whom they have not believed? How shall they believe on him, of whom they have not heard? How shall they hear without a preacher? and how shall they preach, except they be sent? As it is written, how beauti-

ful are the feet of them which bring tidings of peace, and bring tidings of good things! But they have not all obeyed to the gospel: for Esay saith, Lord, who hath believed our sayings? So then faith cometh by hearing, and hearing cometh by the word of God. But I ask, Have they not heard? No doubt their sound went out into all lands, and their words into the ends of the world. But I demand, whether Israel did know or not? First Moses saith, I will provoke you to envy by them that are no people, by a foolish nation I will anger you. Esay after that is bold, and saith, I am found of them that sought me not: I am manifest unto them that asked not after me. But against Israel he saith, All day long have I stretched forth my hands unto a people that believeth not, but speaketh against me.

### *The Gospel.* Matt. iv.

As Jesus walked by the sea of Galilee, he saw two brethren, Simon, which was called Peter, and Andrew his brother, casting a net into the sea, (for they were fishers;) and he said unto them, Follow me, and I will make you to become fishers of men. And they straightway left their nets, and followed him. And when he was gone forth from thence, he saw other two brethren, James the son of Zebede, and John his brother, in the ship with Zebede their father, mending their nets; and he called them. And they immediately left the ship and their father, and followed him.

## Saint Thomas the Apostle.

### At the Communion.

*Beati omnes.* Psalm cxxviii.

BLESSED are all they that fear the Lord : and walk in his ways.

For thou shalt eat the labours of thine hands : O well is thee, and happy shalt thou be.

Thy wife shall be as the fruitful vine: upon the walls of thine house.

Thy children like the olive branches: round about thy table.

Lo, thus shall the man be blessed: that feareth the Lord.

The Lord from out of Syon shall so bless thee: that thou shalt see Jerusalem in prosperity all thy life long.

Yea, that thou shalt see thy childer's children: and peace upon Israel.

Glory be to the Father, and to the Son: and to the Holy Ghost.

As it was in the beginning, is now, and ever shall be : world without end. Amen.

### The Collect.

ALMIGHTY everliving God, which for the more confirmation of the faith didst suffer thy holy Apostle Thomas to be doubtful in thy Son's resurrection; Grant us so perfectly, and without all doubt, to believe in thy Son Jesus Christ, that our faith in thy sight never be reproved. Hear us, O Lord, through the same Jesus Christ; to whom, with thee and the Holy Ghost, be all honour, etc.

### The Epistle. Eph. ii.

Now ye are not strangers nor foreigners, but citizens with the saints, and of the household of God; and are built upon the foundation of the apostles and prophets,

Jesus Christ himself being the head corner-stone; in whom what building soever is coupled together, it groweth unto an holy temple in the Lord; in whom ye also are built together to be an habitation of God through the Holy Ghost.

*The Gospel.* John xx.

THOMAS, one of the twelve, which is called Didimus, was not with them when Jesus came. The other disciples therefore said unto him, We have seen the Lord. But he said unto them, Except I see in his hands the print of the nails, and put my finger into the print of the nails, and thrust my hand into his side, I will not believe. And after eight days again his disciples were within, and Thomas with them. Then came Jesus, when the doors were shut, and stood in the midst, and said, Peace be unto you. And after that, he said to Thomas, Bring thy finger hither, and see my hands; and reach hither thy hand, and thrust it into my side; and be not faithless, but believing. Thomas answered and said unto him, My Lord and my God. Jesus said unto him, Thomas because thou hast seen me, thou hast believed; blessed are they that have not seen, and yet have believed. And many other signs truly did Jesus in the presence of his disciples, which are not written in this book. These are written that ye might believe that Jesus is Christ the Son of God; and that (in believing) ye might have life through his Name.

# The Conversion of Saint Paul.

## At Matins.

### THE SECOND LESSON, Acts xxii: 1-22.

*Confitebor tibi.* Psalm cxxxviii.

I WILL give thanks unto thee, O Lord, with my whole heart: even before the gods will I sing praises unto thee.

I will worship toward thy holy temple, and praise thy Name, because of thy loving kindness and truth: for thou hast magnified thy Name, and thy word, above all things.

When I called upon thee, thou heardest me: and enduedst my soul with much strength.

All the kings of the earth shall praise thee, O Lord: for they have heard the words of thy mouth.

Yea, they shall sing in the ways of the Lord: that great is the glory of the Lord.

For though the Lord be high yet hath he respect unto the lowly: as for the proud, he beholdeth them afar off.

Though I walk in the midst of trouble, yet shalt thou refresh me: thou shalt stretch forth thine hand upon the furiousness of mine enemies, and thy right hand shall save me.

The Lord shall make good his loving-kindness toward me: yea, thy mercy, O Lord, endureth for ever; despise not then the works of thine own hands.

Glory be to the Father, and to the Son: and to the Holy Ghost.

As it was in the beginning, is now, and ever shall be: world without end. Amen.

### The Collect.

GOD, which hast taught all the world through the preaching of thy blessed apostle Saint Paul; Grant, we beseech thee, that we which have his wonderful conversion in remembrance, may follow and fulfil the holy doctrine that he taught; through Jesus Christ our Lord.

### The Epistle. Acts ix.

AND Saul, yet breathing out threatenings and slaughter against the disciples of the Lord, went unto the high priest, and desired of him letters to carry to Damasco to the synagogues, that, if he found any of this way, (whether they were men or women,) he might bring them bound unto Jerusalem. And when he journeyed, it fortuned that as he was come nigh to Damasco, suddenly there shined round about him a light from heaven, and he fell to the earth, and heard a voice, saying to him, Saul, Saul, why persecutest thou me? And he said, What art thou, Lord? And the Lord said, I am Jesus, whom thou persecutest: it is hard for thee to kick against the prick. And he, both trembling and astonied, said, Lord, what wilt thou have me do? And the Lord said unto him, Arise, and go into the city, and it shall be told thee what thou must do. The men which journeyed with him stood amazed, hearing a voice, but seeing no man. And Saul arose from the earth, and when he opened his eyes, he saw no man; but they led him by the hand, and brought him into Damasco. And he was three days without sight, and neither did eat nor drink. And there was a certain disciple at Damasco, named Ananias, and to him said the Lord in a vision, Ananias. And he said, Behold, I am here, Lord. And the Lord said unto him, Arise, and go into the street, (which is called Straight,) and seek in the house of Judas after one called Saul, of Tharsus: for behold he prayeth, and hath seen in a vision a man named Ananias, coming in to him, and putting his hands on him, that he might receive his sight. Then Ananias answered, Lord, I have heard by many of this man, how much evil he hath done to thy saints at Jerusalem; and here he hath authority of the high priests to bind all that call on thy Name. The Lord said unto him, Go thy way; for he is a chosen vessel unto me, to bear my Name before the Gentiles, and kings, and the children of Israel: for I will shew him how great things he must suffer for my Name's sake. And Ananias went his way, and entered into the house, and put his hands on him, and said, Brother Saul, the Lord that appeared unto thee in the way as thou camest, hath sent me, that thou mightest receive thy sight, and be filled with the Holy Ghost. And immediately there fell from his eyes as it had been scales; and he received sight, and arose, and was baptized, and received meat, and was comforted. Then was Saul a certain days with the disciples which were at Damasco. And straightway he preached Christ in the synagogues, how that he was the Son of God. But all that heard him were amazed, and said, Is not this he that spoiled them which called on this Name in Jerusalem, and came hither for that intent, that he might bring them bound unto the high priests? But Saul increased the more in strength, and confounded the Jews which dwelt at Damasco, affirming that this was very Christ.

*The Gospel.* Matt. xix.

PETER answered and said unto Jesus, Behold, we have forsaken all, and followed thee; what shall we have therefore? Jesus said unto them, Verily I say unto you, that when the Son of Man shall sit in the seat of his majesty, ye that have followed me in the regeneration shall sit also upon twelve seats, and judge the twelve tribes of Israel. And every one that forsaketh house, or brethren, or sisters, or father, or mother, or wife, or children, or lands, for my Name's sake, shall receive an hundred-fold, and shall inherit everlasting life. But many that are first shall be last, and the last shall be first.

## At Evensong.

### THE SECOND LESSON, Acts xxvi.

# The Purification of Saint Mary the Virgin.

## At the Communion.

*Ecce nunc benedicite.*
### Psalm cxxxiv.

BEHOLD (now) praise the Lord: all ye servants of the Lord ;

Ye that by night stand in the house of the Lord ; (even in the courts of the house of our God.)

Lift up your hands in the sanctuary: and praise the Lord.

The Lord that made heaven and earth: give thee blessing out of Syon.

Glory be to the Father, and to the Son: and to the Holy Ghost.

As it was in the beginning, is now, and ever shall be: world without end. Amen.

### *The Collect.*

ALMIGHTY and everlasting God, we humbly beseech thy Majesty, that as thy only begotten Son was this day presented in the temple in the substance of our flesh: so grant that we may be presented unto thee with pure and clear minds, by Jesus Christ our Lord.

### *The Epistle.*

THE same that is appointed for the Sunday.

### *The Gospel.* Luke ii.

WHEN the time of their purification (after the law of Moses) was come, they brought him to Hierusalem, to present him to the Lord ; (as it is written in the law of the Lord, every man child that first openeth the matrix shall be called holy to the

Lord;) and to offer (as it i said in the law of the Lord) a pair of turtle doves, or two young pigeons. And behold, there was a man in Hierusalem, whose name was Simeon; and the same man was just and godly, and looked for the consolation of Israel: and the Holy Ghost was in him. And an answer had he received of the Holy Ghost, that he should not see death, except he first saw the Lord's Christ. And he came by inspiration into the temple.

# Saint Matthias's Day.

## At the Communion.

*Eripe mê.* Psalm cxl.

DELIVER me, O Lord, from the evil man: and preserve me from the wicked man.

Which imagine mischief in their hearts: and stir up strife all the day long.

They have sharpened their tongues like a serpent: adder's poison is under their lips.

Keep me, O Lord, from the hands of the ungodly: preserve me from the wicked men, which are purposed to overthrow my goings.

The proud have laid a snare for me, and spread a net abroad with cords: yea, and set traps in my way.

I said unto the Lord, Thou art my God: hear the voice of my prayers, O Lord.

O Lord God, thou strength of my health: thou hast covered my head in the day of battle.

Let not the ungodly have his desire, O Lord: let not his mischievous imagination prosper, lest they be too proud.

Let the mischief of their own lips fall upon the head of them: that compass me about.

Let hot burning coals fall upon them: let them be cast into the fire, and into the pit, that they never rise up again.

A man full of words shall not prosper upon the earth: evil shall hunt the wicked person to overthrow him.

Sure I am that the Lord will avenge the poor: and maintain the cause of the helpless.

The righteous also shall give thanks unto thy Name: and the just shall continue in thy sight.

Glory be to the Father, and to the Son: and to the Holy Ghost.

As it was in the beginning, is now, and ever shall be : world without end. Amen.

### The Collect.

ALMIGHTY God, which in the place of the traitor Judas didst choose thy faithful serv- ant Matthias to be of the num- ber of thy twelve Apostles ; Grant that thy Church, being alway preserved from false Apostles, may be ordered and guided by faithful and true pastors; through Jesus Christ our Lord.

### The Epistle. Acts i.

IN those days Peter stood up in the midst of the disci- ples, and said, (the number of names that were together were about an C. xx.,) Ye men and brethren, this scrip- ture must needs have been fulfilled, which the Holy Ghost through the mouth of David spake before of Judas, which was guide to them that took Jesus : for he was num- bered with us, and had ob- tained fellowship in this min- istration. And the same hath now possessed a plat of ground with the reward of iniquity ; and when he was hanged, he burst asunder in the midst, and all his bowels gushed out. And it is known unto all the inhabiters of Hierusalem, insomuch as the same field is called in their mother tongue, Acheldama, that is to say, The bloody field. For it is written in the book of Psalms, His habita- tion be void, and no man be dwelling therein; and, His bishopric let another take. Wherefore, of these men which have companied with us (all the time that the Lord Jesus had all his conversation among us, beginning at the baptism of John, unto that same day that he was taken up from us) must one be or- dained to be a witness with us of his resurrection. And they appointed two, Joseph which is called Barsabas, (whose surname was Justus,) and Matthias. And when they prayed, they said, Thou, Lord, which knowest the hearts of all men, shew whether of these two thou hast chosen, that he may take the room of this minis- tration and apostleship, from which Judas by transgression fell, that he might go to his own place. And they gave forth their lots; and the lot fell on Matthias, and he was counted with the eleven Apos- tles.

### The Gospel. Matt. xi.

IN that time Jesus answered and said, I thank thee, (O

Father,) Lord of heaven and earth, because thou hast hid these things from the wise and prudent, and hast shewed them unto babes. Verily, Father, even so was it thy good pleasure. All things are given over unto me of my Father: and no man knoweth the Son but the Father; neither knoweth any man the Father, save the Son, and he to whomsoever the Son will open him. Come unto me, all ye that labour, and are laden, and I will ease you. Take my yoke upon you, and learn of me; for I am meek and lowly in heart: and ye shall find rest unto your souls. For my yoke is easy, and my burden is light.

# The Annunciation of the Virgin Mary.

## At the Communion.

*Domine, non est.*
### Psalm cxxxi.

LORD, I am not high-minded: I have no proud looks.

I do not exercise myself in great matters: which are too high for me.

But I refrain my soul, and keep it low, like as a child that is weaned from his mother: yea, my soul is even as a weaned child.

O Israel, trust in the Lord: from this time forth for evermore.

Glory be to the Father, and to the Son: and to the Holy Ghost.

As it was in the beginning, is now, and ever shall be: world without end. Amen.

### The Collect.

WE beseech thee, Lord, pour thy grace into our hearts; that, as we have known Christ thy Son's incarnation, by the message of an angel, so by his cross and passion we may be brought unto the glory of his resurrection; through the same Christ our Lord.

### The Epistle. Isaiah vii.

GOD spake once again unto Ahaz, saying, Require a token of the Lord thy God; whether it be toward the depth beneath, or toward the height above. Then said Ahaz, I will require none, neither will I tempt the Lord. And he said, Hearken to me, ye of the house of David; is it not enough for you that ye be grievous unto men, but ye must grieve my God also? And therefore the Lord shall give you a token; Behold, a Virgin shall conceive, and bear a son, and his mother shall call his Name Emanuel. Butter and honey shall he eat, that he may know to refuse the evil, and choose the good.

*The Gospel.* Luke i.

AND in the sixth month the angel Gabriel was sent from God unto a city of Galilee named Nazareth, to a Virgin spoused to a man whose name was Joseph, of the house of David; and the Virgin's name was Mary. And the angel went in unto her, and said, Hail, full of grace, the Lord is with thee; Blessed art thou among women. When she saw him, she was abashed at his saying, and cast in her mind what manner of saluta-tion that should be. And the angel said unto her, Fear not, Mary; for thou hast found grace with God. Behold, thou shalt conceive in thy womb, and bear a son, and shalt call his name JESUS. He shall be great, and shall be called the Son of the High-est; and the Lord God shall give unto him the seat of his father David: and he shall reign over the house of Jacob for ever; and of his kingdom there shall be none end. Then said Mary unto the angel, How shall this be, seeing I know not a man? And the angel answered and said unto her, The Holy Ghost shall come upon thee, and the power of the Highest shall overshadow thee: therefore also that holy thing which shall be born shall be called the Son of God. And behold, thy cousin Elizabeth, she hath also conceived a son in her age; and this is her sixth month, which was called barren: for with God shall nothing be unpossible. And Mary said, Behold the hand-maid of the Lord; be it unto me according to thy word. And the angel departed from her.

# Saint Mark's Day.

## At the Communion.

*Domine, clamavi.*

### Psalm cxli.

Lord, I call upon thee, haste thee unto me: and consider my voice when I cry unto thee.

Let my prayer be set forth in thy sight as the incense: and let the lifting up of my hands be an evening sacrifice.

Set a watch, O Lord, before my mouth: and keep the door of my lips.

O let not mine heart be inclined to any evil thing: let me not be occupied in ungodly works with the men that work wickedness, lest I eat of such things as please them.

Let the righteous rather smite me friendly: and reprove me.

But let not their precious balms break mine head: yea, I will pray yet against their wickedness.

Let their judges be overthrown in stony places: that they may hear my words, for they are sweet.

Our bones lie scattered before the pit: like as when one breaketh and heweth wood upon the earth.

But mine eyes look unto thee, O Lord God: in thee is my trust, O cast not out my soul.

Keep me from the snare which they have laid for me: and from the traps of the wicked doers.

Let the ungodly fall into their own nets together: and let me ever escape them.

Glory be to the Father, and to the Son: and to the Holy Ghost.

As it was in the beginning, is now, and ever shall be: world without end.　Amen.

### The Collect.

Almighty God, which hast instructed thy holy Church with the heavenly doctrine of thy Evangelist Saint Mark; Give us grace so to be established by thy holy Gospel, that we be not, like children, carried away with every blast of vain doctrine; through Jesus Christ our Lord.

### The Epistle. Eph. iv.

Unto every one of us is given grace according to the measure of the gift of Christ. Wherefore he saith, When he went up an high, he led captivity captive, and gave gifts unto men. That he ascended, what meaneth it but that he also descended first into the lowest parts of the earth? He that descended is even the same also that ascended up above all heavens, to fulfil all things. And the very same made some apostles, some prophets, some evangelists, some shepherds and teachers; to the edifying of the saints, to the work and ministration, even to the edifying of the body of Christ; till we all come to the unity of faith, and knowledge of the Son of God, unto a perfect man, unto the measure of the full perfect age of Christ. That we henceforth should be no more children, wavering and carried about with every wind of doctrine, by the wiliness of men, through craftiness, whereby they lay await for us to deceive us; but let us follow the truth in love, and in all things grow in him, which is the head, even Christ, in whom if all the body be coupled and knit together throughout every joint, wherewith one ministereth to another, (according to the operation, as every part hath his measure,) he increaseth the body, unto the edifying of itself through love.

*The Gospel.* John xv.

I AM the true vine, and my Father is an husbandman. Every branch that beareth not fruit in me, he will take away; and every branch that beareth fruit, will he purge, that it may bring forth more fruit. Now are ye clean through the words which I have spoken unto you. Bide in me, and I in you. As the branch cannot bear fruit of itself, except it bide in the vine, no more can ye, except ye abide in me. I am the vine, ye are the branches. He that abideth in me, and I in him, the same bringeth forth much fruit For without me can ye do nothing. If a man bide not in me, he is cast forth as a branch, and is withered; and men gather them, and cast them into the fire, and they burn. If ye bide in me, and my words abide in you, ask what ye will, and it shall be done for you. Herein is my Father glorified, that ye bear much fruit, and become my disciples. As the Father hath loved me, even so have I also loved you: continue ye in my love. If ye keep my commandments, ye shall bide in my love, even as I have kept my Father's commandments, and abide in his love. These things have I spoken unto you, that my joy might remain in you, and that your joy might be full.

## Saints Philip and James.

### At Matins.
THE SECOND LESSON, Acts viii: 1-14.

### At the Communion,

*Ecce, quam, bonum!*
Psalm cxxxiii.

BEHOLD, how good and joyful a thing it is: brethren, to dwell together in unity.

It is like the precious ointment upon the head, that ran down unto the beard: even unto Aaron's beard, and went down to the skirts of his clothing.

Like the dew of Hermon: which fell upon the hill of Sion.

For there the Lord promised his blessing: and life for evermore.

Glory be to the Father, and to the Son: and to the Holy Ghost.

As it was in the beginning, is now, and ever shall be: world without end. Amen.

### The Collect.

ALMIGHTY God, whom truly to know is everlasting life; Grant us perfectly to know thy Son Jesus Christ to be the way, the truth, and the life; as thou hast taught Saint Philip and other the Apostles; through Jesus Christ our Lord.

### The Epistle. James i.

JAMES, the servant of God, and of the Lord Jesus Christ, sendeth greeting to the twelve tribes which are scattered abroad. My brethren, count it for an exceeding joy when ye fall into divers temptations; knowing this, that the trying of your faith gendereth patience: and let patience have her perfect work, that ye may be perfect and sound, lacking nothing. If any of you lack wisdom, let him ask of him that giveth it, even God, which giveth to all men indifferently, and casteth no man in the teeth, and it shall be given him. But let him ask in faith, and waver not;

for he that doubteth is like a wave of the sea, which is tossed of the winds, and carried with violence. Neither let that man think that he shall receive any thing of the Lord. A wavering-minded man is unstable in all his ways. Let the brother which is of low degree rejoice when he is exalted. Again, let him that is rich rejoice when he is made low; for even as the flower of the grass shall he pass away. For as the sun riseth with heat, and the grass withereth, and his flower falleth away, and the beauty of the fashion of it perisheth; even so shall the rich man perish in his ways. Happy is the man that endureth temptation; for when he is tried, he shall receive the crown of life, which the Lord hath promised to them that love him.

*The Gospel.* John xiv.

AND Jesus said unto his disciples, Let not your heart be troubled; ye believe in God, believe also in me. In my Father's house are many mansions; if it were not so, I would have told you. I go to prepare a place for you: and if I go to prepare a place for you I will come again, and receive you even unto myself, that where I am, there may ye be also. And whither I go ye know, and the way ye know. Thomas saith unto him Lord, we know not whither thou goest, and how is it possible for us to know the way? Jesus saith unto him, I am the way, and the truth, and the life: no man cometh unto the Father but by me. If ye had known me, ye had known my Father also: and now ye know him, and have seen him. Philip saith unto him, Lord, shew us the Father, and it sufficeth us. Jesus saith unto him, Have I been so long time with you, and yet hast thou not known me, Philip? He that hath seen me hath seen my Father; and how sayest thou then, Shew us the Father? Believest thou not that I am in the Father, and the Father in me? The words that I speak unto you I speak not of myself; but the Father that dwelleth in me is he that doeth the works. Believe me, that I am in the Father, and the Father in me; or else believe me for the works' sake. Verily, verily I say unto you, He that believeth on me, the works that I do, the same shall he do also; and greater works than these shall he do; because I go unto my Father.

And whatsoever ye ask in my Name, that will I do, that the Father may be glorified by the Son. If ye shall ask any thing in my Name, I will do it.

# Saint Barnabas Apostle.

## At Matins.

THE SECOND LESSON, Acts xiv.

## At the Communion.

*Voce mea ad Dominum.*

### Psalm cxlii.

I CRIED unto the Lord with my voice : yea, even unto the Lord did I make my supplication.

I poured out my complaints before him : and shewed him of my trouble.

When my spirit was in heaviness thou knewest my path : in the way wherein I walked have they privily laid a snare for me.

I looked also upon my right hand : and see, there was no man that would know me.

I had no place to fly unto : and no man cared for my soul.

I cried unto thee, O Lord, and said : Thou art my hope and my portion in the land of the living.

Consider my complaint : for I am brought very low.

O deliver me from my persecutors : for they are too strong for me.

Bring my soul out of prison, that I may give thanks unto thy Name : which thing if thou wilt grant me, then shall the righteous resort unto my company.

Glory be to the Father, and to the Son : and to the Holy Ghost.

As it was in the beginning, is now, and ever shall be : world without end. Amen.

### The Collect.

LORD Almighty, which hast indued thy holy Apostle Barnabas with singular gifts of thy Holy Ghost; let us not be destitute of thy manifold gifts, nor yet of grace to use them alway to thy honour and glory; through Jesus Christ our Lord.

*The Epistle.* Acts xi.

TIDINGS of these things came unto the ears of the congregation which was in Jerusalem; and they sent forth Barnabas, that he should go unto Antioch. Which, when he came, and had seen the grace of God, was glad; and exhorted them all, that with purpose of heart they would continually cleave unto the Lord. For he was a good man, and full of the Holy Ghost and of faith; and much people was added unto the Lord. Then departed Barnabas to Tharsus, for to seek Saul. And when he had found him, he brought him unto Antioch. And it chanced, that a whole year they had their conversation with the congregation there, and taught much people, insomuch that the disciples of Antioch were the first that were called Christen. In those days came prophets from the city of Jerusalem unto Antioch. And there stood up one of them, name Agabus, and signified by the Spirit, that there should be great dearth throughout all the world, which came to pass in the Emperor Claudius' days. Then the disciples, every man according to his habilitie, purposed to send succour unto the brethren which dwelt in Jewry: which thing they also did, and sent it to the elders by the hands of Barnabas and Saul.

*The Gospel.* John xv.

THIS is my commandment, that ye love together, as I have loved you. Greater love hath no man than this, that a man bestow his life for his friends. Ye are my friends, if ye do whatsoever I command you. Henceforth call I you not servants; for the servant knoweth not what his lord doeth; but you have I called friends: for all things that I have heard of my Father have I opened to you. Ye have not chosen me, but I have chosen you, and ordained you, to go and bring forth fruit, and that your fruit should remain: that whatsoever ye ask of the Father in my Name, he may give it you.

## At Evensong.

THE SECOND LESSON, Acts xv: 1-36.

# Saint John Baptist.

## Proper Lessons at Matins.

THE FIRST LESSON, Mal. iii.     THE SECOND LESSON, Matt. iii.

## At the Communion,

*Domine, exaudi.*
### Psalm cxliii.

HEAR my prayer, O Lord, and consider my desire: hearken unto me for thy truth and righteousness' sake.

And enter not into judgment with thy servant: for in thy sight shall no man living be justified.

For the enemy hath persecuted my soul; he hath smitten my life down to the ground: he hath laid me in the darkness, as the men that have been long dead.

Therefore is my spirit vexed within me: and my heart within me is desolate.

Yet do I remember the time past; I muse upon all thy works: yea, I exercise myself in the works of thy hands.

I stretch forth my hands unto thee: my soul gaspeth unto thee as a thirsty land.

Hear me, O Lord, and that soon, for my spirit waxeth faint: hide not thy face from me, lest I be like unto them that go down into the pit.

O let me hear thy loving-kindness betimes in the morning, for in thee is my trust: shew thou me the way that I should walk in, for I lift up my soul unto thee.

Deliver me, O Lord, from mine enemies: for I fly unto thee to hide me.

Teach me to do the thing that pleaseth thee, for thou art my God: let thy loving Spirit lead me forth unto the land of righteousness.

Quicken me, O Lord, for thy Name's sake: and for thy righteousness' sake bring my soul out of trouble.

And of thy goodness slay mine enemies: and destroy all them that vex my soul; for I am thy servant.

Glory be to the Father, and to the Son: and to the Holy Ghost.

As it was in the beginning, is now, and ever shall be: world without end.   Amen.

### The Collect.

ALMIGHTY God, by whose

providence thy servant John Baptist was wonderfully born, and sent to prepare the way of thy Son our Saviour, by preaching of penance; Make us so to follow his doctrine and holy life, that we may truly repent according to his preaching, and after his example constantly speak the truth, boldly rebuke vice, and patiently suffer for the truth's sake; through Jesus Christ our Lord.

*The Epistle.* Isaiah xl.

BE of good cheer, my people: O ye prophets, comfort my people, saith your God; comfort Jerusalem at the heart, and tell her, that her travail is at an end, that her offence is pardoned, that she hath received of the Lord's hand sufficient correction for all her sins. A voice crieth in wilderness, Prepare the way of the Lord in the wilderness, make straight the path for our God in the desert. Let all valleys be exalted, and every mountain and hill be laid low: whatso is crooked, let it be made straight, and let the rough be made plain fields. For the glory of the Lord shall appear, and all flesh shall at once see it: for why? The mouth of the Lord hath spoken it. The same voice spake, Now cry. And the prophet answered, What shall I cry? That all flesh is grass, and that all the goodliness thereof is as the flower of the field. The grass is withered, the flower falleth away: even so is the people as grass, when the breath of the Lord bloweth upon them. Nevertheless, whether the grass wither, or that the flower fade away, yet the word of our God endureth for ever. Go up unto the high hill, (O Sion,) thou that bringest good tidings; lift up thy voice with power, O thou preacher, Jerusalem; lift it up without fear, and say unto the cities of Juda, Behold your God: Behold the Lord God shall come with power, and bear rule with his arm: behold, he bringeth his treasure with him, and his works go before him. He shall feed his flock like an herdman; he shall gather the lambs together with his arm, and carry them in his bosom, and shall kindly entreat those that bear young.

*The Gospel.* Luke i.

ELIZABETH's time came that she should be delivered, and she brought forth a son. And her neighbours and her cousins heard how the Lord had shewed great mercy upon her; and they rejoiced with her.

And it fortuned, that in the eight day they came to circumcise the child, and called his name Zacharias, after the name of his father. And his mother answered and said, Not so; but he shall be called John. And they said unto her, There is none in thy kynred that is named with this name. And they made signs to his father, how he would have him called. And he asked for writing tables, and wrote, saying, His name is John. And they marvelled all. And his mouth was opened immediately, and his tongue also, and he spake and praised God. And fear came on all them that dwelt nigh unto them: and all these sayings were noised abroad throughout all the hill country of Jewry. And all they that heard them laid them up in their hearts saying, What manner of child shall this be? And the hand of the Lord was with him. And his father Zacharias was filled with the Holy Ghost, and prophesied, saying, Praised be the Lord God of Israel: for he hath visited and redeemed his people, and hath raised up an horn of salvation unto us in the house of his servant David; even as he promised by the mouth of his holy prophets, which were since the world began; that we should be saved from our enemies, and from the hand of all that hate us; that he would deal mercifully with our fathers, and remember his holy covenant; and that he would perform the oath which he sware to our father Abraham for to give us, that we, delivered out of the hands of our enemies, might serve him without fear all the days of our life, in such holiness and righteousness as are acceptable before him. And thou, child, shalt be called the prophet of the Highest: for thou shalt go before the face of the Lord to prepare his ways; to give knowledge of salvation unto his people, for the remission of sins, through the tender mercy of our God, whereby the day-spring from an high hath visited us; to give light to them that sat in darkness and in the shadow of death, to guide our feet into the way of peace. And the child grew, and waxed strong in spirit; and was in wilderness till the day came when he should shew himself unto the Israelites.

## Proper Lessons at Evensong.

THE FIRST LESSON, Mal. iv: 1-13.  THE SECOND LESSON, Matt. xiv.

# Saint Peter's Day.

## At Matins.
THE SECOND LESSON, Acts iii.

# At the Communion.

*Benedictus Dominus.*
Psalm cxliv.

BLESSED be the Lord my strength: which teacheth my hands to war, and my fingers to fight.

My hope and my fortress, my castle and deliverer, my defender in whom I trust: which subdueth my people that is under me.

Lord, what is man, that thou hast such respect unto him: or the son of man, that thou so regardest him?

Man is like a thing of nought: his time passeth away like a shadow.

Bow thy heavens, O Lord, and come down: touch the mountains, and they shall smoke.

Cast forth the lightning, and tear them: shoot out thine arrows, and consume them.

Send down thine hand from above: deliver me, and take me out of the great waters, from the hand of strange children;

Whose mouth talketh of vanity: and their right hand is a right hand of wickedness.

I will sing a new song unto thee, O God: and sing praises unto thee upon a ten-stringed lute.

Thou that givest victory unto kings: and hast delivered David thy servant from the peril of the sword.

Save me, and deliver me from the hand of strange children: whose mouth talketh of vanity, and their right hand is a right hand of iniquity.

That our sons may grow up as the young plants: and that our daughters may be as the polished corners of the temple.

That our garners may be full and plenteous with all manner of store: that our sheep may bring forth thousands and ten thousands in our streets.

That our oxen may be strong to labour, that there be no decay: no leading into captivity, and no complaining in our streets.

Happy are the people that be in such a case: yea, blessed are the people which have the Lord for their God.

Glory be to the Father, and to the Son: and to the Holy Ghost.

As it was in the beginning, is now, and ever shall be: world without end. Amen

### The Collect.

ALMIGHTY God, which by thy Son Jesus Christ hast given to thy Apostle Saint Peter many excellent gifts, and commandedst him earnestly to feed thy flock; Make, we beseech thee, all bishops and pastors diligently to preach thy holy word, and the people obediently to follow the same, that they may receive the crown of everlasting glory; through Jesus Christ our Lord.

### The Epistle. Acts xii.

AT the same time Herod the king stretched forth his hands to vex certain of the congregation. And he killed James the brother of John with the sword. And, because he saw that it pleased the Jews, he proceeded farther and took Peter also. Then were the days of sweet bread.

And when he had caught him, he put him in prison also, and delivered him to four quaternions of soldiers, to be kept; intending after Easter to bring him forth to the people. And Peter was kept in prison; but prayer was made without ceasing of the congregation unto God for him. And when Herod would have brought him out unto the people, the same night slept Peter between two soldiers, bound with two chains; and the keepers before the door kept the prison. And behold, the angel of the Lord was there present, and a light shined in the habitation; and he smote Peter on the side, and stirred him up, saying, Arise up quickly. And his chains fell off from his hands. And the angel said unto him, Gird thyself, and bind on thy sandals: and so he did. And he saith unto him, Cast thy garment about thee, and follow me. And he came out, and followed him; and wist not that it was truth which was done by the angel; but thought he had seen a vision. When they were past the first and the second watch, they came unto the iron gate that leadeth unto the city, which opened to them by the own accord; and they went out, and passed through one street, and forthwith the angel departed from him. And when Peter was come to himself, he said, Now I know of a surety that the Lord hath sent his angel, and hath delivered me out of the hand of Herod, and from all the waiting for of the people of the Jews.

*The Gospel.* Matt. xvi.

WHEN Jesus came into the coasts of the city which is called Cesarea Philippi, he asked his disciples, saying, Whom do men say that I the Son of Man am? They said, Some say that thou art John Baptist, some Helias, some Jeremias, or one of the number of the prophets. He saith unto them, But whom say ye that I am? Simon Peter answered and said, Thou art Christ, the Son of the living God. And Jesus answered and said unto him, Happy art thou, Simon, the son of Jonas: for flesh and blood hath not opened that unto thee, but my Father which is in heaven. And I say also unto thee, That thou art Peter, and upon this rock I will build my congregation: and the gates of hell shall not prevail against it. And I will give unto thee the keys of the kingdom of heaven: and whatsoever thou bindest in earth shall be bound in heaven; and whatsoever thou loosest in earth shall be loosed in heaven.

At Evensong.
THE SECOND LESSON, Acts iv.

## Saint Mary Magdalene.
### At the Communion.

*Lauda, anima mea.*
Psalm cxlvi.

PRAISE the Lord, O my soul: while I live will I praise the Lord, yea, as long as I have any being, I will sing praises unto my God.

O put not your trust in princes, nor in any child of man: for there is no help in them.

For when the breath of man goeth forth he shall turn again to his earth: and then all his thoughts perish.

Blessed is he that hath the God of Jacob for his help:

and whose hope is in the Lord his God;

Which made heaven and earth, the sea, and all that therein is: which keepeth his promise for ever;

Which helpeth them to right that suffer wrong: which feedeth the hungry.

The Lord looseth men out of prison: the Lord giveth sight to the blind.

The Lord helpeth them up that are fallen: the Lord careth for the righteous.

The Lord careth for the strangers; he defendeth the fatherless and widow: as for the way of the ungodly, he turneth it upside down.

The Lord thy God, O Sion, shall be king for evermore: and throughout all generations.

Glory be to the Father, and to the Son: and to the Holy Ghost.

As it was in the beginning, is now, and ever shall be: world without end. Amen.

### The Collect.

MERCIFUL Father, give us grace, that we never presume to sin through the example of any creature; but if it shall chance us at any time to offend thy divine Majesty, that then we may truly repent, and lament the same, after the example of Mary Magdalene, and by lively faith obtain remission of all our sins; through the only merits of thy Son our Saviour Christ.

### The Epistle. Prov. xxxi.

WHOSOEVER findeth an honest faithful woman, she is much more worth than pearls. The heart of her husband may safely trust in her, so that he shall fall in no poverty. She will do him good and not evil all the days of her life. She occupieth wool and flax, and laboureth gladly with her hands. She is like a merchant's ship that bringeth her vitailes from afar. She is up in the night season, to provide meat for her household, and food for her maidens. She considereth land, and buyeth it; and with the fruit of her hands she planteth a vineyard. She girdeth her loins with strength and courageth her arms. And if she perceive that her huswifery doeth good, her candle goeth not out by night. She layeth her fingers to the spindle, and her hand taketh hold of the distaff. She openeth her hand to the poor; yea, she stretcheth forth her hands to such as have need. She feareth not that the cold of winter shall hurt her house: for all her household folks are clothed with scarlet. She maketh herself fair ornaments; her clothing is white silk and purple. Her husband is much set by in the gates, when he sitteth among the rulers of the land. She maketh cloth of silk, and selleth it; and delivereth girdles unto the merchant. Strength and honour is her clothing; and in the latter day she shall rejoice. She openeth her mouth with wisdom, and in her tongue is the law of grace. She looketh well to the ways of her household, and eateth not her bread with idleness. Her children shall arise, and call her blessed; and her husband shall make much of her. Many daughters there be that gather riches together; but thou goest above them all. As for favour it is deceitful, and beauty is a vain thing: but a woman that feareth the Lord, she is worthy to be praised. Give her of the fruit of her hands, and let her own works praise her in the gates.

*The Gospel.* Luke vii.

AND one of the Pharisees desired Jesus that he would eat with him. And he went into the Pharisee's house, and sat down to meat. And behold, a woman in that city, (which was a sinner,) as soon as she knew that Jesus sat at meat in the Pharisee's house, she brought an alabaster box of ointment, and stood at his feet behind him weeping, and began to wash his feet with tears, and did wipe them with the hairs of her head, and kissed his feet, and anointed them with the ointment. When the Pharisee (which had bidden him) saw that, he spake within himself, saying, If this man were a prophet, he would surely know who and what manner of woman this is that touched him: for she is a sinner. Jesus answered and said unto him, Simon, I have somewhat to say unto thee. And he said, Master say on. There was a certain lender which had two debtors: the one ought him five hundred pence, and the other fifty. When they had nothing to pay, he forgave them both. Tell me therefore, which of them will love him most? Simon answered and said, I suppose that he to whom he forgave most. And he said unto him, Thou hast truly judged. And he turned to the woman, and said unto Simon, Seest thou this woman? I entered into thy house, thou gavest me no water for my feet: but she hath washed my feet with tears, and wiped them with the hairs of her head. Thou gavest me no kiss: but she since the time I came in hath not ceased to kiss my feet. My head with oil thou didst not anoint: but she hath anointed my feet with ointment. Wherefore I say unto thee, Many sins are forgiven her; for she loved much: to whom less is forgiven, the same doth less love. And he said unto her, Thy sins are forgiven thee. And they that sat at meat with him began to say within themselves, Who is this which forgiveth sins also? And he said to the woman, Thy faith hath saved thee; go in peace.

# Saint James the Apostle.
## At the Communion.

*Laudate Dominum de cœlis.*
Psalm cxlviii.

O PRAISE the Lord of heaven: praise him in the height.

Praise him, all ye angels of his: praise him, all his host.

Praise him, sun and moon: praise ye him, all ye stars and light.

Praise him, all ye heavens: and ye waters that be above the heavens.

Let them praise the Name of the Lord: for (he spake the word, and they were made;) he commanded, and they were created.

He hath made them fast for ever and ever: he hath given them a law which shall not be broken.

Praise the Lord upon the earth: ye dragons, and all deeps;

Fire and hail, snow and vapours: wind and storm, fulfilling his word;

Mountains and all hills: fruitful trees and all cedars;

Beasts and all cattle: worms and feathered fowls;

Kings of the earth and all people: princes and all the judges of the world;

Young men and maidens, old men and children, praise the Name of the Lord; for his Name only is excellent, and his praise above heaven and earth.

He shall exalt the horn of his people; all his saints shall praise him: even the children of Israel, even the people that serveth him.

Glory be to the Father, and to the Son: and to the Holy Ghost.

As it was in the beginning, is now, and ever shall be: world without end. Amen.

### The Collect.

GRANT, O merciful God, that as thine holy Apostle James, leaving his father and all that he had, without delay was obedient unto the calling of thy Son Jesus Christ, and followed him; so we, forsaking all worldly and carnal affections, may be evermore ready to follow thy commandments; through Jesus Christ our Lord.

### The Epistle. Acts xi. xii.

IN those days came prophets from the city of Jerusalem unto Antioch. And there stood up one of them named Agabus, and signified by the Spirit that there should be great dearth throughout all the world; which came to pass in the Emperor Claudius' days. Then the disciples, every man according to his habilitie, purposed to send succour unto the brethren which dwelt in Jewry: which thing they also did, and sent it to the elders by the hands of Barnabas and Saul. At the same time Herod the king stretched forth his hands to vex certain of the congregation. And he killed James the brother of John with the sword. And, because he saw that it pleased the Jews, he proceeded farther and took Peter also.

### The Gospel. Matt. xx.

THEN came to him the mother of Zebede's children with her sons, worshipping him and desiring a certain thing of him. And he said unto her, What wilt thou? She said unto him, Grant that these my two sons may sit, the one on thy right hand, and the other on thy left, in thy kingdom. But Jesus answered and said, Ye wot not what ye ask. Are ye able to drink of the cup that I shall drink of, and to be baptized with the baptism that I am baptized with? They said unto him, We are. He said unto them, Ye shall drink indeed of my cup, and be baptized with the baptism that I am baptized with: but to sit on my right hand, and on my left, is not mine to give; but it shall chance unto them that it is prepared for of my Father. And when the ten heard this, they disdained at the two brethren. But Jesus called them unto him, and said, Ye know that the princes of the nations have dominion over them, and they that are great men exercise authority upon them. It shall not be so among you: but whosoever will be great among you, let him be your minister; and whosoever will be chief among you, let him be your servant: even as the Son of Man came not to be ministered unto, but to minister, and to give his life a redemption for many.

# Saint Bartholomew.

## At the Communion.

*Non nobis, Domine.*
Psalm cxv.

Not unto us, (O Lord,) not unto us, but unto thy Name, give the praise: for thy loving mercy, and for thy truth's sake.

Wherefore shall the heathen say: Where is now their God?

As for our God, he is in heaven: he hath done whatsoever pleased him.

Their idols are silver and gold: even the work of men's hands.

They have mouths, and speak not: eyes have they, and see not.

They have ears, and hear not: noses have they, and smell not.

They have hands, and handle not; feet have they, and walk not: neither speak they through their throat.

They that make them are like unto them: and so are all such as put their trust in them.

But the house of Israel, trust thou in the Lord: he is their succour and defence.

Ye house of Aaron, put your trust in the Lord: he is their helper and defender.

Ye that fear the Lord, trust ye in the Lord: he is their helper and defender.

The Lord hath been mindful of us, and he shall bless us: even he shall bless the house of Israel, he shall bless the house of Aaron.

He shall bless them that fear the Lord: both small and great.

The Lord shall increase you more and more : you and your children.

Ye are the blessed of the Lord : which made heaven and earth.

All the whole heavens are the Lord's : the earth hath he given unto the children of men.

The dead praise not thee (O Lord:) neither all they that go down into the silence.

But we will praise the Lord: from this time forth for evermore.

Glory be to the Father, and to the Son : and to the Holy Ghost.

As it was in the beginning, is now, and ever shall be: world without end.    Amen.

### The Collect.

O ALMIGHTY and everlasting God, which hast given grace to thy Apostle Bartholomew truly to believe and to preach thy word; Grant, we beseech thee, unto thy Church, both to love that he believed, and to preach that he taught; through Christ our Lord.

### The Epistle. Acts v.

BY the hands of the Apostles were many signs and wonders shewed among the people. And they were all together with one accord in Salomon's porch.   And of other durst no man join himself to them : nevertheless the people magnified them : the number of them that believed in the Lord, both of men and women, grew more and more : insomuch that they brought the sick into the streets, and laid them on beds and couches, that at the least way the shadow of Peter, when he came by, might shadow some of them, (and that they might all be delivered from their infirmities.)   There came also a multitude out of the cities round about unto Jerusalem, bringing sick folks, and them which were vexed with unclean spirits; and they were healed every one.

### The Gospel. Luke xxii.

AND there was a strife among them, which of them should seem to be the greatest. And he said unto them, The kings of nations reign over them; and they that have authority upon them are called gracious lords. But ye shall not be so : but he that is greatest among you, shall be as the younger; and he that is chief, shall be as he that doth minister.   For whether is greater, he that sitteth at meat, or he that serveth? is not he that sitteth at meat? But I am among you as he that ministereth. Ye are they which have bidden with me in my temptations. And I appoint unto you a kingdom, as my Father hath appointed to me; that ye may eat and drink at my table in my kingdom, and sit on seats judging the twelve tribes of Israel.

# Saint Matthew.

## At the Communion.

*Laudate Dominum omnes gentes.* Psalm cxvii.

O PRAISE the Lord, all ye heathen : praise him, all ye nations.

For his merciful kindness is ever more and more toward us: and the truth of the Lord endureth for ever.

Glory be to the Father, and to the Son : and to the Holy Ghost.

As it was in the beginning, is now, and ever shall be: world without end. Amen.

### The Collect.

ALMIGHTY God, which by thy blessed Son diddest call Matthew from the receipt of custom to be an Apostle and Evangelist: Grant us grace to forsake all covetous desires and inordinate love of riches, and to follow thy said Son Jesus Christ; who liveth and reigneth, etc.

*The Epistle.* 2. Cor. iv.

SEEING that we have such an office, even as God hath had mercy on us, we go not out of kind; but have cast from us the clokes of unhonesty, and walk not in craftiness, neither handle we the word of God deceitfully, but open the truth, and report ourselves to every man's conscience in the sight of God. If our gospel be yet hid, it is hid among them that are lost: in whom the god of this world hath blinded the minds of them which believe not, lest the light of the gospel of the glory of Christ (which is the image of God) should shine unto them. For we preach not ourselves, but Christ Jesus to be the Lord; and ourselves your servants for Jesu's sake. For it is God, that commanded the light to shine out of darkness, which hath shined in our hearts, for to give the light of the knowledge of the glory of God, in the face of Jesus Christ.

*The Gospel.* Matt. ix.

AND as Jesus passed forth from thence, he saw a man (named Matthew) sitting at the receipt of custom; and he said unto him, Follow me. And he arose, and followed him. And it came to pass, as Jesus sat at meat in his house, behold, many publicans also and sinners that came, sat down with Jesus and his disciples. And when the Pharisees saw it, they said unto his disciples, Why eateth your Master with publicans and sinners? But when Jesus heard that, he said unto them, They that be strong need not the physician, but they that are sick. Go ye rather and learn what that meaneth, I will have mercy and not sacrifice; for I am not come to call the righteous, but sinners to repentance.

# Saint Michael and all Angels.

## At the Communion.

*Laudate, pueri.*
Psalm cxiii.

PRAISE the Lord (ye servants): O praise the Name of the Lord.

Blessed be the Name of the Lord: from this time forth for evermore.

The Lord's Name is praised: from the rising up of the sun unto the going down of the same.

The Lord is high above all heathen: and his glory above the heavens.

Who is like unto the Lord our God, that hath his dwelling so high: and yet humbleth himself to behold the things that are in heaven and earth?

He taketh up the simple out of the dust: and lifteth the poor out of the mire;

That he may set him with the princes: even with the princes of his people.

He maketh the barren woman to keep house: and to be a joyful mother of children.

Glory be to the Father, and to the Son: and to the Holy Ghost.

As it was in the beginning,

is now, and ever shall be: world without end. Amen.

### The Collect.

EVERLASTING God, which hast ordained and constituted the services of all Angels and men in a wonderful order; Mercifully grant, that they which alway do thee service in heaven, may by thy appointment succour and defend us in earth: through Jesus Christ our Lord, etc.

### The Epistle. Rev. xii.

THERE was a great battle in heaven: Michael and his angels fought with the dragon, and the dragon fought and his angels; and prevailed not, neither was their place found any more in heaven. And the great dragon, that old serpent, called the Devil and Sathanas, was cast out, which deceiveth all the world. And he was cast into the earth, and his angels were cast out also with him. And I heard a loud voice, saying. In heaven is now made salvation and strength, and the kingdom of our God, and the power of his Christ. For the accuser of our brethren is cast down, which accused them before our God day and night. And they overcame him by the blood of the Lamb, and by the word of their testi-mony; and they loved not their lives unto the death. Therefore rejoice, heavens, and ye that dwell in them. Woe unto the inhabiters of the earth, and of the sea: for the devil is come down unto you, which hath great wrath, because he knoweth that he hath but a short time.

### The Gospel. Matt. xviii.

AT the same time came the disciples unto Jesus, saying, Who is the greatest in the kingdom of heaven? Jesus called a child unto him, and set him in the midst of them, and said, Verily I say unto you, Except ye turn, and become as children, ye shall not enter into the kingdom of heaven. Whosoever therefore humbleth himself as this child, the same is the greatest in the kingdom of heaven. And whosoever receiveth such a child in my Name, receiveth me. But whoso doth offend one of these little ones which believe in me, it were better for him that a millstone were hanged about his neck, and that he were drowned in the depth of the sea. Woe unto the world because of offences: necessary it is that offences come: but woe unto the man by whom the offence cometh.

Wherefore if thy hand or thy foot hinder thee, cut him off, and cast it from thee: it is better for thee to enter into life halt or maimed, rather than thou shouldest (having two hands or two feet) be cast into everlasting fire. And if thine eye offend thee, pluck it out, and cast it from thee: it is better for thee to enter into life with one eye, rather than (having ii. eyes) to be cast into hell fire. Take heed that ye despise not one of these little ones; for I say unto you, That in heaven their angels do always behold the face of my Father which is in heaven.

# Saint Luke Evangelist.

## At the Communion.

*Super flumina.* Psalm cxxxvii.

By the waters of Babylon we sat down and wept: when we remembered (thee, O) Sion.

As for our harps, we hanged them up: upon the trees that are therein.

For they that led us away captive required of us then a song, and melody, in our heaviness: Sing us one of the songs of Sion.

How shall we sing the Lord's song: in a strange land?

If I forget thee, O Jerusalem: let my right hand forget her cunning.

If I do not remember thee, let my tongue cleave to the roof of my mouth: yea, if I prefer not Jerusalem in my mirth.

Remember the children of Edom, O Lord, in the day of Jerusalem, how they said: Down with it, down with it, even to the ground.

O daughter of Babylon, wasted with misery: yea, happy shall he be that rewardeth thee, as thou hast served us.

Blessed shall he be that taketh thy children, and throweth them against the stones.

Glory be to the Father, and to the Son: and to the Holy Ghost.

As it was in the beginning, is now, and ever shall be: world without end. Amen.

### The Collect.

ALMIGHTY God, which calledst Luke the physician, whose praise is in the Gospel, to be a physician of the soul: it may please thee, by the wholesome medicines of his doctrine, to heal all the diseases of our souls; through thy Son Jesus Christ our Lord.

### The Epistle. 2. Tim. iv.

WATCH thou in all things, suffer afflictions, do the work throughly of an Evangelist, fulfil thine office unto the utmost: be sober. For I am now ready to be offered, and the time of my departing is at hand. I have fought a good fight, I have fulfilled my course, I have kept the faith. From henceforth there is laid up for me a crown of righteousness, which the Lord (that is a righteous Judge) shall give me at that day: not to me only, but unto all them also that love his coming. Do thy diligence that thou mayest come shortly unto me: for Demas hath forsaken me, and loveth this present world, and is departed unto Thessalonica; Crescens is gone to Galacia, Titus unto Dalmacia: only Luke is with me. Take Mark and bring him with thee; for he is profitable unto me for the ministration. And Tychicus have I sent to Ephesus. The cloke that I left at Troada with Carpus, when thou comest, bring with thee; and the books, but specially the parchment. Alexander the coppersmith did me much evil; the Lord reward him according to his deeds: of whom be thou ware also, for he hath greatly withstand our words.

### The Gospel. Luke x.

THE Lord appointed other seventy (and two) also, and sent them two and two before him into every city and place whither he himself would come. Therefore said he unto them, The harvest is great, but the labourers are few: pray ye therefore the Lord of the harvest to send forth labourers into his harvest. Go your ways; behold I send you forth as lambs among wolves. Bear no wallet, neither scrip, nor shoes, and salute no man by the way. Into whatsoever house ye enter, first say, Peace be to this house. And if the son of peace be there, your peace shall rest upon him: if not, it shall return to you again. And in the same house tarry still, eating and drinking such as they give: for the labourer is worthy of his reward.

# Symon and Jude Apostles.

## At the Communion.

*Laudate Dominum.*
Psalm cl.

O PRAISE God in his holiness: praise him in the firmament of his power.

Praise him in his noble acts: praise him according to his excellent greatness.

Praise him in the sound of the trumpet: praise him upon the lute and harp.

Praise him in the cymbals and dance: praise him upon the strings and pipe.

Praise him upon the welltuned cymbals: praise him upon the loud cymbals.

Let every thing that hath breath: praise the Lord.

Glory be to the Father, and to the Son: and to the Holy Ghost.

As it was in the beginning, is now, and ever shall be: world without end. Amen.

### The Collect.

ALMIGHTY God, which hast builded thy congregation upon the foundation of the Apostles and Prophets, Jesu Christ himself being the head corner-stone; Grant us so to be joined together in unity of spirit by their doctrine, that we may be made an holy temple acceptable to thee: through Jesu Christ our Lord.

### The Epistle. Jude i.

JUDAS, the servant of Jesu Christ, the brother of James, to them which are called and sanctified in God the Father, and preserved in Jesu Christ: Mercy unto you, and peace, and love be multiplied. Beloved, when I gave all diligence to write unto you of the common salvation, it was needful for me to write unto you to exhort you that ye should continually labour in the faith which was once given unto the saints. For there are certain ungodly men craftily crept in, of which it was written aforetime unto such judgment. They turn the grace of our God unto wantonness, and deny God, (which is the only Lord,) and our Lord Jesus Christ. My mind is therefore to put you in remembrance, forasmuch as ye once knew this, how that the Lord (after that he had delivered the people out of Egypt) destroyed them which afterward believed not. The angels also which kept not their first estate, but left their own habitation, he hath reserved in everlasting chains under darkness unto the judgment of the great day. Even as Sodom and Gomor, and the cities about them, which in like manner defiled themselves with fornication, and followed strange flesh, are set forth for an example, and suffer the pain of eternal fire. Likewise these being deceived by dreams defile the flesh, despise rulers, and speak evil of them that are in authority.

*The Gospel.* John xv.

THIS command I you, that ye love together. If the world hate you, ye know that it hated me before it hated you. If ye were of the world, the world would love his own: howbeit, because ye are not of the world, but I have chosen you out of the world, therefore the world hateth you. Remember the word that I said unto you, The servant is not greater than the lord: if they have persecuted me, they will also persecute you; if they have kept my saying, they will keep yours also. But all these things will they do unto you for my Name's sake, because they have not known him that sent me. If I had not come and spoken unto them, they should have had no sin: but now have they nothing to cloke their sin withal. He that hateth me hateth my Father also. If I had not done among them the works which none other man did, they should have had no sin; but now have they both seen and hated not only me, but also my Father. But this happeneth that the saying might be fulfilled that is written in their law, They hated me without a cause. But when the Comforter is come, whom I will send unto you from the Father, even the Spirit of truth, (which proceedeth of the Father,) he shall testify of me. And ye shall bear witness also, because ye have been with me from the beginning.

# All Saints' Day.

### Proper Lessons at Matins.

THE FIRST LESSON, Wisdom iii. THE SECOND LESSON, Heb. xi: 32 to xii: 17.

## At the Communion.

*Cantate Domino.*

### Psalm cxlix.

O SING unto the Lord a new song : let the congregation of saints praise him.

Let Israel rejoice in him that made him : and let the children of Sion be joyful in their king.

Let them praise his Name in the dance : let them sing praises unto him with tabret and harp.

For the Lord hath pleasure in his people : and helpeth the meek-hearted.

Let the saints be joyful with glory : let them rejoice in their beds.

Let the praises of God be in their mouth : and a two-edged sword in their hands ;

To be avenged of the heathen : and to rebuke the people.

To bind their kings in chains : and their nobles with links of iron.

That they may be avenged of them, as it is written : Such honour have all his saints.

Glory be to the Father, and to the Son : and to the Holy Ghost.

As it was in the beginning, is now, and ever shall be : world without end. Amen.

### The Collect.

ALMIGHTY God, which hast knit together thy elect in one communion and fellowship, in the mystical body of thy Son Christ our Lord : Grant us grace so to follow thy holy Saints in all virtues and godly living, that we may come to those unspeakable joys, which thou hast prepared for all them that unfeignedly love thee ; through Jesus Christ.

### The Epistle. Rev. vii.

BEHOLD, I John saw another angel ascend from the rising of the sun, which had the seal of the living God ; and he cried with a loud voice to the four angels, (to whom power was given to hurt the earth and the sea,) saying, Hurt not the earth, neither the sea, neither the trees, till we have sealed the servants of our God in their foreheads. And I heard the number of them which were sealed; and there were sealed an C. and xliv. M. of all the tribes of the children of Israel.

Of the tribe of Juda were sealed xii. M.

Of the tribe of Ruben were sealed xii. M.

Of the tribe of Gad were sealed xii. M.

Of the tribe of Aser were sealed xii. M.

Of the tribe of Naptalim were sealed xii. M.

Of the tribe of Manasses were sealed xii. M.

Of the tribe of Symeon were sealed xii. M.

Of the tribe of Levi were sealed xii. M.

Of the tribe of Isachar were sealed xii. M.

Of the tribe of Zabulon were sealed xii. M.

Of the tribe of Joseph were sealed xii. M.

Of the tribe of Benjamin were sealed xii. M.

After this I beheld, and lo, a great multitude, (which no man could number,) of all nations, and people, and tongues, stood before the seat, and before the Lamb, clothed with long white garments, and palms in their hands;

and cried with a loud voice, saying, Salvation be ascribed to him that sitteth upon the seat of our God, and unto the Lamb. And all the angels stood in the compass of the seat, and of the elders, and of the four beasts, and fell before the seat on their faces, and worshipped God, saying, Amen; Blessing, and glory, and wisdom, and thanks, and honour, and power, and might, be unto our God for evermore. Amen.

*The Gospel.* Matt. v.

JESUS, seeing the people, went up into the mountain; and when he was set, his disciples came to him. And after that he had opened his mouth, he taught them, saying, Blessed are the poor in spirit; for theirs is the kingdom of heaven. Blessed are they that mourn: for they shall receive comfort. Blessed are the meek: for they shall receive the inheritance of the earth. Blessed are they which hunger and thirst after righteousness: for they shall be satisfied. Blessed are the merciful: for they shall obtain mercy. Blessed are the pure in heart: for they shall see God. Blessed are the peacemakers: for they shall be called the children of God. Blessed are they which suffer persecution for righteousness' sake: for theirs is the kingdom of heaven. Blessed are ye when men revile you, and persecute you, and shall falsely say all manner of evil sayings against you for my sake. Rejoice, and be glad; for great is your reward in heaven: for so persecuted they the prophets which were before you.

### Proper Lessons at Evensong.

THE FIRST LESSON, Wisdom v.
THE SECOND LESSON, Rev. xix: 1-17.

✠

# THE SUPPER OF THE LORD.

AND

## The Holy Communion,

COMMONLY CALLED

## ✠ The Mass. ✠

So many as intend to be partakers of the holy Communion, shall signify their names to the Curate over night, or else in the morning, afore the beginning of Matins, or immediately after.

And if any of those be an open and notorious evil liver, so that the congregation by him is offended, or have done any wrong to his neighbours by word or deed; the Curate shall call him and advertise him in any wise not to presume to the Lord's Table, until he have openly declared himself to have truly repented and amended his former naughty life, that the congregation may thereby be satisfied, which afore were offended; and that he have recompensed the parties, whom he hath done wrong unto, or at the least be in full purpose so to do, as soon as he conveniently may.

The same order shall the Curate use with those betwixt whom he perceiveth malice and hatred to reign; not suffering them to be partakers of the Lord's Table, until he know them to be reconciled. And if one of the parties so at variance be content to forgive from the bottom of his heart all that the other hath trespassed against him, and to make amends for that he himself hath offended; and the other party will not be persuaded to a godly unity, but remain still in his frowardness and malice: the Minister in that case ought to admit the penitent person to the holy Communion, and not him that is obstinate.

Upon the day, and at the time appointed for the ministration of the holy Communion, the Priest that shall execute the holy ministry, shall put upon him the vesture appointed for that ministration, that is to say, a white Albe plain, with a Vestment or Cope And where there be many Priests, or Deacons, there so many shall be ready to help the Priest in the ministration, as shall be requisite; and shall have upon them likewise the vestures appointed for their ministry, that is to say, Albes with Tunicles. Then shall the Clerks sing in English, for the Office or Introit, (as they call it,) a Psalm appointed for that day.

The Priest standing humbly afore the midst of the Altar, shall say the Lord's Prayer, with this Collect.

ALMIGHTY God, unto whom all hearts be open, and all desires known, and from whom no secrets are hid; Cleanse the thoughts of our hearts by the inspiration of thy Holy Spirit, that we may perfectly love thee, and worthily magnify thy holy Name; through Christ our Lord. Amen.

Then shall he say a Psalm appointed for the Introit; which Psalm ended, the Priest shall say, or else the Clerks shall sing,

iii. Lord have mercy upon us.

iii. Christ have mercy upon us.

iii. Lord have mercy upon us.

Then the Priest, standing at God's board, shall begin,

Glory be to God on high.

*The Clerks.*

And in earth peace, good will towards men.

We praise thee, we bless thee, we worship thee, we glorify thee, we give thanks to thee for thy great glory, O Lord God, heavenly King, God the Father Almighty.

O Lord, the only-begotten Son, Jesu Christ, O Lord God, Lamb of God, Son of the Father, that takest away the sins of the world, have mercy upon us: thou that takest away the sins of the world, receive our prayer.

Thou that sittest at the right hand of God the Father, have mercy upon us; for thou only art holy, thou only art the Lord. Thou only, (O Christ,) with the Holy Ghost, art most high in the glory of God the Father. Amen.

Then the Priest shall turn him to the people, and say,

The Lord be with you.

*The Answer.*

And with thy spirit.

*The Priest.*

Let us pray.

Then shall follow the Collect of the day, with one of these two Collects following. for the king.

ALMIGHTY God, whose kingdom is everlasting, and power infinite; have mercy upon the whole congregation; and so rule the heart of thy chosen servant Edward the Sixth, our king and governor, that he (knowing whose minister he is) may above all things seek thy honour and glory: and that we, his subjects, (duly considering whose authority he hath,) may faithfully serve, honour, and humbly obey him, in thee, and for thee, according to thy blessed word and ordinance; through Jesus Christ our Lord, who with thee and the Holy Ghost liveth and reigneth, ever one God, world without end. Amen.

ALMIGHTY and everlasting God, we be taught by thy holy word, that the hearts of kings are in thy rule and governance, and that thou dost dispose and turn them as it seemeth best to thy godly wisdom: we humbly beseech thee so to dispose and govern the heart of Edward the Sixth, thy servant, our king and governor, that in all his thoughts, words, and works, he may ever seek thy honour and glory, and study to preserve thy people committed to his charge, in wealth, peace, and godliness: Grant this, O merciful Father, for thy dear Son's sake, Jesus Christ our Lord. Amen.

The Collects ended, the Priest, or he that is appointed, shall read the Epistle in a place assigned for the purpose, saying,

THE Epistle of Saint Paul written in the chapter of      to the

The Minister then shall read the Epistle. Immediately after the Epistle ended, the Priest, or one appointed to read the Gospel, shall say,

THE holy Gospel, writen in the      chapter of

The Clerks and people shall answer,

GLORY be to thee, O Lord.

The Priest or Deacon then shall read the Gospel. After the Gospel ended, the Priest shall begin,

I BELIEVE in One God.

The Clerks shall sing the rest.

THE Father Almighty, Maker of heaven and earth, And of all things visible and invisible: And in one Lord Jesu Christ, the only-begotten Son of God, Begotten of his Father before all worlds, God of God, Light of Light, Very God of very God, Begotten, not made, Being of one Substance with the Father, By whom all things were made : Who for us men, and for our salvation, came down from heaven, And was incarnate by the Holy Ghost of the Virgin Mary, And was made man, And was crucified also for us under Pontius Pilate. He suffered and was buried, And the third day he arose again according to the Scriptures, And ascended into heaven, And sitteth at the right hand of the Father. And he shall come again with glory to judge both the quick and the dead.

And I believe in the Holy Ghost, the Lord and Giver of life, Who proceedeth from the Father and the Son, Who with the Father and the Son together is worshipped and glorified, Who spake by the prophets. And I believe one Catholick and Apostolick Church. I acknowledge one Baptism for the remission of sins, And I look for the Resurrection of the dead, And the life of the world to come. Amen.

After the Creed ended, shall follow the Sermon or Homily, or some portion of one of the Homilies, as they shall be hereafter divided : wherein if the people be not exhorted to the worthy receiving of the holy Sacrament of the Body and Blood of our Saviour Christ, then shall the Curate give this exhortation to those that be minded to receive the same.

DEARLY beloved in the Lord, ye that mind to come to the holy Communion of the Body and Blood of our Saviour Christ, must consider what S. Paul writeth to the Corinthians, how he exhorteth all persons diligently to try and examine themselves, before they presume to eat of that Bread and drink of that Cup. For as the benefit is great, if with a truly penitent heart and lively faith we receive that holy Sacrament; (for then we spiritually eat the flesh of Christ, and drink his Blood ; then we dwell in Christ, and Christ in us; we be made one with Christ, and Christ with us;) so is the danger great, if we receive the same unworthily. For then we become guilty of the Body and Blood of Christ our Saviour; we eat and drink our own damnation, not considering the Lord's Body; we kindle God's wrath over us; we provoke him to plague us with divers diseases, and sundry kinds of death. Therefore, if any here be a blasphemer, adulterer, or be in malice, or envy, or in any other grievous crime, (except he be truly sorry therefore, and earnestly minded to leave the same vices, and do trust himself to be reconciled to Almighty God, and in charity with all the world,) let him bewail his sins, and not come to that holy Table, lest after the taking of that most blessed Bread, the devil enter into him, as he did into Judas, to fill him full of all iniquity, and bring him to destruction, both of body and soul. Judge therefore yourselves, (brethren), that ye be not judged of the Lord. Let your mind be without desire to sin; repent you truly for your sins past; have an earnest and lively faith in Christ our Saviour; be in perfect charity with all men; so shall ye be meet partakers of those holy Mysteries. And above all things ye must give most humble and hearty thanks to God the Father, the Son, and the Holy Ghost, for the redemption of the world by the Death and Passion of our Saviour Christ, both God and man; who did humble himself, even to the death upon the Cross, for us, miserable sinners; which lay in darkness and shadow of death, that he might make us the children of God, and exalt us to everlasting life. And to the end that we should alway remember the exceeding love of our Master, and only Saviour, Jesu Christ, thus dying for us, and the innumerable benefits which (by his precious blood-shedding) he hath obtained to us; he hath left in those holy Mysteries, as a pledge of his love, and a continual remembrance of the same, his own blessed Body and precious Blood, for us to feed upon spiritually, to our endless comfort and consolation. To him therefore, with the Father and the Holy Ghost, let us give (as we are most bounden) continual thanks; submitting ourselves wholly to his holy will and pleasure, and studying to serve him in true holiness and righteousness all the days of our life. Amen.

In Cathedral churches, or other places where there is daily Communion, it shall be sufficient to read this exhortation above written once in a month. And in Parish churches, upon the week days, it may be left unsaid.

And if upon the Sunday or Holyday the people be negligent to come to the Communion, then shall the priest earnestly exhort his Parishioners to dispose themselves to the receiving of the holy Communion more diligently, saying these or like words unto them.

Dear friends, and you especially upon whose souls I have cure and charge, on        next I do intend, by God's grace, to offer to all such as shall be godly disposed the most comfortable Sacrament of the Body and Blood of Christ, to be taken of them in the remembrance of his most fruitful and glorious Passion: by the which Passion we have obtained remission of our sins, and be made partakers of the kingdom of heaven; whereof we be assured and ascertained, if we come to the said Sacrament with hearty repentance for our offences, stedfast faith in God's mercy, and earnest mind to obey God's will, and to offend no more. Wherefore our duty is to come to these holy Mysteries with most hearty thanks to be given to Almighty God for his infinite mercy and benefits given and bestowed upon us his unworthy servants, for whom he hath not only given his Body to death, and shed his Blood, but also doth vouchsafe, in a Sacrament and Mystery, to give us his said Body and Blood to feed upon spiritually. The which Sacrament being so divine and holy a thing, and so comfortable to them which receive it worthily, and so dangerous to them that will presume to take the same unworthily: my duty is to exhort you, in the mean season, to consider the greatness of the thing, and to search and examine your own consciences, and that not lightly, nor after the manner of dissimulers with God, but as they which should come to a most godly and heavenly banquet; not to come but in the marriage garment required of God in Scripture; that you may (so much as lieth in you) be found worthy to come to such a Table. The ways and means thereto is,

First, that you be truly repentant of your former evil life; and that you confess with an unfeigned heart to Almighty God, your sins and unkindness towards his Majesty committed, either by will, word, or deed, infirmity or ignorance; and that with inward sorrow and tears you bewail your offences, and require of Almighty God mercy and pardon, promising to him (from the bottom of your hearts) the amendment of your former life. And among all others, I am commanded of God especially to move and exhort you to reconcile yourselves to your neighbours, whom you have offended, or who hath offended you, putting out of your hearts all hatred and malice against them, and to be in love and charity with all the world, and to forgive other as you would that God should forgive you. And if any man have done wrong to any other, let him make satisfaction and due restitution of all lands and goods wrongfully taken away or withholden, before he come to God's board; or at the least be in full mind and purpose so to do, as soon as he is able; or else let him not come to this holy Table, thinking to deceive God, who seeth all men's hearts. For neither the Absolution of the Priest can any thing avail them, nor the receiving of this holy Sacrament doth any thing but increase their damnation. And if there be any of you whose conscience is troubled and grieved in any thing, lacking comfort or counsel, let him come to me, or to some other discreet and learned Priest, taught in the law of God, and confess and open his sin and grief secretly, that he may receive such ghostly counsel, advice, and comfort, that his conscience may be relieved, and that of us (as of the Ministers of God and of the Church) he may receive comfort and Absolution, to the satisfaction of his mind, and avoiding of all scruple and doubtfulness; requiring such as shall be satisfied with a general Confession not to be offended with them that do use, to their further satisfying, the auricular and secret Confession to the Priest; nor those also which think needful or convenient, for the quietness of their own consciences, particularly to open their sins to the Priest, to be offended with them that are satisfied with their humble confession to God, and the general Confession to the Church; but in all things to follow and keep the rule of charity; and every man to be satisfied with his own conscience, not judging other men's minds or consciences; whereas he hath no warrant of God's Word to the same.

*Then shall follow for the Offertory one or more of these sentences of Holy Scripture, to be sung whiles the people do offer; or else one of them to be said by the Minister immediately afore the offering.*

LET your light so shine before men, that they may see your good works, and glorify your Father which is in heaven.—(*Matt.* v.)

Lay not up for yourselves treasure upon the earth, where the rust and moth doth corrupt, and where thieves break through and steal: but lay up for yourselves treasures in heaven, where neither rust nor moth doth corrupt, and where thieves do not break through nor steal.—(*Matt.* vi.)

Whatsoever you would that men should do unto you, even so do you unto them: for this is the law and the prophets.—(*Matt.* vii.)

Not every one that saith unto me, Lord, Lord, shall enter into the kingdom of heaven: but he that doeth the will of my Father which is in heaven.—(*Matt.* vii.)

Zachæus stood forth, and said unto the Lord, Behold, Lord, the half of my goods I give to the poor; and if I have done any wrong to any man, I restore fourfold.—(*Luke* xix.)

Who goeth a warfare at any time at his own cost? who planteth a vineyard, and eateth not of the fruit thereof? or who feedeth a flock, and eateth not of the milk of the flock?—(1. *Cor.* ix.)

If we have sown unto you spiritual things, is it a great matter if we shall reap your worldly things?—(1. *Cor.* ix.)

Do ye not know, that they which minister about holy things live of the sacrifice? they which wait of the altar are partakers with the altar? Even so hath the Lord also ordained that they which preach the gospel should live of the gospel.—(1. *Cor.* ix.)

He which soweth little shall reap little; and he that soweth plenteously shall reap plenteously. Let every man do according as he is disposed in his heart; not grudgingly or of necessity: for God loveth a cheerful giver.—(2. *Cor.* ix.)

Let him that is taught in the word minister unto him that teacheth in all good things. Be not deceived; God is not mocked: for whatsoever a man soweth, that shall he reap.—(*Gal.* vi.)

While we have time, let us do good unto all men, and specially unto them which are of the household of faith. —(*Gal.* vi.)

Godliness is great riches, if a man be contented with that he hath. For we brought nothing into the world, neither may we carry any thing out.—(1. *Tim.* vi.)

Charge them which are rich in this world, that they be ready to give, and glad to distribute; laying up in store for themselves a good foundation against the time to come, that they may attain eternal live.—(1. *Tim.* vi.)

God is not unrighteous that he will forget your works and labour that proceedeth of love, which love ye have shewed for his Name's sake, which have ministered unto the saints and yet do minister.—(*Heb.* vi.)

To do good and to distribute forget not, for with such sacrifices God is pleased.—(*Heb.* xiii.)

Whoso hath this world's good, and seeth his brother have need, and shutteth up his compassion from him, how dwelleth the love of God in him?—(1. *John* iii.)

Give alms of thy goods, and turn never thy face from any poor man, and then the face of the Lord shall not be turned away from thee.— (*Tobit* iv.)

Be merciful after thy power. If thou hast much, give plenteously; if thou hast little, do thy diligence gladly to give of that little; for so gatherest thou thyself a good reward in the day of necessity.—(*Tobit* iv.)

He that hath pity upon the poor lendeth unto the Lord; and look, what he layeth out shall be paid him again.— (*Prov.* xix.)

Blessed be the man that provideth for the sick and needy; the Lord shall deliver him in the time of trouble.— (*Psalm* xli.)

Where there be Clerks, they shall sing one or many of the sentences above written, according to the length and shortness of the time that the people be offering. In the mean time, whiles the Clerks do sing the Offertory, so many as are disposed shall offer to the poor men's box every one according to his ability and charitable mind. And at the offering days appointed, every man and woman shall pay to the Curate the due and accustomed offerings.

Then so many as shall be partakers of the Holy Communion shall tarry still in the Quire, or in some convenient place nigh the Quire, the men on the one side, and the women on the other side. All other (that mind not to receive the said Holy Communion) shall depart out of the Quire, except the Ministers and Clerks.

Then shall the Minister take so much Bread and Wine as shall suffice for the persons appointed to receive the Holy Communion, laying the Bread upon the Corporas, or else in the Paten, or in some other comely thing prepared for that purpose: and putting the Wine into the Chalice, or else in some fair or convenient cup prepared for that use, (if the Chalice will not serve,) putting thereto a little pure and clean Water, and setting both the Bread and Wine upon the Altar. Then the Priest shall say,

The Lord be with you.

*Answer.*

And with thy spirit.

*Priest.*

Lift up your hearts.

*Answer.*

We lift them up unto the Lord.

*Priest.*

Let us give thanks to our Lord God.

*Answer.*

It is meet and right so to do.

*The Priest.*

It is very meet, right, and our bounden duty, that we should at all times and in all places give thanks to thee, O Lord, holy Father,

Almighty Everlasting God.

Here shall follow the proper Preface, according to the time, (if there be any specially appointed,) or else immediately shall follow,

Therefore with Angels, etc.

## PROPER PREFACES.

### Upon Christmas Day.

BECAUSE thou diddest give Jesus Christ thine only Son to be born as this day for us; who, by the operation of the Holy Ghost, was made very man of the substance of the Virgin Mary his Mother; and that without spot of sin, to make us clean from all sin. Therefore etc.

### Upon Easter Day.

BUT chiefly are we bound to praise thee for the glorious Resurrection of thy Son Jesus Christ our Lord: for he is the very Paschal Lamb, which was offered for us, and hath taken away the sin of the world; who by his Death hath destroyed death, and by his rising to life again hath restored to us everlasting Life. Therefore etc.

### Upon the Ascension Day.

THROUGH thy most dear beloved Son Jesus Christ our Lord; who, after his most glorious Resurrection, manifestly appeared to all his disciples, and in their sight ascended up into Heaven to prepare a place for us; that where he is, thither might we also ascend, and reign with him in glory. Therefore etc.

### Upon Whitsunday.

THROUGH Jesus Christ our Lord; according to whose most true promise the Holy Ghost came down this day from Heaven with a sudden great sound, as it had been a mighty wind, in the likeness of fiery tongues, lighting upon the Apostles, to teach them, and to lead them to all truth, giving them both the gift of divers languages, and also boldness with fervent zeal constantly to preach the gospel unto all nations; whereby we are brought out of darkness and error into the clear light and true knowledge of thee, and of thy Son Jesus Christ. Therefore, etc.

Upon the Feast of the Trinity.

It is very meet, right, and our bounden duty, that we should at all times, and in all places, give thanks to thee, O Lord, Almighty, Everlasting God, which art One God, One Lord; not one only Person, but three Persons in one Substance. For that which we believe of the Glory of the Father, the same we believe of the Son, and of the Holy Ghost, without any difference or inequality. Whom the angels etc.

After which Preface shall follow immediately,

Therefore with Angels and Archangels, and with all the holy company of Heaven, we laud and magnify thy glorious Name: evermore praising thee, and saying,

Holy, holy, holy, Lord God of hosts, Heaven and earth are full of thy glory. Osanna in the highest. Blessed is he that cometh in the Name of the Lord. Glory be to thee, O Lord, in the highest.

This the Clerks shall also sing.

When the Clerks have done singing, then shall the Priest or Deacon turn him to the people, and say,

Let us pray for the whole state of Christ's Church.

Then the Priest, turning him to the Altar, shall say or sing, plainly and distinctly, this prayer following:

Almighty and everliving God, which by thy holy Apostle hast taught us to make prayers and supplications, and to give thanks for all men; We humbly beseech thee most mercifully to receive these our prayers, which we offer unto thy divine Majesty; beseeching thee to inspire continually the universal Church with the spirit of truth, unity, and concord: and grant, that all they that do confess thy holy Name may agree in the truth of thy holy Word, and live in unity and godly love.

Specially we beseech thee to save and defend thy servant Edward our king; that under him we may be godly and quietly governed: and grant unto his whole Council, and to all that be put in authority under him, that they may truly and indifferently minister justice, to the punishment of wickedness and vice, and to the maintenance of God's true religion and virtue.

Give grace (O heavenly Father) to all Bishops, Pastors, and Curates, that they may both by their life and doctrine set forth thy true and lively word, and rightly and duly administer thy holy Sacraments. And to all ·thy people give thy heavenly grace; that with meek heart and due reverence, they may hear and receive thy holy Word, truly serving thee in holiness and righteousness all the days of their life. And we most humbly beseech thee of thy goodness (O Lord) to comfort and succour all them, which in this transitory life be in trouble, sorrow, need, sickness, or any other adversity. And especially we commend unto thy merciful goodness this congregation, which is here assembled in thy Name, to celebrate the commemoration of the most glorious Death of thy Son. And here we do give unto thee most high praise, and hearty thanks, for the wonderful grace and virtue declared in all thy Saints, from the beginning of the world; and chiefly in the glorious and most blessed Virgin Mary, Mother of thy Son Jesu Christ our Lord and God; and in the holy Patriarchs, Prophets, Apostles, and Martyrs, whose examples (O Lord) and stedfastness in thy faith, and keeping thy holy commandments, grant us to follow. We commend unto thy mercy (O Lord) all other thy servants, which are departed hence from us with the sign of faith, and now do rest in the sleep of peace: grant unto them, we beseech thee, thy mercy and everlasting peace; and that, at the day of the general Resurrection, we and all they which be of the Mystical Body of thy Son, may altogether be set on his right hand, and hear that his most joyful voice: Come unto me, O ye that be blessed of my Father, and possess the kingdom, which is prepared for you from the beginning of the world. Grant this, O Father, for Jesus Christ's sake, our only Mediator and Advocate.

O God, heavenly Father, which of thy tender mercy diddest give thine only Son Jesu Christ to suffer death upon the Cross for our redemption; who made there (by his one oblation once offered) a full, perfect, and sufficient sacrifice, oblation, and satisfaction, for the sins of the whole world; and did institute, and in his holy Gospel command us to celebrate a perpetual memory of that his precious Death, until his coming again:

Hear us (O merciful Father) we beseech

thee; and with thy Holy Spirit and word vouchsafe to bl⚒ess and sanc⚒tify these thy gifts and creatures of Bread and Wine, that they may be unto us the Body and Blood of thy most dearly beloved Son Jesus Christ: Who, in the same night that Here the Priest must take the Bread into his hands. he was betrayed, took Bread; and when he had blessed, and given thanks, he brake it, and gave it to his disciples, saying, Take, eat; this is My Body which is given for you: Do this in remembrance of Me.

Likewise after supper he Here the Priest shall take the Cup into his hands. took the Cup, and when he had given thanks, he gave it to them, saying, Drink ye all of this; for this is My Blood of the new Testament, which is shed for you and for many for remission of sins: Do this, as oft as you shall drink it, in remembrance of Me.

These words before rehearsed are to be said, turning still to the Altar, without any elevation or shewing the Sacrament to the people.

WHEREFORE, O Lord and heavenly Father, according to the institution of thy dearly beloved Son our Saviour Jesu Christ, we thy humble servants do celebrate and make here before thy divine Majesty, with these thy holy gifts, the memorial which thy Son hath willed us to make: having in remembrance his blessed Passion, mighty Resurrection, and glorious Ascension: rendering unto thee most hearty thanks for the innumberable benefits procured unto us by the same; entirely desiring thy fatherly goodness mercifully to accept this our Sacrifice of praise and thanksgiving; most humbly beseeching thee to grant, that by the Merits and Death of thy Son Jesus Christ, and through faith in his Blood, we and all thy whole Church may obtain remission of our sins, and all other benefits of his Passion. And here we offer and present unto thee (O Lord) ourself, our souls and bodies, to be a reasonable, holy, and lively sacrifice unto thee; humbly beseeching thee, that whosoever shall be partakers of this holy Communion may worthily receive the most precious Body and Blood of thy Son Jesus Christ; and be fulfilled with thy grace and heavenly benediction, and made one body with thy Son Jesu Christ, that he may dwell in them, and they in him. And although we be unworthy (through our manifold sins) to offer unto thee any Sacrifice, yet we beseech thee to accept this our bounden duty and service, and command these our prayers and supplications, by the ministry of thy holy Angels, to be brought up into thy holy Tabernacle before the sight of thy divine Majesty; not weighing our merits, but pardoning our offences, through Christ our Lord; by whom, and with whom, in the unity of the Holy Ghost, all honour and glory be unto thee, O Father Almighty, world without end. Amen.

Let us pray.

As our Saviour Christ hath commanded and taught us, we are bold to say: Our Father, which art in heaven, hallowed be thy Name. Thy kingdom come. Thy will be done in earth, as it is in heaven. Give us this day our daily bread. And forgive us our trespasses, as we forgive them that trespass against us. And lead us not into temptation.

*The Answer.*

But deliver us from evil. Amen.

Then shall the Priest say,

The peace of the Lord be alway with you.

*The Clerks.*

And with thy spirit.

*The Priest.*

Christ our Paschal Lamb is offered up for us once for all, when he bare our sins on his Body upon the Cross; for he is the very Lamb of God that taketh away the sins of the world: wherefore let us keep a joyful and holy feast with the Lord.

Here the Priest shall turn him toward those that come to the holy Communion, and shall say,

You that do truly and earnestly repent you of your sins to Almighty God, and be in love and charity with your neighbours, and intend to lead a new life, following the commandments of God, and walking from henceforth in his holy ways; Draw near, and take this holy Sacrament to your comfort; make your humble confession to Almighty God, and to his holy Church here gathered together in his Name, meekly kneeling upon your knees.

Then shall this general Confession be made, in the name of all those that are minded to receive the holy Communion, either by one of them, or else by one of the Ministers, or by the Priest himself, all kneeling humbly upon their knees.

ALMIGHTY God, Father of

our Lord Jesus Christ, Maker of all things, Judge of all men; we knowledge and bewail our manifold sins and wickedness, which we, from time to time, most grievously have committed, by thought, word, and deed, against thy divine Majesty, provoking most justly thy wrath and indignation against us. We do earnestly repent, and be heartily sorry for these our misdoings; the remembrance of them is grievous unto us; the burthen of them is intolerable. Have mercy upon us, have mercy upon us, most merciful Father; for thy Son our Lord Jesus Christ's sake, forgive us all that is past; and grant that we may ever hereafter serve and please thee in newness of life, to the honour and glory of thy Name; through Jesus Christ our Lord.

Then shall the Priest stand up, and turning himself to the people, say thus:

ALMIGHTY God, our heavenly Father, who of his great mercy hath promised forgiveness of sins to all them which with hearty repentance and true faith turn unto him; Have mercy upon you; pardon and deliver you from all your sins; confirm and strengthen you in all good-

ness; and bring you to everlasting life; through Jesus Christ our Lord. Amen.

Then shall the Priest also say,

Hear what comfortable words our Saviour Christ saith to all that truly turn to him.

COME unto me all that travail, and be heavy laden, and I shall refresh you. So God loved the world, that he gave his only-begotten Son, to the end that all that believe in him should not perish, but have life everlasting.

Hear also what Saint Paul saith.

This is a true saying, and worthy of all men to be received, that Jesus Christ came into this world to save sinners.

Hear also what Saint John saith.

If 'any man sin, we have an Advocate with the Father, Jesus Christ the righteous; and he is the propitiation for our sins.

Then shall the Priest, turning him to God's board, kneel down, and say in the name of all them that shall receive the Communion, this prayer following:

WE do not presume to come to this thy Table (O merciful Lord) trusting in our own righteousness, but in thy manifold and great mercies: We be not worthy so much as to gather up the crumbs under thy Table: but thou art the same Lord whose property is always to have mercy: Grant us therefore (gracious Lord) so to eat the flesh of thy dear Son Jesus Christ, and to drink his Blood, in these holy Mysteries, that we may continually dwell in him, and he in us, that our sinful bodies may be made clean by his Body, and our souls washed through his most precious Blood. Amen.

Then shall the Priest first receive the Communion in both kinds himself, and next deliver it to other Ministers, if any be there present, (that they may be ready to help the chief Minister,) and after to the people.

And when he delivereth the Sacrament of the Body of Christ, he shall say to every one these words:

The Body of our Lord Jesus Christ, which was given for thee, preserve thy body and soul unto everlasting life.

And the Minister delivering the Sacrament of the Blood, and giving every one to drink once, and no more, shall say,

The Blood of our Lord Jesus Christ, which was shed for thee, preserve thy body and soul unto everlasting live.

If there be a Deacon or other Priest, then shall he follow with the Chalice; and as the Priest ministereth the Sacrament of the Body, so shall he (for more expedition) minister the Sacrament of the Blood, in form before written.

In the Communion time the Clerks shall sing.

ii. O Lamb of God, that takest away the sins of the world: Have mercy upon us.

O Lamb of God, that takest away the sins of the world: Grant us thy peace.

Beginning so soon as the Priest doth receive the holy Communion: and when the Communion is ended, then shall the Clerks sing the post-Communion.

Sentences of Holy Scripture to be said or sung, every day one, after the holy Communion, called the post-Communion.

If any man will follow me, let him forsake himself, and take up his cross and follow me.—(*Matt.* xvi.)

Whosoever shall endure unto the end, he shall be saved.—(*Mark* xiii.)

Praised be the Lord God of Israel; for he hath visited and redeemed his people. Therefore let us serve him all the days of our life, in holiness and righteousness accepted before him.—(*Luke* i.)

Happy are those servants whom the Lord (when he cometh) shall find waking. —(*Luke* xii.)

Be ye ready, for the Son of

Man will come at an hour when ye think not.

The servant that knoweth his master's will, and hath not prepared himself, neither hath done according to his will, shall be beaten with many stripes.—(*Luke* xii.)

The hour cometh, and now it is, when true worshippers shall worship the Father in spirit and truth.—(*John* iv.)

Behold, thou art m a d e whole; sin no more, lest any w o r s e thing happen u n t o thee.—(*John* v.)

If ye shall continue in my word, then are ye my very disciples; and ye shall know the truth, and the truth shall make you free.—(*John* viii.)

While ye have light, believe on the light, that ye may be the children of light.—(*John* xii.)

He that hath my commandments, and keepeth them, the same is he that loveth me.—(*John* xiv.)

If any man love me, he will keep my word; and my Father will love him, and we will come unto him, and dwell with him.—(*John* xiv.)

If ye shall bide in me, and my word shall abide in you, ye shall ask what ye will, and it shall be done to you.—(*John* xv.)

Herein is my Father glori-fied, that ye bear much fruit, and become my disciples.—(*John* xv.)

This is my commandment. that you love together, as I have loved you.—(*John* xv.)

If God be on our side, who can be against us? which did not spare his own Son, but gave him for us all.—(*Rom.* viii.)

Who shall lay any thing to the charge of God's chosen? it is God that justifieth; who is he that can condemn?—(*Rom.* viii.)

The night is past, and the day is at hand; let us therefore cast away the deeds of darkness, and put on t h e armour of light.-(*Rom.* xiii.)

Christ Jesus is made of God unto us wisdom, and righteousness, and sanctifying, and redemption: that (according as it is written) He which rejoiceth should rejoice in the Lord.—(1. *Cor.* i.)

Know ye not that ye are the temple of God, and that the Spirit of God dwelleth in you? If any man defile the temple of God, him shall God destroy.—(1. *Cor.* iii.)

Ye are dearly b o u g h t; therefore glorify God in your bodies, and in your spirits, for they belong to God.—(1. *Cor.* vi.)

Be you followers of God, as dear children; and walk in love, even as Christ loved us, and gave himself for us an offering and a sacrifice of a sweet savour to God.— (*Eph.* v.)

Then the Priest shall give thanks to God, in the name of all them that have communicated, turning him first to the people and saying,

The Lord be with you.

*The Answer.*

And with thy spirit.

*The Priest.*

Let us pray.

ALMIGHTY and everliving God, we most heartily thank thee, for that thou hast vouchsafed to feed us in these holy Mysteries, with the spiritual food of the most precious Body and Blood of thy Son our Saviour Jesus Christ; and hast assured us (duly receiving the same) of thy favour and goodness toward us; and that we be very members incorporate in thy Mystical Body, which is the blessed company of all faithful people, and heirs through hope of thy everlasting kingdom, by the merits of the most precious Death and Passion of thy dear Son. We therefore most humbly beseech

thee, O heavenly Father, so to assist us with thy grace, that we may continue in that holy fellowship, and do all such good works us as thou hast prepared for us to walk in; through Jesus Christ our Lord, to whom, with thee and the Holy Ghost, be all honour and glory, world without end.

Then the Priest, turning him to the people, shall let them depart with this blessing:

THE peace of God (which passeth all understanding) keep your hearts and minds in the knowledge and love of God, and of his Son Jesus Christ our Lord. And the blessing of God Almighty, the Father, the Son, and the Holy Ghost, be amongst you, and remain with you alway.

Then the people shall answer,

Amen.

Where there are no Clerks, there the Priest shall say all things appointed here for them to sing.

When the holy Communion is celebrate on the workday, or in private houses, then may be omitted the Gloria in excelsis, the Creed, the Homily, and the exhortation, beginning,

Dearly beloved, etc.

Collects to be said after the Offertory, when there is no Communion, every such day one.

ASSIST us mercifully, O Lord, in these our supplications and prayers, and dispose the way of thy servants toward the attainment of everlasting salvation; that, among all the changes and chances of this mortal life, they may ever be defended by thy most gracious and ready help; through Christ our Lord. Amen.

O ALMIGHTY Lord, and everliving God, vouchsafe, we beseech thee, to direct, sanctify, and govern, both our hearts and bodies, in the ways of thy laws, and in the works of thy commandments; that through thy most mighty protection, both here and ever, we may be preserved in body and soul; through our Lord and Saviour Jesus Christ. Amen.

GRANT, we beseech thee, Almighty God, that the words which we have heard this day with our outward ears, may through thy grace be so grafted inwardly in our hearts, that they may bring forth in us the fruit of good living, to the honour and praise of thy Name; through Jesus Christ our Lord. Amen.

PREVENT us, O Lord, in all our doings with thy most gracious favour, and further us with thy continual help; that in all our works begun, continued, and ended in thee, we may glorify thy holy Name, and finally by thy mercy obtain everlasting life; through etc.

ALMIGHTY God, the fountain of all wisdom, which knowest our necessities before we ask, and our ignorance in asking; We beseech thee to have compassion upon our infirmities; and those things, which for our unworthiness we dare not, and for our blindness we cannot ask, vouchsafe to give us, for the worthiness of thy Son Jesu Christ our Lord. Amen.

ALMIGHTY God, which hast promised to hear the petitions of them that ask in thy Son's Name; we beseech thee mercifully to incline thine ears to us that have made now our prayers and supplications unto thee; and grant that those things which we have faithfully asked according to thy will, may effectually be obtained, to the relief of our necessity, and to the setting forth of thy glory; through Jesus Christ our Lord.

For rain.

O GOD, heavenly Father, which by thy Son Jesu Christ hast promised to all them that seek thy kingdom, and the righteousness thereof, all things necessary to the bodily sustenance; Send us (we beseech thee) in this our necessity, such moderate rain and showers, that we may receive the fruits of the earth to our comfort and to thy honour; through Jesus Christ our Lord.

### For fair weather.

O LORD God, which for the sin of man, didst once drown all the world, except eight persons, and afterward, of thy great mercy, didst promise never to destroy it so again; We humbly beseech thee, that although we for our iniquities have worthily deserved this plague of rain and waters, yet, upon our true repentance, thou wilt send us such weather whereby we may receive the fruits of the earth in due season, and learn both by thy punishment to amend our lives, and by the granting of our petition, to give thee praise and glory; through Jesu Christ our Lord.

Upon Wednesdays and Fridays the English Litany shall be said or sung in all places, after such form as is appointed by the king's majesty's Injunctions; or as is or shall be otherwise appointed by his Highness. And though there be none to communicate with the Priest, yet these days (after the Litany ended) the Priest shall put upon him a plain Albe or Surplice, with a Cope, and say all things at the Altar, (appoiuted to be said at the celebration of the Lord's Supper,) until after the Offertory: And then shall add one or two of the Collects afore written, as occasion shall serve, by his discretion. And then, turning him to the people, shall let them depart with the accustomed Blessing.

And the same order shall be used all other days, whensoever the people be customably assembled to pray in the Church, and none disposed to communicate with the Priest.

Likewise in Chapels annexed, and all other places, there shall be no celebration of the Lord's Supper, except there be some to communicate with the Priest. And in such Chapels annexed, where the people hath not been accustomed to pay any holy Bread, there they must either make some charitable provision for the bearing of the charges of the Communion, or else (for receiving of the same) resort to their Parish Church.

For avoiding of all matters and occasion of dissension, it is meet that the Bread prepared for the Communion be made through all this Realm after one sort and fashion; that is to say, unleavened, and round, as it was afore, but without all manner of print, and something more larger and thicker than it was, so that it may be aptly divided in divers pieces; and every one shall be divided in two pieces at the least, or more, by the discretion of the Minister, and so distributed. And men must not think less to be received in part than in the whole, but in each of them the whole Body of our Saviour Jesu Christ.

And forsomuch as the Pastors and Curates within this Realm shall continually find at their costs and charges in their Cures, sufficient Bread and Wine for the Holy Communion, (as oft as their Parishioners shall be disposed for their spiritual comfort to receive the same,) it is therefore ordered, that in recompense of such costs and charges the Parishioners of every Parish shall offer every Sunday, at the time of the Offertory, the just value and price of the holy loaf, (with all such money and other things as were wont to be offered with the same,) to the use of their Pastors and Curates, and that in such order and course as they were wont to find and pay the said holy loaf.

Also, that the receiving of the Sacrament of the blessed Body and Blood of Christ may be most agreeable to the institution thereof, and to the usage of the Primitive Church ; in all Cathedral and Collegiate Churches there shall always some communicate with the Priest that ministereth. And that the same may be also observed every where abroad in the country, some one at the least of that house in every Parish, to whom by course, after the ordinance herein made, it appertaineth to offer for the charges of the Communion, or some other whom they shall provide to offer for them, shall receive the holy Communion with the Priest : the which may be the better done, for that they know before when their course cometh, and may therefore dispose themselves to the worthy receiving of the Sacrament. And with him or them who doth so offer the charges of the Communion, all other who be then godly disposed thereunto, shall likewise receive the Communion. And by this means the Minister, having always some to communicate with him, may accordingly solemnize so high and holy Mysteries with all the Suffrages and due order appointed for the same. And the Priest on the week day shall forbear to celebrate the Communion, except he have some that will communicate with him.

Furthermore, every man and woman to be bound to hear and be at the Divine Service, in the Parish Church where they be resident, and there with devout prayer, or godly silence and meditation, to occupy themselves ; there to pay their Duties, to communicate once in the year at the least, and there to receive and take all other Sacraments and Rites in this Book appointed. And whosoever willingly, upon no just cause, doth absent themselves, or doth ungodly in the Parish Church occupy themselves ; upon proof thereof, by the Ecclesiastical laws of the Realm to be excommunicate, or suffer other punishment, as shall to the Ecclesiastical Judge (according to his discretion) seem convenient.

And although it be read in ancient writers that the people many years past received at the Priest's hands the Sacrament of the Body of Christ in their own hands, and no commandment of Christ to the contrary ; yet forasmuch as they many times conveyed the same secretly away, kept it with them, and diversely abused it to superstition and wickedness : lest any such thing hereafter should be attempted, and that an uniformity might be used throughout the whole Realm, it is thought convenient the people commonly receive the Sacrament of Christ's Body in their mouths, at the Priest's hand.

# The Litany and Suffrages.

O God the Father, of heaven: have mercy upon us miserable sinners.

*O God the Father, of heaven: have mercy upon us miserable sinners.*

O God the Son, Redeemer of the world: have mercy upon us miserable sinners.

*O God the Son, Redeemer of the world: have mercy upon us miserable sinners.*

O God, the Holy Ghost, proceeding from the Father and the Son: have mercy upon us miserable sinners.

*O God, the Holy Ghost, proceeding from the Father and the Son: have mercy upon us miserable sinners.*

O holy, blessed, and glorious Trinity, three Persons and one God: have mercy upon us miserable sinners.

*O holy, blessed, and glorious Trinity, three Persons and one God: have mercy upon us miserable sinners.*

Remember not, Lord, our offences, nor the offences of our forefathers; neither take thou vengeance of our sins: spare us, good Lord, spare thy people, whom thou hast redeemed with thy most precious Blood, and be not angry with us forever.

*Spare us, good Lord.*

From all evil and mischief; from sin, from the crafts and assaults of the devil; from thy wrath, and from everlasting damnation,

*Good Lord, deliver us.*

From blindness of heart; from pride, vainglory, and hypocrisy; from envy, hatred, and malice, and all uncharitableness,

*Good Lord, deliver us.*

From fornication, and all other deadly sin; and from all the deceits of the world, the flesh, and the devil,

*Good Lord, deliver us.*

From lightning and tempest; from plague, pestilence, and famine; from battle and murther, and from sudden death,

*Good Lord, deliver us.*

From all sedition and privy conspiracy: from the tyranny of the Bishop of Rome, and all his detestable enormities; from all false doctrine and heresy; f r o m hardness of heart, and contempt of thy word and commandment,

*Good Lord, deliver us.*

By the mystery of thy holy Incarnation; by thy holy Nativity and Circumcision; by thy Baptism, Fasting, and Temptation,

*Good Lord, deliver us.*

By thine Agony and bloody Sweat, by thy Cross and Passion; by thy precious Death and Burial; by thy glorious Resurrection and Ascension; by the coming of the Holy Ghost,

*Good Lord, deliver us.*

In all time of our tribulation; in all time of our wealth; in the hour of death, in the day of judgment,

*Good Lord, deliver us.*

We sinners do beseech thee to hear us (O Lord God;) and that it may please thee to rule and govern thy holy Church universal in the right way;

*We beseech thee to hear us, good Lord.*

That it may please thee to keep Edward the vi., thy servant our king and governor;

*We beseech thee to hear us, good Lord.*

That it may please thee to rule his heart in thy faith, fear, and love, that he may always have affiance in thee, and ever seek thy honour and glory;

*We beseech thee to hear us, good Lord.*

That it may please thee to be his defender and keeper, giving him the victory over all his enemies;

*We beseech thee to hear us, good Lord.*

That it may please thee to illuminate all Bishops, pastors, and ministers of the Church with true knowledge and understanding of t h y word; and that both by their preaching and living they may set it forth, and shew it accordingly;

*We beseech thee to hear us, good Lord.*

That it may please thee to endue the lords of the Council, and all the nobility, with grace, wisdom, and understanding;

*We beseech thee to hear us, good Lord.*

That it may please thee to bless and keep the magistrates, giving them grace to execute justice, and to maintain truth;

*We beseech thee to hear us, good Lord.*

That it may please thee to bless and keep all thy people;

*We beseech thee to hear us, good Lord.*

That it may please thee to give to all nations unity, peace, and concord:

*We beseech thee to hear us, good Lord.*

That it may please thee to give us an heart to love and dread thee, and diligently to live after thy commandments;

*We beseech thee to hear us, good Lord.*

That it may please thee to give all thy people increase of grace to hear meekly thy word, and to receive it with pure affection, and to bring forth the fruits of the Spirit;

*We beseech thee to hear us, good Lord.*

That it may please thee to bring into the way of truth all such as have erred, and are deceived;

*We beseech thee to hear us, good Lord.*

That it may please thee to strengthen such as do stand; and to comfort and help the weak-hearted; and to raise up them that fall; and finally to beat down Sathan under our feet.

*We beseech thee to hear us, good Lord.*

That it may please thee to succour, help, and comfort all that be in danger, necessity, and tribulation;

*We beseech thee to hear us, good Lord.*

That it may please thee to preserve all that travel by land or by water, all women labouring of child, all sick persons, and young children; and to shew thy pity upon all prisoners and captives;

*We beseech thee to hear us, good Lord.*

That it may please thee to defend and provide for the fatherless children, and widows, and all that be desolate and oppressed;

*We beseech thee to hear us, good Lord.*

That it may please thee to have mercy upon all men;

*We beseech thee to hear us, good Lord.*

That it may please thee to forgive our enemies, persecutors, and slanderers, and to turn their hearts;

*We beseech thee to hear us, good Lord.*

That it may please thee to give and preserve to our use the kindly fruits of the earth, so as in due time we may enjoy them;

*We beseech thee to hear us, good Lord.*

That it may please thee to give us true repentance; to forgive us all our sins, negligences, and ignorances; and to endue us with the grace of thy holy Spirit to amend our lives according to thy holy word;

*We beseech thee to hear us, good Lord.*

Son of God: we beseech thee to hear us.

*Son of God: we beseech thee to hear us.*

O Lamb of God: that takest away the sins of the world;

*Grant us thy peace.*

O Lamb of God; that takest away the sins of the world;

*Have mercy upon us.*

O Christ, hear us.

*O Christ, hear us.*

Lord, have mercy upon us.

*Lord, have mercy upon us.*

Christ, have mercy upon us.

*Christ, have mercy upon us.*

Lord, have mercy upon us.

*Lord, have mercy upon us.*

Our Father, which art in heaven.

With the residue of the *Pater noster.*

And lead us not into temptation.

*But deliver us from evil. Amen.*

The Versicle.

O Lord, deal not with us after our sins.

The Answer.

*Neither reward us after our iniquities.*

Let us pray.

O GOD, merciful Father, that despisest not the sighing of a contrite heart, nor the desire of such as be sorrowful; Mercifully assist our prayers that we make before thee in all our troubles and adversities, whensoever they oppress us; and graciously hear us, that those evils, which the craft and subtilty of the devil or man worketh against us, be brought to nought; and by the providence of thy goodness they may be dispersed; that we thy servants, being hurt by no persecutions, may evermore give thanks unto thee in thy holy Church; through Jesu Christ our Lord.

*O Lord, arise, help us, and deliver us for thy Name's sake.*

O GOD, we have heard with our ears, and our fathers have declared unto us, the noble works that thou diddest in their days, and in the old time before them.

*O Lord, arise, help us, and deliver us for thy honour.*

Glory be to the Father, and to the Son: and to the Holy Ghost.

As it was in the beginning, is now, and ever shall be: world without end. Amen.

From our enemies defend us, O Christ.

*Graciously look upon our afflictions.*

Pitifully behold the sorrows of our heart.

*Mercifully forgive the sins of thy people.*

Favourably with mercy hear our prayers.

*O Son of David, have mercy upon us.*

Both now and ever vouchsafe to hear us, Christ.

*Graciously hear us, O Christ.*

*Graciously hear us, O Lord Christ.*

The Versicle.

O Lord, let thy mercy be shewed upon us.

The Answer.

As we do put our trust in thee.

Let us pray.

WE humbly beseech thee, O Father, mercifully to look upon our infirmities; and for the glory of thy Name' sake turn from us all those evils that we most righteously have deserved; and grant that in all our troubles we may put our whole trust and confidence in thy mercy, and evermore serve thee in pureness of living, to thy honour and glory; through our only Mediator and Advocate Jesus Christ our Lord. Amen.

ALMIGHTY God, which hast given us grace at this time with one accord to make our common supplications unto thee; and dost promise, that when two or three be gathered in thy Name thou wilt grant their requests; Fulfil now, O Lord, the desires and petitions of thy servants, as may be most expedient for them; granting us in this world knowledge of thy truth, and in the world to come life everlasting. Amen.

✠

# OF THE

# Administration of Public Baptism

## TO BE USED IN THE CHURCH.

IT appeareth by ancient writers, that the Sacrament of Baptism in the old time was not commonly ministered but at two times in the year, at Easter and Whitsuntide : at which times it was openly ministered in the presence of all the congregation : Which custom, (now being grown out of use,) although it cannot for many considerations be well restored again, yet it is thought good to follow the same as near as conveniently may be. Wherefore the people are to be admonished, that it is most convenient that Baptism should not be ministered but upon Sundays and other Holy-days, when the most number of people may come together : as well for that the congregation there present may testify the receiving of them that be newly baptized into the number of Christ's Church ; as also because in the Baptism of infants every man present may be put in remembrance of his own profession made to God in his Baptism. For which cause also it is expedient that Baptism be ministered in the English tongue. Nevertheless (if necessity so require) children ought at all times be baptized, either at the Church or else at home.

## Public Baptism.

When there are children to be baptized upon the Sunday or Holy-day, the parents shall give knowledge overnight, or in morning afore the beginning of Matins, to the Curate. And then the Godfathers, Godmothers, and people, with the children, must be ready at the Church door, either immediately afore the last Canticle at Matins, or else immediately afore the last Canticle at Evensong, as the Curate by his discretion shall appoint. And then, standing there, the Priest shall ask whether the children be baptized or no. If they answer, No, then shall the Priest say thus :

DEAR beloved, forasmuch as all men be conceived and born in sin, and that no man born in sin can enter into the kingdom of God, (except he be regenerate and born anew of Water and the Holy Ghost;) I beseech you to call upon God the Father, through our Lord Jesus Christ, that of his bounteous mercy he will grant to these children that thing which by nature they cannot have; that is to say, they may be baptized with the Holy Ghost, and received into Christ's holy Church, and be made lively members of the same.

Then the Priest shall say,

Let us pray.

ALMIGHTY and everlasting God, which of thy justice didst destroy by floods of water the whole world for sin, except viii. persons, whom of thy mercy (the same time) thou didst save in the ark; and when thou didst drown in the Red sea wicked king Pharaoh, with all his army, yet (at the same time) thou didst lead thy people the children of Israel safely through the midst thereof; whereby thou didst figure the washing of thy holy Baptism; and by the Baptism of thy well-beloved Son Jesus Christ thou didst sanctify the flood Jordan, and all other waters, to this mystical washing away of sin: We beseech thee (for thy infinite mercies) that thou

wilt mercifully look upon these children, and sanctify them with thy Holy Ghost; that by this wholesome laver of regeneration, whatsoever sin is in them may be washed clean away; that they, being delivered from thy wrath, may be received into the ark of Christ's Church, and so saved from perishing: and being fervent in spirit, steadfast in faith, joyful through hope, rooted in charity, may ever serve thee; and finally attain to everlasting life, with all thy holy and chosen people. This grant us, we beseech thee, for Jesus Christ's sake, our Lord. Amen.

Here shall the Priest ask what shall be the name of the child; and when the Godfathers and Godmothers have told the name, then he shall make a Cross upon the child's forehead and breast, saying,

N. Receive the sign of the holy Cross, both in thy forehead and in thy breast, in token that thou shalt not be ashamed to confess thy faith in Christ crucified, and manfully to fight under his banner against sin, the world, and the devil, and to continue his faithful soldier and servant unto thy life's end. Amen.

And this he shall do and say to as many children as be present to be baptized, one after another.

_persons_

234           *PUBLIC BAPTISM.*

Let us pray.

ALMIGHTY and immortal God, the aid of all that need, the helper of all that flee to thee for succour, the Life of them that believe, and the Resurrection of the dead; We call upon thee for these ~~infants,~~ that they, coming to thy holy Baptism, may receive remission of their sins by spiritual regeneration. Receive them, (O Lord,) as thou hast promised by thy well-beloved Son, saying, Ask, and you shall have; seek, and you shall find; knock, and it shall be opened unto you: so give now unto us that ask; let us that seek find; open thy gate unto us that knock; that these infants may enjoy the everlasting benediction of thy heavenly washing, and may come to the eternal kingdom which thou hast promised by Christ our Lord. Amen.

Then let the Priest, looking upon the children, say,

I COMMAND thee, unclean spirit, in the Name of the Father, of the Son, and of the Holy Ghost, that thou come out, and depart from these infants, whom our Lord Jesus Christ hath vouchsafed to call to his holy Baptism, to be made members of his Body, and of his holy congregation. Therefore, thou cursed spirit, remember thy sentence, remember thy judgment, remember the day to be at hand wherein thou shalt burn in fire everlasting, prepared for thee and thy angels. And presume not hereafter to exercise any tyranny toward these ~~infants,~~ whom Christ hath bought with his precious Blood, and by this his holy Baptism calleth to be of his flock.

Then shall the Priest say,

The Lord be with you.

*The People.*

And with thy spirit.

*The Minister.*

Hear now the Gospel written by S. Mark.

*Mark* x.

AT a certain time they brought children to Christ, that he should touch them; and his disciples rebuked those that brought them. But when Jesus saw it he was displeased, and said unto them: Suffer little children to come unto me, and forbid them not; for to such belongeth the kingdom of God. Verily I say unto you, Whosoever doth not receive the kingdom of God as a little child, he shall not enter therein. And when he had taken them up in his arms, he put his hands upon them, and blessed them.

After the Gospel is read, the Minister shall make this brief exhortation upon the words of the Gospel.

FRIENDS, you hear in this Gospel the words of our Saviour Christ, that he commanded the children to be brought unto him; how he blamed those that would have kept them from him; how he exhorteth all men to follow their innocency. Ye perceive how by his outward gesture and deed he declared his good-will toward them; for he embraced them in his arms, he laid his hands upon them, and blessed them. Doubt ye not therefore, but earnestly believe, that he will likewise favourably receive these present infants; that he will embrace them with the arms of his mercy; that he will give unto them the blessing of eternal life, and make them partakers of his everlasting kingdom. Wherefore we being thus persuaded of the good-will of our heavenly Father toward these infants, declared by his Son Jesus Christ; and nothing doubting but that he favourably alloweth this charitable work of ours in bringing these children to his holy Baptism; let us faithfully and devoutly give thanks unto him, and say the Prayer which the Lord himself taught. And in declaration of our faith, let us also recite the Articles contained in our Creed.

Here the Minister, with the Godfathers, Godmothers, and people present, shall say,

Our Father, which art in heaven, hallowed be thy Name, etc.

And then shall say openly,

I believe in God, the Father Almighty, etc.

The Priest shall add also this prayer.

ALMIGHTY and everlasting God, heavenly Father, we give thee humble thanks, that thou hast vouchsafed to call us to knowledge of thy grace, and faith in thee: Increase and confirm this faith in us evermore: Give thy Holy Spirit to these infants, that they may be born again, and be made heirs of everlasting salvation; through our Lord Jesus Christ, who liveth and reigneth with thee and the Holy Spirit, now and for ever. Amen.

Then let the Priest take one of the children by the right hand, the other being brought after him. And coming into the Church toward the Font, say,

THE Lord vouchsafe to receive you into his holy household, and to keep and govern you alway in the same, that you may have everlasting life. Amen.

Then, standing at the Font, the Priest shall speak to the Godfathers and Godmothers on this wise:

WELLBELOVED friends, ye have brought these children here to be baptized; ye have prayed that our Lord Jesus Christ would vouchsafe to receive them, to lay his hands upon them, to bless them, to release them of their sins, to give them the kingdom of heaven, and everlasting life. Ye have heard also that our Lord Jesus Christ hath promised in his Gospel to grant all these things that ye have prayed for: which promise he, for his part, will most surely keep and perform. Wherefore, after this promise made by Christ, these infants must also faithfully, for their part, promise by you that be their Sureties, that they will forsake the devil and all his works, and constantly believe God's holy Word, and obediently keep his Commandments.

Then shall the Priest demand of the child (which shall be first baptized) these questions following; first naming the child, and saying,

N. Dost thou forsake the devil and all his works?

*Answer.*

I forsake them.

*Minister.*

Dost thou forsake the vain pomp and glory of the world, with all the covetous desires of the same?

*Answer.*

I forsake them.

*Minister.*

Dost thou forsake the carnal desires of the flesh, so that thou wilt not follow nor be led by them?

*Answer.*

I forsake them.

*Minister.*

Dost thou believe in God the Father Almighty, Maker of heaven and earth?

*Answer.*

I believe.

*Minister.*

Dost thou believe in Jesus Christ his only begotten Son

our Lord? and that he was conceived by the Holy Ghost; born of the Virgin Mary; that he suffered under Pontius Pilate, was crucified, dead, and buried; that he went down into hell, and also did rise again the third day; that he ascended into Heaven, and sitteth on the right hand of God the Father Almighty; and from thence shall come again at the end of the world, to judge the quick and the dead? Dost thou believe this?

*Answer.*

I believe.

*Minister.*

Dost thou believe in the Holy Ghost; the Holy Catholick Church; the Communion of Saints; Remission of sins; Resurrection of the flesh; and Everlasting Life after death?

*Answer.*

I believe.

*Minister.*

What dost thou desire?

*Answer.*

Baptism.

*Minister.*

Wilt thou be baptized?

*Answer.*

I will.

Then the Priest shall take the child in his hands, and ask the name; and naming the child, shall dip it in the Water thrice.

First, dipping the right side; second, the left side; the third time dipping the face toward the Font: so it be discreetly and warily done; saying,

N. I baptize thee in the Name of the Father, and of the Son, and of the Holy Ghost. Amen.

And if the child be weak, it shall suffice to pour Water upon it, saying the foresaid words.

N. I baptize thee, etc.

Then the Godfathers and Godmothers shall take and lay their hands upon the child: and the Minister shall put upon him his white vesture, commonly called the Crisome, and say,

Take this white vesture for a token of the innocency which, by God's grace, in this holy Sacrament of Baptism, is given unto thee; and for a sign whereby thou art admonished, so long as thou livest, to give thyself to innocency of living, that, after this transitory life, thou mayest be partaker of the life everlasting. Amen.

Then the Priest shall anoint the infant upon the head, saying,

Almighty God, the Father of our Lord Jesus Christ, who hath regenerate thee by Water and the Holy Ghost, and hath given unto thee remission of all thy sins; He vouchsafe to anoint thee with the Unction of his Holy

Spirit, and bring thee to the inheritance of everlasting life. Amen.

When there are many to be baptized, this order of demanding, baptizing, putting on the Crisome, and anointing, shall be used severally with every child; those that be first baptized departing from the Font, and remaining in some convenient place within the Church until all be baptized. At the last end, the Priest, calling the Godfathers and Godmothers together, shall say this short exhortation following:

FORASMUCH as these children have promised by you to forsake the devil and all his works, to believe in God, and to serve him; you must remember, that it is your parts and duty to see that these infants be taught, as soon as they shall be able to learn, what a solemn vow, promise, and profession, they have made by you. And that they may know these things the better, ye shall call upon them to hear Sermons; and chiefly you shall provide that they may learn the Creed, the Lord's Prayer, and the Ten Commandments, in the English tongue, and all other things which a Christian man ought to know and believe to his soul's health: And that these children may be virtuously brought up to lead a godly and Christian life; remembering always, that Baptism doth represent unto us our profession; which is, to follow the example of our Saviour Christ, and to be made like unto him; that, as he died, and rose again for us, so should we (which are baptized) die from sin, and rise again unto righteousness; continually mortifying all our evil and corrupt affections, and daily proceeding in all virtue and godliness of living.

The Minister shall command that the Crisomes be brought to the Church, and delivered to the Priests after the accustomed manner, at the purification of the mother of every child; and that the children be brought to the Bishop to be confirmed of him, so soon as they can say in their vulgar tongue the Articles of the Faith, the Lord's Prayer, and the Ten Commandments; and be further instructed in the Catechism set forth for that purpose, accordingly as it is there expressed.

And so let the congregation depart in the Name of the Lord.

Note, that if the number of children to be baptized, and multitude of people present be so great that they cannot conveniently stand at the Church door, then let them stand within the Church, in some convenient place, nigh unto the Church door; and there all things be said and done, appointed to be said and done at the Church door.

# OF THEM THAT BE

# Baptized in Private Houses,

## IN TIME OF NECESSITY.

The Pastors and Curates shall oft admonish the people, that they defer not the Baptism of infants any longer than the Sunday or other Holy Day next after the child be born, unless upon a great and reasonable cause, declared to the Curate, and by him approved.

And also they shall warn them, that without great cause and necessity they baptize not children at home in their houses. And when great need shall compel them so to do. that then they minister it on this fashion.

First, let them that be present call upon God for his grace, and say the Lord's Prayer, if the time will suffer. And then one of them shall name the child, and dip him in the water, or pour water upon him, saying these words:

N. I baptize thee in the Name of the Father, and of the Son, and of the Holy Ghost. Amen.

And let them not doubt, but that the child so baptized is lawfully and sufficiently baptized, and ought not to be baptized again in the Church. But yet nevertheless, if the child, which is after this sort baptized, do afterward live, it is expedient that he be brought into the Church, to the entent the Priest may examine and try whether the child be lawfully baptized or no. And if those that bring any child to the Church do answer that he is already baptized then shall the Priest examine them further.

By whom the child was baptized?

Who was present when the child was baptized?

Whether they called upon God for grace and succour in that necessity?

With what thing, or what matter, they did baptize the child?

With what words the child was baptized?

Whether they think the child to be lawfully and perfectly baptized?

And if the Minister shall prove by the answers of such as brought the child that all things were done as they ought to be, then shall not he christen the child again, but shall receive him as one of the flock of the true Christian people, saying thus:

I CERTIFY you, that in this case ye have done well, and according unto due order, concerning the baptizing of this child; which being born in original sin, and in the wrath of God, is now, by the laver of regeneration in Baptism, made the child of God, and heir of everlasting life: for our Lord Jesus Christ doth not deny his grace and mercy unto such infants, but most lovingly doth call them unto him: As the holy Gospel doth witness to our comfort on this wise.

### Mark x.

AT a certain time they brought children unto Christ, that he should touch them: and his disciples rebuked those that brought them. But when Jesus saw it, he was displeased, and said unto them, Suffer little children to come unto me, and forbid them not, for to such belongeth the kingdom of God. Verily I say unto you, Whosoever doth not receive the kingdom of God as a little child, he shall not enter therein. And when he had taken them up in his arms, he put his hands upon them and blessed them.

After the Gospel is read, the Minister shall make this exhortation upon the words of the Gospel.

FRIENDS, ye hear in this Gospel the words of our Saviour Christ, that he commanded the children to be brought unto him; how he blamed those that would have kept them from him; how he exhorted all men to follow their innocency. Ye perceive how by his outward gesture and deed he declared his goodwill toward them; for he embraced them in his arms, he laid his hands upon them, and blessed them. Doubt you not therefore, but earnestly believe, that he hath likewise favourably received this present infant; that he hath embraced him with the arms of his mercy; that he hath given unto him the blessing of eternal life, and made him partaker of his everlasting kingdom. Wherefore, we being thus persuaded of the goodwill of our heavenly Father, declared by his son Jesus Christ, towards this infant, let us faithfully and devoutly give thanks unto him, and say the Prayer, which the Lord himself taught; and in declaration of our faith, let us also recite the Articles contained in our Creed.

Here the Minister, with the Godfathers and Godmothers, shall say,

OUR Father, which art in heaven, hallowed be thy Name. Thy kingdom come, etc.

Then shall they say the Creed; and then the Priest shall demand the name of the child, which being by the Godfathers and Godmothers pronounced, the Minister shall say,

N. Dost thou forsake the devil and all his works?

*Answer.*

I forsake them.

*Minister.*

Dost thou forsake the vain pomp and glory of the world, with all the covetous desires of the same?

*Answer.*

I forsake them.

*Minister.*

Dost thou forsake the carnal desires of the flesh, so that thou wilt not follow and be led by them?

*Answer.*

I forsake them.

*Minister.*

Dost thou believe in God the Father Almighty, Maker of heaven and earth?

*Answer.*

I believe.

*Minister.*

Dost thou believe in Jesus Christ his only begotten Son our Lord? and that he was conceived by the Holy Ghost; born of the Virgin Mary; that he suffered under Pontius Pilate, was crucified, dead, and buried; that he went down into hell, and also did arise again the third day; that he ascended into Heaven, and sitteth on the right hand of God the Father Almighty; and from thence shall come again at the end of the world to judge the quick and the dead? Dost thou believe thus?

*Answer.*

I believe.

*Minister.*

Dost thou believe in the Holy Ghost, the Holy Catholic Church; the Communion of Saints; Remission of sins; Resurrection of the flesh; and Everlasting Life after death?

*Answer.*

I believe.

Then the Minister shall put the white vesture, commonly called the Crisome, upon the child, saying,

TAKE this white vesture for a token of the innocency which, by God's grace in the holy Sacrament of Baptism, is given unto thee: and for a sign whereby thou art admonished, so long as thou shalt live, to give thyself to innocency of living, that, after this transitory life, thou mayest be partaker of the life everlasting. Amen.

Let us pray.

ALMIGHTY and everlasting God, heavenly Father, we give thee humble thanks, that thou hast vouchsafed to call us to the knowledge of thy grace, and faith in thee; increase and confirm this faith in us evermore. Give thy Holy Spirit to this infant, that he, being born again, and being made heir of everlasting salvation, through our Lord Jesus Christ, may continue thy servant, and attain thy promises, through the same our Lord Jesus Christ thy Son, who liveth and reigneth with thee in unity of the same Holy Spirit everlastingly. Amen.

Then shall the Minister make this exhortation to the Godfathers and Godmothers:

FORASMUCH as this child hath promised by you to forsake the devil and all his works, to believe in God, and to serve him; you must remember that it is your parts and duty to see that this infant be taught, so soon as he shall be able to learn, what a solemn vow, promise, and profession he hath made by you. And that he may know these things the better, ye shall call upon him to hear Sermons; and chiefly ye shall provide, that he may learn the Creed, the Lord's

Prayer, and the Ten Commandments in the English tongue, and all other things which a Christian man ought to know and believe to his soul's health; and that this child may be virtuously brought up to lead a godly and Christian life; remembering alway, that Baptism doth represent unto us our profession; which is, to follow the example of our Saviour Christ, and to be made like unto him: that, as he died and rose again for us, so should we which are baptized, die from sin, and rise again unto righteousness; continually mortifying all our evil and corrupt affections, and daily proceeding in all virtue and godliness of living.

&c. as in Public Baptism.

But if they which bring the infants to the Church do make an uncertain answer to the Priest's questions, and say that they cannot tell what they thought, did, or said, in that great fear and trouble of mind; (as oftentimes it chanceth;) then let the Priest baptize him in form above written concerning Public Baptism, saving that at the dipping of the child in the Font, he shall use this form of words:

IF thou be not baptized already, N. I baptize thee in the Name of the Father, and of the Son, and of the Holy Ghost. Amen.

The Water in the Font shall be changed every month once at the least; and afore any child be baptized in the Water so changed, the Priest shall say at the Font these prayers following:

O MOST merciful God our Saviour Jesu Christ, who hast ordained the element of Water for the regeneration of thy faithful people, upon whom, being baptized in the river of Jordan, the Holy Ghost came down in the likeness of a dove; Send down, we beseech thee, the same thy Holy Spirit to assist us, and to be present at this our Invocation of thy holy Name. Sanctify ✠ this fountain of Baptism, thou that art the Sanctifier of all things, that by the power of thy word all those that shall be baptized therein may be spiritually regenerated, and made the children of everlasting adoption. Amen.

O MERCIFUL God, grant that the old Adam in them that shall be baptized in this fountain, may be so buried, that the new man may be raised up again. Amen.

GRANT that all carnal affections may die in them; and that all things belonging to the Spirit may live and grow in them. Amen.

GRANT to all them which at this fountain forsake the devil and all his works, that they may have power and strength to have victory, and to triumph against him, the world, and the flesh. Amen.

WHOSOEVER shall confess thee, O Lord, recognise him also in thy kingdom. Amen.

GRANT that all sin and vice here may be so extinct, that they never have power to reign in thy servants. Amen.

GRANT that whosoever here shall begin to be of thy flock, may evermore continue in the same. Amen.

GRANT that all they which for thy sake in this life do deny and forsake themselves, may win and purchase thee, (O Lord,) which art everlasting treasure. Amen.

GRANT that whosoever is here dedicated to thee by our office and ministry, may also be endued with heavenly virtues, and everlastingly rewarded through thy mercy, O blessed Lord God, who dost live and govern all things world without end. Amen.

The Lord be with you.

*Answer.*

And with thy spirit.

ALMIGHTY everliving God, whose most dearly beloved Son Jesus Christ, for the forgiveness of our sins, did shed out of his most precious Side both Water and Blood, and gave commandment to his disciples that they should go teach all nations, and baptize them in the Name of the Father, the Son, and the Holy Ghost; Regard, we beseech thee, the supplications of thy congregation, and grant that all thy servants which shall be baptized in this Water prepared for the ministration of thy holy Sacrament, may receive the fulness of thy grace, and ever remain in the number of thy faithful and elect children, through Jesus Christ our Lord.

# Confirmation,

## WHEREIN IS CONTAINED

## A Catechism for Children.

To the end that Confirmation may be ministered to the more edifying of such as shall receive it, (according to Saint Paul's doctrine, who teacheth that all things should be done in the Church to the edification of the same,) it is thought good that none hereafter shall be confirmed, but such as can say in their mother tongue the Articles of the Faith, the Lord's Prayer, and the Ten Commandments; and can also answer to such questions of this short Catechism, as the Bishop (or such as he shall appoint) shall by his discretion appose them in. And this order is most convenient to be observed for divers considerations.

First, because that when children come to the years of discretion, and have learned what their Godfathers and Godmothers promised for them in Baptism, they may then, themselves, with their own mouth, and with their own consent, openly before the Church, ratify and confess the same; and also promise, that by the grace of God they wil evermore endeavour themselves faithfully to observe and keep such things as they by their own mouth and confession have assented unto.

Secondly, forasmuch as Confirmation is ministered to them that be baptized, that by imposition of hands and prayer they may receive strength and defence against all temptations to sin, and the assautes of the world and the devil; it is most meet to be ministered when children come to that age. that partly by the frailty of their own flesh, partly by the assautes of the world and the devil, they begin to be in danger to fall into sin.

Thirdly, for that it is agreeable with the usage of the Church in times past, whereby it was ordained that Confirmation should be ministered to them that were of perfect age, that they, being instructed in Christ's

Religion, should openly profess their own faith, and promise to be obedient unto the will of God.

And that no man shall think that any detriment shall come to children by deferring of their Confirmation, he shall know for truth, that it is certain by God's Word that children being baptized, (if they depart out of this life in their infancy,) are undoubtedly saved.

✠

# A Catechism,

THAT IS TO SAY

## An Instruction to be learned of every Child,

BEFORE HE BE BROUGHT TO BE CONFIRMED OF THE BISHOP.

*Question.*

What is your name?

*Answer.*

N. or M.

*Question.*

Who gave you this name?

*Answer.*

My Godfathers and Godmothers in my Baptism; wherein I was made a member of Christ, the child of God, and an inheritor of the kingdom of heaven.

*Question.*

What did your Godfathers and Godmothers then for you?

*Answer.*

They did promise and vow three things in my name. First, that I should forsake the devil, and all his works and pomps, the vanities of the wicked world, and all the sinful lusts of the flesh. Secondly, that I should believe all the Articles of the Christian Faith. And thirdly, that I should keep God's holy will and commandments, and walk in the same all the days of my life.

*Question.*

Dost thou not think that thou art bound to believe, and to do, as they have promised for thee?

*Answer.*

Yes, verily; and by God's help so I will. And I heartily thank our heavenly Father, that he hath called me to this state of salvation, through Jesus Christ our Saviour. And I pray God to give me his grace, that I may continue in the same unto my life's end.

*Question.*

Rehearse the Articles of thy belief.

*Answer.*

I believe in God the Father Almighty, Maker of heaven and earth: And in Jesus Christ his only Son our Lord, which was conceived by the Holy Ghost, born of the Virgin Mary, suffered under Pontius Pilate, was crucified, dead, and buried, he descended into hell; the third day he arose again from the dead; he ascended into heaven, and sitteth on the right hand of God the Father Almighty; from thence shall he come to judge the quick and the dead. I believe in the Holy Ghost; the Holy Catholick Church; the Communion of Saints; the Forgiveness of sins; the Resurrection of the Body; and the Life everlasting. Amen.

*Question.*

What dost thou chiefly learn in these Articles of thy belief?

*Answer.*

First, I learn to believe in God the Father, who hath made me and all the world.

Secondly, in God the Son, who hath redeemed me and all mankind.

Thirdly, in God the Holy Ghost, who sanctifieth me and all the elect people of God.

*Question.*

You said that your Godfathers and Godmothers did promise for you that ye should keep God's commandments. Tell me how many there be.

*Answer.*

Ten.

*Question.*

Which be they?

*Answer.*

Thou shalt have none other gods but me.

II. Thou shalt not make to thyself any graven image, nor the likeness of any thing that is in heaven above, or in the earth beneath, nor in the water under the earth; thou shalt not bow down to them, nor worship them.

III. Thou shalt not take the Name of the Lord thy God in vain

IV. Remember that thou keep holy the Sabbath day.

v. Honour thy father and thy mother.

vi. Thou shalt do no murder.

vii. Thou shalt not commit adultery.

viii. Thou shalt not steal.

ix. Thou shalt not bear false witness against thy neighbour.

x. Thou shalt not covet thy neighbour's wife, nor his servant, nor his maid, nor his ox, nor his ass, nor any thing that is his.

### Question.

What dost thou chiefly learn by these commandments?

### Answer.

I learn two things: my duty towards God, and my duty towards my neighbour.

### Question.

What is thy duty towards God?

### Answer.

My duty towards God is to believe in him, to fear him, and to love him with all my heart, with all my mind, with all my soul, and with all my strength; to worship him, to give him thanks, to put my whole trust in him, to call upon him, to honour his holy Name and his Word, and to serve him truly all the days of my life.

### Question.

What is thy duty towards thy neighbour?

### Answer.

My duty towards my neighbour is to love him as myself, and to do to all men as I would they should do to me: to love, honour, and succour my father and mother: to honour and obey the king and his ministers: to submit myself to all my governors, teachers, spiritual pastors, and masters: to order myself lowly and reverently to all my betters: to hurt nobody by word nor deed: to be true and just in all my dealing: to bear no malice nor hatred in my heart: to keep my hands from picking and stealing, and my tongue from evil speaking, lying, and slandering: to keep my body in temperance, soberness, and chastity: not to covet nor desire other men's goods; but learn and labour truly to get my own living, and to do my duty in that state of life, unto which it shall please God to call me.

### Question..

My good son, know this, that thou art not able to do these things of thyself, nor to walk in the commandments of God, and to serve him, without his special grace, which thou must learn at all times to call for by diligent prayer. Let me hear therefore if thou canst say the Lord's Prayer.

*Answer.*

Our Father, which art in heaven, hallowed be thy Name. Thy kingdom come. Thy will be done in earth, as it is in heaven. Give us this day our daily bread. And forgive us our trespasses, as we forgive them that trespass against us. And lead us not into temptation; but deliver us from evil. Amen.

*Question.*

What desirest thou of God in this prayer?

*Answer.*

I desire my Lord God our heavenly Father, who is the giver of all goodness, to send his grace unto me, and to all people: that we may worship him, serve him, and obey him, as we ought to do.

And I pray unto God, that he will send us all things that be needful both for our souls and bodies: and that he will be merciful unto us, and forgive us our sins; and that it will please him to save and defend us in all dangers ghostly and bodily: and that he will keep us from all sin and wickedness, and from our ghostly enemy, and from everlasting death. And this I trust he will do of his mercy and goodness, through our Lord Jesu Christ. And therefore I say, Amen, so be it.

So soon as the children can say in their mother tongue the Articles of the Faith, the Lord's Prayer, and the Ten Commandments, and also can answer to such questions of this short Catechism, as the Bishop (or such as he shall appoint) shall by his discretion appose them in; then shall they be brought to the Bishop by one that shall be his Godfather or Godmother, that every child may have a witness of his Confirmation.

And the Bishop shall confirm them on this wise.

## Confirmation.

Our help is in the Name of the Lord.

*Answer.*

Which hath made both heaven and earth.

*Minister.*

Blessed is the Name of the Lord.

*Answer.*

Henceforth world without end.

*Minister.*

The Lord be with you.

*Answer.*

And with thy spirit.

Let us pray.

ALMIGHTY and everliving God, who hast vouchsafed to regenerate these thy servants of Water and the Holy Ghost, and hast given unto them forgiveness of all their sins: Send down from heaven, we beseech thee, (O Lord,) upon them thy Holy Ghost the Comforter, with the manifold gifts of grace; the spirit of wisdom and understanding; the spirit of counsel and ghostly strength: the spirit of knowledge and true godliness; and fulfil them (O Lord) with the spirit of thy holy fear.

*Answer.*

Amen.

*Minister.*

Sign them (O Lord) and mark them to be thine for ever, by the virtue of thy holy Cross and Passion. Confirm and strength them with the inward Unction of thy Holy Ghost mercifully unto everlasting life. Amen.

Then the Bishop shall cross them in the forehead, and lay his hand upon their head, saying,

N. I sign the with the sign of the Cross, and lay my hand upon thee. In the Name of the Father, and of the Son, and of the Holy Ghost. Amen.

And thus shall he do to every child, one after another. And when he hath laid his hand upon every child, then shall he say,

The peace of the Lord abide with you.

*Answer.*

And with thy spirit.

Let us pray.

ALMIGHTY everliving God, which makest us both to will and to do those things that be good and acceptable unto thy Majesty; We make our humble supplications unto thee for these children, upon whom (after the example of thy holy Apostles) we have laid our hands, to certify them (by this sign) of thy favour and gracious goodness toward them. Let thy fatherly hand (we beseech thee) ever be over them; let thy Holy Spirit ever be with them; and so lead them in the knowledge and obedience of thy word, that in the end they may obtain the life everlasting; through our Lord Jesus Christ, who with thee and

Holy Ghost liveth and reigneth, one God, world without end. Amen.

Then shall the Bishop bless the children, thus saying,

The blessing of God Almighty, the Father, the Son, and the Holy Ghost, be upon you, and remain with you for ever. Amen.

The Curate of every Parish, once in six weeks at the least, upon warning by him given, shall, upon some Sunday or Holy Day, half an hour before Evensong, openly in the Church instruct and examine so many children of his Parish sent unto him, as the time will serve, and as he shall think convenient, in some part of this Catechism. And all fathers, mothers, masters, and dames, shall cause their children, servants, and prentises, (which are not yet confirmed,) to come to the Church at the day appointed, and obediently hear and be ordered by the Curate, until such time as they have learned all that is here appointed for them to learn.

And whensoever the Bishop shall give knowledge for children to be brought afore him to any convenient place for their Confirmation, then shall the Curate of every Parish either bring or send in writing the names of all those children of his Parish which can say the Articles of their Faith, the Lord's Prayer, and the Ten Commandments; and also how many of them can answer to the other questions contained in this Catechism.

And there shall none be admitted to the holy Communion until such time as he be confirmed.

# The Form of Solemnization of Matrimony.

First the Banns must be asked three several Sundays or Holy Days in the Service time, the people being present, after the accustomed manner.

And if the persons that would be married dwell in divers Parishes, the Banns must be asked in both Parishes; and the Curate of the one Parish shall not solemnize Matrimony betwixt them, without a certificate of the Banns being thrice asked, from the Curate of the other Parish.

At the day appointed for Solemnization of Matrimony, the persons to be married shall come into the body of the Church with their friends and neighbours: and there the Priest shall thus say: .

DEARLY beloved friends, we are gathered together here in the sight of God, and in the face of his congregation, to join together this Man and this Woman in holy Matrimony; which is an honourable estate, instituted of God in Paradise, in the time of man's innocency, signifying unto us the mystical union that is betwixt Christ and his Church; which holy estate Christ adorned and beautified with his presence, and first miracle that he wrought, in Cana of Galilee; and is commended of Saint Paul to be honourable among all men: and therefore is not to be enterprised, nor taken in hand unadvisedly, lightly, or wantonly, to satisfy men's carnal lusts and appetites, like brute beasts that have no understanding; but reverently, discreetly, advisedly, soberly, and in the fear of God; duly considering the causes for the which Matrimony was ordained. One cause was the procreation of children, to be brought up in the fear and nurture of the Lord, and praise of God. Secondly, it was ordained for a remedy against sin, and to avoid fornication; that such persons as be married might live chastely in matrimony, and keep themselves undefiled members of Christ's body. Thirdly, for the mutual society, help, and comfort, that the one ought to have of the other both in prosperity and adversity. Into the which holy estate these two persons present come now to be joined. Therefore if any man can shew any just cause why they may not lawfully be joined so together, let him now speak, or else hereafter for ever hold his peace.

And also speaking to the persons that shall be married, he shall say,

I require and charge you, (as you will answer at the dreadful day of judgment, when the secrets of all hearts shall be disclosed,) that if either of you do know any impediment why ye may not be lawfully joined together in Matrimony, that ye confess it. For be ye well assured, that so many as be coupled together otherwise than God's word doth allow, are not joined of God, neither is their Matrimony lawful.

At which day of Marriage, if any man do allege any impediment why they may not be coupled together in Matrimony; and will be bound, and Sureties with him to the parties; or else put in a Caution to the full value of such charges as the persons to be married do sustain, to prove his allegation: then the Solemnization must be deferred unto such time as the truth be tried. If no impediment be alleged, then shall the Curate say unto the Man,

N. Wilt thou have this Woman to thy wedded wife, to live together after God's ordinance in the holy estate of Matrimony? Wilt thou love her, comfort her, honour, and keep her in sickness and in health; and, forsaking all other, keep thee only to her so long as you both shall live?

The Man shall answer,

I will.

Then shall the Priest say to the Woman,

N. Wilt thou have this Man to thy wedded husband, to live together after God's ordinance in the holy estate of Matrimony? Wilt thou obey him, and serve him, love, honour, and keep him in sickness and in health; and, forsaking all other, keep thee only to him, so long as you both shall live?

The Woman shall answer.

I will.

Then shall the Minister say,

Who giveth this Woman to be married to this Man?

And the Minister, receiving the Woman at her father or friend's hands, shall cause the Man to take the Woman by the right hand, and so either to give their troth to other; the Man first saying,

I N. take thee N. to my wedded wife, to have and to hold from this day forward, for better for worse, for richer for poorer, in sickness and in health, to love and to cher-

ish, till death us depart: according to God's holy ordinance: And thereto I plight thee my troth.

Then shall they loose their hands; and the Woman, taking again the Man by the right hand, shall say;

I N. take thee N. to my wedded husband, to h a v e and to hold from this day forward, for better for worse, for richer for poorer, in sickness and in health, to love, cherish, and to o b e y, till death us depart: according to God's h o l y ordinance: And thereto I give thee my troth.

Then shall they again loose their hands; and the Man shall give unto the Woman a Ring, and other tokens of Spousage, as gold or silver, laying the same upon the Book. And the Priest taking the Ring, shall deliver it unto the Man; to put it upon the fourth finger of the Woman's left hand. And the Man, taught by the Priest, shall say,

With this Ring I thee wed: this gold and silver I thee give: with my body I thee worship: and with all my worldly goods I thee endow. In the Name of the Father, and of the Son, and of the Holy Ghost. Amen.

Then the Man leaving the Ring upon the fourth finger of the Woman's left hand, the Minister shall say,

Let us pray.

O ETERNAL God, Creator and Preserver of all mankind, Giver of all spritual grace, the Author of everlasting life: Send thy blessing upon these thy servants, this Man and this Woman, whom we bless in thy Name; that as Isaac and Rebecca (after bracelets and Jewels of gold given of the one to the other for tokens of their matrimony) lived faithfully together, so these persons may surely perform and keep the vow and covenant betwixt them made, whereof this Ring given and received is a token and pledge. And may ever remain in perfect love and peace together: and live according to t h y laws: through Jesus Christ our Lord. Amen.

Then shall the Priest join their right l.ands together, and say,

Those whom God h a t h joined together let no man put asunder.

Then shall the Minister speak unto the people.

FORASMUCH as N. and N. have consented together in holy wedlock, and have witnessed the same here before God and this company, and thereto have given and pledged their troth either to other, and have declared the same by giving and receiving gold and silver, and by joining of hands: I pronounce that they be Man and Wife together. In the Name of the Father, of the Son, and of the Holy Ghost. Amen.

And the Minister shall add this blessing.

God the Father bless you. ✣ God the Son keep you: God the Holy Ghost lighten your understanding. The Lord mercifully with his favour look upon you; and so fill you with all spiritual benediction and grace, that you may have remission of your sins in this life, and in the world to come life everlasting. Amen.

Then shall they go into the Quire, and the Ministers or Clerks sha'l say or sing this Psalm following.

*Beati omnes.* Psalm cxxviii.

BLESSED are all they that fear the Lord: and walk in his way.

For thou shalt eat the labour of thy hands: O well is thee, and happy shalt thou be.

Thy wife shall be as the fruitful vine: upon the walls of thy house.

Thy children like the olive-branches: round about thy table.

Lo, thus shall the man be blessed: that feareth the Lord.

The Lord from out of Sion

shall so bless thee: that thou shalt see Hierusalem in prosperity all thy life long.

Yea, that thou shalt see thy childer's children: and peace upon Israel.

Glory be to the Father, and to the Son: and to the Holy Ghost.

As it was in the beginning, is now, and ever shall be: world without end. Amen.

Or else this Psalm following.

*Deus misereatur nostri.*
Psalm lxvii.

GOD be merciful unto us, and bless us, and shew us the light of his countenance: and be merciful unto us.

That thy way may be known upon earth: thy saving health among all nations.

Let the people praise thee, (O God): yea, let all people praise thee.

O let the nations rejoice and be glad, for thou shalt judge the folk righteously: and govern the nations upon earth.

Let the people praise thee, (O God): let all people praise thee.

Then shall the earth bring forth her increase: and God, even our own God, shall give us his blessing.

God shall bless us: and all the ends of the world shall fear him.

Glory be to the Father, and to the Son: and to the Holy Ghost.

As it was in the beginning, is now, and ever shall be: world without end. Amen.

The Psalm ended, and the Man and Woman kneeling afore the Altar, the Priest standing at the Altar, and turning his face toward them, shall say,

Lord, have mercy upon us.

*Answer.*

Christ, have mercy upon us.

*Minister.*

Lord, have mercy upon us.
Our Father, which art in heaven, etc.

And lead us not into temptation.

*Answer.*

But deliver us from evil. Amen.

*Minister.*

O Lord, save thy servant, and thy handmaid;

*Answer.*

Which put their trust in thee.

*Minister.*

O Lord, send them help from they holy place.

*Answer.*

And evermore defend them.

*Minister.*

Be unto them a tower of strength.

*Answer.*

From the face of their enemy.

*Minister.*

O Lord, hear my prayer.

*Answer.*

And let my cry come unto thee.

*The Minister.*

Let us pray.

O God of Abraham, God of Isaac, God of Jacob, bless these thy servants, and sow the seed of eternal life in their minds, that whatsoever in thy holy Word they shall profitably learn, they may in deed fulfil the same. Look, O Lord, mercifully upon them from heaven, and bless them. And as thou diddest send thy angel Raphael to Thobie and Sara, the daughter of Raguel, to their great comfort: so vouchsafe to send thy blessing upon these thy servants, that they, obeying thy will, and alway being in safety under thy protection, may abide in thy love unto their lives' end: through Jesu Christ our Lord. Amen.

This prayer following shall be omitted where the Woman is past childbirth.

O merciful Lord, and heavenly Father, by whose gracious gift mankind is increased: We beseech thee assist with thy blessing these two persons, that they may both be fruitful in procreation of children, and also live together so long in godly love and honesty, that they may see their childer's children unto the third and fourth generation, unto thy praise and honour: through Jesus Christ our Lord. Amen.

O God, which by thy mighty power hast made all things of naught; which also, after other things set in order, diddest appoint that out of man (created after thine own image and similitude) woman should take her beginning; and, knitting them together, didst teach that it should never be lawful to put asunder those whom thou by Matrimony hadst made one: O God, which hast consecrated the state of Matrimony to such an excellent mystery, that in it is signified and represented the spiritual marriage and unity betwixt Christ and his Church; Look mercifully upon these thy servants, that both this Man may love his Wife, according to thy word, (as Christ doth love his spouse the Church, who gave himself for it, loving and cherishing it even as his own flesh:) and also that this Woman may be loving and amiable to her husband as Rachael, wise as Rebecca, faithful and obedient as Sara; and in all quietness, sobriety, and peace, be a follower of holy and godly matrons. O Lord, bless them both, and grant them to inherit thy everlasting kingdom; through Jesus Christ our Lord. Amen.

Then shall the Priest bless the Man and the Woman, saying,

ALMIGHTY God, which at the beginning did create our first parents Adam and Eve, and did sanctify and join them together in marriage: Pour upon you the riches of his grace, sanctify and ✠ bless you, that ye may please him both in body and soul: and live together in holy love unto your lives' end. Amen.

Then shall be said after the Gospel a Sermon, wherein ordinarily (so oft as there is any Marriage) the office of Man and Wife shall be declared, according to holy Scripture. Or if there be no Sermon, the Minister shall read this that followeth.

ALL ye which be married, or which intend to take the holy estate of Matrimony upon you, hear what holy Scripture doth say as touching the duty of husbands toward their wives, and wives toward their husbands.

Saint Paul, (in his Epistle to the Ephesians, the fifth chapter,) doth give this commandment to all married men:

Ye husbands, love your wives, even as Christ loved the Church, and hath given himself for it, to sanctify it, purging it in the fountain of water, through the word; that he might make it unto himself a glorious Congregation, not having spot, or wrinkle, or any such thing; but that it should be holy and blameless. So men are bound to love their own wives as their own bodies. He that loveth his own wife loveth himself: for never did any man hate his own flesh, but nourisheth and cherisheth it, even as the Lord doth the congregation: for we are members of his body, of his flesh, and of his bones. For this cause shall a man leave father and mother, and shall be joined unto his wife, and they two shall be one flesh. This mystery is great; but I speak of Christ and the Congregation. Nevertheless, let every one of you so love his own wife even as himself.

Likewise the same Saint

Paul, (writing to the Colossians,) speaketh thus to all men that be married; Ye men, love your wives, and be not bitter unto them.-(*Coloss.* iii.)

Hear also what Saint Peter, the apostle of Christ, (which was himself a married man,) saith unto all men that are married; Ye husbands, dwell with your wives according to knowledge; giving honour unto the wife, as unto the weaker vessel, and as heirs together of the grace of life, so that your prayers be not hindered.—(1. *Pet.* iii.)

Hitherto ye have heard the duty of the husband toward the wife. Now likewise, ye wives, hear and learn your duty toward your husbands, even as it is plainly set forth in holy Scripture.

Saint Paul (in the forenamed Epistle to the Ephesians), teacheth you thus; Ye women, submit yourselves unto your own husbands, as unto the Lord. For the husband is the wife's head, even as Christ is the head of the Church: and he also is the Saviour of the whole body. Therefore as the Church or Congregation is subject unto Christ, so likewise let the wives also be in subjection unto their own husbands in all things. And again

he saith, Let the wife reverence her husband. (*Eph.* v.) And (in his Epistle to the Colossians)Saint Paul giveth you this short lesson; Ye wives submit yourselves unto your own husbands as it is convenient in the Lord.-(*Coloss.* iii.)

Saint Peter also doth instruct you very godly,(1.*Peter* iii.,)thus saying; Let wives be subject to their own husbands; so that, if any obey not the Word, they may be won without the Word by the conversation of the wives; while they behold your chaste conversation coupled with fear. Whose apparel, let it not be outward, with broided hair and trimming about with gold either in putting on of gorgeous apparel; but let the hid man, which is in the heart, be without all corruption; so that the spirit be mild and quiet, which is a precious thing in the sight of God. For after this manner (in the old time did the holy women,) which trusted in God, apparel themselves, being subject to their own husbands: as Sara obeyed Abraham, calling him lord; whose daughters ye are made, doing well, and being not dismayed with any fear.

The new married persons (the same day of their Marriage) must receive the holy Communion.

✠

## THE ORDER

### For the Visitation of the Sick,

#### AND THE COMMUNION OF THE SAME.

The Priest, entering into the sick person's house, shall say,

Peace be in this house, and to all that dwell in it.

When he cometh into the sick man's presence, he shall say this Psalm.

*Domine exaudi.*

Psalm cxliii.

HEAR my prayer (O Lord) and consider my desire: hearken unto me for thy truth and righteousness' sake.

And enter not into judgment with thy servant: for in thy sight shall no man living be justified.

For the enemy hath persecuted my soul; he hath smitten my life down to the ground: he hath laid me in the darkness, as the men that have been long dead.

Therefore is my spirit vexed within me: and my heart within me is desolate.

Yet do I remember the time past; I muse upon all thy works: yea, I exercise myself in the works of thy hands.

I stretch forth mine hands unto thee: my soul gaspeth unto thee as a thirsty land.

Hear me, (O Lord,) and that soon, for my spirit waxeth faint: hide not thy face from me, lest I be like unto them that go down into the pit.

O let me hear thy loving-kindness betimes in the morning, for in thee is my trust: shew thou me the way that I should walk in, for I lift up my soul unto thee.

Deliver me (O Lord) from mine enemies: for I fly unto thee to hide me.

Teach me to do the thing that pleaseth thee, for thou art my God: let thy loving Spirit lead me forth into the land of righteousness.

Quicken me (O Lord) for thy Name's sake: and for thy righteousness' sake bring my soul out of trouble.

And of thy goodness slay mine enemies: and destroy all them that vex my soul; for I am thy servant.

Glory be to the Father, and to the Son: and to the Holy Ghost.

As it was in the beginning, is now, and ever shall be: world without end. Amen.

With this Anthem,

REMEMBER not, Lord, our iniquities, nor the iniquities of our forefathers. Spare us, good Lord, spare thy people, whom thou hast redeemed with thy most precious Blood, and be not angry with us for ever.

Lord, have mercy upon us.

Christ, have mercy upon us.

Lord, have mercy upon us.

Our Father, which art in heaven, etc.

And lead us not into temptation.

*Answer.*

But deliver us from evil. Amen.

*The Minister.*

O Lord, save thy servant;

*Answer.*

Which putteth his trust in thee.

*Minister.*

Send him help from thy holy place.

*Answer.*

And evermore mightily defend him.

*Minister.*

Let the enemy have none advantage of him;

*Answer.*

Nor the wicked approach to hurt him.

*Minister.*

Be unto him, O Lord, a strong tower,

*Answer.*

From the face of his enemy.

*Minister.*

Lord, hear my prayer,

*Answer.*

And let my cry come unto thee.

*Minister.*

Let us pray.

O LORD, look down from heaven, behold, visit, and relieve this thy servant. Look upon him with the eyes of thy mercy, give him comfort and sure confidence in thee, defend him from the danger of the enemy, and keep him in perpetual peace and safety; through Jesus Christ our Lord. Amen.

HEAR us, Almighty and most merciful God and Saviour; extend thy accustomed goodness to this thy servant, which is grieved with sickness. Visit him, O Lord, as thou diddest visit Peter's wife's mother and the Captain's servant. And as thou preservedst Thobie and Sara by thy angel from danger, so restore unto this sick person his former health, (if it be thy will,) or else give him grace so to take thy correction, that, after this painful life ended, he may dwell with thee in life everlasting. Amen.

Then shall the Minister exhort the sick person after this form, or other like.

DEARLY beloved, know this, that Almighty God is the Lord over life and death, and over all things to them pertaining; as youth, strength, health, age, weakness, and sickness. Wherefore, whatsoever your sickness is, know you certainly, that it is God's visitation. And for what cause soever this sickness is sent unto you: whether it be to try your patience for the example of other, and that your faith may be found in the day of the Lord, laudable, glorious, and honourable, to the increase of glory and endless felicity; or else it be sent unto you to correct and amend in you whatsoever doth offend the eyes of our heavenly Father; know you certainly, that if you truly repent you of your sins, and bear your sickness patiently, trusting in God's mercy, for his dear Son Jesus Christ's sake, and render unto him humble thanks for his fatherly visitation, submitting yourself wholly to his will, it shall turn to your profit, and help you forward in the right way that leadeth unto everlasting life.* Take *If the person visited be very sick, then the Curate may end his exhortation at this place.\** therefore in good worth the chastement of the Lord: for whom the Lord loveth he chastiseth; yea, (as Saint Paul saith,) he scourgeth every son which he receiveth. If you endure chastisement, he offereth himself unto you as unto his own children. What son is he that the father chastiseth not? If ye be not under correction, (whereof all the true children are partakers,) then are ye bastards and not children. Therefore seeing that when our carnal fathers do correct us, we reverently obey them; shall we not now much rather be obedient to our spiritual Father, and so live? And they for a few days do chastise us after their own pleasure; but he doth chastise us for our profit, to the intent he may make us partakers of his holiness. These words, good brother, are God's words, and written in holy

Scripture for our comfort and instruction; that we should patiently, and with thanksgiving, bear our heavenly Father's correction, whensoever by any manner of adversity it shall please his gracious goodness to visit us. And there should be no greater comfort to Christian persons, than to be made like unto Christ, by suffering patiently adversities, troubles, and sicknesses. For he himself went not up to joy, but first he suffered pain; he entered not into his glory before he was crucified. So truly our way to eternal joy is to suffer here with Christ; and our door to enter into eternal life is gladly to die with Christ; that we may rise again from death, and dwell with him in everlasting life. Now therefore, taking your sickness, which is thus profitable for you, patiently, I exhort you, in the Name of God, to remember the profession which you made unto God in your Baptism. And forasmuch as after this life there is account to be given unto the righteous Judge, of whom all must be judged without respect of persons, I require you to examine yourself and your state, both toward God and man, so that

accusing and condemning yourself for your own faults, you may find mercy at our heavenly Father's hand for Christ's sake, and not be accused and comdemned in that fearful judgment. Therefore I shall shortly rehearse the 'Articles of our Faith, that ye may know whether you do believe as a Christian man should believe, or no.

Here the Minister shall rehearse the Articles of the Faith, saying thus,

DOST thou believe in God the Father Almighty?

And so forth, as it is in Baptism.

Then shall the Minister examine whether he be in charity with all the world; exhorting him to forgive, from the bottom of his heart, all persons that have offended him; and if he have offended other, to ask them forgiveness; and where he hath done injury or wrong to any man, that he make amends to his uttermost power. And if he have not afoi e disposed his goods, let him then make his Will. (But men must be oft admonished that they set an order for their temporal goods and lands when they be in health.) And also to declare his debts, what he oweth, and what is owing unto him; for discharging of his conscience, and

*This may be done before the Minister begins his prayers, as he shall see caus.*

quietness of his exe-
cutors. The Minister
may not forget nor
omit to move the sick
person, (and that
most earnestly,) to
liberality toward the
poor.

Here shall the sick person make a
special Confession, if he feel his
conscience troubled with any
weighty matter. After which
Confession the Priest shall absolve him after this form; and
the same form of Absolution
shall be used in all private Con-
fessions.

Our Lord Jesus Christ, who hath left power to his Church to absolve all sinners which truly repent and believe in him: of his great mercy forgive thee thine offences: and by his authority committed to me, I absolve thee from all thy sins, in the Name of the Father, and of the Son, and of the Holy Ghost. Amen.

And then the Priest shall say the
Collect following.

Let us pray.

O most merciful God, which according to the multitude of thy mercies, dost so put away the sins of those which truly repent, that thou remember-est them no more; Open thy eye of mercy upon this thy servant, who most earnestly desireth pardon and forgive-ness. Renew in him, most loving Father, whatsoever hath been decayed by the fraud and malice of the devil, or by his own carnal will and frailness; preserve and con-tinue this sick member in the unity of thy Church; consider his contrition, accept his tears, assuage his pain, as shall be seen to thee most expedient for him. And forasmuch as he putteth his full trust only in thy mercy, impute not unto him his former sins, but take him unto thy favour; through the merits of thy most dearly beloved Son Je-sus Christ. Amen.

Then the Minister shall say this
Psalm.

*In te, Domine, speravi.*

Psalm lxxi.

In thee, O Lord, have I put my trust; let me never be put to confusion, but rid me, and deliver me in thy righteous-ness: incline thine ear unto me, and save me.

Be thou my strong hold, (whereunto I may alway re-sort), thou hast promised to help me: for thou art my house of defence, and my castle.

Deliver me (O my God) out of the hand of the ungod-ly: out of the hand of the un-righteous and cruel man.

For thou (O Lord God) art the thing that I long for:

thou art my hope even from my youth.

Through thee have I been holden up ever since I was born: thou art he that took me out of my mother's womb; my praise shall be alway of thee.

I am become as it were a monster unto many: but my sure trust is in thee.

O let my mouth be filled with thy praise: (that I may sing of thy glory) and honour all the day long.

Cast me not away in the time of age: forsake me not when my strength faileth me.

For mine enemies speak against me, and they that lay wait for my soul take their counsel together, saying: God hath forsaken him, persecute him, and take him; for there is none to deliver him.

Go not far from me, O God: my God, haste thee to help me.

Let them be confounded and perish that are against my soul: let them be covered with shame and dishonour that seek to do me evil.

As for me, I will patiently abide alway: and will praise thee more and more.

My mouth shall daily speak of thy righteousness and salvation: for I know no end thereof.

I will go forth in the strength of the Lord God: and will make mention of thy righteousness only.

Thou (O God) hast taught me from my youth up until now: therefore will I tell of thy wondrous works.

Forsake me not (O God) in mine old age, when I am grayheaded: until I have shewed thy strength unto this generation, and thy power to all them that are yet for to come.

Thy righteousness (O God) is very high, and great things are they that thou hast done: O God, who is like unto thee?

O what great troubles and adversities hast thou shewed me! and yet didst thou turn and refresh me: yea, and broughtest me from the deep of the earth again.

Thou hast brought me to great honour: and comforted me on every side.

Therefore will I praise thee and thy faithfulness, (O God,) playing upon an instrument of music: unto thee will I sing upon the harp, O thou holy cne of Israel.

My lips will be fain when I sing unto thee: and so will my soul, whom thou hast delivered.

My tongue also shall talk of thy righteousness all the day long: for they are confounded and brought unto shame that seek to do me evil.

Glory be to the Father, and to the Son, and to the Holy Ghost.

As it was in the beginning, is now, etc.

Adding this Anthem,

O SAVIOUR of the world, save us, which by thy Cross and precious Blood hast redeemed us, help us, we beseech thee, O God.

Then shall the Minister say,

THE Almighty Lord, which is a most strong tower to all them that put their trust in him, to whom all things in heaven, in earth, and under earth, do bow and obey, be now and evermore thy defence; and make thee know and feel, that there is no other Name under heaven given to man, in whom, and through whom, thou mayest receive health and salvation, but only the Name of our Lord Jesus Christ. Amen.

If the sick person desire to be anointed, then shall the Priest anoint him upon the forehead or breast only, making the sign of the Cross, saying thus,

As with this visible oil thy body outwardly is anointed, so our heavenly Father, Almighty God, grant of infinite goodness that thy soul inwardly may be anointed with the Holy Ghost, who is the Spirit of all strength, comfort, relief, and gladness. And vouchsafe for his great mercy (if it be his blessed will) to restore unto thee thy bodily health and strength, to serve him; and send thee release of all thy pains, troubles, and diseases, both in body and mind. And howsoever his goodness (by his divine and unsearchable Providence) shall dispose of thee; we his unworthy Ministers and servants, humbly beseech the eternal Majesty to do with thee according to the multitude of his innumerable mercies, and to pardon thee all thy sins and offences committed by all thy bodily senses, passions, and carnal affections; who also vouchsafe mercifully to grant unto thee ghostly strength, by his Holy Spirit, to withstand and overcome all temptations and assaults of thine adversary, that in no wise he prevail against thee; but that thou mayest have perfect victory and triumph against the devil, sin, and death; through Christ our Lord: who by his death hath overcomed the prince of death; and with the Father and the Holy Ghost evermore liveth and reigneth God, world without end. Amen.

*Usque quo, Domine?*
### Psalm xiii.

How long wilt thou forget me, (O Lord,) for ever: how long wilt thou hide thy face from me?

How long shall I seek counsel in my soul, and be so vexed in mine heart: how long shall mine enemy triumph over me?

Consider, and hear me, (O Lord my God)· lighten mine eyes, that I sleep not in death.

Lest mine enemy say, I have prevailed against him: for if I be cast down, they that trouble me will rejoice at it.

But my trust is in thy mercy: and my heart is joyful in thy salvation.

I will sing of the Lord, because he hath dealt so lovingly with me: yea, I will praise the Name of the Lord the most Highest.

Glory be to the Father, and to the Son: and to the Holy Ghost.

As it was in the beginning, is now, and ever shall be: world without end. Amen.

Here follows immediately THE COMMUNION OF THE SICK.

# The Communion of the Sick.

FORASMUCH as all mortal men be subject to many sudden perils, diseases, and sicknesses, and ever uncertain what time they shall depart out of this life; therefore, to the intent they may be always in a readiness to die, whensoever it shall please Almighty God to call them, the Curates shall diligently from time to time, but specially in the Plague time, exhort their Parishioners to the oft receiving (in the Church) of the Holy Communion of the Body and Blood of our Saviour Christ; which (if they do) they shall have no cause, in their sudden visitation, to be unquieted for the lack of the same. But if the sick person be not able to come to the Church, and yet is desirous to receive the Communion in his house, then he must give knowledge over night, or else early in the morning, to the Curate, signifying also how many be appointed to communicate with him. And if the same day there be a celebration of the Holy Communion in the Church, then shall the Priest reserve (at the open Communion) so much of the Sacrament of the Body and Blood as shall serve the sick person, and so many as shall communicate with him, (if there b·any.) And so soon as he conveniently may, after the open Communion ended in the Church, shall go and minister the same, first to those that are appointed to communicate with the sick, (if there be any,) and last of all to the sick person himself. But before the Curate distribute the Holy Communion, the appointe l *general Confession* must be made in the name of the communicants, the Curate adding the *Absolution, with the comfortable sentences of Scripture* following in the open Communion. And after the Communion ended, the Collect.

ALMIGHTY and everliving God, we most heartily thank thee, etc.

But if the day be not appointed for the open Communion in the Church, then (upon convenient warning given) the Curate shall come and visit the sick person afore noon. And having a convenient place in the sick man's house, (where he may reverently celebrate,) with all things nece-sary for the same, and not being otherwise letted with the public Service, or any other just impediment, he shall there celebrate the Holy Communion after such form and sort as hereafter is appointed.

✠

# THE CELEBRATION

## OF THE

# Holy Communion for the Sick.

O PRAISE the Lord, all ye nations; laud him, all ye people: for his merciful kindness is confirmed toward us, and the truth of the Lord endureth for ever.

Glory be to the Father, and to the Son: and to the Holy Ghost.

As it was in the beginning, is now, and ever shall be: world without end. Amen.

Lord, have mercy upon us.
Christ, have mercy upon us.
Lord, have mercy upon us.

*Without any more repetition.*

*The Priest.*

The Lord be with you.
*Answer.*
And with thy spirit.
Let us pray.

ALMIGHTY everliving God, Maker of mankind, which dost correct those whom thou dost love, and chastisest every one whom thou dost receive: We beseech thee to have mercy upon this thy servant visited with thy hand, and to grant that he may take his sickness patiently, and recover his bodily health, (if it be thy gracious will;) and whensoever his soul shall depart from the body, it may without spot be presented unto thee; through Jesus Christ our Lord. Amen.

*The Epistle.* Heb. xii.

MY son, despise not the correction of the Lord, neither faint when thou art rebuked of him. For whom the Lord loveth, him he correcteth; yea, and he scourgeth every son whom he receiveth.

*The Gospel.* John v.

VERILY, verily, I say unto you, He that heareth my word, and believeth on him that sent me, hath everlasting life, and shall not come unto damnation; but he passeth from death unto life.

*The Preface.*

The Lord be with you.

*Answer.*

And with thy spirit.

Lift up your hearts, etc.

Unto the end of the Canon.

At the time of the distribution of the Holy Sacrament, the Priest shall first receive the Communion himself, and after minister to them that be appointed to communicate with the sick, (if there be any) and then to the sick person. And the sick person shall always desire some, either of his own house or else of his neighbours, to receive the Holy Communion with him, for that shall be to him a singular great comfort, and of their part a great token of charity.

And if there be more sick to be visited the same day that the Curate doth celebrate in any sick man's house, then shall the Curate (there) reserve so much of the Sacrament of the Body and Blood as shall serve the other sick persons, and such as be appointed to communicate with them, (if there be any;) and shall immediately carry it, an l minister it unto them.

But if any man, either by reason of extremity of sickness, or for lack of warning given in due time to the Curate, or by any other just impediment do not receive the Sacrament of Christ's Body and Blood; then the Curate shall instruct him, that if he do truly repent him of his sins, and stedfastly believe that Jesus Christ hath suff red death upon the Cross for him, and shed his Blood for his redemption, earnestly remembering the benefits he hath thereby, and giving him hearty thanks therefore, he doth eat and drink spiritually the Body a d Blood of our Saviour Christ profitably to his soul's health, although he do not receive the Sacrament with his mouth.

When the sick person is visited and receiveth the holy Communion all at one time, then the Priest, for more expedition, shall use this order at the Visitation.

The Anthem.

Remember not, Lord, etc.

Lord, have mercy upon us.

Christ, have mercy upon us.

Lord, have mercy upon us.

Our Father which art in heaven, etc.

And lead us not into temptation.

*Answer.*

But deliver us from evil. Amen.

Let us pray.

O Lord, look down from heaven, etc.

With the first part of the exhortation, and all other things unto the Psalm.

In thee, O Lord, have I put my trust, etc.

And if the sick person desire to be anointed, then shall the Priest use the appointed prayer without any Psalm.

THE ORDER FOR

# The Burial of the Dead.

The Priest, meeting the Corpse at the Church stile, shall say, or else the Priests and Clerks shall sing, and so go either into the Church, or towards the Grave.

I AM the Resurrection and the life, (saith the Lord:) he that believeth in me, yea, though he were dead, yet shall he live: and whosoever liveth and believeth in me shall not die for ever.—(*John* xi.)

I KNOW that my Redeemer liveth, and that I shall rise out of the earth in the last day, and shall be covered again with my skin, and shall see God in my flesh: yea, and I myself shall behold him, not with other but with these same eyes.—(*Job.* xix.)

WE brought nothing into this world, neither may we carry any thing out of this world. The Lord giveth, and the Lord taketh away. Even as it pleaseth the Lord, so cometh things to pass. Blessed be the Name of the Lord. —(1. *Tim.* vi; *Job.* i.)

When they come at the Grave, whiles the Corpse is made ready to be laid into the earth, the Priest shall say, or else the Priests and Clerks shall sing.

MAN that is born of a woman hath but a short time to live, and is full of misery. He cometh up, and is cut down, like a flower; he flieth as it were a shadow, and never continueth in one stay. —(*Job.* ix.)

In the midst of life we be in death: of whom may we seek for succour, but of thee,

O Lord, which for our sins justly art moved? Yet, O Lord God most holy, O Lord most mighty, O holy and most merciful Saviour, deliver us not into the bitter pains of eternal death. Thou knowest, Lord, the secrets of our hearts; shut not up thy merciful eyes to our prayers: but spare us, Lord most holy, O God most mighty, O holy and merciful Saviour, thou most worthy Judge eternal, suffer us not, at our last hour, for any pains of death, to fall from theé.

Then the Priest, casting earth upon the Corpse, shall say,

I COMMEND thy soul to God the Father Almighty, and thy body to the ground: earth to earth, ashes to ashes, dust to dust; in sure and certain hope of resurrection to eternal life, through our Lord Jesus Christ; who shall change our vile body, that it may be like to his glorious body, according to the mighty working, whereby he is able to subdue all things to himself.

Then shall be said or sung,

I HEARD a voice from heaven, saying unto me: Write, Blessed are the dead which die in the Lord: even so saith the Spirit; that they rest from their labours.— (*Rev.* xiv.)

Let us pray.

WE commend into thy hands of mercy (most merciful Father) the soul of this our brother departed, N. And his body we commit to the earth; beseeching thine infinite goodness to give us grace to live in thy fear and love, and to die in thy favour: that when the Judgment shall come, which thou hast committed to thy well-beloved Son, both this our brother and we may be found acceptable in thy sight, and receive that blessing which thy well-beloved Son shall then pronounce to all that love and fear thee, saying, Come, ye blessed children of my Father, receive the kingdom prepared for you before the beginning of the world. Grant this, merciful Father, for the honour of Jesu Christ our only Saviour, Mediator, and Advocate. Amen.

This prayer shall also be added.

ALMIGHTY God, we give thee hearty thanks for this thy servant, whom thou hast delivered from the miseries of this wretched world, from the body of death, and all temptation; and, as we trust, hast brought his soul, which he committed into thy holy hands, into sure consolation and rest. Grant we beseech thee, that at the day of Judgment his soul, and all the souls of thy elect departed out of this life, may with us and we with them, fully receive thy promises, and be made perfect altogether through the glorious resurrection of thy Son Jesus Christ our Lord.

These Psalms, with other suffrages following. are to be said in the Church. either before or after the burial of the Corpse.

*Dilexi, quoniam.*
Psalm cxvi.

I AM well pleased that the Lord hath heard the voice of my prayer.

That he hath inclined his ear unto me : therefore will I call upon him as long as I live.

The snares of death compassed me round about, and the pains of hell gat hold upon me : I shall find trouble and heaviness, and I shall call upon the Name of the Lord, (O Lord) I beseech thee, deliver my soul.

Gracious is the Lord, and righteous: yea, our God is merciful.

The Lord preserveth the simple : I was in misery, and he helped me.

Turn again then unto thy rest, O my soul : for the Lord hath rewarded thee.

And why? thou hast delivered my soul from death : mine eyes from tears, and my feet from falling.

I will walk before the Lord: in the land of the living.

I believed, and therefore will I speak : but I was sore troubled.

I said in my haste : all men are liars.

What reward shall I give unto the Lord : for all the benefits that he hath done unto me?

I will receive the cup of salvation : and call upon the Name of the Lord.

I will pay my vows now in the presence of all his people : right dear in the sight of the Lord is the death of his saints.

Behold (O Lord) how that I am thy servant : I am thy servant, and the son of thy handmaid ; thou hast broken my bonds in sunder.

I will offer to thee the sacrifice of thanksgiving : and will call upon the Name of the Lord.

I will pay my vows unto the Lord in the sight of all his people : in the courts of the Lord's house, even in the midst of thee, O Hierusalem.

Glory be to the Father, and

to the Son: and to the Holy Ghost.

As it was in the beginning, is now, and ever shall be: world without end.   Amen.

*Domine, probasti.*

Psalm cxxxix.

O LORD, thou hast searched me out: and known me.

Thou knowest my down-sitting and mine up-rising: thou understandest my thoughts long before.

Thou art about my path and about my bed: and spiest out all my ways.

For lo, there is not a word in my tongue: but thou (O Lord) knowest it altogether.

Thou hast fashioned me behind and before: and laid thine hand upon me.

Such knowledge is too wonderful and excellent for me: I cannot attain unto it.

Whither shall I go then from thy Spirit: or whither shall I go then from thy Presence?

If I climb up into heaven, thou art there: if I go down to hell, thou art there also.

If I take the wings of the morning: and remain in the uttermost parts of the sea;

Even there also shall thy hand lead me: and thy right hand shall hold me.

If I say, Peradventure the darkness shall cover me: then shall my night be turned to day.

Yea, the darkness is no darkness with thee: but the night is all clear as the day, the darkness and light to thee are both alike.

For my reins are thine, thou hast covered me in my mother's womb, I will give thanks unto thee: for I am fearfully and wondrously made, marvellous are thy works, and that my soul knoweth right well.

My bones are not hid from thee: though I be made secretly, and fashioned beneath in the earth.

Thine eyes did see my substance, yet being unperfect: and in thy book were all my members written;

Which day by day were fashioned: when as yet there was none of them.

How dear are thy counsels unto me, O God: O how great is the sum of them.

If I tell them, they are more in number than the sand: when I wake up I am present with thee.

Wilt thou not slay the wicked, O God: depart from me, ye bloodthirsty men.

For they speak unrighteously against thee: and

thine enemies take thy Name in vain.

Do not I hate them, O Lord, that hate thee: and am not I grieved with those that rise up against thee?

Yea, I hate them right sore: even as though they were mine enemies.

Try me, O God, and seek the ground of mine heart: prove me, and examine my thoughts.

Look well if there be any way of wickedness in me: and lead me in the way everlasting.

Glory be to the Father, and to the Son: and to the Holy Ghost.

As it was in the beginning, is now, and ever shall be: world without end. Amen.

*Lauda, anima mea.*

### Psalm cxlvi.

PRAISE the Lord, (O my soul;) while I live will I praise the Lord: yea, as long as I have any being I will sing praises unto my God.

O put not your trust in princes, nor in any child of man, for there is no help in them.

For when the breath of man goeth forth he shall turn again to his earth: and then all his thoughts perish.

Blessed is he that hath the God of Jacob for his help: and whose hope is in the Lord his God;

Which made heaven and earth, the sea, and all that therein is: which keepeth his promise for ever;

Which helpeth them to right that suffer wrong: which feedeth the hungry.

The Lord looseth men out of prison: the Lord giveth sight to the blind.

The Lord helpeth them up that are fallen: the Lord careth for the righteous.

The Lord careth for the strangers; he defendeth the fatherless and widow: as for the way of the ungodly, he turneth it upside down.

The Lord thy God, O Zion, shall be King for evermore: and throughout all generations.

Glory be to the Father, and to the Son: and to the Holy Ghost.

As it was in the beginning, is now, and ever shall be: world without end. Amen.

Then shall follow this Lesson, taken out of the xv. chapter to the Corinthians, the first Epistle.

CHRIST is risen from the dead, and become (1. *Cor.* xv.) the first fruits of them that slept. For by a man came death, and by a man came the resurrection of the dead. For as by Adam all die, even so by Christ shall all be made alive. But every man in his own order : the first is Christ, then they that are Christ's at his coming. Then cometh the end, when he hath delivered up the kingdom to God the Father; when he hath put down all rule, and all authority, and power. For he must reign, till he have put all his enemies under his feet. The last enemy that shall be destroyed is death. For he hath put all things under his feet. But when he saith, all things are put under him, it is manifest that he is excepted, which did put all things under him. When all things are subdued unto him, then shall the Son also himself be subject unto him that put all things under him, that God may be all in all. Else what do they which are baptized over the dead, if the dead rise not at all ? Why are they then baptized over them ? yea, and why stand we alway then in jeopardy ? By our rejoicing which I have in Christ Jesu our Lord, I die daily. That I have fought with beasts at Ephesus after the manner of men, what advantageth it me, if the dead rise not again ? Let us eat and drink, for to-morrow we shall die. Be not ye deceived : evil words corrupt good manners. Awake truly out of sleep, and sin not ; for some have not the knowledge of God. I speak this to your shame. But some man will say, How arise the dead? with what body shall they come ? Thou fool, that which thou sowest is not quickened, except it die. And what sowest thou ? Thou sowest not that body that shall be, but bare corn, as of wheat or of some other : but God giveth it a body at his pleasure, to every seed his own body. All flesh is not one manner of flesh ; but there is one manner of flesh of men, another manner of flesh of beasts, another of fishes, and another of birds. There are also celestial bodies, and there are bodies terrestrial ; but the glory of the celestial is one, and the glory of the terrestrial is another. There is one manner of glory of the sun, and another glory of the moon, and another glory of the stars ; for one star differeth from another in glory. So is the resurrection of the dead : it is sown in corruption ; it riseth again in incorruption : it is sown in dishonour ; it riseth again in honour : it is sown in weakness ; it riseth again in power:

it is sown a natural body; it riseth again a spiritual body. There is a natural body, and there is a spiritual body: as it is also written, The first man Adam was made a living soul; and the last Adam was made a quickening spirit. Howbeit, that is not first which is spiritual, but that which is natural; and then that which is spiritual. The first man is of the earth, earthy: the second man is the Lord from heaven (heavenly). As is the earthy, such are they that are earthy: and as is the heavenly, such are they that are heavenly. And as we have borne the image of the earthy, so shall we bear the image of the heavenly. This say I, brethren, that flesh and blood cannot inherit the kingdom of God; neither doth corruption inherit uncorruption. Behold, I shew you a mystery: we shall not all sleep, but we shall all be changed, and that in a moment, in the twinkling of an eye, by the last trump; for the trump shall blow, and the dead shall rise incorruptible, and we shall be changed. For this corruptible must put on incorruption, and this mortal must put on immortality. When this corruptible hath put on incorruption, and this mortal hath put on immortality; then shall be brought to pass the saying that is written, Death is swallowed up in victory. Death, where is thy sting? Hell, where is thy victory? The sting of death is sin, and the strength of sin is the law. But thanks be unto God, which hath given us victory through our Lord Jesus Christ. Therefore, my dear brethren, be ye stedfast and unmovable, always rich in the work of the Lord, forasmuch as ye know how that your labour is not in vain in the Lord.

The Lesson ended, then shall the Priest say,

Lord, have mercy upon us.

Christ, have mercy upon us.

Lord, have mercy upon us.

Our Father which art in heaven, etc.

And lead us not into temptation.

*Answer.*

But deliver us from evil. Amen.

*Priest.*

Enter not (O Lord) into judgment with thy servant.

*Answer.*

For in thy sight no living creature shall be justified.

*Priest.*

From the gates of hell.

*Answer.*

Deliver their souls, O Lord.

*Priest.*

I believe to see the goodness of the Lord.

*Answer.*

In the land of the living.

*Priest.*

O Lord, graciously hear my prayer.

*Answer.*

And let my cry come unto thee.

Let us pray.

O LORD, with whom do live the spirits of them that be dead, and in whom the souls of them that be elected, after they be delivered from the burden of the flesh, be in joy and felicity; Grant unto this thy servant, that the sins which he committed in this world be not imputed unto him; but that he, escaping the gates of hell, and pains of eternal darkness, may ever dwell in the region of light, with Abraham, Isaac, and Jacob, in the place where is no weeping, sorrow, nor heaviness: and when that dreadful Day of the general Resurrection shall come, make him to rise also with the just and righteous, and receive this body again to glory, then made pure and incorruptible. Set him on the right hand of thy Son Jesus Christ, among thy holy and elect, that then he may hear with them these most sweet and comfortable words; Come to me, ye blessed of my Father, possess the kingdom which hath been prepared for you from the beginning of the world. Grant this. we beseech thee, O merciful Father, through Jesus Christ our Mediator and Redeemer. Amen.

✠

## THE CELEBRATION

OF THE

# 𝔥𝔬𝔩𝔶 ℭ𝔬𝔪𝔪𝔲𝔫𝔦𝔬𝔫 𝔴𝔥𝔢𝔫 𝔱𝔥𝔢𝔯𝔢 𝔦𝔰 𝔞 𝔅𝔲𝔯𝔦𝔞𝔩 𝔬𝔣 𝔱𝔥𝔢 𝔇𝔢𝔞𝔡.

*Quemadmodum.* Psalm xlii.

Like as the hart desireth the water-brooks: so longeth my soul after thee, O God.

My soul is athirst for God, yea, even for the living God: When shall I come to appear before the presence of God?

My tears have been my meat day and night: while they daily say unto me, Where is now thy God?

Now when I think thereupon, I pour out my heart by myself: for I went with the multitude, and brought them forth unto the house of God;

In the voice of praise and thanksgiving: among such as keep holy day.

Why art thou so full of heaviness, (O my soul:) and why art thou so unquiet within me?

Put thy trust in God: for I will yet give him thanks for the help of his countenance.

My God, my soul is vexed within me: therefore will I remember thee concerning the land of Jordan, and the little hill of Hermonim.

One deep calleth another, because of the noise of thy water-pipes: all thy waves and storms are gone over me.

The Lord hath granted his loving-kindness on the day-time: and in the night season did I sing of him, and made my prayer unto the God of my life.

I will say unto the God of my strength, Why hast thou forgotten me: why go I thus heavily, while the enemy oppresseth me?

My bones are smitten asunder, while mine enemies (that trouble me) cast me in the teeth: namely, while they say daily unto me, Where is now thy God?

Why art thou so vexed, (O my soul:) and why art thou so disquieted within me?

O put thy trust in God, for I will yet thank him: which is the help of my countenance, and my God.

Glory be to the Father, and to the Son: and to the Holy Ghost.

As it was in the beginning, is now, and ever shall be: world without end. Amen.

### Collect.

O MERCIFUL God, the Father of our Lord Jesu Christ, who is the Resurrection and the Life: in whom whosoever believeth shall live, though he die: and whosoever liveth, and believeth in him, shall not die eternally: who also hath taught us (by his holy Apostle Paul) not to be sorry, as men without hope, for them that sleep in him: We meekly beseech thee (O Father) to raise us from the death of sin unto the life of righteousness; that, when we shall depart this life, we may sleep in him, ~~(as our hope is this our brother doth;)~~ and at the ~~general~~ Resurrection ~~in the last Day~~, both we, and this our brother departed, receiving again our bodies, and rising again in thy most gracious favour, may, with all thine elect Saints, obtain eternal joy. Grant this, O Lord God, by the means of our Advocate Jesus Christ; which, with thee and the Holy Ghost, liveth and reigneth one God for ever. Amen.

### The Epistle. 1. Thess. iv.

I WOULD not, brethren, that ye should be ignorant concerning them which are fallen asleep, that ye sorrow not as other do which have no hope. For if we believe that Jesus died, and rose again, even so them also which sleep by Jesus will God bring again with him. For this say we unto you in the word of the Lord, that we which shall live, and shall remain in the coming of the Lord, shall not come ere they which sleep. For the Lord himself shall descend from heaven with a shout, and the voice of the archangel, and trump of God: and the dead in Christ shall arise first: then we which shall live (even we which shall remain) shall be caught up with them also in the clouds, to meet the Lord in the air: and so shall we ever be with the Lord. Wherefore comfort yourselves one another with these words.

### The Gospel. John vi.

JESUS said to his disciples and to the Jews, All that the Father giveth me shall come to me; and he that cometh to me I cast not away. For I came down from heaven, not to do that I will, but that he will which hath sent me.

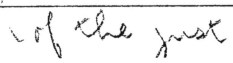

*of the just*

And this is the Father's will which hath sent me, that of all which he hath given me I shall lose nothing, but raise them up again at the last day. And this is the will of him that sent me, that every one which seeth the Son, and believeth on him, have everlasting life: and I will raise him up at the last day.

# THE ORDER

## OF THE

# Purification of Women.

The Woman shall come into the Church, and there shall kneel down in some convenient place nigh unto the Quire door; and the Priest standing by her, shall say these words, or such like, as the case shall require.

FORASMUCH as it hath pleased Almighty God of his goodness to give you safe deliverance: and your child Baptism, and hath preserved you in the great danger of childbirth; ye shall therefore give hearty thanks unto God, and pray.

Then shall the Priest say this Psalm.

*Levavi oculos.* Psalm cxxi.

I HAVE lifted up mine eyes unto the hills: from whence cometh my help.

My help cometh even from the Lord: which hath made heaven and earth.

He will not suffer thy foot to be moved: and he that keepeth thee will not sleep.

Behold he that keepeth Israel: shall neither slumber nor sleep.

The Lord himself is thy keeper: the Lord is thy defence upon thy right hand;

So that the sun shall not burn thee by day: neither the moon by night.

The Lord shall preserve thee from all evil: yea, it is even he that shall keep thy soul.

The Lord shall preserve thy going out and thy coming in: from this time forth for evermore.

Glory be to the Father, and to the Son: and to the Holy Ghost,

As it was in the beginning, is now, etc.

Lord, have mercy upon us.

Christ, have mercy upon us.

Lord, have mercy upon us.

Our Father which art in heaven, etc.

And lead us not into temptation.

*Answer.*

But deliver us from evil. Amen.

*Priest.*

O Lord, save this woman thy servant.

*Answer.*

Which putteth her trust in thee.

*Priest.*

Be thou to her a strong tower.

*Answer.*

From the face of her enemy.

*Priest.*

Lord, hear our prayer.

*Answer.*

And let our cry come to thee.

*Priest.*

Let us pray.

O ALMIGHTY God, which has delivered this woman thy servant from the great pain and peril of childbirth: Grant, we beseech thee, (most merciful Father,) that she, through thy help, may both faithfully live and walk in her vocation, according to thy will, in this life present: and also may be partaker of everlasting glory in the life to come: through Jesus Christ our Lord. Amen.

The Woman that is purified must offer her Crisome, and other accustomed offerings. And if there be a Communion, it is convenient that she receive the holy Communion.

## The First Day of Lent,

COMMONLY CALLED

## Ashwednesday.

After Matins ended, the people being called together by the ringing of a Bell, and assembled in the Church, the English Litany shall be said after the accustomed manner, which ended, the Priest shall go into the Pulpit, and say thus:

BRETHREN, in the primitive Church there was a godly discipline, that, at the beginning of Lent, such persons as were notorious sinners were put to open penance, and punished in this world, that their souls might be saved in the day of the Lord; and that other, admonished by their example, might be more afraid to offend. In the stead whereof, until the said discipline may be restored again, (which thing is much to be wished,) it is thought good that at this time (in your presence) should be read the general sentences of God's cursing against impenitent sinners, gathered out of the xxvii. chapter of Deuteronomy, and other places of Scripture; and that ye should answer to every sentence, Amen: to the intent that you, being admonished of the great indignation of God against sinners, may the rather be called to earnest and true repentance; and may walk more warily in these dangerous days; fleeing from such vices for the which ye affirm with your own mouths the curse of God to be due.

CURSED is the man that maketh any carved or molten image, an abomination to the Lord, the work of the hands of the craftsman, and putteth it in a secret place to worship it.

And the people shall answer and say,

Amen.

*Minister.*

Cursed is he that curseth his father and mother.

*Answer.*

Amen.

*Minister.*

Cursed is he that removeth away the mark of his neighbour's land.

*Answer.*

Amen.

*Minister.*

Cursed is he that maketh the blind to go out of his way.

*Answer.*

Amen.

*Minister.*

Cursed is he that letteth in judgment the right of the stranger, of them that be fatherless, and of widows.

*Answer.*

Amen.

*Minister.*

Cursed is he that smiteth his neighbour secretly.

*Answer.*

Amen.

*Minister.*

Cursed is he that lieth with his neighbour's wife.

*Answer.*

Amen.

*Minister.*

Cursed is he that taketh reward to slay the soul of innocent blood.

*Answer.*

Amen.

*Minister.*

Cursed is he that putteth his trust in man, and taketh man for his defence, and in his heart goeth from the Lord.

*Answer.*

Amen.

*Minister.*

Cursed are the unmerciful, the fornicators and adulterers, the covetous persons, the worshippers of images, slanderers, drunkards, and extortioners.

*Answer.*

Amen.

*The Minister.*

Psalm cxviii. Now seeing that all they be accursed (as the prophet David beareth witness) which do err and go astray from the commandments of God: let us (remembering the dreadful judgment hanging over our heads, and being always at hand) return unto our Lord God, with all contrition and meekness of heart; bewailing and lamenting our sinful life, knowledging and confessing our offences, and seeking to bring forth worthy fruits of penance. For even now is the Matt. iii. axe put unto the root of the trees, so that every tree which bringeth not forth good fruit is hewn down, and cast into the fire. It is a fearful Heb. x. thing to fall into the hands of the living God: he shall pour down rain upon the sinners, snares, fire and brimstone, storm and tempest; this Psalm x. shall be their portion to drink. For lo, the Lord is Isa. xxvi. cummen out of his place to visit the wickedness of such as dwell upon the earth. But who may abide Mal iii. the day of his coming? Who shall be able to endure when he appeareth? His fan Matt. iii. is in his hand, and he will purge his floor, and gather his wheat into the barn; but he will burn the chaff with unquenchable fire. The 1. Thess. v. day of the Lord cometh as a thief upon the night: and when men shall say, Peace, and all things are safe, then shall sudden destruction come upon them, as sorrow cometh upon a woman travailing with child, and they shall not escape. Then shall appear the wrath of God in the day of vengeance, which obstinate sinners, through the stubbornness of their heart, have heaped upon themselves; which despised Rom. ii. the goodness, patience, and long-sufferance of God, when he called them continually to repentance. Then Prov. i. shall they call upon me, (saith the Lord,) but I will not hear; they shall seek me early, but they shall not find me; and that, because they hated knowledge, and received not the fear of the Lord, but abhorred my counsel, and despised my correction. Then shall it be too late to knock when the door shall be shut; and too late to cry for mercy when it is the time of justice. O terrible voice of most just judgment, which shall be pronounced upon them, when it shall be said unto them, Go, ye cursed, Matt. xxv. into the fire everlasting, which is prepared for the devil and his angels. Therefore, brethren, take we heed by time, while the day of salvation lasteth; for the night 2. Cor. vi. cometh when none can work. But let us, while John ix. we have the light, believe in the light, and walk as the children of the light;

that we be not cast into the utter darkness, where is Matt. xxv. weeping and gnashing of teeth. Let us not abuse the goodness of God, which calleth us mercifully to amendment, and of his endless pity promiseth us forgiveness of that which is past if (with a whole mind and a true heart) we return unto him. For though our sins be Isa. i. red as scarlet, they shall be as white as snow; and though they be like purple, yet shall they be as white as wool. Turn you clean (saith Ezek. xviii. the Lord) from all your wickedness, and your sin shall not be your destruction. Cast away from you all your ungodliness that ye have done: make you new hearts, and a new spirit: wherefore will ye die, O ye house of Israel? seeing I have no pleasure in the death of him that dieth (saith the Lord God). Turn you then, and you shall live. Although 1 John i. we have sinned, yet have we an Advocate with the Father, Jesus Christ the righteous; and he it is that obtaineth grace for our sins: Isa. liii. for he was wounded for our offences, and smitten for our wickedness. Let us therefore return unto him, who is the merciful receiver of all true penitent sinners; assuring ourselves that he is ready to receive us, and most willing to pardon us if we come to him with faithful repentance; if we will submit ourselves unto him, and from henceforth walk in his ways; Matt. xi. if we will take his easy yoke and light burden upon us, to follow him in lowliness, patience, and charity, and be ordered by the governance of his Holy Spirit; seeking always his glory, and serving him duly in our vocation with thanksgiving. This if we do, Christ will deliver us from the curse of the law, and from the extreme malediction which shall light upon them that shall be set on the left hand; and he will set us on Matt. xxv. his right hand, and give us the blessed benediction of his Father, commanding us to take possession of his glorious kingdom: unto the which he vouchsafe to bring us all, for his infinite mercy. Amen.

Then shall they all kneel upon their knees; and the Priest and Clerks kneeling (where they are accustomed to say the Litany) shall say this Psalm.

*Miserere mei, Deus.*
Psalm li.

HAVE mercy upon me, (O God,) after thy great good-ness: according unto the multitude of thy mercies do away mine offences.

Wash me throughly from my wickedness: and cleanse me from my sin.

For I knowledge my faults: and my sin is ever before me.

Against thee only have I sinned, and done this evil in thy sight: that thou mightest be justified in thy saying, and clear when thou art judged.

Behold, I was shapen in wickedness: and in sin hath my mother conceived me.

But lo, thou requirest truth in the inward parts: and shalt make me to understand wisdom secretly.

Thou shalt purge me with hyssop, and I shall be clean: thou shalt wash me, and I shall be whiter than snow.

Thou shalt make me hear of joy and gladness: that the bones which thou hast broken may rejoice.

Turn thy face from my sins: and put out all my misdeeds.

Make me a clean heart, (O God:) and renew a right spirit within me.

Cast me not away from thy Presence: and take not thy Holy Spirit from me.

O give me the comfort of thy help again: and stablish me with thy free Spirit.

Then shall I teach thy ways unto the wicked: and sinners shall be converted unto thee.

Deliver me from bloodguiltiness, (O God,) thou that art the God of my health: and my tongue shall sing of thy righteousness.

Thou shalt open my lips, (O Lord:) my mouth shall shew thy praise.

For thou desirest no sacrifice, else would I give it thee: but thou delightest not in burnt-offering.

The sacrifice of God is a troubled spirit: a broken and a contrite heart, (O God) shalt thou not despise.

O be favourable and gracious unto Sion: build thou the walls of Hierusalem.

Then shalt thou be pleased with the sacrifice of righteousness, with the burnt-offerings and oblations: then shall they offer young bullocks upon thine altar.

Glory be to the Father, and to the Son: and to the Holy Ghost.

As it was in the beginning, is now, and ever shall be: world without end. Amen.

Lord, have mercy upon us.

Christ, have mercy upon us.

Lord, have mercy upon us.

Our Father, which art in heaven, etc.

And lead us not into temptation.

*Answer.*

But deliver us from evil. Amen.

*Minister.*

O Lord, save thy servants.

*Answer.*

Which put their trust in thee.

*Minister.*

Send unto them help from above.

*Answer.*

And evermore mightily defend them.

*Minister.*

Help us, O God, our Saviour.

*Answer.*

And for the glory of thy Name's sake deliver us; be merciful unto us sinners, for thy Name's sake.

*Minister.*

O Lord, hear my prayer.

*Answer.*

And let my cry come to thee.

Let us pray.

O Lord, we beseech thee, mercifully hear our prayers, and spare all those which confess their sins to thee; that they, (whose consciences by sin are accused,) by thy merciful pardon may be absolved; through Christ our Lord. Amen.

O MOST mighty God, and merciful Father, which hast compassion of all men, and hatest nothing that thou hast made; which wouldest not the death of a sinner, but that he should rather turn from sin, and be s a v e d; Mercifully forgive us our trespasses: receive and comfort us, which be grieved and wearied with the burden of our sin. Thy property is to have mercy; to thee only it appertaineth to forgive sins. Spare us t h e r e f o r e good L o r d, spare thy people, whom thou hast redeemed; enter not into judgment with thy servants which be vile earth, and miserable sinners; but so turn thy ire from us, which meekly knowledge our vileness, and truly repent us of our fautes : so make haste to help us in this world, that we may ever live with thee in the world to come; through Jesus Christ our Lord. Amen.

Then shall this Anthem be said or sung.

TURN thou us, good Lord, and so shall we be turned. Be favourable, (O Lord,) be favourable to t h y people, which turn to thee in weeping, fasting, and praying. For thou art a merciful God, full of compassion, longsuffering, and of a great pity. Thou sparest when we deserve punishment, and in thy wrath thinkest upon mercy. Spare thy people, good Lord, spare them, and let not thine heritage be brought to confusion. Hear us (O Lord,) for thy mercy is great, and after the multitude of thy mercies look upon us.

## OF CEREMONIES,

### why some be abolished and some retained.

OF such Ceremonies as be used in the Church, and have had their beginning by the institution of man, some at the first were of godly intent and purpose devised, and yet at length turned to vanity and superstition; some entered into the Church by undiscreet devotion, and such a zeal as was without knowledge: and forbecause they were winked at in the beginning, they grew daily to more and more abuses, which, not only for their unprofitableness, but also because they have much blinded the people, and obscured the glory of God, are worthy to be cut away, and clean rejected. Other there be, which although they have been devised by man, yet it is thought good to reserve them still, as well for a decent order in the Church, (for the which they were first devised,) as because they pertain to edification; whereunto all things done in the Church (as the Apostle teacheth) ought to be referred. And although the keeping or omitting of a Ceremony (in itself considered) is but a small thing, yet the wilful and contemptuous trangression, and breaking of a common order and discipline, is no small offence before God. Let all things be done among you (saith Saint Paul) in a seemly and due order: the appointment of the which order pertaineth not to private men. Therefore, no man ought to take in hand nor presume to appoint or alter any public or common order in Christ's Church, except he be lawfully called and authorized thereunto. And whereas, in this our time, the minds of men be so diverse, that some think it a great matter of conscience to depart from a piece of the least of their Ceremonies (they be so addicted to their old customs;) and again, on the other side, some be so new fangle, that they would innovate all thing, and so do despise the old that nothing can like them but that is new: It was thought expedient not so much to have respect how to please and satisfy either of these parties, as how to please God, and profit them both. And yet, lest any man should be offended, (whom good reason might satisfy,) here be certain causes rendered why some of the accustomed Ceremonies be put away, and some be retained and kept still.

Some are put away because the great excess and multitude of them hath so increased in these latter days, that the burden of them was intolerable: whereof Saint Augustine in his time complained that they were grown to such a number, that the state of Christian people was in worse case (concerning that matter) than were the Jews: and he counselled, that such yoke and burden should be taken away, as time would serve quietly to do it. But what would Saint Augustine have said, if he had seen the Ceremonies of late days used among us, whereunto the multitude used in his time was not to be compared? This our excessive multitude of Ceremonies was so great, and many of them so dark, that they did more confound and darken than declare and set forth Christ's benefits unto us. And besides this, Christ's Gospel is not a ceremonial law, (as much of Moses' law was,) but it is a religion to serve God, not in bondage of the figure or shadow, but in the freedom of spirit, being content only with those Ceremonies which do serve to a decent order and godly discipline, and such as be apt to stir up the dull mind of man to the remembrance of his duty to God, by some notable and special signification, whereby he might be edified

Furthermore, the most weighty cause of the abolishment of certain Ceremonies was, that they were so far abused, partly by the superstitious blindness of the rude and unlearned, and partly by the unsatiable avarice of such as sought more their own lucre than the glory of God, that the abuses could not well be taken away, the thing remaining still. But now, as concerning those persons which peradventure will be offended for that some of the old Ceremonies are retained still; if they consider, that without some Ceremonies it is not possible to keep any order or quiet discipline in the Church, they shall easily perceive just cause to reform their judgments. And if they think much that any of the old do remain, and would rather have all devised anew, then such men (granting some Ceremonies convenient to be had) surely where the old may be well used, there they cannot reasonably reprove the old, (only for their age,) without bewraying of their own folly. For in such a case they ought rather to have reverence unto them for their antiquity, if they will declare themselves to be more studious of unity and concord than of innovations and newfangleness, which (as much as may be with the true setting forth of Christ's religion) is always to be eschewed. Furthermore, such shall have no just cause with the Ceremonies reserved to be offended; for as those be taken away which were most abused, and did burden men's consciences without any cause, so the other that remain are retained for a discipline and order, which (upon just causes) may be altered and changed, and therefore are not to be esteemed equal with God's law. And moreover, they be neither dark nor dumb Ceremonies, but are so set forth that every man may understand what they do mean, and to what use they do serve: so that it is not like that they, in time to come, should be abused as the other have been. And in these all our doings we condemn no other nations, nor prescribe any thing but to our own people only. For we think it convenient that every country should use such Ceremonies as they shall think best to the setting forth of God's honour and glory, and to the reducing of the people to a most perfect and godly living, without error or superstition: and that they should put away other things which from time to time they perceive to be most abused, as in men's ordinances it often chanceth diversely in diverse countries.*

# CERTAIN NOTES

## For the more plain explication and decent ministration of things contained in this Book.

In the saying or singing of Matins and Evensong, Baptizing and Burying, the Minister, in Parish Churches and Chapels annexed to the same, shall use a Surplice. And in all Cathedral Churches and Colleges, the Archdeacons, Deans, Provosts, Masters, Prebendaries, and Fellows, being Graduates, may use in the Quire, beside their Surplices, such Hoods as pertaineth to their several Degrees, which they have taken in any University within this Realm. But in all other places, every Minister shall be at liberty to use any Surplice or no. It is also seemly, that Graduates when they do preach, should use such Hoods as pertaineth to their several Degrees.

And whensoever the Bishop shall celebrate the Holy Communion in the Church, or execute any other public Ministration, he shall have upon him, beside his Rochette, a Surplice or Albe, and a Cope or Vestment; and also his Pastoral Staff in his hand, or else borne or holden by his Chaplain.

As touching kneeling, crossing, holding up of hands, knocking upon the breast, and other gestures, they may be used or left, as every man's devotion serveth, without blame.

Also upon Christmas Day, Easter Day, the Ascension Day, Whitsunday, and the Feast of the Trinity, may be used any part of holy Scripture hereafter to be certainly limited and appointed, in the stead of the Litany.

If there be a Sermon, or for other great cause, the Curate by his discretion, may leave out the Litany, Gloria in Excelsis, the Creed, the Homily, and the exhortation to the Communion.

FINIS.

Imprinted at London in
Fletestrete, at the signe of the Sunne ouer against
the conduyte, by EdVVarde VVhitchurche.
The xvi. daye of Iune, the
yeare of our Lorde,
1549.

# The Kings Maiestie, by

THE ADVISE OF HIS MOSTE DERE UNCLE THE LORDE PROTECTOR AND
OTHER HIS HIGHNES COUNSELL, STREIGHTLY CHARGETH AND
COMMANDETH, THAT NO MANER OF PERSON DOE SELL THYS
PRESENTE BOOKE UNBOUNDE, ABOVE THE PRICE OF II
SHYLYNGES AND II PENCE THE PIECE.  AND THE
SAME BOUNDE IN PASTE OR IN BOORDES
COVERED WITH CALVES LEATHER,
NOT ABOVE THE PRICE OF IIII
SHILLINGES THE PIECE.

# God Saue the King.

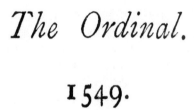

# *The Ordinal.*

## 1549.

# THE FORME

## and maner of makyng and consecratyng of Archebishoppes, Bishoppes, Priests and Deacons, M. D. xlix.

## THE PREFACE.

IT is evident unto all men, diligently reading holy Scripture, and ancient authors, that from the Apostles' time there hath been these Orders of Ministers in Christ's Church, Bishops, Priests, and Deacons: which Offices were evermore had in such reverent estimation, that no man by his own private authority might presume to execute any of them, except he were first called, tried, examined, and known to have such qualities as were requisite for the same. And also, by public prayer, with imposition of hands, approved and admitted thereunto. And therefore, to the intent these Orders should be continued, and reverently used, and esteemed, in this Church of England, it is requisite that no man (not being at this present Bishop, Priest, nor Deacon) shall execute any of them, except he be called, tried, examined, and admitted, according to the form hereafter following. And none shall be admitted a Deacon, except he be xxi. years of age at the least. And every man which is to be admitted a Priest shall be full xxiv. years old. And every man which is to be consecrated a Bishop, shall be fully thirty years of age. And the Bishop, knowing, either by himself or by sufficient testimony, any person to be a man of virtuous conversation, and without Crime, and after examination and trial, finding him learned in the Latin tongue, and sufficiently instructed in Holy Scripture, may, upon a Sunday or Holy Day, in the face of the Church, admit him a Deacon, in such manner and form as hereafter followeth.

# ✠
# THE FORM AND
## 𝕸𝖆𝖓𝖓𝖊𝖗 𝖔𝖋 𝕺𝖗𝖉𝖊𝖗𝖎𝖓𝖌 𝖔𝖋 𝕯𝖊𝖆𝖈𝖔𝖓𝖘.

First, when the day appointed by the Bishop is come, there shall be an exhortation, declaring the duty and office of such as come to be admitted Ministers, how necessary such Orders are in the Church of Christ, and also how the people ought to esteem them in their Vocation.

After the exhortation ended, the Archdeacon, or his deputy, shall present such as come to be admitted, to the Bishop: Every one of them that are presented having upon him a plain Albe; and the Archdeacon, or his deputy, shall say these words.

REVEREND Father in God, I present unto you these persons present, to be admitted Deacons.

*The Bishop.*

Take heed that the persons whom ye present unto us be apt and meet, for their learning and godly conversation, to exercise their Ministry duly, to the honour of God, and edifying of his Church.

The Archdeacon shall answer.

I have inquired of them, and also examined them, and think them so to be.

And then the Bishop shall say unto the people.

BRETHREN, if there be any of you who knoweth any impediment or notable crime in any of these persons presented to be ordered Deacons, for the which he ought not to be admitted to the same, let him come forth in the Name of God, and shew what the crime or impedient is.

And if any great crime or impediment be objected, the Bishop shall surcease from ordering that person, until such time as the party accused shall try himself clear of that crime.

Then the Bishop, commending such as shall be found meet to be ordered to the prayers of the congregation, with the Clerks and people present, shall say or sing the Litany as followeth.

## 𝕿𝖍𝖊 𝕷𝖎𝖙𝖆𝖓𝖞 𝖆𝖓𝖉 𝕾𝖚𝖋𝖋𝖗𝖆𝖌𝖊𝖘.

O GOD the Father, of heaven : have mercy upon us miserable sinners.

*O God the Father, of heav-* en : *have mercy upon us miserable sinners.*

O God the Son, Redeemer of the world : have mercy

upon us miserable sinners.

*O God the Son, Redeemer of the world: have mercy upon us miserable sinners.*

O God, the Holy Ghost, proceeding from the Father and the Son: have mercy upon us miserable sinners.

*O God, the Holy Ghost, proceeding from the Father and the Son: have mercy upon us miserable sinners.*

O holy, blessed, and glorious Trinity, three Persons and one God: have mercy upon us miserable sinners.

*O holy, blessed, and glorious Trinity, three Persons and one God: have mercy upon us miserable sinners.*

Remember not, Lord, our offences, nor the offences of our forefathers; neither take thou vengeance of our sins: spare us, good Lord, spare thy people, whom thou hast redeemed with thy most precious Blood, and be not angry with us forever.

*Spare us, good Lord.*

From all evil and mischief; from sin, from the crafts and 'assaults of the devil; from thy wrath, and from everlasting damnation,

*Good Lord, deliver us.*

From blindness of heart; from pride, vainglory, and hypocrisy; from envy, hatred, and malice, and all uncharitableness,

*Good Lord, deliver us.*

From fornication, and all deadly sin; and from all the deceits of the world, the flesh, and the devil.

*Good Lord, deliver us.*

From lightning and tempest; from plague, pestilence, and famine; from battle and murther, and from sudden death.

*Good Lord, deliver us.*

From all sedition and privy conspiracy: from the tyranny of the Bishop of Rome, and all his detestable enormities; from all false doctrine and heresy; from hardness of heart, and contempt of thy word and commandment.

*Good Lord, deliver us.*

By the mystery of thy holy Incarnation; by thy holy Nativity and Circumcision; by thy Baptism, Fasting, and Temptation.

*Good Lord, deliver us.*

By thine Agony and bloody Sweat, by thy Cross and Passion; by thy precious Death and Burial; by thy glorious Resurrection and Ascension; by the coming of the Holy Ghost.

*Good Lord, deliver us.*

In all time of our tribulation; in all time of our wealth; in the hour of death, in the day of judgment,

*Good Lord, deliver us.*

We sinners do beseech thee to hear us (O Lord God;) and that it may please thee to rule and govern thy holy Church universal in the right way.

*We beseech thee to hear us, good Lord.*

That it may please thee to keep Edward the vi., thy servant our king and governor.

*We beseech thee to hear us, good Lord.*

That it may please thee to rule his heart in thy faith, fear, and love, that he may always have affiance in thee, and ever seek thy honour and glory.

*We beseech thee to hear us, good Lord.*

That it may please thee to be his defender and keeper, giving him the victory over all his enemies.

*We beseech thee to hear us, good Lord.*

That it may please thee to illuminate all Bishops, pastors, and ministers of the Church with true knowledge and understanding of thy word; and that both by their preaching and living they may set it forth, and shew it accordingly.

*We beseech thee to hear us, good Lord.*

That it may please thee to bless these men, and send thy grace upon them, that they may duly execute the Office now to be committed unto them, to the edifying of thy Church, and to thy honour, praise, and glory.

*We beseech thee to hear us, good Lord.*

That it may please thee to endue the lords of the Council, and all the nobility, with grace, wisdom, and understanding.

*We beseech thee to hear us, good Lord.*

That it may please thee to bless and keep the magistrates, giving them grace to execute justice, and to maintain truth.

*We beseech thee to hear us, good Lord.*

That it may please thee to bless and keep all thy people.

*We beseech thee to hear us, good Lord.*

That it may please thee to give to all nations unity, peace, and concord.

*We beseech thee to hear us, good Lord.*

That it may please thee to give us an heart to love and dread thee, and diligently to live after thy commandments.

*We beseech thee to hear us, good Lord.*

That it may please thee to give all thy people increase of grace to hear meekly thy word, and to receive it with pure affection, and to bring forth the fruits of the Spirit.

*We beseech thee to hear us, good Lord.*

That it may please thee to bring into the way of truth all such as have erred, and are deceived.

*We beseech thee to hear us, good Lord.*

That it may please thee to strengthen such as do stand; and to comfort and help the weak-hearted; and to raise up them that fall; and finally to beat down Sathan under our feet.

*We beseech thee to hear us, good Lord.*

That it may please thee to succour, help, and comfort all that be in danger, necessity, and tribulation.

*We beseech thee to hear us, good Lord.*

That it may please thee to preserve all that travel by land or by water, all women la-

bouring of child, all sick persons, and young children; and to shew thy pity upon all prisoners and captives.

*We beseech thee to hear us, good Lord.*

That it may please thee to defend and provide for the fatherless children, and widows, and all that be desolate and oppressed.

*We beseech thee to hear us, good Lord.*

That it may please thee to have mercy upon all men.

*We beseech thee to hear us, good Lord.*

That it may please thee to forgive our enemies, persecutors, and slanderers, and to turn their hearts.

*We beseech thee to hear us, good Lord.*

That it may please thee to give and preserve to our use the kindly fruits of the earth, so as in due time we may enjoy them.

*We beseech thee to hear us, good Lord.*

That it may please thee to give us true repentance; to forgive us all our sins, negligences, and ignorances; and to endue us with the grace of thy holy Spirit to amend our lives according to thy holy word.

*We beseech thee to hear us, good Lord.*

Son of God: we beseech thee to hear us.

*Son of God: we beseech thee to hear us.*

O Lamb of God: that takest away the sins of the world.

*Grant us thy peace.*

O Lamb of God; that takest away the sins of the world.

*Have mercy upon us.*

O Christ, hear us.

*O Christ, hear us.*

Lord, have mercy upon us.

*Lord, have mercy upon us.*

Christ, have mercy upon us.

*Christ, have mercy upon us.*

Lord, have mercy upon us.

*Lord, have mercy upon us.*

Our Father, which art in heaven.

With the residue of the *Pater noster.*

And lead us not into temptation.

*But deliver us from evil.*

*The Versicle.*

O Lord, deal not with us after our sins.

*The Answer.*

*Neither reward us after our iniquities.*

Let us pray.

O GOD, merciful Father, that despisest not the sighing of a contrite heart, nor the desire of such as be sorrowful; Mercifully assist our prayers that we make before thee in all our troubles and adversities, whensoever they oppress us: and graciously hear us, that those evils, which the craft and subtilty of the devil or man worketh against us, be brought to nought; and by the providence of thy goodness they may be dispersed; that we thy servants, being hurt by no persecutions, may evermore give thanks unto thee in thy holy Church: through Jesu Christ our Lord.

*O Lord, arise, help us, and deliver us for thy Name's sake.*

O GOD, we have heard with our ears, and our fathers have declared unto us, the noble works that thou diddest in their days, and in the old time before them.

*O Lord, arise, help us, and deliver us for thy honour.*

Glory be to the Father, and to the Son: and to the Holy Ghost; as it was in the beginning, is now, and ever shall be: world without end. Amen.

From our enemies defend us, O Christ.

*Graciously look upon our afflictions.*

Pitifully behold the dolour of our heart.

*Mercifully forgive the sins of thy people.*

Favourably with mercy hear our prayers.

*O Son of David, have mercy upon us.*

Both now and ever vouchsafe to hear us, O Christ.

*Graciously hear us, O Christ.*

*Graciously hear us, O Lord Christ.*

### The Versicle.

O Lord, let thy mercy be shewed upon us.

### The Answer.

As we do put our trust in thee.

### Let us pray.

WE humbly beseech thee, O Father, mercifully to look upon our infirmities; and for the glory of thy Name' sake turn from us all those evils that we most righteously have deserved: And grant that in all our troubles we may put our whole trust and confidence in thy mercy, and evermore serve thee in pureness of living, to thy honour and glory; through our only Mediator and advocate Jesus Christ our Lord.

ALMIGHTY God, which hast given us grace at this time with one accord to make our supplications unto thee, and dost promise that when two or three be gathered in thy Name, thou wilt grant their requests: Fulfil now, O Lord, the desires and petitions of thy servants, as may be most expedient for them, granting us in this world knowledge of thy truth, and in the world to come life everlasting. Amen.

ALMIGHTY God, which by thy divine Providence hast appointed diverse Orders of Ministers in the Church, and diddest inspire thine holy Apostles to choose unto this Order of Deacons thy first martyr Saint Stephen, with other: Mercifully behold these thy servants, now called to the like Office and ministration: replenish them so with the truth of thy doctrine, and innocency of life, that, both by word and good example, they may faithfully serve thee in this Office, to the glory of thy Name, and profit of the congregation: through the merits of our Saviour Jesu Christ, who liveth and reigneth with thee and the Holy Ghost now and ever. Amen.

Then shall be sung or said the Communion of the day, saving the Epistle shall be read out of Timothy, as followeth.

### 1. *Tim.* iii.

LIKEWISE must the Ministers be honest, not double-tongued, not given unto much wine, neither greedy of filthy lucre; but holding the mystery of the faith with a pure conscience. And let them first be proved, and then let them minister, so that no man be able to reprove them. Even so must their wives be honest, not evil speakers, but sober and faithful in all things. Let the Deacons be the husbands of one wife, and such as rule their children well, and their own households. For they that minister well get themselves a good degree and a great liberty in the faith which is in Christ Jesu.

These things write I unto thee, trusting to come shortly unto thee: but and if I tarry long, that then thou mayest yet have knowledge how thou oughtest to behave thyself in the house of God, which is the Congregation of the living God, the pillar and ground of truth. And without doubt great is that mystery of Godliness: God was shewed in the flesh, was justified in the Spirit, was seen among the angels, was preached unto the Gentiles, was believed on in the world, and received up in glory.

Or else this, out of the vi. of the Acts.

THEN the xii. called the multitude of the disciples together, and said, It is not meet that we should leave the word of God, and serve tables. Wherefore, brethren, look ye out among you seven men of honest report, and full of the Holy Ghost and wisdom, to whom we may commit this business: but we will give ourselves continually to prayer, and to the administration of the word. And the saying pleased the whole multitude: and they chose Stephen, a man full of faith and full of the Holy Ghost, and Philip, and Procorus, and Nichanor, and Tymon, and Permenas, and Nicholas, a convert of Antioche. These they set before the Apostles: and when they had prayed, they laid their hands on them. And the word of God increased : and the number of the disciples multiplied in Jerusalem greatly ; and a great company of the priests were obedient unto the faith.

And before the Gospel, the Bishop, sitting in a Chair, shall cause the Oath of the King's supremacy, and against the usurped power and authority of the Bishop of Rome, to be ministered unto every one of them that are to be ordered.

## The Oath of the King's supremacy.

I FROM henceforth shall utterly renounce, refuse, relinquish, and forsake the Bishop of Rome, and his authority, power, and jurisdiction. And I shall never consent nor agree that the Bishop of Rome shall practise, exercise, or have any manner of authority, jurisdiction, or power within this Realm, or any other of the King's dominions, but shall resist the same at all times to the uttermost of my power. And I from henceforth will accept, repute, and take the King's Majesty to be the only supreme head in earth of the Church of England : And to my cunning, wit, and uttermost of my power, without guile, fraud, or other undue mean, I will observe, keep, maintain, and defend the whole effects and contents of all and singular Acts and Statutes made and to be made within this Realm, in derogation, extirpation, and extinguishment of the Bishop of Rome, and his authority; and all other Acts and Statutes made or to be made, in reformation and corroboration of the King's power, of the supreme head in earth of the Church of England : and this I will do against all manner of persons, of what estate, dignity, or degree, or condition they be; and in no wise do, nor attempt, nor to my power suffer to be done or attempted, directly or indirectly, any thing or things, privily or apertly, to the let, hinderance, damage, or derogation thereof, or any part thereof, by any manner of means, or for any manner of pretence. And in case any Oath be made, or hath been made by me, to any person or persons, in maintenance, defence, or favour of the Bishop of Rome, or his authority, jurisdiction, or power, I repute the same as vain and annihilate, so help me GOD, all Saints, and the holy Evangelist.

Then shall the Bishop examine every one of them that are to be ordered, in the presence of the people, after this manner following.

Do you trust that you are inwardly moved by the Holy Ghost to take upon you this Office and ministration, to serve God, for the promoting of his glory, and the edifying of his people?

*Answer.*

I trust so.

*The Bishop.*

Do ye think that ye truly be called, according to the will of our Lord Jesus Christ, and the due order of this Realm, to the ministry of the Church?

*Answer.*

I think so.

*The Bishop.*

Do ye unfeignedly believe all the Canonical Scriptures of the Old and New Testament?

*Answer.*

I do believe.

*The Bishop.*

Will you diligently read the same unto the people assembled in the church where you shall be appointed to serve?

*Answer.*

I will.

*The Bishop.*

It pertaineth to the Office of a Deacon, to assist the Priest in Divine Service, and specially when he ministereth the holy Communion, and help him in the distribution thereof, and to read ho-

ly Scriptures and Homilies in the congregation, and instruct the youth in the Catechism, and also to baptize and preach, if he be commanded by the Bishop. And furthermore, it is his office to search for the sick, poor, and impotent people of the Parish, and to intimate their estates, names, and places where they dwell, to the Curate, that by his exhortation they may be relieved by the Parish, or other convenient almose. Will you do this gladly and willingly?

*Answer.*

I will so do by the help of God.

*The Bishop.*

Will you apply all your diligence to frame and fashion your own lives, and the lives of all your family according to the doctrine of Christ, and to make both yourselves and them, as much as in you lieth, wholesome examples of the flock of Christ?

*Answer.*

I will so do, the Lord being my helper.

*The Bishop.*

Will you reverently obey your Ordinary and other chief Ministers of the Church, and them to whom the government and charge is committed over you, following with a glad mind and will their godly admonitions!

*Answer.*

I will thus endeavour myself, the Lord being my helper.

Then the Bishop, laying his hands severally upon the head of every one of them, shall say,

Take thou authority to execute the Office of a Deacon in the Church of God committed unto thee: in the Name of the Father, the Son, and the Holy Ghost. Amen.

Then shall the Bishop deliver to every one of them the New Testament, saying.

Take thou authority to read the Gospel in the Church of God, and to preach the same, if thou be thereunto ordinarily commanded.

Then one of them, appointed by the Bishop, putting on a Tunicle, shall read the Gospel of that day.

Then shall the Bishop proceed to the Communion, and all that be ordered shall tarry and receive the Holy Communion, the same day with the Bishop.

The Communion ended, after the last Collect and immediately before the Benediction, shall be said this Collect following.

ALMIGHTY God, giver of all good things, which of thy great goodness has vouchsafed to accept and take these thy servants unto the Office of Deacons in thy Church: Make them, we beseech thee, O Lord, to be modest, humble, and constant in their ministration, and to have a ready will to observe all spiritual discipline, that they, having always the testimony of a good conscience, and continuing ever stable and strong in thy Son Christ, may so well use themselves in this inferior office, that they may be found worthy to be called unto the higher Ministries in thy Church; through the same thy Son our Saviour Christ, to whom be glory and honour world without end. Amen.

And here it must be shewed unto the Deacon that he must continue in that Office of a Deacon the space of a whole year at the least, (except for reasonable causes it be otherwise seen to his Ordinary,) to the intent he may be perfect, and well expert in the things appertaining to the Ecclesiastical administration; in executing whereof, if he be found faithful and diligent, he may be admitted by his Diocesan to the Order of Priesthood.

# THE FORM

## of Ordering of Priests.

When the exhortation is ended, then shall be sung, for the Introit to the Communion, this Psalm.

*Expectans expectavi Dominum.* Psalm xl.

I WAITED patiently for the Lord: and he inclined unto me, and heard my calling.

He brought me also out of the horrible pit, out of the mire and clay: and set my feet upon the rock, and ordered my goings.

And he hath put a new song in my mouth: even a thanksgiving unto our God.

Many shall see it, and fear: and shall put their trust in the Lord.

Blessed is the man that hath set his hope in the Lord: and turned not unto the proud, and to such as go about with lies.

O Lord my God, great are the wondrous works which thou hast done: like as be also thy thoughts which are to usward, and yet there is no man that ordereth them unto thee.

If I would declare them and speak of them: they should be more than I am able to express.

Sacrifice and meat-offering thou wouldest not have: but mine ears hast thou opened.

Burnt-offerings and sacrifice for sin hast thou not required: then said I, Lo, I come.

In the volume of the book it is written of me, that I should fulfil thy will, O my God: I am content to do it; yea, thy law is within my heart.

I have declared thy righteousness in the great congregation: lo, I will not refrain my lips, O Lord, and that thou knowest.

I have not hid thy righteousness within my heart: my talk hath been of thy truth, and of thy salvation.

I have not kept back thy loving mercy and truth: from the great congregation.

Withdraw not thou thy mercy from me, O Lord: let thy loving kindness and thy truth alway preserve me.

For innumerable troubles are come about me: my sins have taken such hold upon me that I am not able to look up: yea, they are more in number than the hairs of my head, and my heart hath failed me.

O Lord, let it be thy pleasure to deliver me: make haste, O Lord, to help me.

Let them be ashamed and confounded together, that seek after my soul to destroy it: let them be driven backward, and put to rebuke, that wish me evil.

Let them be desolate, and rewarded with shame that say unto me: Fie upon thee, fie upon thee.

Let all those that seek thee be joyful and glad in thee: and let such as love thy salvation say alway, The Lord be praised.

As for me, I am poor and needy: but the Lord careth for me.

Thou art my helper and redeemer: make no long tarrying, O my God.

Glory be to the Father, and to the Son: and to the Holy Ghost.

As it was in the beginning, is now: and ever shall be, world without end. Amen.

Or else this Psalm.

*Memento Domine.*

Psalm cxxxii.

LORD, remember David: and all his trouble;

How he sware unto the Lord: and vowed a vow unto the Almighty God of Jacob;

I will not come within the tabernacle of my house: nor climb up into my bed;

I will not suffer mine eyes to sleep, nor mine eyelids to slumber: neither the temples of my head to take any rest;

Until I find out a place for the temple of the Lord: an habitation for the mighty God of Jacob.

Lo, we heard of the same at Ephrata: and found it in the wood.

We will go into his tabernacle: and fall low on our knees before his footstool.

Arise, O Lord, into thy resting-place: thou, and the ark of thy strength.

Let thy priests be clothed with righteousness: and let thy saints sing with joyfulness.

For thy servant David's sake: turn not away the presence of thine Anointed.

The Lord hath made a faithful oath unto David: and he shall not shrink from it;

Of the fruit of thy body: shall I set upon thy seat.

If thy children will keep my covenant, and my testimonies that I shall learn them : their children also shall sit upon thy seat for evermore.

For the Lord hath chosen Sion to be an habitation for himself : he hath longed for her.

This shall be my rest for ever : here will I dwell, for I have a delight therein.

I will bless her victuals with increase : and will satisfy her poor with bread.

I will deck her priests with health : and her saints shall rejoice and sing.

There shall I make the horn of David to flourish : I have ordained a lantern for mine Anointed.

As for his enemies, I shall clothe them with shame : but upon himself shall his crown flourish.

Glory be to the Father, and to the Son : and to the Holy Ghost.

As it was in the beginning, is now : and ever shall be, world without end. Amen.

Or else this Psalm.

*Laudate Nomen Domini.*
Psalm cxxxv.

O praise the Lord, laud ye the Name of the Lord : praise it, O ye servants of the Lord ;

Ye that stand in the house of the Lord : in the courts of the house of our God.

O praise the Lord, for the Lord is gracious : O sing praises unto his Name, for it is lovely.

For why? the Lord hath chosen Jacob unto himself : and Israel for his own possession.

For I know that the Lord is great : and that our Lord is above all gods.

Whatsoever the Lord pleased, that did he in heaven, and in earth : and in the sea, and in all deep places.

He bringeth forth the clouds from the ends of the world : and sendeth forth lightnings with the rain, bringing the winds out of his treasures.

He smote the first-born of Egypt : both of man and beast.

He hath sent tokens and wonders into the midst of thee, O thou land of Egypt : upon Pharao, and all his servants.

He smote divers nations : and slew mighty kings ;

Sehon king of the Amorites, and Og the king of Basan : and all the kingdoms of Canaan ;

And gave their land to be an heritage : even an heritage unto Israel his people.

Thy Name, O Lord, endureth for ever : so doth thy memorial, O Lord, from one generation to another.

For the Lord will avenge his people: and be gracious unto his servants.

As for the images of the heathen, they are but silver and gold : the work of men's hands.

They have mouths, and speak not: eyes have they, but they see not.

They have ears, and yet they hear not: neither is there any breath in their mouths.

They that make them are like unto them : and so are all they that put their trust in them.

Praise the Lord, ye house of Israel: Praise the Lord, ye house of Aaron.

Praise the Lord, ye house of Levi: ye that fear the Lord, praise the Lord.

Praised be the Lord out of Sion : who dwelleth at Jerusalem.

Glory be to the Father, and to the Son: and to the Holy Ghost.

As it was in the beginning, is now: and ever shall be, world without end.　Amen.

Then shall be read for the Epistle this out of the xx Chapter of the Acts of the Apostles.

FROM Mileto Paul sent messengers to Ephesus, and called the elders of the congregation: which when they were come to him, he said unto them, Ye know that from the first day that I came into Asia, after what manner I have been with you at all seasons, serving the Lord with all humbleness of mind, and with many tears, and temptations, which happened unto me by the layings await of the J e w s : because I would keep back nothing that was profitable unto you, but to shew you and teach you openly throughout every house ; witnessing both to the Jews, and also to the Grekes, the repentance that is toward God, and the faith which is toward our Lord Jesus.　And now behold, I go bound in the Spirit unto Jerusalem, not knowing the things that shall come on me there; but that the H o l y Ghost witnesseth in every city, saying that bands and trouble abide me.　But none of these things move me, neither is my life dear unto myself, that I might fulfil my course with joy, and the ministration of the word, which I have received of the Lord Jesu, to testify the gospel of the grace of God.　And now, behold, I am sure that henceforth ye all (through whom I have gone preaching the kingdom of God) shall see my face no more.　Wherefore

I take you to record this day, that I am pure from the blood of all men. For I have spared no labour, but have shewed you all the counsel of God. Take heed therefore unto yourselves, and to all the flock, among whom the Holy Ghost hath made you overseers, to rule the Congregation of God, which he hath purchased with his Blood. For I am sure of this, that after my departing, shall grievous wolves enter in among you, not sparing the flock. Moreover of your own selves shall men arise, speaking perverse things, to draw disciples after them. Therefore awake, and remember, that by the space of three years I ceased not to warn every one of you night and day with tears.

And now, brethren, I commend you to God, and to the word of his grace, which is able to build farther, and to give you an inheritance among all them which are sanctified. I have desired no man's silver, gold, or vesture. Yea, you yourselves know that these hands have ministered unto my necessities, and to them that were with me. I have shewed you all things, how that so labouring ye ought to receive the weak, and to remember the words of the Lord Jesu, how that he said, It is more blessed to give than to receive.

Or else this third Chapter of the fi st Epistle to Timothy.

THIS is a true saying: If any man desire the office of a Bishop, he desireth an honest work. A Bishop therefore must be blameless, the husband of one wife, diligent, sober, discreet, a keeper of hospitality, apt to teach; not given to overmuch wine, no fighter, not greedy of filthy lucre; but gentle, abhorring fighting, abhorring covetousness; one that ruleth well his own house, one that hath children in subjection with all reverence. For if a man cannot rule his own house, how shall he care for the congregation of God? He may not be a young scholar, lest he swell, and fall into the judgment of the evil speaker. He must also have a good report of them which are without, lest he fall into rebuke, and snare of the evil speaker.

Likewise must the Ministers be honest, not double-tongued, not given unto much wine, neither greedy of filthy lucre; but holding the mystery of the faith with a pure conscience. And let them first be proved, and then let them minister so that no man be able to reprove them.

Even so must their wives be honest, not evil speakers, but sober and faithful in all things. Let the Deacons be the husbands of one wife, and such as rule their children well, and their own households. For they that minister well get themselves a good degree, and great liberty in the faith which is in Christ Jesu.

These things write I unto thee, trusting to come shortly unto thee: but and if I tarry long, that then thou mayest have yet knowledge how thou oughtest to behave thyself in the house of God, which is the congregation of the living God, the pillar and ground of truth. And without doubt, great is that mystery of godliness: God was shewed in the flesh, was justified in the Spirit, was seen among the angels, was preached unto the Gentiles, was believed on in the world, and received up in glory.

After this shall be read for the Gospel a piece of the last Chapter of Matthew as followeth.

JESUS came and spake unto them, saying: All power is given unto me in heaven and in earth. Go ye therefore, and teach all nations, baptizing them in the Name of the Father, and of the Son, and of the Holy Ghost: teaching them to observe all things whatsoever I have commanded you: and, lo, I am with you alway, even until the end of the world.

Or else this that followeth, of the x Chapter of John.

VERILY, verily, I say unto you: He that entereth not in by the door into the sheep-fold, but climbeth up some other way, the same is a thief and a murtherer. But he that entereth in by the door, is the shepherd of the sheep. To him the porter openeth; and the sheep heareth his voice: and he calleth his own sheep by name, and leadeth them out. And when he hath sent forth his own sheep, he goeth before them, and the sheep follow him: for they know his voice. A stranger will they not follow, but will fly from him: for they know not the voice of strangers. This proverb spake Jesus unto them; but they understood not what things they were which he spake unto them. Then said Jesus unto them again, Verily, verily, I say unto you, I am the door of the sheep. All (even as many as come before me) are thieves and murtherers: but the sheep did not hear them. I am the door: by me, if any man enter in, he shall be safe, and go in and out, and find pasture. A thief cometh not, but for to steal, kill, and to destroy: I am come that they might have life, and that they might have it m o r e abundantly. I am the good Shepherd: a good shepherd giveth his life for the sheep. An hired servant, and he which is not the shepherd, (neither the sheep are his own,) seeth the wolf coming, and leaveth the sheep, and flieth: and the wolf catcheth and scattereth the s h e e p. The hired servant flieth, because he is an hired servant, and careth not for the sheep. I am the good shepherd, and know my sheep, and am known of mine. As my Father knoweth me, even so know I also my Father : and I give my life for the sheep. And other sheep I have, which are not of this fold: them also must I bring, and they shall hear my voice; and there shall be one fold and one shepherd.

Or else this, of the xx Chapter of John.

THE same day at night, which was the first day of the sabbaths, when the doors were shut, (where the disci-ples were assembled together for fear of the Jews,) came Jesus and stood in the midst, and said unto them, Peace be unto you. And when he had so said, he shewed unto them his hands and his side. Then were the disciples glad, when they saw the Lord. Then said Jesus unto them again, Peace be unto you: as my Father sent me, even so send I you also. And when he had said those words, he breathed on them, and said unto them, Receive ye the Holy Ghost: whosesoever's sins ye remit, they are remitted unto them. And whosoever's sins ye retain, they are retained.

When the Gospel is ended, then shall be said or sung.

COME, Holy Ghost, eternal God, proceeding from above,
 Both from the Father and the Son, the God of peace and love.
Visit our minds, and into us thy heavenly grace inspire,
 That in all truth and godliness, we may have true desire.
Thou art the very Comforter, in all woe and distress,
 The heavenly gift of God most high, which no tongue can express;
 The fountain and the lively spring of joy celestial,
 The fire so bright, the love

so clear, and unction spiritual.

Thou in thy gifts art manifold, whereby Christ's Church doth stand ;

In faithful hearts writing thy law, the finger of God's hand.

According to thy promise made thou givest speech of grace,

That through thy help the praise of God may sound in every place.

O Holy Ghost, into our wits send down thine heavenly light,

Kindle our hearts with fervent love, to serve God day and night;

Strength and stablish all our weakness, so feeble and so frail,

That neither flesh, the world, nor devil, against us do prevail.

Put back our enemy far from us, and grant us to obtain.

Peace in our hearts with God and man, without grudge or disdain.

And grant, O Lord, that thou, being our Leader and our Guide,

We may eschew the snares of sin, and from thee never slide.

To us such plenty of thy grace, good Lord, grant, we thee pray,

That thou, Lord, mayest be our comfort at the last dreadful day.

Of all strife and dissension, O Lord, dissolve the bands,

And make the knots of peace and love throughout all Christen lands.

Grant us, O Lord, through thee to know the Father most of might,

That of his dear beloved Son we may attain the sight :

And that with perfect faith also we may acknowledge thee.

The Spirit of them both. alway one God in Persons three.

Laud and praise be to the Father, and to the Son equal.

And to the Holy Spirit also, one God coeternal.

And pray we that the only Son vouchsafe his Spirit to send,

To all that do profess his Name unto the world's end. Amen.

*And then the Archdeacon shall present unto the Bishop all them that shall receive the Order of Priesthood that day, every one of them having upon him a plain Albe; the Archdeacon saying.*

REVEREND father in God, I present unto you these persons present, to be admitted to the Order of Priesthood, *Cum interrogatione et respon-*

*sione, ut in Ordine Diacona-tus.*

And then the Bishop shall say to the people.

GOOD people, these be they whom we purpose, God will-ing, to receive this day unto the holy Office of Priesthood. For after due examination we find not the contrary but that they be lawfully called to their function and ministry, and that they be persons meet for the same. But yet if there be any of you which knoweth any impediment, or notable crime in any of them, for the which he ought not to be re-ceived to this holy ministry, now in the Name of God de-clare the same.

And if any great crime or imped-iment be objected, etc., *ut supra in Ordine Diaconatus usque ad finem Letanie cum hac Collecta.*

ALMIGHTY God, giver of all good things, which by thy Holy Spirit hast appointed diverse Orders of Ministers in thy Church: Mercifully behold these thy servants, now called to the Office of Priesthood, and replenish them so with the truth of thy doctrine, and innocency of life, that, both by word and good example, they may faithfully serve thee in this office, to the glory of thy Name, and profit of the con-gregation, through the merits of our Saviour Jesu Christ; who liveth and reigneth, with thee and the Holy Ghost, world without end. Amen.

Then the Bishop shall minister unto every one of them the Oath concerning the King's Su-premacy, as it is set out in the Order of Deacons. And that done, he shall say unto them which are appointed to receive the said Office, as hereafter fol-loweth.

You have heard, brethren, as well in your private exam-ination, as in the exhortation, and in the holy lessons taken out of the Gospel, and of the writings of the Apostles, of what dignity and of how great importance this Office is (whereunto ye be called). And now we exhort you, in the Name of our Lord Jesus Christ, to have in remem-brance into how high a dig-nity, and to how chargeable an office ye be called, that is to say, to be the Messengers, the Watchmen, the Pastors, and Stewards of the Lord; to teach, to premonish, to feed, and provide for the Lord's family; to seek for Christ's sheep that be dispersed abroad, and for his children which be in the midst of this naughty world, to be saved through Christ for ever. Have always, therefore, printed in your remembrance how great a treasure is committed to your charge; for they be the sheep of Christ which be bought with his death, and for whom he shed his Blood. The Church and congregation whom you must serve is his Spouse and his body: and if it shall chance the same Church, or any member thereof, to take any hurt or hinderance, by reason of your negligence, ye know the greatness of the fault, and also of the horrible punishment which will ensue. Wherefore consider with yourselves the end of your ministry towards the children of God, toward the Spouse and Body of Christ, and see that ye never cease your labour, your care, and diligence, until you have done all that lieth in you, according to your bounden duty, to bring all such as are or shall be committed to your charge, unto that agreement in faith, and knowledge of God, and to that ripeness and perfectness of age in Christ, that there be no place left among them, either for error in religion or for viciousness in life.

Then, forasmuch as your Office is both of so great excellency and of so great difficulty, ye see with how great care and study ye ought to apply yourselves, as well that you may shew yourselves kind to that Lord, who hath placed you in so high a dignity, as also to beware that neither you yourselves offend, neither be occasion that other offend. Howbeit ye cannot have a mind and a will thereto of yourselves; for that power and ability is given of God alone. Therefore ye see how ye ought and have need earnestly to pray for his Holy Spirit. And seeing that ye cannot by any other means compass the doing of so weighty a work pertaining to the salvation of man, but with doctrine and exhortation taken out of holy Scripture, and with a life agreeable unto the same; ye perceive how studious ye ought to be in reading and learning the holy Scriptures, and in framing the manners both of yourselves and of them that specially pertain unto you, according to the rule of the same Scriptures. And for this selfsame cause ye see how you ought to forsake and set aside (as much as you may) all worldly cares and studies.

We have a good hope that you have well weighed and pondered these things with yourselves long before this time, and that you have clearly determined, by God's grace, to give yourselves wholly to this vocation, whereunto it hath pleased God to call you, so that (as much as lieth in you) you apply yourselves wholly to this one thing, and draw all your cares and studies this way, and to this end: And that you will continually pray for the heavenly assistance of the Holy Ghost from God the Father, by the mediation of our only Mediator and Saviour Jesus Christ, that by daily reading and weighing of the Scriptures ye may wax riper and stronger in your Ministry. And that ye may so endeavour yourselves, from time to time, to sanctify the lives of you and yours, and to fashion them after the rule and doctrine of Christ; and that ye may be wholesome and godly examples and patterns for the rest of the congregation to follow. And that this present congregation of Christ, here assembled, may also understand your minds and wills in these things;

And that this your promise shall more move you to do your duties, ye shall answer plainly to these things, which we, in the name of the congregation, shall demand of you, touching the same.

Do you think in your heart that you be truly called, according to the will of our Lord Jesus Christ, and the order of this Church of England, to the ministry of Priesthood?

*Answer.*

I think it.

*The Bishop.*

Be you persuaded that the holy Scriptures contain sufficiently all doctrine required of necessity for eternal salvation, through faith in Jesu Christ? And are you determined with the said Scriptures to instruct the people committed to your charge, and to teach nothing, as required of necessity to eternal salvation, but that you shall be persuaded may be concluded and proved by the Scripture?

*Answer.*

I am so persuaded, and have so determined by God's grace.

*The Bishop.*

Will you then give your faithful diligence always so to minister the doctrine and Sacraments, and the discipline of Christ, as the Lord hath commanded, and as this

Realm hath received the same, according to the commandments of God, so that ye may teach the people committed to your cure and charge with all diligence to keep and observe the same?

*Answer.*

I will so do, by the help of the Lord.

*The Bishop.*

Will you be ready, with all faithful diligence, to banish and drive away all erroneous and strange doctrines contrary to God's Word, and to use both public and private monitions and exhortations, as well to the sick as to the whole, within your Cures, as need shall require and occasion be given?

*Answer.*

I will, the Lord being my helper.

*The Bishop.*

Will you be diligent in prayers, and in reading of the holy Scriptures, and in such studies as help to the knowledge of the same, laying aside the study of the world and the flesh?

*Answer.*

I will endeavour myself so to do, the Lord being my helper.

*The Bishop.*

Will you be diligent to frame and fashion your own selves and your families according to the doctrine of Christ, and to make both yourselves and them (as much as in you lieth) wholesome examples and spectacles to the flock of Christ?

*Answer.*

I will so apply myself, the Lord being my helper.

*The Bishop.*

Will you maintain and set forwards (as much as lieth in you) quietness, peace, and love among all Christen people, and specially among them that are, or shall be, committed to your charge?

*Answer.*

I will so do, the Lord being my helper.

*The Bishop.*

Will you reverently obey your Ordinary, and other chief Ministers, unto whom the government and charge is committed over you, following with a glad mind and will their godly admonition, and submitting yourselves to their godly judgments?

*Answer.*

I will so do, the Lord being my helper.

Then shall the Bishop say,

ALMIGHTY God, who hath given you this will to do all these things; Grant also unto you strength and power to perform the same, that he may accomplish his work which he hath begun in you, until the time he shall come at the latter day to judge the quick and the dead.

After this, the congregation shall be desired, secretly in their prayers, to make humble supplications to God for the foresaid things: for the which prayers there shall be a certain space kept in silence.

That done, the Bishop shall pray in this wise.

The Lord be with you. •

*Answer.*

And with thy spirit.

Let us pray.

ALMIGHTY God and Heavenly Father, which of thy infinite love and goodness towards us, hast given to us thy only and most dear beloved Son Jesus Christ, to be our Redeemer and Author of everlasting life: who, after he had made perfect our redemption by his death, and was ascended into heaven, sent abroad into the world his Apostles, Prophets, Evangelists, Doctors, and Pastors; by whose labour and ministry he gathered together a great flock in all the parts of the world, to set forth the eternal praise of thy holy Name. For these so great benefits of thy eternal goodness, and for that thou hast vouchsafed to call these thy servants here present to the same Office and Ministry of the salvation of mankind, we render unto thee most hearty thanks, we worship and praise thee; and we humbly beseech thee, by the same thy Son, to grant unto all us which either here or elsewhere call upon thy Name, that we may shew ourselves thankful to thee for these and all other thy benefits, and that we may daily increase and go forwards in the knowledge and faith of thee, and thy Son, by the Holy Spirit. So that as well by these thy Ministers, as by them to whom they shall be appointed Ministers, thy holy Name may be always glorified, and thy blessed kingdom enlarged; through the same thy Son our Lord Jesus Christ, which liveth and reigneth with thee, in the unity of the same Holy Spirit world without end. Amen.

When this prayer is done, the Bishop with the Priests present shall lay their hands severally upon the head of every one that receiveth Orders. The receivers humbly kneeling u p o n their knees, and the Bishop saying.

RECEIVE the Holy Ghost, whose sins thou dost forgive, they are forgiven. And whose sins thou dost retain, they are retained : and be thou a faithful dispenser of the Word of God, and of his holy Sacraments: In the Name of the Father, and of the Son, and of the Holy Ghost. Amen.

The Bishop shall deliver to every one of them the Bible in the one hand, and the Chalice or Cup with the Bread, in the other hand, and say.

TAKE thou authority to preach the Word of God, and to minister the holy Sacraments, in this Congregation.

When this is done the Congregation shall sing the Creed, and also they shall go to the Communion, which all they that receive Orders shall take together, and remain in the same place where the hands were laid upon them, until such time as they have received the Communion.

The Communion being done, after the last Collect, and immediately before the Benediction, shall be said this Collect:

MOST merciful Father, we beseech thee so to send upon these thy servants thy heavenly blessing, that they may be clad about with all justice, and that thy word spoken by their mouths may have such success, that it may never be spoken in vain. Grant also that we may have grace to hear and receive the same as thy most holy word, and the means of our salvation, that in all our words and deeds we may seek thy glory, and the increase of thy kingdom; through Jesus Christ our Lord. Amen.

If the Orders of Deacon and Priesthood be given both upon one day, then shall the Psalm for the Introit and other things at the holy Communion be used as they are appointed at the ordering of Priests. Saving that for the Epistle the whole iii. Chapter of the first to Timothy shall be read as it is set out before in the Order of Priests. And immediately after the Epistle, the Deacons shall be ordered. And it shall suffice the Litany to be said once.

# ✠
# THE FORM OF
## Consecrating of an Archbishop or Bishop.

The Psalm for the Introit at the Communion, as at the Ordering of Priests.

*The Epistle.* 1. Tim. iii.

THIS is a true saying, If a man desire the Office of a Bishop, he desireth an honest work. A Bishop therefore must be blameless, the husband of one wife, diligent, sober, discreet a keeper of hospitality, apt to teach; not given to overmuch wine, no fighter, not greedy of filthy lucre; but gentle, abhorring fighting, abhorring covetousness; one that ruleth well his own house; one that hath children in subjection with all reverence; for if a man cannot rule his own house, how shall he care for the Congregation of God? He may not be a young scholar, lest he swell, and fall into the judgment of the evil speaker. He must also have a good report of them which are without, lest he fall into rebuke and snare of the evil speaker.

*The Gospel.* John xxi.

JESUS said to Simon Peter, Simon Johanna, lovest thou me more than these? He said unto him, Yea, Lord; thou knowest that I love thee. He said unto him, Feed my lambs. He said to him again the second time, Simon Johanna, lovest thou me? He said unto him, Yea, Lord; thou knowest that I love thee. He said unto him, Feed my sheep. He said unto him the third time, Simon Johanna, lovest thou me? Peter was sorry because he said unto him the third time, Lovest thou me? And he said unto him, Lord, thou knowest all things; thou knowest that I love thee. Jesus said unto him, Feed my sheep.

Or else out of the X. Chapter of John, as before in the Order of Priests.

After the Gospel and *Credo* ended, first the elected Bishop, having upon him a Surplice and a Cope, shall be presented by two Bishops (being also in Surplices and Copes, and having their Pastoral Staves in their hands) unto the Archbishops of that Province, or to some other Bishop appointed by his commission, the Bishops that present saying:

MOST reverend Father in God, we present unto you this godly and well learned man to be consecrated Bishop.

And then the King's Mandate to the Archbishop for the Consecration shall be read. And the Oath touching the knowledging of the King's supremacy shall be ministered to the person elected, as it is set out in the o r d e r of Deacons. And then shall be ministered also the Oath of due obedience unto the Archbishop, as followeth.

The Oath of due obedience to the Archbishop.

In the Name of God, Amen. I, N. chosen Bishop of the Church and See of N. do profess and promise all due reverence and obedience to the Archbishop and to the Metropolitical Church of N. and to their successors, so help me God and his holy Gospel.

Then the Archbishop shall move the congregation p r e s e n t to pray ; saying thus to them:

BRETHREN, it is written in the Gospel of Saint Luke that our Saviour Christ continued the whole night in prayer, or ever that he did choose and sent forth his xii. Apostles. It is written also in the Acts of the Apostles, that the disciples which were at Antioch did fast and pray, or ever they laid hands upon or sent forth Paul and Barnabas. Let us, therefore, following the example of our Saviour Christ and his Apostles, first fall to prayer, or that we admit and send forth this person presented unto us to the work whereunto we trust the Holy Ghost hath called him.

And then shall be said the Litany, as afore in the Order of Deacons. And a f t e r this place, *That it may please thee to illuminate all Bishops,&c.* he shall say,

THAT it may please thee to bless this our brother elected, and to send thy grace upon him, that he may duly execute the Office whereunto he is called, to the edifying of thy Church, and to the honour, praise, and glory of thy Name.

*Answer.*

We beseech thee to hear us, good Lord.

Concluding the Litany in the end with this prayer.

ALMIGHTY God, giver of all good things, which by thy Holy Spirit hast appointed divers Orders of Ministers in thy Church; Mercifully behold this thy servant, now called to the work and ministry of a Bishop; and replenish him so with the truth of thy doctrine, and innocency of life, that both by word and deed he may faithfully serve thee in this Office, to the glory of thy Name, and profit of thy Congregation; through the merits of our Saviour Jesu Christ, who liveth and reigneth with thee and the Holy Ghost world without end. Amen.

Then the Archbishop, sitting in a Chair shall say this to him that is to be consecrated.

BROTHER, forasmuch as holy Scripture and the old Canons commandeth that we should not be hasty in laying on hands, and admitting of any person to the government of the Congregation of Christ, which he hath purchased with no less price than the effusion of his own Blood; afore that I admit you to this administration whereunto ye are called, I will examine you in certain articles, to the end the congregation present may have a trial and bear witness how ye be minded to behave yourself in the Church of God.

Are you persuaded that you be truly called to this ministration, according to the will of our Lord Jesus Christ, and the order of this Realm?

*Answer.*

I am so persuaded.

*The Archbishop.*

Are you persuaded that the holy Scriptures contain suffi-

ciently all doctrine required of necessity for eternal salvation, through the faith in Jesu Christ; And are you determined with the same holy Scriptures to instruct the people committed to your charge, and to teach or maintain nothing, as required of necessity to eternal salvation, but that you shall be persuaded may be concluded and proved by the same?

*Answer.*

I am so persuaded and determined by God's grace.

*The Archbishop.*

Will you then faithfully exercise yourself in the said holy Scriptures, and call upon God by prayer for the true understanding of the same, so as ye may be able by them to teach and exhort with wholesome doctrine, and to withstand and convince the gainsayers?

*Answer.*

I will so do, by the help of God.

*The Archbishop.*

Be you ready, with all faithful diligence, to banish and drive away all erroneous and strange doctrine contrary to God's word, and both privately and openly to call upon and encourage other to the same?

*Answer.*

I am ready, the Lord being my helper.

*The Archbishop.*

Will you deny all ungodliness, and worldly lusts, and live soberly, righteously, and godly in this world, that you may shew yourself in all things an example of good works unto other; that the adversary may be ashamed, having nothing to lay against you?

*Answer.*

I will so do, the Lord being my helper.

*The Archbishop.*

Will you maintain and set forward (as much as shall lie in you) quietness, peace, and love among all men? and such as be unquiet, disobedient, and criminous within your Diocese, correct and punish, according to such authority as ye have by God's word, and as to you shall be committed by the ordinance of this Realm?

*Answer.*

I will so do, by the help of God.

*The Archbishop.*

Will you shew yourself gentle, and be merciful for Christ's sake, to poor and needy people, and to all strangers destitute of help?

*Answer.*

I will so shew myself, by God's grace.

*The Archbishop.*

Almighty God, our heavenly Father, who hath given you a good will to do all these things; Grant also unto you strength and power to perform the same, that he accomplishing in you the good work which he hath begun, ye may be found perfect and irreprehensible at the latter day: through Jesu Christ our Lord. Amen.

Then shall be sung or said, *Come, Holy Ghost,* &c, as it is set out in the order of Priests.

That ended, the Archbishop shall say,

The Lord be with you.

*Answer.*

And with thy spirit.

Let us pray.

ALMIGHTY God, and most merciful Father, which of thy infinite goodness hast given to us thy only and most dear beloved Son Jesus Christ to be our Redeemer and Author of everlasting life, who after that he had made perfect our redemption by his death, and was ascended into heaven, poured down his gifts abundantly upon men, making some Apostles, some Prophets, some Evangelists, some Pastors and Doctors, to the edifying and making perfect of his congregation; Grant, we beseech thee, to this thy servant such grace, that he may be evermore ready to spread abroad thy gospel, and glad tidings of reconcilement to God, and to use the authority given unto him, not to destroy, but to save; not to hurt, but to help; so that he, as a faithful and a wise servant, giving to thy family meat in due season, may at the last day be received into joy; through Jesu Christ our Lord, who with thee and the Holy Ghost, liveth and reigneth one God, world without end. Amen.

Then the Archbishop and Bishops present shall lay their hands upon the head of the elect Bishop, the Archbishop saying,

TAKE the Holy Ghost, and remember that thou stir up the grace of God which is in thee, by imposition of hands: for God hath not given us the spirit of fear, but of power, and love, and of soberness.

Then the Archbishop shall lay the Bible upon his neck, saying,

GIVE heed unto reading, exhortation, and doctrine. Think upon those things contained in this Book, be diligent in them, that the increase coming thereby may be manifest unto all men. Take heed unto thyself, and unto teaching, and be diligent in doing them; for by doing this thou shalt save thyself and them that hear thee, through Jesus Christ our Lord.

Then shall the Archbishop put into his hand the Pastoral Staff, saying:

Ezek. xxxiv. BE to the flock of Christ a shepherd, not a wolf; feed them, devour them not. Hold up the weak, heal the sick, bind together the broken, bring again the outcast, seek the lost. Be so merciful, that you be not too remiss; so minister discipline, that ye forget not mercy; that when the chief Shepherd shall come, ye may receive the immercessible crown of glory; through Jesus Christ our Lord.

Then the Archbishop shall proceed to the Communion, with whom the new consecrated Bishop shall also communicate. And after the last Collect, immediately afore the Benediction shall be said this prayer.

MOST merciful Father, we beseech thee to send down upon this thy servant thy heavenly blessing; and so endue him with thy Holy Spirit, that he, preaching thy Word, may not only be earnest to reprove, beseech, and rebuke with all patience and doctrine, but also may be to such as believe an wholesome example in word, in conversation, in love, in faith, in chastity, and purity, that, faithfully fulfilling his course, at the latter day he may receive the crown of righteousness laid up by the Lord, the righteous Judge, who liveth and reigneth one God with the Father and the Holy Ghost, world without end. Amen.

RICHARDVS GRAFTON

typographus Regius

excudebat.

*Mense Martii*

*A. M. D. XLIX.*

*Cum priuilegio ad imprimendum solum.*

# The Order of the Communion,

# 1548.

# The Proclamation.

EDWARD by the grace of God king of England, France, and Ireland, defender of the faith, and of the Church of England and Ireland in earth the supreme head: to all and singular our loving subjects, greeting. Forsomuch as in our High Court of Parliament lately holden at Westminster, it was by us, with the consent of the lords spiritual and temporal and Commons there assembled, most godly and agreeably to Christ's holy institution enacted that the most blessed Sacrament of the Body and Blood of our Saviour Christ should from henceforth be commonly delivered and ministered unto all persons within our Realm of England and Ireland, and other our dominions, under both kinds, that is to say, of Bread and Wine, (except necessity other ways require,) lest every man phantasyng and devising a sundry way by himself, in the use of this most blessed Sacrament of unity, there might thereby arise any unseemly and ungodly diversity: Our pleasure is, by the advice of our most dear uncle the Duke of Somerest, governor of our person, and Protector of all our Realms, dominions, and subjects, and other of our Privy Council, that the said blessed Sacrament be ministered unto our people only after such form and manner as hereafter, by our authority, with the advice before mentioned, is set forth and declared: willing every man, with due reverence and Christian behaviour to come to this holy Sacrament and most blessed Communion, lest that by the unworthy receiving of so high mysteries they become guilty of the Body and Blood of the Lord, and so eat and drink their own damnation; but rather diligently trying themselves, that they may so come to this holy Table of Christ, and so be partakers of this holy Communion, that they may dwell in Christ, and have Christ dwelling in them. And also with such obedience and conformity to receive this our ordinance, and most godly direction, that we may be encouraged from time to time further to travail for the reformation, and setting forth of such godly orders, as may be most to God's glory, the edifying of our subjects, and for the advancement of true religion. Which thing we (by the help of God) most earnestly entend to bring to effect, willing all our loving subjects in the mean time to stay and quiet themselves with this our direction, as men content to follow authority, (according to the bounden duty of subjects), and not enterprising to run afore, and so by their rashness become the greatest hinderers of such things as they more arrogantly than godly would seem (by their own private authority) most hotly to set forward. We would not have our subjects so much to mislike our judgment, so much to mistrust our zeal, as though we either could not discern what were to be done, or would not do all things in due time. God be praised, we know both what by his word is meet to be redressed and have an earnest mind, by the advice of our most dear uncle, and other of our Privy Council, with all diligence and convenient speed so to set forth the same, as it may most stand with God's glory, and edifying and quietness of our people : which we doubt not but all our obedient and loving subjects will quietly and reverently tarry for.

### God save the King.

✠

# The Order of the Communion.

First, the Parson, Vicar or Curate, the next Sunday or Holy-day, or at the least one day before he shall minister the Communion, shall give warning to his Parishioners, or those which be present, that they prepare themselves thereto, saying to them openly and plainly as hereafter followeth, or such like.

DEAR friends, and you especially upon whose souls I have cure and charge, upon           day next I do intend, by God's grace, to offer to all such as shall be thereto godly disposed, the most comfortable Sacrament of the Body and Blood of Christ; to be taken of them in the remembrance of his most fruitful and glorious Passion: by the which Passion we have obtained remission of our sins, and be made partakers of the kingdom of heaven, whereof we be assured and ascertained, if we come to the said Sacrament with hearty repentance of our offences, stedfast faith in God's mercy, and earnest mind to obey God's will, and to offend no more: wherefore our duty is, to come to these holy Mysteries with most hearty thanks to be given to Almighty God for his infinite mercy and benefits given and bestowed upon us, his unworthy servants, for whom he hath not only given his Body to death, and shed his Blood, but also doth vouchsafe, in a Sacrament and Mystery, to give us his said Body and Blood spiritually to feed and drink upon. The which Sacrament being so divine and holy a thing. and so comfortable to them which receive it worthily, and so dangerous to them that will presume to take the same unworthily; my duty is to exhort you in the mean season to consider the greatness of the thing, and to search and examine your own consciences, and that not lightly, nor after the manner of dissimulers with God; but as they which should come to a most godly and heavenly banquet; not to come but in the marriage garment required of God in Scripture, that you may, so much as lieth in you, be found worthy to come to such a Table. The ways and mean thereto is,

First, That you be truly repentant of your former evil

life, and that you confess with an unfeigned heart to Almighty God your sins and unkindness towards his Majesty, committed either by will, word, or deed, infirmity or ignorance; and that with inward sorrow and tears you bewail your offences, and require of Almighty God mercy and pardon, promising to him, from the bottom of your hearts, the amendment of your former life. And among all others, I am commanded of God especially to move and exhort you to reconcile yourselves to your neighbours whom you have offended, or who hath offended you, putting out of your hearts all hatred and malice against them, and to be in love and charity with all the world, and to forgive other, as you would that God should forgive you. And if there be any of you whose conscience is troubled and grieved in any thing, lacking comfort or counsel, let him come to me, or to some other discreet and learned Priest taught in the law of God, and confess and open his sin and grief secretly; that he may receive such ghostly counsel, advice, and comfort, that his conscience may be relieved, and that of us, as a Minister of God, and of the Church, he may receive comfort and Absolution, to the satisfaction of his mind, and avoiding of all scruple and doubtfulness: requiring such as shall be satisfied with a general Confession not to be offended with them that doth use, to their further satisfying, the auricular and secret Confession to the Priest; nor those also, which think needful or convenient, for the quietness of their own consciences, particularly to open their sins to the Priest. to be offended with them which are satisfied with their humble confession to God, and the general Confession to the Church: but in all these things to follow and keep the rule of charity; and every man to be satisfied with his own conscience, not judging other men's minds or acts, where as he hath no warrant of God's Word for the same.

The time of the Communion shall be immediately after that the Priest himself hath received the Sacrament, without the varying of any other rite or ceremony in the Mass, (until other order shall be provided.) but as heretofore usually the Priest hath done with the Sacrament of the Body, to prepare, bless, and consecrate so much as will serve the people; so it shall yet continue still after the same manner and form, save that he shall bless and consecrate the biggest Chalice or some fair and convenient Cup or Cups full of Wine, with some Water put unto it. And that day not drink it up all himself, but taking only sup or draught, leave the rest upon the Altar covered, and turn to them that are disposed to be partakers of the Communion, and shall thus exhort them as followeth.

DEARLY beloved in the Lord, ye, coming to this holy Communion, must consider what S. Paul writeth to the Corinthians, how he exhorteth all persons diligently to try and examine themselves, or ever they presume to eat of this Bread and drink of this Cup. For as the benefit is great, if with a truly penitent heart and lively faith we receive this holy Sacrament; (for then we spiritually eat the Flesh of Christ, and drink his Blood: then we dwell in Christ, and Christ in us; we be made one with Christ, and Christ with us): So is the danger great, if we receive the same unworthily; for then we become guilty of the Body and Blood of Christ our Saviour; we eat and drink our own damnation, because we make no difference of the Lord's Body; we kindle God's wrath over us; we provoke him to plague us with divers diseases, and sundry kinds of death. Judge therefore yourselves (brethren), that ye be not judged of the Lord; let your mind be without desire to sin; repent you truly for your sins past; have an earnest and lively faith in Christ our Saviour; be in perfect charity with all men; so shall ye be meet partakers of these holy Mysteries. But above all things you must give most humble and hearty thanks to God, the Father, the Son, and the Holy Ghost, for the redemption of the world by the Death and Passion of our Saviour Christ, both God and Man; who did humble himself, even to the death upon the Cross, for us miserable sinners, lying in darkness and the shadow of death; that he might make us the children of God, and exalt us to everlasting Life. And to the end that we alway should remember the exceeding love of our Master and only Saviour Jesus Christ, thus doing for us, and the innumerable benefits which by his precious blood-shedding he hath obtained to us; he hath left in these holy Mysteries, as a pledge of his love, and a continual remembrance of the same, his own blessed Body and precious

Blood, for us spiritually to feed upon, to our endless comfort and consolation. To him therefore, with the Father and the Holy Ghost, let us give, as we are most bound, continual thanks; submitting ourselves wholly to his holy will and pleasure, and studying to serve him in true holiness and righteousness all the days of our life. Amen.

Then the Priest shall say to them that be ready to take the Sacrament,

IF any man here be an open blasphemer, a d u l t e r e r, in malice, or envy, or any other notable crime, and be not t r u l y sorry therefore, and earnestly minded to leave the same vices, or that doth not trust himself to be reconciled to Almighty God, and in charity with all the world, let him yet a while bewail his sins, and not come to this holy Table, lest, after the taking of this most blessed Bread, the devil enter into him, as he did into Judas, to fulfil in him all iniquity, and to bring him to destruction, both of body and soul.

Here the Priest shall pause a while, to see if any man will withdraw himself: and if he perceive any so to do, then let him common with him privily at convenient leisure, and see whether he can with good exhortation bring him to grace. And after a little pause, the Priest shall say:

You that do truly and earnestly repent you of your sins and offences committed to Almighty God, and be in love and charity with your neighbours, and intend to lead a new life, and heartily to follow the commandments of God, and to walk from henceforth in his holy ways; draw near, and take this holy Sacrament to your comfort, make your humble Confession to Almighty God, and to his holy Church, here gathered together in his Name, meekly kneeling upon your knees.

Then shall a general Confession be made, in the name of all those that are minded to receive the holy Communion, either by one of them, or else by one of the Ministers, or by the Priest himself; all kneeling humbly upon their knees.

ALMIGHTY God, Father of our Lord Jesus Christ, Maker of all things, Judge of all men; we knowledge and bewail our manifold sins and wickedness, which we, from time to time, most grievously have committed by thought, word, and deed, against thy divine Majesty, provoking most justly thy wrath and indignation against us. We do earnestly repent, and be heartily sorry for these our misdoings; the remembrance of them is grievous unto us; the burthen of them is intolerable. Have mercy upon us, have mercy upon us, most merciful Father; for thy Son our Lord Jesus Christ's sake forgive us all that is past; and grant that we may ever hereafter serve and please thee in newness of life, to the honour and glory of thy Name; through Jesus Christ our Lord.

*Then shall the Priest stand up, and turning him to the people, say thus:*

Our blessed Lord, who hath left power to his Church to absolve penitent sinners from their sins, and to restore to the grace of the heavenly Father such as truly believe in Christ; Have mercy upon you; pardon and deliver you from all sins; confirm and strength you in all goodness; and bring you to everlasting life.

*Then shall the Priest stand up, and turning him to the people, say thus:*

Hear what comfortable words our Saviour Christ saith to all that truly turn to him.

Come unto me all that travail and be heavy loaden, and I shall refresh you. So God loved the world, that he gave his only-begotten Son, to the end that all that believe in him should not perish, but have life everlasting.

Hear also what S. Paul saith.

This is a true saying, and worthy of all men to be embraced and received, That Jesus Christ came into this world to save sinners.

Hear also what S. John saith.

If any man sin, we have an Advocate with the Father, Jesus Christ the righteous: he it is that obtaineth grace for our sins.

*Then shall the Priest kneel down and say, in the name of all them that shall receive the Communion, this prayer following:*

We do not presume to come to this thy Table (O merciful Lord) trusting in our own righteousness, but in thy manifold and great mercies. We be not worthy so much as to gather up the crumbs under thy Table. But thou art the same Lord, whose property is always to have mercy: Grant us therefore, gracious Lord, so to eat the Flesh of thy dear Son Jesus Christ, and to drink his Blood, in these holy Mysteries, that we may continually dwell in him, and he in us, that our sinful bodies may be made clean by his Body, and our souls washed through his most precious Blood. Amen.

Then shall the Priest rise, the people still reverently kneeling, and the Priest shall deliver the Communion first to the Ministers, if any be there present, that they may be ready to help the Priest. and after to the other. And when he doth deliver the Sacrament of the body of Christ, he shall say to every one these words following :

THE Body of our Lord Jesus Christ which was given for thee, preserve thy body unto everlasting life.

And the Priest, delivering the Sacrament of the Blood, and giving every one to drink once and no more, shall say :

THE Blood of our Lord Jesus Christ which was shed for thee, preserve thy soul unto everlasting life.

If there be a Deacon, or other P r i e s t, then shall he follow with the Chalice ; and as the Priest ministereth the Bread, so shall he, for more expedition, minister the wine, in form before written.

Then shall the Priest turning him to the people, let the people depart with this blessing :

· THE peace of God, which passeth all understanding, keep your hearts and minds in the knowledge and love of God, and of his Son Jesus Christ our Lord.

To the which the people shall answer,

Amen.

NOTE.—That the Bread that shall be consecrated shall be such as heretofore hath been accustomed. And every of the said consecrated Breads shall be broken in two pieces, at the least, or more, by the discretion of the Minister, and so distributed. And men must not think less to be received in part than in the whole, but in each of them the whole Body of our Saviour Jesu Christ.

NOTE.—That if it doth so chance that the Wine hallowed and consecrate doth not suffice or be enough for them that do take the Communion, the Priest, after the first Cup or Chalice be emptied, may go again to the Altar, and reverently and devoutly prepare and consecrate another, and so the third, or more likewise, beginning at these words, *Simili modo postquam cœnatum est,* and ending at these words, *Qui pro vobis et pro multis effundetur in remissionem peccatorum,* and without any levation or lifting up.

IMPRINTED AT LONDON, THE VIII DAYE OF MARCHE. IN THE
SECONDE YERE OF THE REIGNE OF OUR SOUEREIGNE
LORDE KYNG EDWARDE THE SIXT: BY RICH-
ARD GRAFTON, PRINTER TO HIS
MOSTE ROYALL MAIESTIE.

*In the yere of our Lord*
*M.D.XLVIII.*

*Cum priuilegio ad imprimendum solum.*

SD - #0020 - 220223 - C0 - 229/152/21 - PB - 9781313009188 - Gloss Lamination